Studies in Philosophy and the History of Philosophy

Founded in 1960 by John K. Ryan

Studies in Philosophy and the History of Philosophy

Volume 6

HEIRS AND ANCESTORS

Edited by

John K. Ryan

THE CATHOLIC UNIVERSITY OF AMERICA PRESS

Consortium Press

Washington, D.C.

1973

The paper used in this publication meets the minimum requirements of the American National Standards for Information Science – Permanence of paper for Printed Library Materials, ANSI Z39.48-1984.
∞

Cataloging-in-Publication Data available from the Library of Congress

ISBN 978-0-8132-3102-0 (pbk)

TABLE OF CONTENTS

FOREWORD

Among the many thinkers discussed as to one or another aspect of their work in Volume 6 of *Studies in Philosophy and the History of Philosophy* are Sartre, Frankl, Hartshorne, Ortega, Kant, Leibniz, Descartes, John of St. Thomas, Anselm, Bonaventure, Augustine, Plotinus, and Aristotle. The philosophers, both of the modern era, now drawing to a close, and of the postmodern era that is just beginning, differ among themselves and from their predecessors both near and remote. Yet great as the differences are, they do not annul the affinity that has always held within what Dante rightly calls "la filosofica famiglia." The Greeks and Romans and their medieval descendants saw the great problems, gave their answers to them, developed methods of investigation and ways of exposition, and thus helped to form the modern mind. Assuredly there are great differences between individual thinkers and between the various schools of thought, but whether for good or for evil, each generation of thinkers is heir to those who went before it and stands as ancestor to other generations to come.

John K. Ryan

1

THE ALIENATING AND THE MEDIATING THIRD IN THE SOCIAL PHILOSOPHY OF JEAN-PAUL SARTRE

> For today there are only two ways of speaking about the self: the third person singular and the first person plural. We must know how to say "we" in order to say "I"—that is beyond question. But the opposite is also true. If some tyranny, in order to establish the "we" first, deprives individuals of the subjective image, all "interiority" disappears and all reciprocal relations with it.
>
> —Sartre's foreword to André Gorz's *The Traitor*[1]

The present essay may be considered an extended gloss on these remarks by Sartre. For it is a critical examination of his defense of interiority in the midst of collective action by distinguishing two uses of the concept of the third person or simply the "Third" (*le tiers*). After a brief review of this concept in *Being and Nothingness* (hereafter BN) where it is introduced, our attention will focus on *The Critique of Dialectical Reason* and that apocalyptic moment when the group emerges. It is only then that Sartre differentiates between the alienating and the mediating Third.

If Sartre's reputation as a social philosopher has been uneven, this is due in large part to his early failure to appreciate that dimension of interpersonal relations which the Third reveals. As we shall see, his original understanding of the Third was no less objectifying and alienating than was his concept of the Other. It was for this reason that his idea of the social subject, the We-subject, was so sketchy and inadequate. In fact, it was Sartre's development of the mediating role of the Third in the '40s and '50s which

[1]André Gorz. *The Traitor,* with a Foreword by Jean-Paul Sartre, trans. by Richard Howard (New York: Simon and Schuster, 1959), p. 35.

enabled him to formulate a social theory which, if not contrary to BN, was scarcely its logical outgrowth. Thus the career of this concept could provide a valid indicator of his philosophic evolution.

But our present concern is more analytic than historical. We wish to determine the function of the Third in Sartre's current social philosophy. To do this, we must first examine in detail both uses of this concept and then observe his employment of the mediating Third to resolve the difficulties he encounters as he attempts to construct a "theory of practical ensembles," his subtitle for the *Critique*.

These problems are of two kinds, ontological and methodological. The former involves the individual–group relationship and the ontological status of each of its terms. The latter refers to current conflict between methodological holists and individualists and to the opposition between sociological and psychological explanations in the social sciences.[2]

After a close examination of Sartre's treatment of the Third in the apocalyptic genesis of the group (II), we shall evaluate the success of the mediating Third in resolving these problems which must be faced by any adequate social philosophy (III). But first let us observe Sartre's initial use of the term in BN.

I

The dismal conclusion of *No Exit,* "Hell is other people," has long been taken for the epitaph on the tomb of Sartre's social philosophy.

[2]Psychologism is, of course, only one species of methodological individualism, as Arthur Danto points out in his perceptive *Analytical Philosophy of History* (London: Cambridge University Press, 1968), p. 270. The same is true of sociologism as an instance of methodological holism. For important distinctions between the methodological and the ontological aspects of the holist/individualist controversy see Chapter XII of the Danto volume, "Methodological Individualism and Methodological Socialism," as well as the articles by Ernest Gellner, Maurice Mandelbaum, and J.W.N. Watkins respectively in Patrick Gardiner, ed., *Theories of History* (Glencoe: The Free Press, 1959). Alasdair MacIntyre considers the key problem of contemporary social theory to be that of relating sociological explanations to explanations in terms of individual psychology, i.e., the problem of Marx and Freud. He admits that Sartre has grappled with this problem in the *Critique,* though he feels that Sartre's "reluctance to look at facts" leaves his answers extremely general and, in fact, constitutes "his tragedy as a theorist." See "Sartre as a Social Theorist," *The Listener,* March 22, 1962, pp. 512-513.

The tendency to read his analysis of interpersonal relations in BN as normal, indeed as inevitable, led many commentators of the '40s and '50s to conclude that Sartre's social thought was bankrupt, that he offered no escape from the mutually destructive relations so vividly described in BN. This was their view despite the famous footnote in BN where he spoke of a radical conversion, offering salvation from the bad faith described in the corpus of the text.[3] It is true that Sartre himself lent scant support to alternative interpretations in the '40s. His plays of that "existentialist" period, *The Flies* and *No Exit,* for example, are individualistic and socially pessimistic. But as the decade moved into its second half, there was evidence that Sartre had begun to have second thoughts on the nature of social interaction and responsibility. This first emerged in that embarrassing lecture, *Existentialism is a Humanism* (1946), replete with the overstatements and inconsistencies which mark a thinker in the process of reassessing his stand. But it became clearest in his plays of the next ten years, especially in *The Devil and the Good Lord* (1951).[4] These two works would be essential for any study of the evolution of Sartre's social thought.

[3]See *L'Etre et le néant* (Paris: Gallimard, 1943), p. 484, n. 1, hereafter EN, or the English translation by Hazel Barnes, *Being and Nothingness* (New York: Philosophical Library, 1956), p. 412, n. 14, hereafter BN. Although all citations are from EN and the translations are my own, the corresponding page in BN is listed for the convenience of those using the Barnes translation. Francis Jeanson's *Le problème moral et la pensée de Sartre* (2nd ed.; Paris: Seuil, 1965), which first appeared in 1947, is a notable exception to this common misunderstanding. He discusses the possibility of deliverance from bad faith via Sartre's concept of a "purifying reflection." See pp. 238 ff. Herbert Spiegelberg, writing in 1954, had already noticed a move by Sartre away from BN toward a form of socialist democracy and social revolution "not unlike that of John Dewey." See his "French Existentialism: Its Social Philosophy," *Kenyon Review,* XVI (Summer, 1954), pp. 446-462. Now it is commonly admitted that the relations described in BN were intended to refer to life in a certain type of society, viz., the bourgeois, or to certain not insuperable personal conditions. For an example of the former, see Marie-Denise Boros, *Un séquestré. L'Homme sartrien* (Paris: Nizet, 1968), pp. 92-93. Hazel Barnes offers us the latter interpretation in her *An Existentialist Ethics* (New York: Knopf, 1967), p. 320.

[4]Joseph H. McMahon, in one of the best written and most comprehensive studies of Sartre yet to have appeared in English, finds this play "profoundly autobiographical." See his *Humans Being. The World of Jean-Paul Sartre* (Chicago: The University of Chicago Press, 1971), especially pp. 227 ff. McMahon lends support to our remarks about Sartre's crucial discovery of the Third in the '40s and '50s when he characterizes Nasty, a protagonist in the

Sartre's systematic introduction of the Third occurs in Part III of BN as a development of the category "for-others" (*pour-autrui*). The Other, he writes, "has established me in a new type of being which can support new qualifications."[5] These qualifications are the well-known relations of fear, pride, shame, alienation of possibilities, and the like, which the look *(le regard)* of the Other brings into play. But the Other's look at best constitutes a duality of mutually objectifying consciousnesses, each transcending the other, each the internal negation of the other.[6] The embodied consciousness which the look reveals sets the limit to any relation between individual consciousnesses. Because I exist my body, in Sartre's phrase, I remain vulnerable to objectification by the Other. My status as internal negation of the embodied Other not only makes true unity impossible[7] but expresses itself in three original, antisocial attitudes, viz., sadism, masochism, and hatred. These are the fundamental projects of the *pour-soi* with regard to Others.[8] Sartre insists that all men's complex patterns of conduct toward one another are merely enrichments of these attitudes. A synthesis of self and Other is impossible. In what seems to be a final effort to salvage a semblance of social forms, Sartre at this point introduces the Third.[9]

We first discover the Third as the alienating presence who objectifies two lovers by his look, fixing their mutual relationship into a set of dead possibilities. Whatever they may do, he is always there to qualify their plans, to give them a meaning which they cannot control. In Sartre's metaphor, he "robs" them of their freedom. We shall call this use of the concept "the alienating

---

play, as incarnating "a new category in the Sartrean system, a kind of harmonization of the subject-object conflict" (p. 242).

[5]EN 276; BN 222.

[6]Recall that in BN the For-itself *(pour-soi)* or consciousness *is* the nihilation (néantization) of the In-itself *(en-soi)* or nonconsciousness which it is, and is the internal negation of the In-itself which it is not, viz., its being-for-others. See EN 360-363 and 502; BN 298-301 and 429. For a close study of the internal negation of the Other which the For-itself is, see Klaus Hartmann, *Sartre's Ontology* (Evanston: Northwestern University Press, 1966), pp. 119-121.

[7]EN 433; BN 365-366.

[8]See EN 477; BN 407.

[9]Throughout this essay we shall use "the Third" to refer both to the concept and to the concrete agent in this role. The distinction, unimportant for our argument, will be clear from the context, especially from the corresponding pronouns.

Third," for its major features are common to the Other, the chief agent of alienation in BN. The Third merely establishes a "more complex modality of being-for-others."[10] In fact, Sartre argues that my relation to the Other (duality) is predicated on the limitless ground of my relation and his to *all* Others, i. e., to what he calls the quasi-totality of all consciousnesses.[11] Thus the intervention of the Third remains a constant possibility in every duality.

We must insist on Sartre's claim that the Third constitutes only a "more complex mode" of being-for-others, since it is precisely this similarity between Other and Third in Sartre's "existentialist" analysis, we shall argue, that accounts for the concept's poverty in social discourse. It will be supplemented in the *Critique* by a richer (in terms of explanatory force) and qualitatively different use. So let us review in detail the characteristics of the alienating Third. There are six which we can garner from Sartre's description in BN.

First of all, the Third is essentially *extrinsic* to the dual.[12] As such, he confers on the For–itself and the Other a being–outside their reciprocity. He is Other to them. Correspondingly, they are constituted a "them" for him, and this integration comes necessarily from without.

Secondly, the Third is a *transcending* consciousness, a freedom that drains reciprocal projects of their freedom the way a kibitzer spoils the mutuality of two chess players. By his presence their strategy is globally modified. They suddenly exist *for* him (for his entertainment, his vanity, etc.).

Furthermore, the Third *synthesizes* or totalizes these reciprocal projects into a *single project.* Before his appearance I could say (to myself), "I am against the Other" or "I am playing him and he is playing me." But now I must say, "We are playing each Other." Note that the "We" is no internally unified collective subject. The totalization is entirely *ab extra.* It is a status of which I become aware.

[10]See EN 493; BN 421.

[11]See EN 487; BN 415

[12]We use "dual" here, as Sartre does occasionally, to refer to the relationship. For-itself/Other, it forms one of the terms of the subsequent relationship, dual/Third. The dual need not be limited to two consciousnesses. Indeed, in one of Sartre's favorite examples of the dual/Third, class consciousness, it is not.

But, fourthly, this totalization confers on the dual the unity of an object *(unité-objet),* not that of a subject. It is the *Us-object,* as Sartre calls it, which the Third reveals to us in our condition of being "looked-at" by a consciousness which escapes us. As in the case of the Other, the Third's look fixes me in immobility. This is probably the chief weakness of the concept of the Third in BN since it is entailed by the other three. It constitutes the main obstacle to dialogue and renders community *(Gemeinschaft)* impossible. Yet in the context of almost universal bad faith which BN presumes, the very limitations of the alienating Third suggest the possibility that it may be the context and not the concept as such which is the hindrance.

The object–unity which every Third effects is a *unity of equivalence* wherein each loses his identity and individuality in a common equation with every Other. The result is what Sartre calls a "community of equivalence" between me and the Other.[13] Sartre will ascribe this feature to serial unity in the *Critique*. Indeed, the entire discussion of the series in that later work falls heir to the description of the Us–object in BN.

Finally, the Third *alienates* the dual in a twofold sense which summarizes the five other characteristics. It does this first by objectifying it, deadening its possibilities, constituting it a transcended transcendence in the same manner as the Other alienates the For–itself. Secondly, by establishing an equivalence between the For–itself and the Other, the Third forces the former to assume responsibility for a totality "which it is not, although it forms an integral part of it."[14] Belonging to the Us–object is thus felt to be a still more radical alienation of the For–itself than simple being–for–others.

We have examined the six characteristics of the Third/dual relationship so as to bring into sharp relief its similarity to the Other/For–itself correlatives. In both cases the relation is extrinsic,[15] transcending, totalizing, objectifying, and alienating. What

[13]EN 489; BN 418. The "community," of course, is a creature of the Third in the same way that "the Jew" is a product of the anti-Semite. See Sartre's essay *Anti-Semite and Jew,* trans. by George J. Becker (New York: Schoken Books, 1948), especially p. 69: "The Jew is one whom other men consider a Jew."

[14]EN 490; BN 419.

[15]It is extrinsic in the sense of "coming from without," and should not be confused with "external" which is the contradictory of "internal" or "con-

distinguishes the dual from the solitary For-itself (and hence the Third from the Other) is the *plurality* of consciousnesses and situations which are welded together by the look of the Third. Sartre calls this the "internal reciprocity of the situation."[16] But his only attempt to account for it is his implicit appeal to that mutual internal negation which constituted the For-itself/Other relationship in the first place.

Sartre continues his discussion of what he terms being-with others by a consideration of the We-subject. This need not detain us because the Third figures only obliquely in this analysis. Significantly, however, Sartre writes the We-subject off as a mere "subjective *Erlebnis*," a purely psychological phenomenon lacking the ontological grounding in being-for-others which supported the Us-object.[17] The Third as a mode of being-for-others shares in its ontological status as part of a real, objective, concrete "situation form" in relation to the Us-object which it constitutes.[18] But the very relationship of looking/looked-at which accounts for the reality of the Third also precludes any nonobjectifying, nonalienating exchange such as a real, intrinsic unity of subjectivities would require. Although the look may succeed in overcoming solipsism in Sartre's ontology, the net gain for social thought is practically nil. For the Others whose existence is apodictically evident in shame consciousness are radically out of reach from me and from each other.[19]

Such, then, is the concept of the alienating Third as introduced in BN. It does not significantly allay the extreme individualism of that book since it merely raises to another power Sartre's famous dyadic opposition looking/looked-at.[20] As the preceding analysis has indicated, the crux of the problem of Sartre's would-be social philosophy is that he has not yet adequately dis-

stitutive." For, as we have seen, the For-itself is an internal negation of the Other and vice versa; but this is true of the dual/Third as well (see EN 502-503; BN 429-430).

[16]EN 490; BN 418.

[17]See EN 502; BN 429.

[18]EN 489; BN 418.

[19]See EN 498; BN 425.

[20]"So there are two radically different forms of the *Nous* (we/us) experience, and they correspond exactly to being-as-looking and being-looked-at which constitute the fundamental relations of the For-itself with the Other" (EN 486; BN 415).

tinguished the Third from the Other in his phenomenological ontology. Until he does, his social philosophy, to the extent that it is systematic at all, remains a pale reflection of his powerful psychological descriptions. A different use of the Third is required to overcome this asymmetry between *the* ontologically grounded Us–object and the merely psychological We–subject. Its introduction in *the Critique* marks a major advance both ontologically and methodologically in Sartre's social thought.

II

If a preponderance of dyadic relationships (including the covert dyad, Dual/Third) marks BN as severely limited in social scope,[21] the abundance of triads in the *Critique* signals a new phase in Sartre's social philosophy. Paradigmatic of dyadic opposition in BN is the sadomasochistic circle which revolves incessantly and without advance like the alternating relations of the characters in *No Exit*. Though it would be an exaggeration to claim that the *Critique* introduces dialectic into Sartre's philosophic method for the first time,[22] this work does present his first *ex professo* treatment of the topic, which henceforth holds a major position in his formal discourse.

As a necessary condition for his explicit use of dialectical discourse in the social sphere, Sartre develops a new use of the

[21]Klaus Hartmann in his extended study of the *Critique, Sartres Sozialphilosophie. Eine Untersuchung zur "Critique de la Raison Dialectique"* (Berlin: Walter de Gruyter, 1966), characterizes BN as a social philosophy "of pairs" *(von Paaren)*, p. 31. This entire work is an interesting attempt by a competent philosopher to demonstrate that Sartre's philosophy both in BN and in the *Critique* is "transcendental" in a way similar to that of the early Heidegger, i.e., not idealistic but ontological or existential; see especially p. 8, n. 3.

[22]L.W. Nauta, for example, points out the beginning of Sartre's dialectical thinking in his studies of the imagination in the '30s; see his "Dialektik bei Sartre," *Studium Generale*, 17 juli, 1968, pp. 591-607. Georges Gurvitch criticizes what he calls Sartre's "domestication" of the dialectic in BN, i.e., its impressment into the service of a "pessimistic individualism"; see his *Dialectique et sociologie* (Paris: Flammarion, 1962), p. 21. If Merleau-Ponty presumes that Sartre has rejected the dialectic in this period, it is the dialectic of nature as well as a date progressive, historical dialectic which he has in mind; see his *Les aventures de la dialectique* (Paris: Gallimard, 1955), p. 135 and passim.

Third, viz., the mediating Third. With this new conceptual instrument in hand, it is not surprising that he now criticizes those philosophers who have sacrificed history to structure by favoring an *organization dualiste* over the dialectical triad.[23] For their penchant reflects on the essentialist plane an error of emphasis which Sartre himself had made on the existentialist level in BN. The alternating dualities of his earlier work never moved in any direction. Like Hegel's "bad infinite," they were without *Aufhebung;* they lacked the synthesizing viewpoint of a nonalienating Third.

In the *Critique* the context is changed. We are plunged into a Hegelian–Marxist world where men and matter provide the mediation, subsuming individuals to communal freedom and dissolving common action into serial isolation and impotence. And the whole progresses from the simple but transcendental fact of scarcity *(la rareté),* i.e., from the fact that there are not enough material goods to go around.[24] It is this fact which gives human history its particular poignancy, rendering men competitors rather than cooperators despite their best intentions. And it is this which explains why class struggle is a fact, indeed why it is the moving force of history.[25] But the "regressive" analysis which Sartre adopts in

[23]*Critique de la raison dialectique, précédé de Question de méthode* tome I, *Théorie des ensembles pratiques* (Paris: Gallimard, 1960), p. 188. (In the notes this work will be cited by the standard abbreviation CRD.) In an interview recorded in *L'Arc,* 30 (1966), Sartre blames Lévi-Strauss for having contributed to "the present discredit of history" in the social sciences by his particular use of structuralism, a method Sartre respects as long as it "remains aware of its limits as a method"; (see pp. 89 and 88 respectively). Lévi-Strauss had previously criticized Sartre's "sociologizing" of the Cogito in the *Critique* whereby he merely "exchanges one prison for another;" see *The Savage Mind* (Chicago: The University of Chicago Press, 1966) which is the English translation of a work published in French four years earlier, p. 249. The final chapter of that work deals with the *Critique.*

[24]Raymond Aron lends support to Hartmann's thesis (see above, n. 21) when he speaks of Sartre's "transcendental deduction" of the class struggle from the fact of scarcity; see his *Marxism and the Existentialists,* trans. by Helen Weaver, Robert Addis, and John Weightman (New York: Harper & Row, 1969), p. 169.

[25]Early in the *Critique* (p. 201) Sartre describes human history as "a desperate battle against scarcity." As he reaches the conclusion of the volume with the discussion of class warfare, he argues that "the only possible intelligibility of human relationships is dialectical" and that "this intelligibility, in a concrete history the real foundation of which is scarcity, can be manifest only as an antagonistic reciprocity. So . . . it is class warfare which, in the

the only volume of the *Critique* ever to have appeared intends to show how class struggle is *possible* (after the manner of Kant's *Prolegomena*).[26] To this end he argues from the "abstract" (in the Hegelian sense of "not fully determined") individual through the isolated series or single group to that concrete nodal point where history actually occurs: the intersection of series and group, of class and organic individual working to fulfill his needs.

Admittedly, a dualistic opposition continues to pervade the *Critique*. But the *pour-soi/en-soi* dichotomy of BN gives way to praxis and the practico-inert. Praxis, a technical term essential to Marxist socioeconomic theory,[27] signifies human activity of any

---

history of human multiplicities occurs necessarily on the basis of historically defined conditions as the realization *en cours* of dialectical rationality" (CRD 744). Thus a recent commentator can conclude that for Sartre "praxis as the praxis of class warfare has become the moving force *(zum Motor)* of history"; see Friedrich von Krosigk, *Philosophie und politische Aktion bei Jean-Paul Sartre* (München: Verlag C. H. Beck, 1969), p. 177.

[26]See CRD 153-154 for Sartre's summary of the progressive-regressive method as it is to be employed in the *Critique*. He hopes to "lay the foundations for 'The Prolegomena to any Future Anthropology.'" As with Kant's version of the regressive method, Sartre argues from the fact to the conditions of its possibility. That fact is "totalization" (CRD 153) or more concretely "the class struggle" (CRD 735); and the necessary conditions for its possibility are the various partial totalizations, detotalizations, and retotalizations along with their abstract structures and functions which dialectical experience, as Sartre terms it, reveals in the course of the *Critique*. Strictly speaking, this dialectical experience terminates not in the historical fact itself (Sartre is not a complete rationalist) but in the "formal milieu in which the concrete, historical fact must necessarily occur" (CRD 637). In other words, he intends to establish "the formal conditions of History" (CRD 743).

Human activity, viewed epistemologically in the *Critique*, is totalizing; it unifies its component elements in terms of a higher viewpoint. Yet it may be misleading to speak of viewpoints, for the "making-whole" is practical, not theoretical. As Hartmann points out, totalization is "not a synthesis in the Kantian manner, but a unification in praxis, in life, and in experience" (*Sartres Sozialphilosophie*, p. 60). Wilfrid Desan offers a good exposition of Sartre's theory of totalization in his *The Marxism of Jean-Paul Sartre* (Garden City, N. Y.: Doubleday Anchor, 1966); see especially pp. 75 ff.

As for the second volume of the *Critique*, Sartre himself has admitted that it will probably never appear; see Michel Contat and Michel Rybalka, eds., *Les Écrits de Sartre* (Paris: Gallimard, 1970), pp. 340 and 481.

[27]For a helpful study of Marx's theory of praxis along with references to its use in Sartre (though unfortunately Sartre's major treatment of this subject, viz., in CRD, is dealt with in two footnotes), see Richard J. Bernstein's *Praxis and Action* (Philadelphia: University of Pennsylvania Press, 1971).

sort for Sartre.[28] As human, this activity is self-originative and purposive. As activity, it is dialectical in that it constantly totalizes its past and present in relation to an objective to be attained in the future.[29] And as dialectical, it is internally related to its negation, the practico-inert. Man the practical organism *gives rise* to the practico-inert field by his praxis. But the chief characteristic of individual praxis from the viewpoint of Sartre's overall strategy in the *Critique* is doubtless its self-translucidity. As constituting dialectic, individual praxis is totally evident to itself just as the *pour-soi* had been in BN. Thus it constitutes the ultimate evidence in Sartre's present system, establishing that link between being and knowing which he wishes to restore with Hegel, while denying the "ideality" of matter, i.e., without turning Hegel once more on end.

The other term of Sartre's duality, the practico-inert, functions as anti-praxis or anti-dialectic making history possible and rendering any overarching master dialectic impossible. The practico-inert is the locus of scarcity, of material objectivity, and of the permanence of human endeavors in their "solid" state as institutions and artifacts (what Sartre terms "worked matter"). But the same practico-inert by its sheer material recalcitrance blocks the progress of any superdialectic. It is never fully subsumable into a noninertial form. So it dissipates practical unities, hardens spontaneity into habit, reverses or deflects projects with its counterfinality, and generally functions as the antithesis of freedom in the *Critique*. In a most perceptive article Dina Dreyfus points out that the practico-inert is the ground of all alienation in the later Sartre, but only in the form of scarcity could it be considered "rad-

[28]Nevertheless, praxis signifies primarily "work" in Sartre's vocabulary, and in this meaning evokes more clearly its counter-concept, the practico-inert. Sartre writes admiringly: "The essential discovery of Marxism is that work as a historical reality and as the utilization of determinate tools in an already determined social and material milieu is the real foundation for the organization of social relations. This discovery can no longer be questioned" (CRD 224-225, n. 1).

In a valuable note to the *Critique* (CRD 286 n. 1), Sartre offers a rough "translation" of the two dichotomies of BN and CRD in terms of each other. Thus he likens praxis in its self-luminosity to "consciousness (of) self"—a technical term in BN (see EN 20; BN liv).

[29]Late in the *Critique* Sartre offers a descriptive definition of praxis: "organizing project moving beyond material conditions toward an end, and imprinting itself by work upon inorganic matter as a reworking of the practical field and a reunification of the means in view of attaining the end" (CRD 687).

ical evil." In other words, Sartre has not lapsed into Manichaeism, as some of his critics have suggested.[30] And yet it constitutes the final necessary condition for sociality in Sartre's system. All social objects, he insists, "are beings of the practico-inert field, at least in their fundamental structures."[31] By introducing the practico-inert as anti-dialectic and by further qualifying it with the fact of scarcity, Sartre has grounded the Marxist dialectic while offering an explanation for the scandal of continued alienation in socialist societies.

What Sartre calls the social field, i.e., the proper domain of sociology, consists of structured ensembles which are always a combination of praxis and the practico-inert, although each is the negation of the other. At either extreme of this polar opposition stands a social ensemble, viz., the collective *(le collectif)* and the group. Sartre defines the collective as "that two-way relationship between a material, inorganic, worked object and a multiplicity which finds its 'external unity' *(unité d'exteriorité)* in it."[32] The group, on the contrary, is defined by its common enterprise which provides a practical unity and a specific intelligibility for its praxis. Where the group is conceived as project, praxis, internal unity and dissolution of inertia, the collective is described as passivity, exis, multiplicity, and discrete quantity. At the limits of the social field Sartre speaks of "collectives which have almost entirely adsorbed their groups and groups where passivity tends to disappear completely."[33] But neither of these "pure" types is instantiated in reality. Although Sartre's regressive analysis moves from series to group to "concrete" class struggle, no attempt is made to assign a temporal precedence to one form over another. Conceptually, however, collectives are simultaneously "the matrix of groups and their grave."[34]

[30]Dina Dreyfus, "Jean-Paul Sartre et le mal radical," *Mercure de France,* tome 341 (janvier, 1961), pp. 154-167.

[31]CRD 306.

[32]CRD 319. The multiplicity so united would be what Sartre calls the "series" and the relations between individuals in a series or in a collective are designated "serial." Sartre tends to use the terms "collective" and "series" without respecting his distinction. Though this may lead to a certain amount of confusion, it leaves the general argument intact.

[33]CRD 307.

[34]CRD 608.

The practical ensembles of the social field are relational. Sartre writes: "When I wish to find my location in the social world, I discover ternary and binary formations around me. The former are in constant dissolution and the latter appear on the ground of a revolving totalization and can be integrated into a trinity at any moment."[35] Throughout the *Critique* Sartre is tireless in affirming that these relations are ever *en cours,* that the totalities which praxis effects are really "totalizings," and that the ensembles which social science studies are *practical* unities and not metaphysical hypostases. We shall now turn to the dual in the *Critique* in order the better to understand Sartre's claim that "the *real* relation of men among themselves is necessarily ternary."[36]

In Sartre's regressive analysis the dual, being more "abstract," must precede the triple. Of course, it is individual praxis which by its projects determines its reciprocal ties with every other, and its does this via the *material conditions* of the situation which this project brings to the fore—this is the basic thesis of the *Critique.* The gardener and the road-mender, for example, recognize in each other the similar social task which an Other has assigned them. But what is role-playing in BN (where the milieu is one of bad faith and inauthenticity) has become *social role* in the *Critique.* And the latter is determined as much by material conditions, e.g., by dress, tools, etc., as by the express intention of the Other. In fact, it is the "quasi-totality" called "worked matter" *(matière ouvrée)* which forms the inert, negative ground upon which reciprocity appears. "This means that it always appears on an inert base of institutions and instruments by which each man is already defined and alienated."[37] Unlike BN, however, it is not the binary relationship itself but its material base which is the chief source of alienation.

Sartre lists four conditions necessary for reciprocity: (1) that the Other be a means to the exact degree that I am a means myself, i.e., that he be the means toward a *transcending* goal and not *my* means; (2) that I recognize the Other as *praxis,* i.e., as totalization *en cours,* at the same time that I integrate him into my totalizing project; (3) that I recognize his movement toward his own ends in the very movement by which I project my self to-

[35]CRD 189.
[36]CRD 189, italics his.
[37]CRD 191.

ward mine; and (4) that I discover myself to be the object and instrument of his ends by the same act which makes him the object and instrument of mine.[38] Although Sartre offers such examples of reciprocity as the boxing match and the exchange of goods and services, it is clear from his writings in the *Critique* and elsewhere that he considers the reciprocity among laborers as the most fruitful instance of this relationship, for it grounds class consciousness and thereby furthers history.[39]

Before we consider these conditions singly, we must understand what reciprocity is not. First of all, Sartre denies that it is an abstract, universal bond such as he believes Christian charity to be. Neither is it the Kantian ideal of treating each man as an end and never as a means alone. Sartre's opposition to the Kantian kingdom of ends is revealing of his own anthropology, for it assumes that only *ideas* can be ends in the unconditional sense which he takes Kant to mean. Against what Sartre rather loosely terms "absolute idealism," he maintains that "man is a material being in the midst of a material world."[40] In other words, he *is* his relationship to matter and he cannot resolve to establish new ones except *via* the dissolution of the present relationships. Thus he himself becomes the instrument or *means* in his present state toward achieving that future condition which he will be. And this in turn clarifies Sartre's opposition to the Kantian imperative as he reads it: since I must treat even myself as a means, I cannot be expected to treat another as an end. Cannot implies ought not.

So the first condition for reciprocity recognizes the fact that every man is a means. But it requires that the goal of this instrumentality be nonexclusive. To the extent that reciprocity is operative, mutually exclusive aims must be suspended. The fact

[38]CRD 192.

[39]Already in BN he had emphasized communal work as an "objective situation-form" which by its "internal reciprocity" was more likely to arouse the experience of the *Nous* than were other situations (EN 489-491; BN 418-419). But it is in his 1946 essay, "Materialism and Revolution," translated by Annette Michelson in *Literary and Philosophical Essays* (New York: Collier, 1962), that Sartre explicitly characterizes the revolutionary as one who "sees human relationships from the point of view of work," and who hopes that "the relationships of solidarity which he maintains with other workers will become the very model of human relationships" (p. 226). Cf. *Situations,* III (Paris: Gallimard, 1949), p. 108.

[40]CRD 191. In fact he criticizes Hegel for having "suppressed matter as a mediation between individuals" (CRD 192).

that this condition is fulfilled quite readily in the example of class consciousness and only with many qualifications (which Sartre does not bother to make) in the case of negative reciprocity as in the boxing match example, suggests that Sartre's primary concern is not reciprocity itself, but the part this concept plays in his overall theory of class conflict.

Especially noteworthy in these conditions is the absence of any features which would generate conflict. Sartre seems to be arguing now that conflict is introduced *ab extra,* that it comes to reciprocity from the fact of material scarcity. This is a major advance over the socially pessimistic conclusions of BN, but, as we shall see, the kind of reciprocity which Sartre is describing at this "abstract" level becomes fully determined and hence "real" only through the mediation of the Third.

The second and third conditions require that I recognise the Other as praxis (Sartre would have said "as freedom" in BN), and that I therefore be aware of the purposive character of his actions as I determine my own. Here the example of the boxing match is particularly apt.

Finally, the recognition must be practical and mutual. It must be achieved in the very act that expresses it, as, for example, the feinting and the jabbing of the boxer. And it cannot be the kind of alternating reciprocity which was described in BN. To the extent that alterity is a function of individuality and exclusivity of goals, it is suspended, if not abolished, in true reciprocity.

What, then, is lacking to this immediate reciprocity within the pair? According to Sartre, genuine, interior *unity* is absent in the binary relationship. Push this mutual integration to the limit and it still remains plural. This very reciprocity is "the negation of unity."[41] True, a sort of unity is supplied by the practico-inert (worked matter) in the form of rules, equipment, etc., but even this reflects the presence of the Third. By itself the mutuality of the pair achieves at best that external unity which a Third imposes or the manufactured article reveals (and to this extent the pair continues to resemble the Us-object of BN).

The fundamental reason why reciprocity implies separation, a reason which has deprived Sartre of a dialogical model to this day, is his insistence that "mutual integration implies the being-

[41]CRD 193.

object of each one for the Other."[42] Sartre has always considered objectification to be the leading form of alienation.[43] Hence, the mutuality which any binary relationship achieves will always be a compromise between agents who recognize that the Other's project exists *outside* their own. They cannot totalize without objectifying. The result is what Sartre calls "disunion in solidarity" as he goes on to argue that the unity of the dyad can only be effected by the totalizing action of the Third.[44]

[42]CRD 193.

[43]In his excellent study entitled "The Existentialist Rediscovery of Hegel and Marx," published in *Phenomenology and Existentialism,* ed. by Edward N. Lee and Maurice Mandelbaum, George Kline argues that for Hegel both alienation and objectification could and should be overcome through the dialectical movement of spirit, whereas for Marx only the former should be overcome through the dialectical movement of history; objectification would remain as a necessary aspect of all production (praxis). In the Sartre of BN, Klein insists, neither alienation nor objectification can be overcome, but in CRD Sartre accepts Marx's position "in a vulgarized form that equates objectification with 'materialization' " (p. 134).

As the general thrust of the present essay should make clear, we cannot fully agree with Klein's interpretation of either stage of Sartre's development. In his assessment of BN Klein does not allow for the possibility of deliverance from bad faith (and from the interpersonal relations which it infects) which Sartre's foot-note to the text suggests (see BN 412 n.; EN 484 n.). Indeed, Klein simply mentions the footnote, which he says "Sartre adds enigmatically" to his discussion of human relations in BN. We have argued, doubtless armed with the wisdom of hindsight, that Sartre's remark leaves the door open for relations which need not be alienating or objectifying. It is with the introduction of the mediating Third in the *Critique* that this possibility is actualized.

As for Klein's interpretation of the *Critique,* we must agree that Sartre has now accepted a form of alienation, viz., scarcity in the practico-inert field, which can be overcome, at least in principle. It is further correct that the practico-inert accounts for a type of objectification which closely resembles Marx's *Vergegenständlichung* (or his *Entäusserung*), though it is certainly not true that Sartre's complex analysis of the practico-inert and its avatars is merely a "vulgarization" of the Marxist view; see, e.g., his discussion of money or of public opinion (CRD 240 ff. and 336 f., or 338 ff. respectively). But we are insisting upon another type of objectification, one that figures primarily in BN and which continues to vitiate binary and ternary relations in the *Critique* to the extent that the latter are constituted by what we have called the alienating Third. This objectification is a function of the transcending and totalizing character of the praxis itself. The mediating Third, as we shall now see, will "totalize without objectifying"—that is its raison d'être in Sartre's system.

[44]See CRD 194. Mikel Dufrenne notes that unmediated reciprocity for Sartre is neither dialectical nor totalizing. It calls for mediation, either of mat-

Deliverance from the separation and the false totalities which duality supports may seem unlikely at the hands of the only Third we have experienced thus far. The alienating Third seems to confirm rather than overcome this objectifying duality. Sartre still retains a place for this function of the Third in his dialectical repertory. Indeed, he seems to admit that this is the basic structure of the Third in general[45]. It is this Third that reestablishes serial division and impotency among the members of a society. It is the other class as exploiter of workers, the colonist as Other to the native, the "they" of public opinion which separates as it links in serial relations, the boss of an institution, and the *Duce* of the fascist mob—all examples of the alienating Third.

Another form of the Third is demanded by the deficiencies of the dual as Sartre describes them. Immediate reciprocity is not unifying because it is objectifying. Nonobjectifying or "free" reciprocity, as Sartre terms it, must be mediated. But the alienating Third suffers from the same defect. Like the collective object which confers an "external unity" on a multiplicity of individuals, the alienating Third "serializes" the relations between the terms which it totalizes. What is required is a Third which *totalizes without objectifying*, i.e., a Third which elicits union *from within* rather than imposing it from without.[46] This Third must render

---

ter, in which case it becomes alienating, or of the Third, which is a liberating totalization proceeding from free praxis; see his review of the *Critique* in *Esprit* (avril, 1961), especially pp. 684-685. Dufrenne has not noted the continued presence of the alienating Third in the *Critique*.

[45]Thus he argues that the original structure of the Third "manifests, in effect, the simple practical power of unifying every multiplicity within its field of action, that is, of totalizing it by passing beyond it (*un dépassement*) toward its ends" (CRD 399). What we have termed the alienating Third, Sartre in one place calls "*un tiers-objet*" or "a Third transcending me" (CRD 406). With the mediating function of the Third, this relationship among group members is "quasi-transcendence." To the extent that totalizing without objectifying is possible, Sartre has overcome a second source of alienation in his system (besides scarcity), a source reaching back to BN. For this variety of objectification is alienating as well; it is a sufficient condition for alterity and it blocks the exercise of freedom by hindering internal, group unity.

[46]Sartre conceives of the mediating Third's totalization as a revealing or "unveiling" of a practical unity already under way. He writes: "I find myself in the midst of the Thirds and without privileged status. But this operation [my totalization by the other mediating Third] does not transform me into an object, since totalization by the Third merely reveals a free praxis as a common unity already there and qualifying it" (CRD 408). Whenever Sartre speaks

every other "the same" *(la même)* in practice without resorting to an abstract idea (the sameness of a universal) on the one hand or a mere nominalistic stipulation on the other. The Third, in effect, must be a *mediating* Third and its mediation must be dialectical. Sartre labels this position "dialectical nominalism."[47] It turns on the notion of the mediating Third.

The collective with its serial relations forms the first degree of sociality for Sartre. The second degree of sociality is the group which is by definition the suppression of seriality in a constitut*ed* praxis, a constitut*ed* dialectic. (Only individual praxis is constitut*ing*, as we have noted above.) Sartre's problem at this juncture is to explain the appearance of this constituted praxis within the limits mentioned in the previous paragraph. This is the *experimentum crucis* for Sartre's dialectical nominalism. He undertakes it by distinguishing three basic components which together can resolve the contradictions of seriality, viz., free individual action, free reciprocity, and the mediating Third.

We have seen that in Sartre's current thought it is axiomatic that individual praxis alone is constituting and self-luminous. It is capable of totalizing every multiplicity which appears in the practical field, but it can do this only from an individual viewpoint. The potential which it bears within itself for union with *all* praxes, and for the higher viewpoint which such a union demands, lies dormant in solitude and even, as we now realize, in reciprocity.[48] "Unity

---

of "objectification" *(l'objectivation)* of the group in its early stages or of the mediating Third, he is referring to its attainment of its material objectives which form a totality external to it (see, e.g., CRD 412). This is a form of the practico-inert objectification we mentioned above (n. 43).

[47] "The dialectic, if it exists, can only be the totalization of concrete totalizations effected by a multiplicity of totalizing individuals *(singularités)*. This is what I shall call 'dialectical nominalism' " (CRD 132).

[48] Sartre is vague, perhaps justifiably so in view of his continued opposition to determinism, as to what actually triggers that "Apocalypse" (Malraux) wherein the series dissolves into the group-in-fusion. Sometimes he assigns this function to the "common danger," perceived as such by the potential Thirds whose status as group members is thereby actualized (see CRD 398). Other times he speaks of "a concurrence of historical circumstances, a dated change in the situation, a danger of death, violence" (CRD 425) as more concrete forms of this common danger. It is always in accord with some "objective exigency" which can be read or misread by the would-be Third that group fusion begins (see CRD 413-414). To this extent, Sartre makes good his commitment to historical materialism with its distinction of base from

in fact can appear as the omnipresent reality of a seriality undergoing total liquidation only if it affects each one in his relations as Third with Others, relations which form one of the structures of his existence in freedom."[49]

The binary relationship which we analyzed in detail was "abstract" because it prescinded from reference to a third element, whether collective object (worked matter), alienating Third or mediating Third. To appreciate what Sartre means by "free reciprocity," we must first consider his distinction between free and serial alterity. The latter designates that object–being and otherness which accrue to binary relations in virtue of reference to a collective object or an alienating Third. To be consistent, we might call such binary relations "serial reciprocity" so as to distinguish them from free reciprocity where "free alterity" obtains. Free alterity is a type of nonalienating otherness which characterizes each individual in a group as distinct though "the same" (in a manner soon to be explained) as every other member. Sartre must account for the fact that the individual is never totally integrated into the group. By insisting that there is a form of alterity which is not inimical to group praxis as is serial alterity, he can defend the primacy of individual praxis and emphasize that group unity is never completed but is ever under way. "Free alterity" is one of a number of paradoxical expressions which Sartre feels constrained to employ as he tries to reconcile the insuperable individuality of the organic agent with the qualitatively richer praxis of the group. The reciprocity which is operative within the group is free because the alterity which, according to Sartre, characterizes *all* reciprocity is in this case free. But the elixir of this freedom is the mediating Third.

It is in relation to dyadic separation and serial impotency that the mediating Third must be understood, for it exists in dialectical opposition to them. Structurally, the Third is "the human mediation by which the multiplicity of epicenters and ends (identical and separated) allows itself *directly* to be organized as determined by

---

superstructure and its concept of "objective contradiction." But Sartre is a Marxist *suo modo;* and it is individual men (in relation), not processes who are the ultimate agents of history. So it is only *as interiorized* by the Third that these objective factors become operative in dissolving seriality.

[49]CRD 398.

a synthetic objective."[50] The free dyadic relationship in which the agents suspend mutually incompatible actions toward individual goals becomes actualized only through the mediating Third. It is as Third that multiplicity is interiorized and alterity rendered harmless in view of a common objective.

Because Sartre's powerful imagination adds flesh to the bare bones of an admittedly abstract and technical analysis, let us view his dialectical nominalism in practice as he explains the origin of the revolutionary group from the serialized mob of the Quartier St.–Antoine on the 14th of July, 1789. We can then appeal to this extended example as we pursue our examination of the mediating Third.

Sartre begins with the serial status of the crowd. Totalized negatively and from without by the army that surrounds Paris, the immediate reaction of the people is panic, i.e., serial dispersion. Each is Other, fleeing for his life at the expense, if need be, of the others. The alienating Third, as the basic structure of any Third, is operative here as well. The army assumes this status in regard to the inhabitants of the quarter. Yet Sartre adds a new aspect to his description when he treats of the resident of the quarter itself who would withdraw himself from the fray. Though he view the panic from his window or in some other way attempt to maintain the position of Other toward the situation as a whole, socioeconomic conditions and historical circumstances conspire to preclude this possibility. This is a striking instance of the praxis/practico–inert relationship which is Sartre's understanding of Engels's dictum: men make their history themselves, but they make it within a given milieu which conditions them.[51] Like it or not, the individual finds himself totalized by the menacing Other. His material membership in the series as well as its passive activity (e.g., its flight) confer on him a status which excludes detachment. For example, he lives in the quarter, he is "standing around" when the crowd starts to move, his dress or accent betrays him. One need only think of the involvement of the "onlookers" in the Kent State affair who by virtue of their curiosity, their attire, their very presence in an area "where the trouble was starting" suddenly found themselves totalized with activist war

[50]CRD 398.

[51]Quoted by Sartre from a letter of Engels to Marx (CRD 30 and 60).

protesters by nervous guardsmen to realize the plausibility of Sartre's descriptive analysis.

Every Third must start as an alienating Third, for each at first grasps the situation as a whole without integrating himself into it. As he starts to move, for example, he notices that the crowd is running through the narrow street. But in that same moment he realizes that his absence from "the crowd" is *risk of death*. The resultant fear is surmounted by his "joining in." But one doesn't "join in" to a serial flight; such flight is contagious, yes, but not unifying. By one and the same act, he constitutes the crowd as more than serial unity and allies himself with it. As Sartre puts it: "There are neither Others nor individuals who flee in his eyes; but flight, conceived as common praxis responding to a common danger, becomes flight as active totality."[52]

In effect, a transformation is taking place. As the awareness grows on the part of each that they are numerous or that death awaits them in total rout, the Third in each is actualized and flight is converted into a free common act. This is no mere change in the individual's way of perceiving the situation or regarding himself, though both elements are doubtless involved. Rather, at this crucial moment each becomes *sovereign;* he becomes the organizer of a common praxis.[53] Now men turn to countercharge or they withdraw only to obtain a better position from which to do battle. This is true of each one, for each is the same as far as the resistance is concerned. In the white heat of mortal combat, the individual has shed his serial alienation and powerlessness: the group is born.

The relationship among individual members which arises with the emergence of the group is at once *transcendent,* each as sovereign synthetically unifies the group, and *immanent,* seriality dissolves only to the degree that unity of objective is interiorized by the practical comprehension of each member. The practical relationship which constitutes the group is in effect a totalizing action on the part of each Third of all the actions ascribable to

[52]CRD 401.

[53]"By 'sovereignty' . . . I mean the absolute practical power of the dialectical organism, that is, its pure and simple praxis as synthesis *en cours* of every given multiplicity in its practical field whether inanimate objects, living beings or men" (CRD 563). Whereas sovereignty was lacking to the collective, in the group-in-fusion every man is sovereign. The only limit to his sovereignty is the sovereignty of the other Third. Thus each is co- or quasi-sovereign, just as each is quasi-transcendence, quasi-subject, and quasi-object.

the group as being "the same" as his own. He unites and coordinates similar or reciprocal actions. He thereby discovers "*our* flight."[54]

But the very act of totalizing cannot include itself as a totalized element. Here we encounter in the action of the mediating Third a gap, a certain lack of coincidence with itself (such as characterized *pour-soi* in BN), a lingering alterity, albeit "free" alterity, parallel to the neccesary being-object which we saw vitiate every attempt at full mutual integration on the abstract level of reciprocity. On the one hand this marks the limit of integration of any individual into the group (We shall treat of this consequence when our analysis reaches the phenomenon of time gap or *dècalage*) and on the other it accounts for the tension which obtains at the heart of the group. Member and member are related to each other and to the group as quasi-object and quasi-subject.[55] However, Sartre believes that it is the error of analytic as distinct from dialectical sociologists to stop at this point and to consider the group as a binary relationship (individual/community) when in reality it is a set of ternary relations dialectically ordered. In effect, they have overlooked the mediating function of the Third.

Sartre refers to two moments in the mediated reciprocity which constitutes the inner life of the group. The first is the mediation of the Third by the group itself.[56] His example is that of a man joining ninety-nine others. Via their numerical presence he renders *each* the hundredth. So the group mediates reciprocity among its members, but it does so as praxis, unlike the practico-inert object which mediates the collective. What was lacking to the collective is available through the mediation of the group, namely, a bond of *interiority* established between the Thirds. Thus interiorized number, to continue Sartre's example, is converted from discrete to intensive quantity, conferring the same degree of power upon all the Thirds in opposition to the enemy. The result of this interiorized quantity is the "objective reality" of the group, as Sartre calls it. It is not sheer number, but number in the service of a specific objective which constitutes the objective reality of the group. It is to this that the prospective member approaches as

[54]See CRD 403 where Sartre discusses "my group" as a kind of synthetic *dèpassement* of the group-subject and the group-object in my practical field.

[55]See CRD 404.

[56]See CRD 404.

he "joins in." And at this apocalyptic stage, the very decision to join is itself efficacious of membership since it consists in acting on the assumption that multiplicity is a *means* toward a common goal.

Sartre's dialectical nominalism comes to the fore as he attempts to explain the specificity of that unity which the group realizes. For he is hard pressed to avoid the claim that the group is a whole with characteristics independent of the sum of its individual parts. He hopes to do this with the help of the concept of "the same" *(la même):* the unity of the group is one of sameness, not of identity, and this sameness is the contrary of serial otherness. Thus he writes: "The Third is no longer Other nor is he my identical: but he comes to the group as I do; he is the same as me."[57] Throughout the *Critique* Sartre distinguishes seriality from group unity in terms of otherness and sameness respectively.

The concept of sameness combines the notions of singularity and ubiquity. "Singularity" refers to the fact that each organic agent retains a certain uniqueness grounded in his totalizing praxis which precludes the possibility of the group's becoming a hyperorganism and which accounts for the free alterity which exists within the group.

"Ubiquity" is Sartre's term for the common character conferred on individual actions by virtue of their being interiorized as means to a common end. Because we are acting together, each action is "here" in the sense of "within the range of my concern and responsibility." To be a group member means to be wherever the group acts, i.e., wherever each member as member acts, for that is "here" for me. By employing a spatial term Sartre calls attention to the *practical* nature of group unity, based as it is on the transformation of numerical power which occurs when multiplicity is interiorized.

By resolving sameness into singularity and ubiquity, Sartre hopes to arrive at a practical, nonsubstantial "We." In so arguing he approximates those nominalists who opt for resemblance theories of universals without realizing that resemblance is itself a uni-

[57]CRD 405. "I see myself coming to the group in him [the Third], and what I see is only lived objectivity." In the group-in-fusion the Third is "my interiorized objectivity. I grasp it in him not as Other but as mine" (CRD 406).

versal in the sense they wish to reject.[58] Not that Sartre has created a substantial "We" *malgré lui;* but his zealous opposition to what he takes to be substantialism in social theory has blinded him to the fact that he, too, has assigned an ontological status to the group, viz., that of a relational entity (though the relations are practical), and that it is in virtue of this status that the group itself operates at this first moment of mediation.[59] Perhaps the chief deficiency in Sartre's theory from the ontological viewpoint is precisely this failure to offer a thoroughgoing ontology of relations. He has never undertaken a systematic analysis of relations themselves, though their distinction from substances and events has been crucial to Sartrean philosophy since BN.

The second moment of mediated reciprocity which Sartre distinguishes obtains between the group and other Thirds on the one hand and the "regulating Third" *(le tiers regulateur)* on the other. Each Third in a sense assumes responsibility for the praxis of the others by designating his own action regulative of the common action, and this prior to any formal organization of the group. "From this perspective I am a free human agent in the eyes of each Third," writes Sartre, "but one *committed* (with the other Thirds and in the group) to a constellation of mediated reciprocities."[60]

[58]This objection against nominalism was perhaps most forcefully pressed by Bertrand Russell both early and late in his career. See his *The Problems of Philosophy*, The Home University Library (London: Thornton Butterworth, 1912), chaps. ix and x; and his William James Lectures, *An Inquiry into Meaning and Truth* (London: George Allen and Unwin, 1940), chap. xxv.

[59]Thus it is at least arguable that Sartre's archenemy in his antisubstantialist battle in social philosophy, Emile Durkheim, held a position regarding the ontological status of the group not unlike that of Sartre himself! For one interpreter, Edward A. Tiryakian, in his *Sociologism and Existentialism* (Englewood Cliffs, N.J.: Prentice-Hall, 1962) insists that "Durkheim's fundamental concern was really to study objectively a *subjective* reality, not, as is sometimes assumed (by existentialists, among others) an *objective* reality. Following his perspective, society may be viewed as a psychic reality, composed of beliefs, values, and ideals . . . It is a reality, however, which does not exist apart from men, and in this sense may be termed an immanent transcendence" (page 163, italics his). Of course, this would require the reconciling of Sartre's numerous strictures against "hyperorganisms" and reification with Durkheim's precept that "the first and most fundamental rule [for the observation of social facts] is: *Consider social facts as things*"; see his *The Rules of Sociological Method,* trans. by Sarah A. Solovay and John H. Mueller, ed. by George E. G. Catlin (8th ed.; New York: The Free Press, 1938), p. 14, italics his.

[60]CRD 408, italics mine. "Committed . . . to" is our rendering of "*engagé . . . dans*"; it seems most in accord with the context.

Each Third moves from totalizing sovereign to totalized sovereign in relation to the other Third as regulating. This occurs not theoretically but in practice by each Third's accommodating his action to the action of the other Third as normative. Sartre explains: "Practically, this means that I am integrated into the common action when the common praxis of the Third is posited as *regulative*."[61] Again, I recognize the action of the other Thirds as "the same," this time through the mediation of the regulating Third. The *mot d'ordre* which the Third emits is really the articulation of my own desires at that moment. In following it I am actually pursuing my own designs. Unlike the worked matter of the collective, the *mot d'ordre* becomes the "vehicle of sovereignty"[62] as it passes from man to man. For in expressing the same direction the I give myself, it realizes my freedom.

In his conception of the mediating reciprocity of the regulating Third and especially in his analysis of the *mot d'ordre* as vehicle of sovereignty, Sartre is doubtless inspired by Rousseau's notion of the general will as conferring freedom on the individual precisely because it involves obedience to a command he has given to himself.[63] And at this stage of the analysis Sartre is probably right. The group member is not coerced from without; neither is he the passive victim of propaganda or other forms of psychological conditioning. (These limitations on freedom will characterize subsequent stages of the group, viz., the organized and the institutionalized group respectively.) For that brief moment when the group is being born, unalloyed freedom and sovereignty appear only to fade before the harsh exigencies of the practico-inert.

That limit which greets every agent of integration in Sartre's social thought makes no exception for the regulating Third. This time Sartre calls it a "time gap" (*décalage*) and he discovers it as an infinitesimal but insuperable distance between totality and totalization, between identity and difference which he had previously tried to capture with the concept of sameness. The Third is able to direct *(régler)* because he is neither Other like the boss of an institution, nor identical, as some part in an organic whole. Sartre thus retains the possibility of evasion or tyranny even in the spontaneous unity of the group-in-fusion.

[61]CRD 408, italics mine.
[62]CRD 409.
[63]See *The Social Contract,* Book II, Chapter 6, "On Law."

With the revolving *décalage* of the regulating Third we witness Sartre's closest approximation to a Hegelian *Aufhebung* of subject and object in the social sphere as well as its necessary failure. If commentators have remarked on the new concept of freedom which Sartre develops in the *Critique,* namely, that the individual is free only in the group, they are probably impressed with Sartre's description of the group–in–fusion.[64] But if they speak of the later Sartre as repudiating the existentialist theory of the primacy of the individual, they have neglected to note the limitations to group integration which Sartre appeals to at every turn. Sartre concludes that the alternating status of each group member as he passes from interiority to "quasi–exteriority" seems to be "the very law of the group–in–fusion."[65]

The foregoing analysis of the alienating and the mediating Third in the *Critique* has reached its term with the two moments of mediated reciprocity in the group–in–fusion. It has emphasized the contribution of the Third to the ontological problem of the genesis of the group and the status of the individual within it. Before undertaking our evaluation of Sartre's success in resolving this problem, however, we shall summarize the major conclusions which the previous pages support regarding the dialectical intel-

[64]Mary Warnock, for example, writes that in CRD "choosing freedom now means choosing to rid ourselves of the impotence caused by living in a collective. Once we have formed a group, then choosing freedom means choosing to take steps to prevent its disintegration"; see her *The Philosophy of Sartre* (London: Hutchinson University Library, 1965), p. 180. Wilfrid Desan interprets Sartre's *"la necessité de la liberté"* (CRD 494) to mean "one cannot not be in a group" (*Marxism,* p. 152). Given the function of the group in the *Critique* to liberate from the practico-inert, Anthony Manser is in fact agreeing with Warnock and Desan when he observes: "Marx realized that the practico-inert presented an important limitation on human action and freedom; instead of following Marx, Sartre seems to leap to the conclusion that there is no freedom because of this feature"; see his *Sartre. A Philosophic Study* (London: The Athlone Press, 1966), p. 207. Manser goes on to add, however, that "it is the problem of freedom which causes Sartre most of his trouble in this book" (p. 219). This is no doubt true, but the concept of the mediating Third, as we have now seen, represents an ingenious attempt to synthesize two apparently conflicting notions of freedom, the Marxist and the existentialist. It places Sartre squarely in another French tradition, that of "libertarian socialism" (anarchism), reaching back to Proudhon and Saint-Simon. Although the question of Sartre's anarchism is beyond the purview of the present essay, his analysis of the mediating Third is obviously vital to any claim he might make for the primacy of voluntary associations.

[65]CRD 409.

ligibility of the group-in-fusion so as to establish the role of the Third in this methodological question as well.

First of all, with the appearance of the group-in-fusion a new reality has entered on the social scene. To the extent that it is constituted by the translucid praxes of individuals, it shares in their intelligibility. But as a "synthetic enrichment" of individual praxis,[66] the group requires an intelligibility of its own. The same Third which mediates the reciprocities that constitute the inner life of the group also establishes the norm for collective action in the group-in-fusion. In other words, at this crucial stage every Third is or can be regulating. The Third thus replaces a collective consciousness/conscience as the source of interior unity proper to the group.

We defined the mediating Third in terms of its ability to organize a multiplicity of agents and ends under a synthetic objective.[67] It is these objectives which provide what we might call the dialectical teleology in Sartre's social thought. To understand the movement of history (and this is the ultimate purpose of the *Critique* as a whole), one must focus on these objectives *as they are conceived by the mediating Thirds.*[68] This may, of course, be different from the "real" significance of the objective as the historian will discover it after the fact.[69] The anatomy of the objective/Third relationship is essentially as we have described it in the threshold instance of the group-in-fusion. The actual content of such objectives, i.e., what gives rise to *this* group here and now, cannot be determined a priori, but remains a matter for empirical study.[70]

With this objective/Third relationship we come to the heart of

[66]CRD 407. Sartre distinguishes two dialectics, viz., those of individual and of group praxis respectively (CRD 359). Though he insists that the intelligibility of the group "as praxis" depends on the intelligibility of individual praxis (as the constituted depends on the constituting), he explains this position in a manner quite in accord with methodological holism: "This dialectic of the group is most certainly *irreducible* to the dialectic of individual work, but it cannot exist by itself" (CRD 432, italics his).

[67]See above pp. 20-21.

[68]"So the first necessity for the situated investigator . . . is to understand *(comprendre)* the comprehension of the regulating Third" (CRD 657).

[69]See CRD 414.

[70]The general content of such objectives, of course, *can* be determined in advance: it is scarcity interiorized (see CRD 752).

Sartre's attempt at dialectical intelligibility, at least as far as the group-in-fusion is concerned. He argues that the ***structure*** of certain objectives (of flight before an organized foe, for example) is understood by the praxis of individuals to require the common unity of *one* praxis for all. It is the historian's task to weigh the urgency, what Sartre calls the "totalizing force," of the objective of any group. He must do this by considering primarily the praxis of the Third in so far as it freely arises in relation to this objective i.e., defines itself in terms of the objective as its common future to be accepted or refused. "It is the tension between this future and the present practice and the progressive and regressive deciphering of this fundamental relation which provide the first elements of intelligibility."[71]

Thus the Third plays a vital role in the progressive-regressive method which Sartre introduced in *A Question of Method* and which, he claims, finds its critical foundation in the *Critique* (though it preceded the latter in time of composition).[72] In the regressive movement, which we have observed in Volume I of the *Critique,* it provides the key concept for a dialectical sociology. In the progressive movement of the once projected second volume, the Third would have enjoyed equal importance. For Sartre intended to demonstrate the (dialectical) rationality of human history by proving that every practical ensemble must totalize itself incessantly

[71]CRD 414. To the extent that personal peculiarities of individual agents contribute to the intelligibility of the leap from series to group, Sartre argues (even at this stage of his regressive analysis) that these circumstances are relevant only as "general particularities," i.e., as attributes which modify the individual precisely in his function *as Third.* As Sartre had once argued that no one *is* cowardly, that each "does" his cowardice by individual cowardly choices (see, e.g., *L'Existentialisme est un humanisme* [Paris: Nagel, 1970], pp. 60-62), so he is now claiming that no one *is* a leader of men, for example, except the men, i.e., the group, in specific circumstances confer this function upon him; see CRD 414-415. This stance is consistent with the mediating role Sartre reserves for the group in regard to the Thirds, but it favors the sociological over the psychological in historical explanation. (In his *A Question of Method,* a prologue to the *Critique,* Sartre scores the Marxists for their inability to get beyond "general particularities" in historical analysis [see CRD 26].) If Sartre will balance these two approaches to the meaning of history (a fortiori, if he will synthesize them), he must apply the fruits of existential psychoanalysis at the moment when the Third mediates the group and other Thirds. At that juncture an appeal to "general particularities" will not suffice.

[72]See Sartre's preface to the Critique (CRD 9).

by interiorizing its multiplicity at every level.[73] The Third, as we have seen, is the neccesary instrument of such interiorization.

Sartre in his preface to Gorz's *The Traitor* had remarked that today there are only two ways of speaking about the self: the third person singular and the first person plural. The point of this central portion of our study has been to demonstrate that for Sartre the secret of the latter is the former: multiplicity is interiorized, i.e., retains its subjectivity, only through the mediation of the Third.

III

As we begin our critical evaluation of the function of the Third in Sartre's social thought, it should be born in mind that our exposition has centered on a single concept extracted from a work which purports to be dialectical in its unity.[74] In fact, we have further limited ourselves by discussing the mediating Third only in that crucial moment of Sartre's regressive analysis where the group is being fused. For we are convinced that the strengths and weaknesses of this concept as Sartre employs it throughout the *Critique* emerge clearly at this juncture. This immediately leaves us vulnerable to a "yes, but" type of criticism. Yet if one is to move from the plane of paraphrase and summary toward a detailed examination of the specific problems which this important work attempts to resolve, the risk of myopic vision must be run.

The genius of the Third, if we may call it that, is its function as a *via media* between atomism and organicism in ontology as well as between simple psychologism and unmitigated sociologism in methodology. Ontologically, we have noted, Sartre is loath to admit that anything like a collective consciousness exists. So only individual praxis is constitut*ing;* group praxis is constitut*ed* and, one might add, always being constituted and reconstituted, totalized and detotalized by individuals in dialectical relation with each other, with other groups, and with the practico-inert.

[73]See CRD 136.

[74]In an interview with Pierre Verstraeten, a young Belgian follower of Sartre's, he defended the *Critique* against criticisms of its prolixity by claiming that "each phrase represents the unity of a dialectical movement"; see "L'écrivain et sa langue," *Revue d'Esthétique*, XVIII (juillet-décembre, 1965), p. 329.

There is a certain prima facie plausibility to Sartre's "solution" to the problem of individual/group relationships stemming from its very attempt to reconcile two traditionally conflicting claims about the nature of social reality. While allowing a "synthetic enrichment" of individual praxis through group membership, Sartre nevertheless insists that each Third is individual and sovereign though "the same" as every other with regard to praxis.

The concept of sameness, we saw, unpacked into "singularity" and "ubiquity." Now the latter is equivalent to the conditional: "If under attack, my fellows will do what I would do if I were there." This is a dispositional use compatible with an atomistic ontology. So far, we cannot claim, as does Mary Warnock, that the *Critique* marks "the disappearance of the individual" from Sartre's philosophic concern.[75] On the contrary, he seems particularly concerned to see that the individual does *not* disappear into some organic totality like the state, the party or even the group.[76] In this he sees a parallel between his existentialist mission to a Marxist "scholasticism of the totality" and Kierkegaard's attack upon Hegelianism in the name of the individual.[77]

When Sartre begins his account of that "synthetic enrichment" which characterizes the mediating Third as group member, however, he becomes increasingly paradoxical and vague. The plausibility of his argument suffers accordingly. This is particularly true of his explanation of mediating reciprocity in its first moment, the mediating of the Thirds by the group. For he is unclear as to how *the group* can mediate between Thirds, even allowing that both come into existence simultaneously. The difficulty, as we suggested, is that Sartre lacks a metaphysics of relations. He is left to fluctuate between denials that the group is a hypostasis and assertions that group praxis is distinct from and less abstract (and thus more "real") than individual praxis. His analysis calls for a real, though relational, group subject which his ontology cannot accommodate.

[75]Warnock, *The Philosophy*, p. 177, where it forms the title for a subsection of her final chapter. Elsewhere in the same volume she writes that Sartre has allowed "the individual to be swallowed up in the group, and existentialism thereby to be swallowed up in Marxism" (p. 134).

[76]Georges Gurvitch has remarked on Sartre's "camouflaged antistatism" (*Dialectique*, p. 170). This is a major feature of what we have called his "libertarian socialism" (above, n.64, p. 28).

[77]See CRD 28 and 108.

It is Sartre's fear of reified abstractions—a common form of alienation, according to Marxists, but one they are often guilty of themselves—which prevents him from mentioning a collective subject. In its stead he offers us the mediating Third which must perform the specific function of a collective subject, namely, that of totalizing without objectifying. As a result the mediating Third and the other Thirds find themselves in the revolving relationships of quasi-subjects and quasi-objects, of quasi--transcendence and immanence. This recourse to contrary descriptions and to paradox need not be disconcerting if we view it as an appeal for dialectical resolution. But this appeal wins only a slight response in the form of the mediating Third, for it relegates the synthetic unity of the Thirds to the status of a regulative idea or ideal. In the absence of a genuine synthesis we are left with the juxtaposition of alternating descriptions, but not with a dialectic.

We have previously alluded to an important sense in which Sartre has never overcome the atomism of BN. This is fundamentally expressed by the inability of the mediating Third to include itself as part of its totalization. Not only does this render the enrichment of individual praxes somewhat less than "synthetic," but the resultant *décalage* harbors the individualistic freedom of BN at the very heart of the group-in-fusion (The agent can still betray or refuse to join). It is as if Sartre were unwilling to leave all the idols of his bourgeois forebears behind as he enters the promised land of collective freedom.

In his discussion of ontological commitment W.V.O. Quine argues that it is reasonable for any philosopher to accept the "existence" of abstract entities if to do so is in accord with "the simplest conceptual scheme into which the ordered fragments of raw experience can be fitted and arranged."[78] And he posits "objects of a special and abstract kind, viz., classes," in order to do higher logic.[79] The example of Quine, who is certainly not noted for the needless multiplication of entities, constitutes a challenge to Sartre in the present problem. Either Sartre accepts the existence of groups, i.e., admits them as values for bound variables (in the language of contemporary logic), or he is left with his present paradox of a group

[78]Willard Van Orman Quine, *From a Logical Point of View,* Harper Torchbooks (2nd ed., rev.; New York: Harper & Row, 1961), p. 16.

[79]Willard Van Orman Quine, *Methods of Logic* (rev. ed.; New York: Holt, Rinehart and Winston, 1959), p. 228.

tarian socialism" (above, n. 64, p. 27).

which is not a subject and a subject which cannot be a group. Dialectic is called for, no doubt; but dialectical nominalism turns out to be self-defeating, since it destroys as nominalism what it aims at establishing as dialectic, namely, a real synthesis of individual actions into group praxis.

But the concept of the Third has a correspondingly important methodological value as well. It justifies Sartre's amalgam of Marxist sociological explanation with insights from existential psychoanalysis. With the former Sartre acquires all the "explanatory force" of dialectical sociology.[80] His regressive analysis explains how classes and class warfare are possible, why groups are less stable than collectives, and why man always seems to witness the work of his hands turn against him in counterfinality.

Yet if man is the victim of history, he is also its agent. To learn the "inside" of history one has the availability of the mediating Third's understanding of the group objective. And existential psychoanalysis provides the historian with a means to achieve that "comprehension" (Sartre's peculiar employment of the *Verstehen* of German historians and social philosophers) of the unique project of the group members which explains the historical event to a degree that mere structural analysis cannot attain. Such an understanding even eludes the Marxists, who must rest content with "situating" a cerain event in its socioeconomic context.[81] The rest for them

[80]Michael and Deena Weinstein locate the *Critique* in the context of the humanist revolt against abstract and formal sociologies which is under way in both Europe and America. They list five hallmarks of the method employed by the humanists: stress on a historical rather than a universalistic approach, multi-variate sociological analysis rather than single-factor social theory, empirical and dynamic methods instead of the method of placing or illustrating, concern with totalization instead of interest in fully defined totalities or pluralistic models, and an emphasis on the practical rather than on the contemplative; see their "Sartre and the Humanist Tradition in Sociology," in *Sartre. A Collection of Critical Essays,* ed. by Mary Warnock, Anchor Books (Garden City, N. Y.: Doubleday & Company, 1971), pp. 357-386.

[81]See CRD 43 ff. Sartre agrees that this method is fine as far as it goes, but that it doesn't go far enough. It hovers at a certain level of abstraction, leaving the explanation of the concrete individual to other disciplines or to chance. Thus in the case of Valéry, the Marxists offer us the "general particularities" of a class, an era, an ideology, etc., but the concrete Valéry eludes them. The latter is discovered only a posteriori and is understood only in terms of an existential psychoanalysis of his childhood, focusing on that "point of insertion of the man into his class, i.e., the particular family as mediation between the universal class and the individual" (CRD 47). "Valéry is a petit-bourgeois

is pure chance. But the rationalist strain in Sartre has always balked at brute facts.[82] So he seeks to discover "the mediations which allow the concrete individual, life, the real dated battle, and the person to come to be out of the *general* contradictions of productive forces and relations of production."[83] At the forefront of these mediations stand worked matter and the Third. By introducing the latter, Sartre has made room for subjectivity in the materialist dialectic once more[84] and has thereby retained a place for existential psychoanalysis in the social sphere.

Despite its laudable aim of humanizing the abstractions of Marxist socioeconomic theory, Sartre's methodological enterprise suffers from the limitations of its component parts. A brief examination of its two leading elements, viz., dialectical sociology and existential psychoanalysis, will make this clear.

Sartre's introduction of the mediating Third, as we saw, was central to his employment of a dialectical sociology. However, the preeminence of that same Third (linked as it is to the denial of a real, collective subject in the ontological realm) seems to have blinded him to the possibility of other forms of dialectical relationships. The late Georges Gurvitch, eminent dialectical sociologist at the Sorbonne, made perhaps the most telling criticism of Sartre in this regard when he concluded his study of the *Critique* with the remark that "Sartre shows himself to be incomparably more dogmatic

---

intellectual, of that there is no doubt. But every petit-bourgeois intellectual is not Valéry. The heuristic insufficiency of contemporary Marxism is contained in those two sentences" (CRD 44). In effect, what Marxism lacks is a "hierarchy of mediations by which to grasp the process which produces the person and his product within a given class and society at a given moment in history" (CRD 44).

82His voluntarist strain, on the contrary, has always thrived on chance and contingency. Iris Murdoch has captured this conflict in his philosophic character with the title of her study, *Sartre. Romantic Rationalist* (New Haven: Yale University Press, 1959).

83CRD 45, italics his.

84We say "once more" because Sartre subscribes to that interpretation of Marx which Alasdair MacIntyre has called "the myth of the plastic figure," i.e., the image of a young Marx, Hegelian and humanist, who later abandons his concern with alienation for socioeconomics; see his collection of essays, *Against the Self-Images of the Age* (London: Duckworth, 1971), pp. 64 ff. For a recent attempt to destroy this myth, using the *Grundrisse* to prove his point, see Bertell Ollman's *Alienation. Marx's Conception of Man in Capitalist Society* (Cambridge: at the University Press, 1971).

than Marx both in his general conception of dialectic and in his application of it to sociology."[85] For Sartre himself had begun the *Critique* with a critical survey of what he called the "dogmatic dialectic" of Marxist philosophers.[86] He went on to affirm a "dialectic within the dialectic" which would afford him a methodological flexibility unavailable to his Marxist counterparts.[87] But in practice he has retained the single, "classic" form of antinomies and syntheses in which the Third is paramount, ignoring the rich variety of dialectical relationships employed by other dialecticians, including Gurvitch himself.[88]

Existential psychoanalysis has been a matter of dispute since Sartre first adopted the term in BN. A species of the phenomenological psychiatry inspired by Husserl and Heidegger, Sartre's version profits from his rich imagination and his descriptive power. But it labors under a burden peculiarly its own. For its rejection of any theory of the unconsious deprives it of the panoply of instincts and complexes usually associated with psychoanalytic theory, while its disregard of experimental psychology bars access to a wealth of scientific research.[89] Sartre's theory hangs perilously by the thread of an initial choice which is neither unconscious nor reflectively conscious. In fact the revolving totalizations of mediating Thirds take place on this prereflective level.[90] But one can reason-

[85]Gurvitch, *Dialectique*, p. 176.

[86]See CRD 115 ff.

[87]CRD 281.

[88]For a detailed typology of such dialectics, see Gurvitch, *Dialectique*, pp. 189 ff.

[89]Sartre's attitude toward Freud is much more qualified now than it had formerly been, although he continues to reject the term "unconscious"; see an interview recorded in *New Left Review*, No. 58 (November-December, 1969), pp. 45 ff. Sylvie Le Bon in the introduction to her critical edition of *La Transcendence de l'Ego* (Paris: Vrin, 1966) goes so far as to claim that Sartre "has totally revised his former conception—his rejection—of the unconscious and of psychoanalytic understanding, and would no longer defend his past suspicions *(préventions)* in this area" (p. 8). In view of the just mentioned interview, so "total" a revision seems unlikely. McMahon, who also considers Le Bon's assertion extreme, points out, however, that the vocabulary of Sartre's work-in-progress on Flaubert "is a perfect representation of Freudian thought"; see McMahon, *Humans Being*, p. 353, n. 10.

[90]This is true of the group-in-fusion. As the common danger subsides, the group becomes *reflectively* conscious: it now acts upon itself by the diversification of roles and functions and, more important, it faces the problem of its permanence. See CRD pp. 435 ff.

ably question the existence of such a fundamental choice in the life of every man as well as its methodological significance in social philosophy. (Perhaps it is no mere coincidence that Sartre has limited his application of this existential phychoanalytic method to the study of artists and men of letters, never applying it to revolutionaries, much less to revolutionary groups.) One should likewise demand evidence justifying Sartre's extensive use of the prereflective level itself, a use which suspiciously resembles that which the Freudians make of the unconscious. This suspicion is heightened when one has to be "told" what he has "consciously" done, a common occurrence in Sartre's analyses and descriptions.

But the difficulties both ontological and methodological which Sartre encounters either stemming from his notion of the Third or deriving from theories such as dialectical sociology and existential psychoanalysis in which this concept figures centrally—these difficulties are not insuperable. Neither are they appreciably worse than those which hinder alternative approaches to social philosophy. As we have suggested, Sartre's dialectical nominalism would be considerably improved if his ontological commitment were extended to include the existence of groups as real, relational entities, i.e., if it ceased to be nominalistic. And his defense of subjectivity within the pale of Marxist materialism would likewise be enhanced by a greater regard for the findings of social psychology.[91] Still, the overall thrust of his social thought continues to display a healthy respect for individual freedom even as it affirms the need

[91]Not that Sartre is ignorant of contemporary studies in group dynamics. J. L. Moreno and Kurt Lewin, for example, are cited occasionally in the *Critique*. But there are numerous studies available in the very areas of Sartre's concern which could provide factual grist for his dialectical mill—empirical research on pressures to uniformity in groups, on power and influence within them, on leadership and motivational processes, to name a few. Of course, these findings could require that Sartre revise his theory substantially or resign himself to a level of analysis much more "abstract" and theoretical than his avowed aim in the *Critique* would allow. As a matter of fact, Sartre has never been at home with empirical research. His "experiments" have always tended to be of the Cartesian, armchair variety favored by phenomenologists. Though it may be disappointing, therefore, it is scarcely surprising that in his polemic against analytical reason in the *Critique* he does not avail himself of aid and comfort from the opposition.

More surprising, perhaps, is Sartre's failure to profit from the writings of more philosophical sociologists like himself. In particular, the absence of any reference to the work of Georg Simmel is curious. For in addition to his emphasis on the dialectical tension which obtains between the individual and

for group action in a less than perfect world. We hope to have shown that the mediating Third is Sartre's vehicle for harmonizing these two values.

* * *

Shortly before the publication of the *Critique* Sartre in an interview with Colette Audry spoke of the need for each man, if he would be *un homme total,* to turn to public affairs while continuing to accept responsibility for his personal life. But by way of *caveat* he added: "Social imperatives and individual destiny are a *true* contradiction; their reconciliation is not obvious."[92] Whether their reconciliation is any more obvious after the seven hundred and fifty-five densely written pages of the *Critique* remains an open question. But the mediating Third, which he introduces there, represents his valiant attempt to bring this very reconciliation more clearly into view. For if hell is other people, Sartre would now have us believe that salvation is the mediating Third.

The Catholic University of America

society, Simmel is noted for his theory of the social significance of sheer quantitative relationships, in particular, for his analysis of the qualitative distinction between *dyadic* and *triadic* relations. See his seminal essay, "Die quantitative Bestimmtheit der Gruppe," which forms the second chapter of his major work, *Soziologie* (5. Auflage, Berlin: Dunker & Humblot, 1968), pp. 32-100. This is available in English translation by Kurt H. Wolff in the latter's *The Sociology of Georg Simmel* (New York: Free Press, 1950), pp. 85-177.

[92]"La démocratie et nous," *L'Express,* le 27 août, 1959, cited by Contat and Rybalka, eds., *Les Écrits* (59/Note), p. 336.

2

THE EXISTENTIALISTIC CONCEPT OF THE HUMAN PERSON IN VIKTOR E. FRANKL'S LOGOTHERAPY

by

Marius G. Schneider, O.F.M.

Existentialistic psychiatrists do not deny the philosophical dependence of their theoretical conceptions. With Viktor E. Frankl they recognize that "there is no psychotherapy without a view of man and Weltanschauung" and that "a phychotherapy which declares itself value-free is actually merely value-blind."[1] Convinced of this inevitable—intended or unintended—philosophical foundation of psychiatry, they strive to become aware of the philosophical principles and implications of their scientific and therapeutic work and to justify the use of their philosophical notions. Thus Frankl maintains that, in contrast to many other therapies, his "logotherapy is based on an explicit philosophy of life"[2] which corresponds "to the full-dimensional reality of the nature of man, that reality which characterizes man and only him."[3] He conceives this human reality in terms of existentialistic philosophical ideas; and thus logotherapy, as an attempt at a psychotherapeutic anthropology, involves existential-analysis, i.e., "an ontological explication of that which is *Existenz*." (Th., 147) "That reality which characterizes man and only him" and which represents the main object of

[1]Viktor E. Frankl, *Theorie und Therapie der Neurosen* (München: Urban & Schwarzenberg, 1956), pp. 147 f. Hereafter referred to in the text as: *Th.*, followed by the page number.

[2]Viktor E. Frankl, *Psychotherapy and Existentialism* (New York: Simon and Schuster, 1968), p. 2. Hereafter referred to in the text as: *Psych.*, followed by the number of the page.

[3]Viktor E. Frankl, *Das Menschenbild der Seelenheilkunde* (Stuttgart: Hippokrates Verlag, 1959), p. 108. Hereafter referred to in the text as: *M.*, followed by the number of the page.

theoretical and practical logotherapeutic concerns is identified with existence, and this with the human person.

It is interesting to grasp the meaning of Frankl's existentialistic concept of the person and to realize the consequences this notion implies for an understanding of human nature and its normal and abnormal manifestations, and for a defense of the dignity of the human person. The use of existentialistic notions is wide-spread today, not only in psychology and psychiatry, but also in literature and even in theological studies. For instance, in writings in moral theology pertaining to the present-day debate about the justification of laws against abortion, one finds occasionally an appeal to the phenomenological or existentialistic concept of person in order to offer a possible excuse for the destruction of human fetal life. Frankl's logotherapeutic view of man certainly is an existentialistic anthropology. The following discussion of his notion of the human person is intended to examine its claim of being the correct view of human nature required for a successful psychotherapy.

The existentialistic concept of the person differs decisively from the traditional ontological understanding of the human individual. In the course of the development of our Western tradition, the term person gradually came to be used to characterize and to distinguish one type of subtantial being, one member of that supreme class of being which, together with accidental being, was considered to differentiate all created reality. It signifies the rational supposit, that being in which, because of its spirituality, the notion of substantiality i.e., of being-in-itself as opposed to the being-in-another as in a subject of inherence of the accident is realized in a most unique and perfect manner. As a supposit or hypostasis, the person is a complete substance totally existing in itself and in no way in another. That is, the person is neither an artificial product of human ingenuity, nor a mere modification or manifestation of some more basic underlying reality, nor an integral or substantial part of a superior whole, but this substantial whole itself as an individual of a determined species subsisting for itself and functioning as support of its properties and characteristics and as a source of its processes and operations. As a *rational* supposit, the individual person is most clearly and uniquely substantial being, inasmuch as he not only *is* in himself, but also is aware or, at least, is able to be aware of himself as a self-subsisting being and as the subject of his nature and individuality, of his character and personality. He is substance in a most perfect way, inasmuch as he is not only the natural static and dynamic substratum of his powers and manifestations, but also the master of his dispositions and activities, freely deciding his present and future. In virtue of his spirituality, the rational hypostasis is, and knows himself to be, destined to a life beyond his physiological death. Thus he is an end in himself and truly a being for himself, endowed with natural rights corresponding to the obligations surpassing his earthly individual and social existence. To differentiate and to extol this "most worthy and most perfect of all creatures,"[4] the term person was introduced in the early Christian centuries and his unique value and dignity were inculcated. The recognition of his natural rights and the respect and reverence due to his superior mode of being are demanded as a serious moral obligation wherever the meaning of the term is realized. Every rational supposit, every individual of the human species, possesses the inalienable rights and dignity of the person, owed to him in virtue of his nature independently of the will or whim of any society or of any conditions and circumstances of his actualisation.

Existentialistic thinkers stress the uniqueness and dignity of human existence; however, they emphatically reject this ontological understanding of the human individual. Existential analysis does not deal with the human being, but with being-human. Existence, the object of existentialistic investigations and exhortations, does not mean being as such, or substantial being, or even the human subject. To refer to man as to a subject, substance, or person implies a reification, according to Heidegger, the initiator of this trend of modern philosophy. Substance is thus declared to be a category only of nonhuman things; and, in order to prevent any association of man with mere objects, the use of such terms as subject, person, or even man is to be avoided when existence is to be discussed.[5] The being of man, existence, or being-in-the--world means "disclosedness," a kind of primarily affective consciousness, and experienced relationship with the world and one's possibilities. It means, therefore, a certain manifestation of human nature, an accident, not this existing nature itself, not the human substance.

Frankl shares Heidegger's existential-analytic approach in his logotherapeutic philosophy of man, even if not his aversion to

[4]St. Thomas Aquinas, *S. Th.*, 1, 29, 3; *De pot.*, *q.*9, *a.*3.

[5]Martin Heidegger, *Being and Time*. Transl. by John Macquarrie and Edward Robinson. (New York: Harper & Row, 1962), p. 72.

the use of the traditional anthropological terms. He intends to study "the being of man, not the existing man,"[6] he writes, introducing one of his philosophical discussions of problems of human existence, and he explicity credits Heidegger with initiating his way of understanding this being. (*Th.,* 170) The substantial character of the human person is repeatedly denied,[7] and the actualistic conception of man is presented as a self-evident truth. The person is said not to be an "ontic" entity, but an "ontological" one (in Heidegger's sense of understanding-being); (*UM.,* 104) his being is determined as a reality of performance. (*UM.,* 98) The person is only in the performance of his acts and is "nothing but this performance."[8] He *is* only in effecting himself: "spiritual actuality is itself activity." (*UM.,* 58) Frankl is so fascinated by the existentialistic view of human reality that he even subscribes to its customary declaration that a mere representation of existence as an object of thought would render the human being a real object, a mere thing. "While speaking of the person," he maintains, "this person always immediately becomes a thing—or as we already said: out of the Ego there immediately becomes an Id." (*UM.,* 101)

The Viennese founder of existentialistic psychiatry is right in admitting his dependence upon the non-substantialistic conception of man of existentialistic philosophy. However, he is mistaken in believing that his logotherapeutic understanding of human existence was conceived "primariry in conformity with Martin Heidegger's conceptual formulation as outlined in his main work 'Being and Time' of 1927." (*Th.,* 170) It is not only that Frankl does not show the least inhibition against the use of the terms person, spirit, or Ego, which Heidegger seems to abhor as an intolerable contamination of the purity of existential-analytic thought; he also indentifies "man's Being," which constitutes the subject matter of his philosophical studies, with merely the spiritual in man, while Heidegger determines "the Being of the whole," that is, of the entire body-mind-spirit unity as this Being and postulates its analysis as the

[6]Viktor E. Frankl, *Der Unbedingte Mensch* (Wien: Deuticke, 1949), p. VII. Hereafter referred to in the text as: *UM.,* followed by the number of the page.

[7]Viktor E. Frankl, *Logos und Existenz* (Wien: Amandus-Verl., 1951), p. 63. Hereafter referred to in the text as: *LE.,* followed by the number of the page.

[8]Viktor E. Frankl, *Der Unbewusste Gott* (Wien: Amandus-Verl., 1948), p. 31. Hereafter referred to in the text as: *UG.,* followed by the number of the page.

foundation of ontology, anthropology, and of any philosophical understanding of life or of the spirit.[9] For Frankl, existence, the spiritual, the Ego, the spiritual person are convertible terms or represent, at most, different aspects of one and the same reality which is existentialistically conceived as a reality of mere performance and considered as the genuine human being. The spiritual is not only one specific dimension, "but also the genuine dimension of man." (*Th.*, 172) Its understanding does not presuppose the idea of "the Being of the whole," but, on the contrary, the unity and wholeness of the human individual, as understood in logotherapy, is known and constituted only by the spiritual person. "The genuine being of man is existence," i.e. spiritual and moral existence.[10] "After all, man is man only in so far and as long as he—as a spiritual being—is *beyond* his somatic and psychic being. Or: man is existential only in so far as he detaches and distances himself from the vital and social." (*HP.*, 35) "It is only this distancing oneself from oneself as psycho-physical organism which constitutes the spiritual person as such, as spiritual," (*Th.* 171) and it is only the spiritual, the person, which "constitutes, grounds, and realizes" the unity and totality of the human being. (*LE.*, 69) It is true that "man is also a vital and social being; however, that which he is essentially, is existential." (*HP.*, 35) The person is not identical with, but "creative" of the human psycho-somatic unity. (*UM.*, 99) The person as the spiritual is not the whole man, but it is the truly and authentically human in a human being.

As the genuine being of man, the person is existence. Existence "means the specifically human mode of being," with self-transcendence as its essence. (*Psych.*, 74) "That is to say, man transcends his environment toward the world; but more than this, he also transcends his being toward an *ought*." (*Psych.*, 136) Existence is the actualisation of the essential logos-orientation of the person, a natural striving for meaning and values. Transcending his environment, man breaks the prison walls of his sensory world, that subjective world which represents the sector of the universe accessible to and through his psycho-somatic constitution, and he ap-

[9]Martin Heidegger, *op. cit.*, pp. 72 ff.

[10]Viktor E. Frankl, *Homo Patiens* (Wien: Deuticke, 1950), p. 101. Hereafter referred to in the text as: HP., followed by page-number.

proaches the objectivity and truth of reality.[11] Transcending himself, he rises spiritually above his psychophysical condition and by "this very act . . . opens and enters the noölogical dimension of being." (*Psych.*, 136)

Frankl further reveals his concrete understanding of this "existential act" by his determination and characterization of its properties, i.e. existentialia of existence: spirituality, freedom, and responsibility. "These three existentialia do not merely characterize man's being, they rather constitute it." (*Th.*, 172)

The essence of spirituality consists in the ability of "being-with" other being. (*UM.*, 28) With other philosophers of existence, Frankl does not consider this general determination of cognition (*LE.*, XII) as the result of an abstraction or generalisation from concrete acts of consciousness, but he defines this universal aspect of individual cognitive operations as the ground and condition of such acts. "Spiritual being's original possibility of 'being with' is the condition of further possibilities, that is, of perceiving, thinking, and speaking." (*UM.*, 29) And in conformity with his actualistic concept of the person, also the reality of spiritual being is seen only in the actualisation of this original possibility, in the actual 'being with' or consciousness. (*UM.*, 26)

Obviously there cannot be an empty "being-with." Consciousness is always a consciousness of something; being-with is identified with intentionality, with object-orientation. "In the ground of his being, spiritual being is intentional, and thus it can be said: spiritual being is *spiritual* being, is being-conscious, is 'with-itself' while being with other being." (*Hdb.*, 673) And this self-understanding through being-with-others is the only type of selfawareness Frankl admits. His existentialistic idea of man's being combined with spatial connotations in relation to 'being-with' does not allow him to grasp the whole phenomenon of spiritual cognition; he recognizes only "an implicit self-understanding" (*Hdb.*, 674), a direct awareness of our mental acts, and denies a perfect self-reflection, which traditionally is considered as an essential characteristic of intellectual knowledge. Existence can understand itself, but not its own self-understanding. For this understanding would have to take place

[11]Viktor E. Frankl, *Grundriss der Existenzanalyse und Logotherapie* in: Frankl, v. Gebsattel, Schultz, *Handbuch der Neurosenlehre und Psychotherapie* (München: Schwarzenberg, 1959), *Vol.* III, p. 683 f. Hereafter referred to in the text as: *Hdb.*, followed by page-number.

on a higher dimension than the original one. (*HP.*, 11, Ftn. 1) Since spiritual being *is* only in the performance of itself, it can never be intended by itself, but must remain transcendent to itself. (*UM.*, 22 Ftn. 1) "As far as it is human, every cognition is bound to a certain position. However, no object can be where there is this position, and thus also the subject can never completely become its own object." (*Hdb.*, 676; *Tt.*, 174)

Frankl adds a rationalization for his limitation of spiritual knowledge which does not improve his phenomenology of human spirituality. Self-reflection is not only impossible, he writes; it is also not necessary. "It pertains to the nature of man to be ordered and directed to something, somebody, to a work or to a human being, to an idea or to a person. And only inasmuch as we are thus intentional, we are existential, only in so far as man is spiritually with something or somebody . . . is man with himself. Man is not here to observe and to mirror himself, but he is here to deliver and to sacrifice himself, to give himself up in cognition and love." (*Hdb.*, 676 f.) As a logotherapist who stresses the healthy in man as opposed to the neurotic and sick, not only in the treatment of his patients but also especially in the interpretation of human existence, Frankl is, of course, aware of the fact that human self-knowledge is not restricted to neurotic or vain forms of self-observation and that the knowing and loving dedication he sees as a demand of human intentionality is impossible without genuine self-knowledge and love.

As his characterization of the inherent tendency of human life reveals, however, spirituality or intentionality is not to be identified merely with intellectual or rational knowledge and truth. In fact, truth as such does not represent a very high value in logotheraphy. Although he is convinced of the need for an objectively true philosophy of man, Frankl knows that even a true philosophical view of human nature can function only as a rather universal frame of reference in psychiatry allowing countless typical and individual concretizations. After all, a materialist does not seem to be more prone to neuroticism than a spiritualist, nor a Christian less than a Buddhist. Thus it is understandable when Frankl expresses the opinion that the psychiatrist as such is not to be concerned so much with the correctness of a cognition as with the sincerity of the confession of the patient. (*HP.*, 8) However, he generalizes this psychiatric experience and, quite in conformity with his existentialistic authorities, defends a subjectivistic epistemology. Objective truth as such is humanly impossible, he maintains; what is accessible is only a subjective perspective of reality. "Thus the *only absoluteness* which truth allows man lies in the *absolute uniqueness* of the perspective in which truth manifests itself to each single individual." (*HP.*, 8 Ftn. 1) Not the recognition of a universally valid truth is decisive for human existence, but the discovery and realization of *his* truth. It is senseless to waste time in searching for a meaning of life or existence in general or of existence as a whole, the grasping of which surpasses human understanding anyway. It is not man who is entitled to ask questions of life, but life which demands his answers in every instant. Thus man has to find the meaning of the concrete situation of his life in order to avoid or to overcome the pathogenic experience of existential frustration. Existence's intentionality is primarily an orientation to meaning and values, and its actualization consists in feeling, emotion, and in love.

This logotherapeutic insistence upon the significance of the emotional is not understood as a decision in the traditional dispute concerning the primacy of either intellect or will. Nor is emotion presented as the natural phase of response after a perception of values in the life cycle of vital functions, nor are love and its happiness seen as the fulfillment of human existence in the conscious possession of a precious good. Intellectual cognition is not conceived as a means for the realization and happy possession of values, and in this sense primacy accorded to the satisfaction of the will. Frankl's ideas about the meaning of existence are too rigoristic to allow any thought about their relation to happiness. The primacy of the intellect is not denied because the intellectual cognition of values is seen to serve the realization of emotion and will, but because such rational knowledge is considered to be impossible. Intentionality of emotional life is identified with a cognitive function of emotions; it is not understood as a mere objective reference of feelings and sentiments.

The emphasis of the "cognitive superiority" (*Th.*, 98) of feeling and emotion is to protect Frankl's existential analysis against the accusation of intellectualism and rationalism. "Not the intellect, nor reason amount to the properly human, to his spirituality; his heart and emotions are much more sensitive than the intellect can ever be." The motional and existential occupy the first rank in the dimension of the specifically human. (*Th.*, 97 f.)

The determination of intentionality as orientation to meaning and values is characteristic of Frankl's logotherapy. It is imposed on him by the starting position of his psychiatric work which "was an opposition . . . against the psychologism in psychotheraphy, as manifested primarily in psychoanalysis." (*HP.*, 19) The Freudian definition of the human person as an unconscious Id drive-determined and regulated by the pleasure principle was the obvious result of a projection of the spiritual onto the merely psychic level, of a deprivation of human acts of their intentionality, (*HP.*, 21) "the sin against the spiritual." (*HP.*, 19) It had to be corrected by a psychiatic view of man which repairs the psychoanalytic suppression of the spirit and replaces the Freudian automatism of the psychic apparatus with the genuine autonomy of human existence. (Cf. *UG.*, 13)

Originally man is not determined by an urge for lust. "The pleasure principle is not a psychological but a pathological principle; where it does hold sway, it is a manifestation not of a normal but of a pathological mental life. For normally man is not intending lust, but always a meaning." (*HP.*, 21) In the place of the primary urge for lust, existential analysis thus stresses the intentionality of the spiritual; to the psychoanalytic drive-determinism it opposes existentiality. Man is not impelled by something drive-like, but he is attracted by values. (*HP.*, 23) His being is "essentially permeated by a will to meaning." (*HP.*, 30) Not a psychoanalytic affect-dynamics of drive-mechanism, but freedom and responsibility specify human existence.

Freedom is an original and irreducible phenomenon of human self-understanding. (*UM.*, 93) It is a fact attested especially by the witness of the psychophysical condition and impotence of the person, the psychiatrist whose professional work depends upon the essential human ability of spiritual antagonism and opposition. (*UM.*, VII f.) For what psychotherapy in the last analysis amounts to is not a Freudian affect-dynamic or drive-energetic transformation, but an existential conversion. (*LE.*, 58) Again and again the defiant power of the spirit has to be appealed to and activated against the seemingly so powerful psychophysical organism. The belief in the ability of the spirit in man "under all conditions and circumstances in some way or other to detach and to posit itself in a fruitful distance to the psychophysical in him" represents an article of faith of Frankl's psychotherapeutic creed. (*LE.*, 62) The spiritual person is essentially free.

Human freedom is conditioned; it is not identical with omnipotence. (*Th.*, 175) However, its dependence upon intrinsic dispositions and external situations is not to be confused with a limitation of its power and exercise. Freedom is integral and indivisible. (*LE.*, 34 f.) It extends itself to every aspect of possible human interest; it is dependent only in so far as it needs an object of its essential opposition. It is a freedom especially with regard to drives, to inheritance, and environment. (*Th.*, 152)

Frankl considers it as a "psychological fact that 'drives as such' never appear in man." "Man has drives—but the drives do not have him. He makes something out of drives, but drives do not make up his being." (*UM.*, 95 f.) The spiritual person is free under all circumstances. "After all, we call 'person' only that which can behave freely—whatever the situation may be. The spiritual person is that in man which in every case and every time *is able to oppose*—against every position: not only extrinsic, but also intrinsic." The person is always in possession of the organism's drives, which are mastered, accepted or rejected, assimilated or integrated. "All driveness, the 'Id', *is always* the Id of an Ego and this ego is—in opposition to Freud—very well 'master in his own house'." The Ego is not a plaything of drives; on the contrary, the ego has "a priori and at any rate" the power of decision. Man may be factually unfree, in spite of his essential facultative freedom. However, "whenever he appears unfree, he has—freely—renounced his freedom. Where he does not have it any more, he has abdicated it. Where man makes the impression of being driven, he lets himself be driven." The person is so absolutely master of his drives that he is even able to betray himself to them; he has freedom always, even when he freely gives it up. (*UM.*, 96 f.)

No less absolutely is the person's rule over his inheritance. "Heredity does not explain anything authentic, and thus truly nothing." The decisive question is: What does the spiritual person do with his inherited psychophysical mass? (*UM.*, 72) Thus Frankl concludes his discussion of the relations between brain physiology and hereditary pathology and human existence. At the first sight, findings of physiological psychology and of genetics seem of offer a strong case for the materialist's epiphenomenalistic and reductionistic explanation of the spiritual in man. Observable correspondences between the somatic and the psychic and spiritual appear to be so numerous and extensive that the body-mind identity seems to be not just an ideal of the materialist's reductionistic endeavors, but an obviously established fact. A closer look at the phenomena, however, reveals merely a primitive confusion of physiological conditions with causes of the human mind. A review of related experimental and biographical data, at least, as presented by Frankl, proves to him beyond any justified doubt that the somatic can merely condition, never effect psychic and spiritual functions. It is true that animal behavior may be exstinguished by the exstirpation of determined nerve centers, or that a mental aphasia may be the result of a determined brain injury. However, the fact that the experimental animals can be retrained to learn the exstinguished behavior or that the mental aphasia patient regains his memory in spite of the perduring damage of its alleged brain center shows that the psychosomatic coordination involved is never strict and final. (*UM,* 37) "What can be localized, can never be psychic performances, but, at most, certain somatic conditions of their occurrence." (*UM.,* 40) The somatic does not produce or originate anything positive; what it perhaps may cause may actually be disturbances of psychic functions. (*UM.,* 41)

The bodily can directly effect and affect only the body and indirectly the psychic, inasmuch as this is by means of the "obligatory psycho-physical parallelism" (*UM.,* 104) necessarily bound up with the physiological in man. And thus heredity, as a biological process, can extend its influence only to "the somatic and together with it to the psychic." (*UM.,* 70) The spiritual person himself stands above and beyond biological causation. "Through their chromosomes the parents determine only and solely . . . the psychophysical organism, but not the spiritual person." For "the spiritual existence is not transferable, it cannot be propagated from the parents to the child . . . What alone can be transferred, are the building stones—not the architect." (*UM.,* 64 f.) The parents do not generate a human being, but "only a 'somatic' child." (*UM.,* 69) Nor can they educate the person of their psychophysical offspring. For faithful to his existentialistic notion of the person, Frankl maintains that "the spiritual cannot be educated: the spiritual must be performed—it is as such only in self-performance, in the 'performance-actuality' of existence." (*UM.,* 70) The parents offer only the material of the person of the child, the somatic conditions of existence and the psychic character, that is, the inherited psychic dispositions. (*UM.,* 99) "This character-disposition, however, is in no way decisive; what is ultimately decisive, is rather always the position the person takes" with regard to his inherited possibilities. (*UM.*, 100) As the studies of identical twins reveal, heredity does not imply a determination of the will. Differences of existence on the basis of the same inheritance, for instance, when one of the twins becomes an outstanding criminal, while his brother is known as an expert criminologist, manifest the autonomy of the spiritual. (*UM.*, 71) The spiritual must be unconditioned, since under identical psychophysical conditions it differs so much. (*UM.*, 58) Heredity as such "explains truly nothing." It presents only conditions of existence, material for the self-realization of the spiritual person. What is important is not that which the person receives from ancestors, but what he does "with the available inherited disposition, with the psycho-physical mass of inheritance." (*UM.*, 72) Only what the being "whose essence consists in being-deciding" decides to be, is decisive, not what man has. (*UM.*, 71)

"Man is essentially a being who transcends necessities;" (*Hdb.*, 681) he is thus always also above the conditions of his environment. And as the superiority over the body and heredity is shown by the difference of spiritual and moral existence in spite of identical psycho-physical conditions, so this existential rule over things and circumstances of the surroundings is evidenced by the different personal encounter of the same physical and social environment. Freud's prediction of a disappearance of all individual differences and of their replacement by a uniform expression of the one unstilled biological urge in case of a sufficient exposition, for instance, to hunger, was tested in a most drastic manner in the living laboratories of the concentration camps and completely disproved. There "we saw how under identical conditions some behaved like swine, while other behaved like saints." (*Th.*, 153) "Man has both these possibilities within himself. Which one he actualizes, depends on decision, not on conditions." (*Psych.*, 35) By nature, the spiritual is never absorbed in a situation; rather instead of being subdued by it, it is always able to detach itself and to gain distance from it, to confront the situation. (*UM.*, 97)

"Man is, therefore, nothing less than a product of heredity and environment. *Tertium datur*: decision—in the last analysis, man determines himself." (*Th.*, 153) As existence, the spiritual person is deciding being. (*HP.*, 60) He is never a slave of his drives or of his society, but under all circumstances lord of his heredity and surroundings. "In every instant of his life, he confronts his natural and social environment, his external surroundings as well as his vital psycho-physical world." (*UM.*, 95) "In every moment, he decides, what in the next he will be." (*LE.*, 57)

As deciding being, the spiritual person has responsibleness as a further existentiale. Decision is possible only as a decision for or against something. Freedom is thus not to be confused with aimlessness or arbitrariness. Human existence is directed to values and meaning; its willing is preceded by a consciously experienced ought, (*HP.*, 23) which has to be faced in responsible decision. "Ultimately, this responsibleness derives from the existential fact that life is a chain of questions which man has to answer by answering for life, to which he has to respond by being responsible, by making decisions, by deciding which answers to give to the individual questions." These questions concern "the specific meaning of a personal life in a given situation," and the answer can thus in each case only be one—"the right one." (*Psych.*, 17) Logotherapy sees in the essential human meaning-orientation a demand for free and responsible meaning confrontation and "in responsibleness the very essence of human existence." (*Psych.*, 13)

And the person "is responsible for all and everything," (*UM.*, 115) even for the existential confrontation of his psychosis. Frankl does not hold a patient responsible for the occurrence of his neurosis or psychosis. He considers "the contention of some psychiatrists that a patient suffering from endogenous depression not only feels guilty but really is guilty . . . and that this is why he is depressed" as "an example of flagrant noölogism." (*Psych.*, 75) As a continental psychiatrist, he considers psychosis as "a somatosis; for it is a pheno-psychic but somatogenic disease." (*UM.*, 55) Endogenous depression, for instance, "represents, as it is known, a hereditary illness and as such proceeds from a specific psycho-physical disposition." (*UM.*, 113) Its consequences for the person are extensive. In psychosis, the spiritual person is invisible and "impotent," inasmuch as the proper use of his instrument, the psychophysical organism, is impossible; he is invisible, in so far as the spirit is only in rare moments able "like lightning to strike through the psycho-physical layer isolating him from us." (*UM.*, 55) Psychosis involves a blocking of the only function the organism has for the person, i.e. its use as an instrument, and thus results in "an impotence of self-manifestation; for in order to manifest himself, the person needs an organism which functions without disturbance both instrumentally and expressively." (*UM.*, 56)

However, "the spiritual person remains untouched even in the psychosis." He is "no more reached by depression than by its theraphy; neither the somatic sickness nor the somatic treatment can approach the spiritual." (*UM*., 54 f.) Disease is a category of organic life; it can apply only to an organism. The spiritual person cannot be sick; he may be prevented by a defective organism from manifesting himself. However, "this impossibility of expressing himself should not be confused with an incapability of the confrontation. This remains possible and is actualized again and again, in virtue of what we call the defiant power of the spirit." (*Th.*, 678) As existence, the person remains unaffected by the disease. And thus logotheraphy holds "him accountable for his attitude" toward his psychosis. (*Psych.*, 75)

The spiritual person is essentially meaning-orientation, responsible, and deciding being. As "that in man which always and at all times is able to oppose," he is to transcend everything somatic, psychic, and social for the fulfillment of meaning and for the realization of values. (*Hdb.*, 684 ff.) He is responsible for all and everything of his being, and he actually freely decides in every instant of his life what in the next he will be. Human freedom is integral and indivisible; responsiblesness of existence is universal and all-inclusive.

Frankl considers his logotherapeutic philosophy of the human person as a necessary revision and amendment of the prevailing psychiatric view of man, demanded by psychotherapeutic needs, especially in our nihilistic age. (*UM*., 116) Every successful case of psychotherapy involves an existential conversion. It thus requires a confrontation of the fatalistic attitude of the neurotic who is wont to ascribe his condition to his constitution or his environment. The neurotic flight from freedom and responsibility has to be met by a consistent logotherapeutic appeal to the human facultative noö-psychic antagonism. Convinced that "the Ego is *never* facticity, but facultative, . . . i.e. always already beyond his own facticity," (*UM*., 103) logotherapy must become an "appelative psychotherapy," calling forth the person's defiant power of the spirit. (*Th.*, 122)

The need for this logotherapeutic appeal to the spiritual in man is the more urgent in our days inasmuch as the neurotic resistance to the categorical imperative of free responsibility is reinforced by the collective neurosis of our age, a "worldwide wave of nihilism" which consists in "being weary and tired of the spirit." (*Psych.*, 121) The deep-seated striving and struggling for a higher and ultimate meaning of human existence is frustrated, and this existential frustration seems to Frankl "today to play, at least, as great a part in the formation of neuroses as formerly the sexual one did." (*Psych.,* 121 f.)

This pathogenic nihilism, this modern resentment of the spiritual, is, however, to a large extent the result of anthropological, especially psychiatric, theories of human existence. "For a long time, psychiatry, psychotherapy, psychoanalysis have presented man as a reflex-being, or a bundle of drives, as conditioned, effected, and determined either by the Oedipus—and other complexes, or by inferiority—or other feelings, have described him as marionette, hanging from external visible or intrinsically running wires. Always man was—it is true—more than nothing; but always he was 'nothing but' something which could restlessly be explained by way of the biological, psychological, or sociological . . . And such biologism, psychologism, and sociologism has always sinned against the spiritual in man." The image of man as of a free, spiritual being was distorted during the past generation, especially in clinical research. It is thus also the duty of psychiatry to help straighten the public vision of the human individual, which really is only a caricature of man, and to replace it with a true image of the person. (*UM.,* 116 f.)

"That is precisely what I have attempted to do with existential analysis and logotherapy," Frankl professes: "to supplement . . . the existing psychotherapy and thereby to make the underlying image of man into a whole, a total image of true man, . . . thus doing justice to that reality which belongs only to man and is called existence." (*Psych.,* 130)

The founder of the third Viennese school of psychiatry is aware that in his "efforts to supplant the unconscious invalid philosophical hypotheses of the Freudians and Adlerians by a conscious philosophy" *(Psych.,* 130) he may be one-sided. As a specific research-trend, his existential analysis is necessarily so, he believes; and he justifies his logotherapeutic obligation "to be partial in the defense of his client," the spiritual person, by quoting Kierkegaard's advice: "Who has to offer a correction, must exactly know the weak sides of the existing and then present the opposite one-sidedly, extremely one-sidedly." However, Frankl is of the opinion that his partiality toward the spiritual in man does in no way affect the truth value of the logotherapeutic image of the human being. An emphasis on existence in research does not imply a false presentation of the spiritual person in the existential analytic anthropological theory. (*HP.*, 14 f.)

It shall not be denied that Frankl's defense of his logotherapeutic vision of man in lectures and writings have made a significant contribution to a revision of biologistic, psychologistic, and sociologistic misunderstandings of human nature and life. His belief that psychotherapy ultimately has "the spiritual person in his uniqueness and individuality" as its subject, (*UM.*, 44) and that consequently psychotherapy has to be supplemented by logotherapy is shared by many clinical psychologists and psychiatrists. What Frankl describes as noögenic neuroses, i.e. "psychological illnesses which are not, as with psychogenic neuroses, rooted in conflicts between different drives" but rather "in collisions between different values, or in the unrewarded longing and groping of man for . . . an ultimate meaning to his life," (*Psych.*, 43) are met in the psychiatrist's office; their cure demands that appelative psychotherapy which logotherapy represents and recommends.

However, it is questionable whether the persuasion about the uniqueness and spirituality of the human person which Frankl certainly communicates to many in his audience is a conviction truly justified by reason. A realistic look at human reality may discover not a few points of disagreement with his logotherapeutic philosophy of man. The justification of some of his most cherished philosophical claims concerning the spiritual person deserves some critical consideration.

The defense of the human spirituality represents the basic aim of Frankl's philosophical endeavors. Motivated by his opposition to the Freudian psychologistic reduction of existence, he attacks the prevailing "psychology without spirit" (*HP.*, 19) whenever possible, and he tries to establish the reality of the spiritual in man as a dimension independent of physiological and psychic layers of his being. But did Frankl ever truly secure the spiritual nature of this supposedly specifically human dimension, or rather is he not prevented from doing so by his method of investigation?

Disappointment at the scarcity and poverty of psychological descriptions in psychiatric literature is almost a common experience. Compared with the wealth and differentiation of psychic phenomena presented in a textbook of phenomenological psychology, for instance, Freud's notions of infantile sexuality and its development must appear as an extremely primitive child psychology. Frankl's characterization of mental phenomena is no exception to this rule of psychiatric psychology. Nowhere in his writings is there even a description of the psychic; only by an analysis of characteristically logotherapeutic doctrines concerning the noöpsychic antagonism and the essential drive-independence of the spiritual person can it be recognized as somewhat identical with the psychoanalytic Id. The spiritual and its three existentialia are better differentiated; however, also with regard to them no phenomenological description, still less an ontological determination, is offered. The nature of the psychic and the spiritual, the manifold manifestations of sensory and intellectual life, their differences and their relationship to one another and to the somatic, for instance, the structure of perception, which is simply listed as an instance of "being-with," are not investigated.

The causal independence of both the psychic and the spiritual from the body and therewith their existence as specific levels of the human individual are assumed to be established by cases of the recovery of mental functions after brain injury; and the independent reality of the spiritual, at least, of freedom, is supposed to be an evident phenomenon of human self-understanding and to be proved by the difference of behavior in spite of identical heredity, the same drive situation, and identical environmental conditions.

Such arguments for the existence of different psychic and intellectual phenomena and their independence of the body may contain useful material for a realistic philosophy of man. As they stand, they will not convince a materialist opponent nor can they satisfy a critical mind. No determinist will deny Frankl's facts; but he will easily find sufficient reasons to reject his conclusions. The recovery of a mental function after brain injury, for instance, may disprove the localization theory for this determined phenomenon; but it cannot be rightly used as a proof for the general denial of physiological centers of mental processes, since sensory phenomena certainly do not only have physiological conditions, but also are causally dependent upon the functioning of certain somatic structures. And since the recovery is admittedly bound up with a "vicariation" (*UM.*, 37) of the injured brain centers by other nervous processes anyway, a mere appeal to facts of brain pathology will not dispose of materialistic explanations of mental life. Nor will differences of behavior of identical twins in similar psychic or social situations be sufficient to prove man's spirituality, since also identical animal twins, which obviously are not spiritual, can be trained to behave differently in similar conditions. And evidence of self-understanding as such can guarantee the existence of human freedom only if the objective value of such evidence is already critically secured. A mere appeal to an immediate awareness of freedom as such does not exclude the possibility of a physiological or psychic determination of human willing. Unless a consideration of the nature of mental and physiological functions establishes their essential difference and thus their causal irreducibility, the assertion of essentially different dimensions of human reality is without a sound philosophical foundation. Frankl's existential-analytic approach does not favor such an ontological investigation; his argumentation for the existence of human spirituality cannot be considered to be truly convincing.

The logotherapeutic understanding of this spirituality as a being or a power of constant and comprehensive defiant opposition does, then, certainly appear to be rather one-sided. It may be useful to insist upon an unrestricted freedom and possibility of the human person in psychotherapy in order to counter-act the self-defeating trends of the neurotic personality. However, it is a rather narrow conception of human spirituality that sees it "essentially" as an opposition to the drives (*UM.*, 104) and finds the person constituting himself only in a self-detachment from himself as psycho-physical organism. (*Th.*, 171) After all, it is not true that the spiritual, "the Ego generally never manifests itself 'as such,' but always only in the shaping and conquest of the Id." (*UM.*, 50) Such a view of human existence may be an expression of the experience of the neurotic described by Freud and of the corresponding psycho-analytic categorical imperative: Where there is Id, Ego shall be! However, in an existentialistic psychiatry which defends the pathogenic influence of an existential frustration and introduces a noögenic neurosis as a specific type of psychological illness, such a fascination with the Freudian anatomy of the mental personality is completely out of place. Human spirituality is a reality of its own and does manifest itself as such; existence as the specifically human mode of being is a concern not primarily with instincts, but with spiritual problems and obligations, and its pathogenic frustration consists in a collision of duties and in moral conflicts, as Frankl himself declares. (Cf. *Psych.*, 43; 122)

No less unrealistic is the logotherapeutic notion of the independence and power of this noö-psychic antagonism. It is admitted that "the functioning of a normal psychophysical organism is no more . . . than the condition of the development of the spiritual person." (*Th.,* 152) However, the stress on this "no more" is intended to exclude any kind of causality on the part of the somatic and psychic dimensions with regard to the spiritual, and also on the part of the body with regard to the psychic. As indicated before, such a denial of a causal relationship is certainly not justified in the case of the sensitive life, the normal manifestation of which is the result of stimulated living organs, not just of a psychic power. It is questionable with regard to spiritual acts also, inasmuch as human spirituality is not endowed with innate ideas and ideals, and thus is dependent upon the functioning of sensitive faculties as the material cause for the presentation of the object of intentionality. Although "the spiritual person" alone is truly the efficient cause of his spiritual operations, the psycho-somatic organism is not merely the condition, but also the material cause of its actualisation.

However, one would think that even a mere psycho-somatic condition of spirituality should render its performance, at least, dependent upon the realization of such condition. Logotherapy disagrees. It combines a dependence of the development of "the spiritual person" upon a normal functioning of the organism with an independence of freedom and responsibility from every physiological and psychic condition. Disease, somatic and mental disturbances affect only the organism, we are told, never the spiritual person. Whatever the psycho-somatic conditions may be, the spiritual is "in every case and always" able to oppose; (*Hdb.* 685) "everywhere and always there remains some share of freedom." (*M.,* 95) Thus "the body does not effect anything." (*Hdb.* 678) Heredity "explains nothing genuine." (*UM.,* 72) "The character, the inherited psychic dispositions are in no way decisive." (*UM.,* 100) And it is merely "typically intellectualistic pride" to consider it possible that something like saintliness or any moral qualification be dependent upon the quality of a brain and have its beginning "only with a determined IQ." (*Th.,* 16) As the born idiot can evidently achieve moral sanctity and the psychotic can and must existentially confront his disease, so the spiritual person is free and responsible under all circumstances to decide what to do with his inherited dispositions.

Frankl resents accusations of spiritualism raised against such logotherapeutic appraisals of human freedom and responsibility. "Spiritualism is not given, when freedom is seen where there is spirit," he defends himself; it "begins only when the human spirit is held responsible for the psycho-somatic disease." (*Th.*, 18 f.) Obviously he is mistaken. To declare an essentially somatogenic or psychogenic disease as spiritogenic and to ascribe its occurrence to the moral guilt of the patient is not the only form of angelism: it finds expression whenever, as in logotherapy, the human spirit is said or demanded to perform activities that surpass the conditions of its incarnate realization.

A real distinction of different dimensions of the human individual does not necessarily guarantee their independent existence and operation. As experience shows, the human spirit does not exist in a lofty sphere of its own, unrelated to the psychic and vegetative levels of human nature. As incarnate spirit, it depends upon the functioning of the human psychosomatic life and thus also upon organic structures and processes for its access to physical and interpersonal social and cultural reality. Therefore, heredity, somatic and psychic dispositions, play a completely different role in the economy of human existence than logotherapy is inclined to allow. Only on the basis of a healthy psychosomatic constitution will the person be able freely to decide the realization of his dispositions. Otherwise inheritance may truly explain everything. And it may well be that it is not the logotherapeutic spiritual person who will be able to determine what to do with the allegedly undecisive psychic dispositions but, on the contrary, these psychosomatic conditions alone that will—as in certain phases of psychosis or in certain cases of cretinism—decide health and disease and even the mere possibility of spiritual existence. It is only the demand of a realistic appraisal of experience, not intellectualistic pride, that a certain quality of the brain is recognized as a condition of moral sanctity or a determined IQ as the natural presupposition of the development of a mature human personality.

It is not surprising that the logotherapeutic idea of the spiritual person has consequences also for the understanding of the unity of the human individual in Frankl's psychiatry. The unity and integrity of man cannot be stressed enough, we read. It is so intimate that it cannot even rightly be called a composition of body, soul, and spirit. "All this he is rather as one." (*UM.*, 60 Ftn. 1) In spite of this intricate union of human nature, however, the boundary between existence, as the genuinely human, and the psychophysical facticity must be drawn "with the most extreme sharpness." (*UG.*, 25) And this is demanded "simply because of the fact, that the spiritual as such is essentially a self-detachment and self-distancing from facticity." (*UM.*, 104)

The integrity of the existing human nature is dictated and determined by the spiritual person. Certainly "a separation and isolation of the spiritual from body and soul can be only heuristic: only in a personal union with the psychophysicum is the spiritual known to us" (*UM.*, 83) and real. (*LE.*, 60) There exists a correlative relationship of mutual need between the person and the organism. "Body and soul may form a unity . . . but this would never be in a position to figure as the human totality; to it, to the whole man, there also belongs the spiritual which pertains to him as his most genuine being" (*UG.*, 28) not only considered statically as an essential component, but especially dynamically as the principle of unification. The spiritual person, who himself represents an undivided and indivisible unique whole, is not only the genuinely human of the three dimensions of man's being; he is also the only unifying and differentiating reality of human life. Only the spiritual constitutes and guarantees unity and integrity. "Wherefrom does this 'manifold in the unity' of man proceed? Wherefrom originates the structure of layers, the hierarchical order of man? Not from the fact that he is composed of body, soul, and spirit, but from the fact that the spiritual confronts the somatic and psychic." (*UM.*, 60, Ftn. 1) The spirit organizes the psychophysical organism and renders it its own by assuming it as its instrument. (*UM.*, 53) And "distancing himself from himself as psychophysical organism, the spiritual person constitutes himself as such, as spiritual." (*Th.*, 171) "Man is a unity; but in this unity the spiritual opposes and confronts the somatic and psychic." (*LE.*, 61 f.)

In logotherapy, the unity and integrity of man is a mere noö-psychosomatic antagonism. It is not a substantial union, the unity of one nature as the source of all human perfections, specified and differentiated by the human soul as the substantial principle of life. In spite of his frequent use of the term in connection with the relationship between the different human dimensions, Frankl never actually speaks of the soul. An existential-analytic psychiatry which receives the material of its investigations in the logotherapeutic process and its philosophical inspiration from existentialistic thought has no possibility of discussing the problem of the ultimate psychological causes of substance and soul. It remains on the level of being-human, i.e. of the manifestations of the human individual, and thus deals only with the psychic and mental operations and their relations. This is implicity admitted by Frankl when he writes that he is using the 'the spiritual' in a pseudo-substantivistic form of expression, avoiding the noun 'the spirit' since this latter could signify a substance. (*Hdb.*, 685) As presented in logotherapy, human reality is not seen as the substantial union of body and soul, but as the dialectic unity (*UM*, 103) of a noö-psychic antagonism. Man is conceived not as the substantial concretization of the human nature of traditional philosophy, but as a battlefield or rather as the struggle of opposing tendencies of human life. Not Aristotle's but Klages' view of the body-mind relationship is endorsed by Frankl. "The spirit as the enemy of the soul" is recognized as a correct expression of the actual relationship of the different layers of the human being; only Klages' sympathy with the oppressed soul has to be replaced by a glorification of the absolutist ruler spirit. (*UM.*, 11)

In this kind of dialectical union, the mutual dependence of the different dimensions of being-human finds its fulfillment. The psychosomatic organism's need for being organized and beaten into submission is satisfied by the defiant power of the spiritual person, and the opposition essential to spirituality is actualized in the constant mastery of drives, inherited dispositions, and social conditions. Only the relative independence of the different levels of human life, exaggerated into the hostile opposition of hypostasized antagonizing forces, is seen in this logotherapeutic vision of the body-mind relationship. The natural coordination of human faculties and the possibility of their mutual cooperation and integration in the development of a mature and happy personality is completely ignored. The result is an unbelievable, unnatural dissection of the human individual, for instance, into the parents' "somatic" child determined by heredity and environment and the offspring's spiritual person ungenerated and self-creative beyond any influence of parental endowment and education; or a ravaged psychotic organism and the spiritual unaffected and untouchable by disease, under all circumstances existentially confronting the psychosis; or a "corrupted 'psychic mechanism', a ruined psychic apparatus or a broken machine" (*Hdb.*, 679 f.) unworthy of a doctor's care and the uninjured and indestructible person standing behind and above all such corruption and decay, deserving the labor and help of the psychiatrist.

Some of these unrealistic differentiations are partly dictated also by Frankl's existentialistic notion of the human person. The superiority and independence of the spiritual seem to be secure on the experiential, phenomenal level, on which alone logotherapy deals with the human being. As actually deciding, human spirituality is obviously different from everything that is decided. Drives, for instance, "could never repress, censure, or sublimate themselves; even if the energy used for the control of drive impulses may—considered merely biologically—be drive-energy, that which uses it cannot itself be derived from drives." (*UG.*, 82 f.) The instance determining the fate of the psychophysical endowment, the spiritual person, cannot himself be organic; it must represent a different dimension of the human being.

However, also this existentialistic concept of the human person has serious shortcomings; it cannot fulfill the hopes set on it in logotherapy. Frankl's logotherapeutic anthropology is not only the theoretical outcome of his professional work. His view of the unique superiority of the human spirit represents a personal conviction, deeply felt and unceasingly defended as the most decisive truth of our age. During his years in the concentration camp, he had lived "the freely and responsibly deciding" of human existence. Its possibility experienced as a powerful reality under the most debasing circumstances of human life had to be defended, and the ideas which made such a cruel, biologistic degradation of human beings possible had to be fought by a defense of the inalienable and inviolable dignity of the human person. "During the past decades, mankind has proved better than necessary, that it has drives." it is now finally time to remind man again that he is a spiritual being. (*Th.*, 148)

And Frankl is of the opinion that a defense of the dignity of the human person is necessarily bound up with his existentialistic understanding of the person, spirit, and existence. Only if the spiritual is mere self-performance, a being self-educating himself and freely deciding the realization of inherited dispositions and social conditions, can the vital and social value of a human being as a "psychophysical individual" be distinguished from the dignity of the individual as a spiritual person, and can a "destruction of life unworthy to live" be consistently rejected. (*UM.*, 56) "Who does not ascribe psychosis to the psychophysical, but seeks it in the person," Frankl believes, "is easily exposed to the danger of denying humanity to the mentally diseased, and enters into a conflict with medical ethos." (*UM.*, 55) "This unconditioned faith in the personal spirit—this 'blind' faith in the 'invisible' but indestructible spiritual person" constitutes his psychiatric creed (*UM.*, 57) The spiritual person is unaffected and indestructible "standing behind the process of the psycho-physical illness." (*UM.*, 56) "The spiritual person . . . *is* there," even in an incurable psychosis, and the faith in his "continued existence . . . alone justifies psychiatric endeavor." (*LE.*, 52 f.) Although "we do not know his wherefrom," (*UM.*, 69) the spiritual person is "present in the moment of conception, already before birth, at least, as a facultative person," (*UM.*, 62) "even if hidden in silence . . . waiting till one day he has taken possession of the organism . . . as his field of expression." (*UM.*, 68) "The interruption of his existence would be equivalent to the destruction of a person as such." (*UM.*, 62) The inviolable dignity of the spiritual person forbids any form of willful abortion and euthanasia.

Frankl's conviction of the unique value of the human person is unquestioned. However, it scarcely has any foundation other than the merely blind faith of his psychiatric creed. Objectively his defense rests on a non-existentialistic use of the terms 'existence' and 'facultative person,' and it cannot consistently justify the sanctity of human life nor the moral evil of abortion and euthanasia as intended in logotherapy.

The "facultative person" whom Frankl asserts to be present already before birth is not identical with the spiritual person of logotherapy. The logotherapeutic facultative person, who is said never to be facticity but "always able to be other than he is," (*UM.*, 103) is not realized at the moment of conception. An interruption of his existence by abortion, that is, an interruption of existence as the logotherapeutic specific mode of being-human is therefore impossible. Moreover, as mere self-performance, the spiritual person can never be affected positively or negatively by any extrinsic influence. According to the logotherapeutic philosophy of man, health and disease, decay and death are categories of vitality, and attacks on human life, injury of a human being, and murder can only affect the psycho-physical organism. The spiritual person, hiding behind the "somatic child" of the parents or silent above a sick and incurable organism, is never subject to such attempts at an interruption of human life. As mere disposal of a "psycho-physical individual" or as a "destruction of life unworthy to live" of a psychosomatic organism, however, abortion and euthanasia cannot be condemned as an offence against the dignity of the human person on the basis of the logotherapeutic anthropology.

Actually Frankl forgets entirely about his existentialistic philosophy of man, when insisting upon the inviolability of the spiritual person. The facultative person of the embryo or of the incurable psychotic patient whose existence is to be protected against any form of interruption is not the actual logotherapeutic person, spirituality or existence, but signifies potential spirituality and, in the last analysis, the substance of the human spirit denied in logotherapy. This incarnate spiritual entity certainly is indestructible and, as destined to a life beyond death, of inviolable dignity; while Frankl's existentialistic spiritual person, as spiritual operation of the human individual, obviously is not indestructible, but can be and is affected, prevented or destroyed by a lack or a disturbance of the required functioning of human psychosomatic life. The existence or reality of such a spiritual potency or substance, however, cannot be consistently maintained by Frankl, especially since he is of the opinion that spiritual existence is known and real only in coexistence with the psycho–physical organism, "as soon and as long as it is united with body and soul." (*UM.*, 84) Considering the complete independence of the spiritual person from the psychosomatic organism, as defended in logotherapy, the mere existence of a seemingly human organism does not permit the prediction of a future spiritual existence nor consequently the recognition of the possibility of a logotherapeutic spiritual person. At any rate, an embryo infected with cretinism, a neonate or a baby with serious birth defects or brain injury, or an incurable psychotic patient in certain phases of the disease certainly does not possess this "facultative person." They will never develop that "freely and responsibly deciding" which logotherapy identifies with spiritual existence and person. According to logotherapeutic reasoning, their destruction truly represents only the disposal of "a mere organism" for which "nobody likes to be a physician." (*UM.*, 55) Logotherapy is in no position to defend consistently the dignity of the human person. Its existentialistic and spiritualistic concept of the human being serves as a justification of the destruction of "unworthy" human life rather than of its inviolability.

One final aspect of the logotherapeutic philosophy of man should not remain unmentioned: the non–phenomenal character of its idea of existence, spirituality, and person. The belief in the actuality of that instance which is said to decide the fate of drives and thus to be irreducible to them is a dictate of common sense; it does not have a place in Frankl's existentialistic theory of the specifically human life. In logotherapy, the person or spirit is known only as being–human, as freely deciding. Even when Scheler's notion of the human person as a spiritual act–center is introduced, this center is immediately interpreted as "mere reality of performance," as identical with spiritual activity. (*UG.*, 31) Such mere reality of performance, however, does not exist. In denying the substantiality of the person, Frankl overlooks the personalness of specifically human activity. A mere deciding or value–orientation is never given as human phenomenon; it is always *my* deciding, *my* performance that is experienced. Consciousness–of . . . is not merely essentially consciousness of an object, but equally also consciousness of a subject. A subject–less human act is as impossible an an object–less intentional activity. The subject of the manifestations of all the dimensions of human reality is ultimately the person of traditional philosophy who, as incarnate spirit, enjoys the personal dignity and natural rights of a human being in every phase of his development, as an embryo as well as in old age, awake or asleep, in health and disease, and as a criminal no less than as a saint. Logotheraphy's existentialistic concept of the spiritual person is not only unrealistic; the logotherapeutic spiritual person or existence simply does not exist.

The logotherapeutic philosophy of man scarcely seems to be the correct view of human nature and existence which Frankl considered to be a requirement of psychiatry and hoped to present with his revision of the prevailing psychiatric systems. His existentialistic vision of the human individual is no less one–sided than the biologistic, psychologistic, and sociologistic notions he intended to correct. However, his failure to realize his philosophical ideal does not eliminate the value of Frankl's theoretical endeavors nor will it prevent the success of his psychiatric work. A cure in psychotherapy is scarcely dependent upon the truth of the anthropological conceptions guiding and motivating the psychiatrist. And even if exaggerated, the logotherapeutic emphasis on the spiritual and existential in psychiatry was necessary and will bear fruit in psychotherapy, especially in cases of existential frustration for which it was primarily advocated. Frankl saw the need for an integration of the spiritual dimension into the psychiatric view of man of his time, and he had the courage to fight for his conviction against the common physiologistic and biologistic trends in his professional field. His logotherapy will be remembered as an important step in the course of the development of psychiatry into an independent, realistic anthropological science.

The Catholic University of America

3

ORIGIN AND NATURE OF PHILOSOPHY ACCORDING TO JOSE ORTEGA Y GASSET[1]

by

Felix Alluntis, O.F.M.

ORIGIN OF PHILOSOPHY

Ortega rejects the opinion, commonly attributed to Aristotle, that the origin of philosophy is due to man's "desire to know," although he observes that the Aristotelian thought on this point has not been as yet properly studied. He believes that Descartes, who states that the relation of the desire to know to philosophy is not the same as that of water to the thirsty but rather that of water to a dropsical person, disagrees with the opinion that the desire to know is the cause of philosophy.[2]

Ortega also rejects Heidegger's opinion as to the origin of philosophy. It is not true, he says, that philosophy originates when man senses himself to be stranger in the world, which happens when things around him that had served him and been his utensils *(Zeugen)* have failed him. Man has always been a stranger in the world, and yet he has not always occupied himself in philosophizing. This initial error proliferates in Heidegger and leads him to assert that man *is* philosophy. Why or how is this? From the failure of the world as a complex of utensils, of things-that-serve, man dis-

[1]The purpose of this article is to expound, not to evaluate in any way, Ortega's final ideas on the origin and nature of philosophy.

[2]*Idea de principio en Leibniz y la evolución de la teoría deductiva,* second ed. (Madrid: El Arquero, Revista de Occidente, 1967), 2 vols., II, p. 91 and note 1. The main works in which Ortega expounds his final ideas on the origin and nature of philosophy are: *Idea de principio en Leibniz, Origen de la filosofía,* and "Prólogo a Historia de la filosofía de E. Bréhier." His *Qué es filosofía?,* which also deals with the origin and nature of philosophy, is a course given by Ortega in 1929. Eventually he abandoned many of the ideas contained in this work.

covers that they are alien to him and therefore have a being of their own, and that his own being consists in inquiring about their being. This is not true; on the contrary, since the fifth century B.C. only a few men in a few places have inquired about being. It can be disputed whether anyone since Plotinus has done so, properly speaking. Certainly the scholastic philosophers did not inquire about being but rather about what Aristotle understood for *ens qua ens,* which is something very different. They did not ask even this question deeply enough. In general, the scholastics did not inquire; they answered, gave solutions to problems they did not see, live, or suffer. Descartes and Leibniz did not inquire about being either, but for something somewhat different. Heidegger's formula "Man has always inquired about being" or "Man is a question for being," makes sense only if for being we understand everything man has inquired about. Not even Heidegger himself, Ortega adds, has restated the problem of being.[3]

The origin of philosophy, according to Ortega, is due to the fact that man lost his faith in traditional beliefs and fell into doubt, while at the same time he believed in a new power, in reason, to rid himself of doubt.[4] To understand the preceding statement it is necessary to explain the specific meaning of the term "beliefs" in Ortega's thought. He distinguishes two types of ideas: idea-ocurrences, or simply ideas, and idea-beliefs, or simply beliefs. Idea-occurrences are thoughts that occur to a person and thoughts occurring to his neighbors that he repeats or adopts. This implies that man has lived before having thought of or adopted these ideas. Now, there is no human life that is not constituted by certain basic beliefs which allow him to deal with himself and the world.[5]

Of idea-occurrences it may be said that we produce, hold, discuss, and propagate them. They are the concrete solutions that each individual and each epoch will have for its own problems. They are acquired either by one's own effort or by the effort of others in order to live authentically.[6] Beliefs, on the other hand, are ideas that have been consolidated in such a way that we automatically and absolutely count on them, even if we do not think of them.

[3]*Idea de principio,* II, pp. 108-109.

[4]*Ibid.,* pp. 131-132.

[5]*Ideas y creencias, Obras completas,* fourth edition (Madrid: Revista de Occidente, 1958), V, pp. 383-384.

[6]*Ibid.,* pp. 381-385; 470; 499-505.

They constitute the foundation of our lives, the ground on which we live. Our whole behavior, including our intellectual behavior, depends on the system of our authentic beliefs. We live, move, and are in them.[7]

What is characteristic of beliefs as opposed to ideas or opinions is that they never appear to us as ideas or opinions, whether personal or collective, but as "reality itself." We not even think of many of our beliefs. They act in us, not as "ideas we have," but as "things we count on or take for granted."[8] To take something for granted without thinking of it, as we take for granted the solidity of the earth or that the sun will rise tomorrow, represents a belief.[9]

The first condition for the origin of philosophy, according to Ortega, is that man loses the "faith of his fathers." When and how does this happen? When man realizes that besides his own beliefs there are others that are contrarily or contradictorily opposed to his own and yet seem to him to be equally worthy of credence. He then wishes to find out which of the two types of beliefs is the one that ultimately deserves to be believed—which means that his beliefs have ceased to be "reality" for him and have become mere ideas. As a consequence he becomes perplexed, insecure, uncertain. He does not know how to act with regard to the world and himself. He has two contradictory or contrary opinions or ideas on them. Each alternatively attracts his adhesion, and oscillates between one and the other. In other words, he doubts.[10] However, his doubt has to be universal to give birth to philosophy for philosophy is a universal kind of knowledge. It becomes universal when one has lost his faith in several beliefs and automatically thinks that having been mistaken in some of them, he cannot trust the others.[11]

Before the rise of philosophy in Greece in the fifth century B.C., man's beliefs were based on religion, mythology, and poetry. The first true philosophers, Parmenides and Heraclitus—the early Ionians were physicists, not philosophers—discovered that prevailing opinions, that is, traditions, were erroneous and, above all, that

[7]*Ibid.*, pp. 397; 384-385; 387-388.

[8]*Idea de principio*, p. 136.

[9]*Ibid.*, pp. 136, 138.

[10]*Ibid.*, pp. 133-142; "Sobre carreras," *Obras completas*, V, p. 177.

[11]*Idea de principio*, II, pp. 97-98.

there were no gods—the foundation and norm of the world—, and that consequently they have been living in a state of deception. Hence the strong reaction with which they sought to find some firm and certain ground.[12]

Yet loss of faith in tradition and the subsequent state of doubt are not enough to give rise to philosophy. Doubt can induce despair and depair leads not to philosophy but to suicide.[13] It is also possible that, having lost his beliefs, man may be left without certitude and in a stupefied state. This has happened in those epochs of general imbecility recorded by history, in which the human mind held captive and its mental life is ruled by superstition.[14] It would have been futile to seek new certitude in religion, mythology, or poetry, on which he had previously based his life. Such an attempt would necessarily have failed, for philosophy originated precisely because man had lost his confidence in these other forms of thought.[15]

The second requirement for the origin of philosophy is a new faith in a new power, namely, in reason. Doubt and belief in a new way or method constitute the historical condition for the historical occupation that philosophy is.[16] It is impossible to stand firmly upon doubt, for doubt consists in a vacillation between one opinion and another, in an incapacity to be content with one opinion. The dictum, "one falls into doubt," expresses it graphically. And the authentic man, who is neither despairing nor superstitious, feels an infinite desire for truth and certitude. He lives disturbed, without inner peace, until he succeeds in "fabricating" true, certain ideas—ideas, not beliefs—which will permit him to live authentically.[17]

[12]*Origin of philosophy*, transl. Toby Talbot (New York: W.W. Norton and Co, 1967), pp. 79 ff; *Idea de principio*, pp. 92-94.

[13]*Idea de principio*, II, p. 104; "Prólogo a historia de filosofía de E. Bréhier," *Obras completas*, VI, p. 405.

[14]*Idea de principio*, II, p. 178.

[15]*Ibid.*, p. 177.

[16]*Ibid.*, p. 104; "Prólogo a Historia de filosofía," p. 406.

[17]*Idea de principio*, II, pp. 138-139; "Prólogo a Historia de filosofía," p. 405; "Sobre las carreras," p. 177-183; "En el centenario de una universidad," *Obras completas*, V, pp. 470-471; *Ideas y creencias*, p. 394; *En torno a Galileo*, *Obras completas*, V, pp. 72; 77. Ortega's words on the necessity of philosophy should be understood in this sense. He refers to the moral necessity or duty the authentic man feels of philosophizing. "Vemos, pues, que la filosofía ni es un don ni es una posibilidad permanente, sino, más bien, un inexcusable deber

The same conditions, loss of faith in tradition and belief in reason, plus the fact that existing philosophies do not satisfy, are necessary for the rebirth of philosophy in any given historical turning point.[18] Ortega points out that unfortunately there is no history either of the form life takes when it is based on beliefs or of the loss of faith in tradition at certain historical times. As long as such a history remains unwritten, he adds, complete clarity on the origin and nature of philosophy will be impossible.[19] He himself tries to show how Parmenides and Heraclitus, the protophilosophers, had no faith in tradition, especially in gods, and also how Descartes' doubt about the world and all human knowledge stemmed from his conviction that the Christian God was an arbitrary and irrationalist deity that had not created a world that was a priori intelligible.[20]

The philosopher who does not truly doubt is not an authentic philosopher. When philosophy emancipates itself from its original utilitarian character, it becomes autonomous and valuable in itself. It is a superfluous activity rather than a humble servant of human life. The present normal situation of philosophy is that it exists as a hobby, as an avocation that attracts many people, as a profession that helps them make a living. Needless to say, such philosophy is not true philosophy and those engaged in it are not true philosophers.[21]

Because he failed to practice this universal doubt, says Ortega, Aristotle's ultimate vocation was not philosophy but science. True, Aristotle recognized the need of starting from a universal doubt, but he himself was unable to follow this imperative. While "he may not have believed in God," he did believe in the sciences. In addition, he accepted the dogmas of the forum, the prevailing opin-

---

que con nosotros mismos tenemos, y por eso no sirve de nada decir que la filosofía también fracasa al intentar servir aquella función constitutiva de la vida que es interpretar el universo. Mientras no haya otra forma nueva y superior, mientras no descubra el hombre la ultra-filosofía, aun siendo un perfecto fracaso, habrá, quiérase o no, que renovar sin pausa su empeño y será forzoso reconocerla como un ensayo necesariamente perpetuo y perpetuamente necesario." *Ibid.*, pp. 179-180.

[18] *Idea de principio*, II, p. 177.

[19] *Ibid.*, p. 132.

[20] *Ibid.*, pp. 92-94.

[21] *Ibid.*, p. 92. This is the social aspect of philosophy. Authentic philosophy must be individual. Cf. "Un rasgo de la vida alemana," *Obras completas*, V, p. 174; "Prólogo a Historia de la filosofía," pp. 395-401.

ions. He believed *(sic)* that the principle of contradiction is an inexorable law of reality. His philosophy is full of prejudices of common sense. Actually Aristotle's works do not make the least use of the inchoative doubt.[22] Nor does Ortega consider scholastic philosophy as an authentic philosophy, since its authors did not really live the philosophical problems and did not practice universal doubt. Contemporary man, Ortega concludes, doubts even what he believed, and in spite of the seemingly antiphilosophical attitude of the present generation, we are at the dawn of the greatest of philosophical epochs.[24]

NATURE OF PHILOSOPHY

From what has been said about the origin of philosophy it follows that it cannot be considered as an occupation that is connatural to man. Before the appearance of philosophy man lived according to other modes of thought—the religious, the mythical, and the poetic. He had to lose faith in tradition and fell into a universal doubt. Philosophy was born on a given day and will disappear, or may disappear, on another day.[25] To Ortega it is surprising that Dilthey did not see that the philosophical attitude was born at a given moment in Greek life.[26] In his *Introduction to the Sciences of the Spirit* Dilthey starts to expound the first philosophical ideas, as if to philosophize were the most natural thing in the world. Ortega sees in this further evidence of the fact that, in spite of his efforts to overcome all naturalism in the study of man, Dilthey never thought of human reality as something strictly historical, but felt back into the traditional idea that man has a nature.[27]

[22]*Idea de principio,* II, pp. 98-99.

[23]*Ibid.,* p. 99. Ortega points out that St. Thomas, in his commentary on Aristotle's *Metaphysics,* recognizes that the philosopher must start from a universal doubt, but that he himself was incapable of fulfilling this imperative. *Ibid.,* pp. 94-95.

[24]*Ibid.,* p. 98. However, in p. 106, Ortega observes that perhaps we are in the dawn of the disappearance of philosophy.

[25]*En torno a Galileo,* pp. 24; 72-78; *Ideas y creencias,* pp. 404-405; "A una edición de sus obras," *Obras completas,* VI, pp. 347-348; "Prólogo a Historia de la filosofía," pp. 392-393; *Idea de principio,* II, pp. 103-104.

[26]*Idea de principio,* II, pp. 103-104.

[27]*Ibid.,* pp. 132-135.

Not only philogenetically but also ontogenetically philosophy is a historical fact. Every philosopher lives before he philosophizes, and life means that the rest of the universe acts in us and we react to its action. *Primum vivere, deinde philosophari.* A man philosophizes when he has a living past and in view of a critical situation he has reached. Philosophy presupposes plenitude of life in the philosopher. Plato and Aristotle realized that philosophy, like politics, is a task for the old.[28]

Between the day on which Parmenides and Heraclitus began to philosophize and the present moment men have realized the great "philosophical experience." "Philosophical experience" is Ortega's designation for the series of systems that philosophically minded men have created over the past twenty-five centuries in order to confront the universe. In this experience each new attempt takes into account the previous ones, especially their errors and limitations. For this reason we can say that the history of philosophy describes a progress. However, Ortega notes, this progress may ultimately consist in the fact that on some future day we will discover not only that all philosophical systems are limited and therefore erroneous, but that philosophizing itself is a limitation, an error, and that "it is necessary to inaugurate another way of intellectually confronting the universe which may be neither philosophy nor any of the ways or modes that preceded it."[29]

Philosophy is a radical as well as a universal form of knowledge. It is the effort to discover the roots of everything else.[30] In past philosophies there have been different levels of radicalism. Today philosophy must be more radical than ever before. Ortega points out that he enuntiated his own radicalism in 1925 by saying, first, that it is necessary to restate radically the traditional problem of being; second, that in this task the phenomenological method should be used, but only insofar as it signifies a synthetic or intuitive form of thinking; thirdly, that a systematic form of thought should be added to this method; fourthly and finally, that for a systematic phenomenological form of thought it is necessary to start from a phenomenon which is in itself a system.

This systematic phenomenon is human life and it is necessary to depart from an analysis of life. Instead of starting from con-

[28]*Ibid.*, pp. 104-105.
[29]*Ibid.*, p. 106.
[30]*Ibid.*, p. 125.

sciousness, as has been done since Descartes, we should start from radical reality, which for each man is his own life. It is not radical in the sense that it is the only reality or the absolute reality. It simply means that every other reality must appear within one's own life. Because human life is the root of every other reality, its study forces us to investigate every other thing in the root in which it originates, namely, in one's own life. This has not been done until now, and for this reason the great traditional problems of philosophy have not been stated in their root form but only in some secondary or derivative form.

Although Ortega admits the phenomenological method in the restricted sense indicated, that is, insofar as it signifies a synthetic and intuitive thought, he rejects Husserl's phenomenology because it is not radical enough. He explains briefly why it is not. Phenomenology consists in describing the phenomenon of natural consciousness—which is in itself positional—from the viewpoint of reflective consciousness which contemplates the first without taking it seriously, that is, suspending its positional character or its executive character in the *epoché*. To this Ortega objects, first, that to suspend the positional or executive character *(vollziehender Character)* of consciousness is to deprive it of its most constitutive element; second, that reflective consciousness has no right to invalidate primary consciousness by suspending its executive character; and, thirdly, that the reflective consciousness, on the contrary, is allowed to be executive and to posit as an absolute being the primary consciousness, which is called *Erlebnis*. This shows precisely that every consciousness has positional value, and consequently that it is not possible, insofar as both are consciousness, for the one to invalidate the other. An act of reasoning can be opposed to an act of consciousness; we do it when we correct an error, for example, an optical illusion. But "normal" consciousness, insofar as it is consciousness—and apart from intermediary reasoning—cannot invalidate "illusory" consciousness. "Hallucination and perception of themselves have equal rights."

As a consequence of these objections, Ortega holds that in a description of the phenomenon "consciousness of...," to say that the act of consciousness is real, but that its object is only intentional and therefore unreal, is not a pure description but a hypothesis. Since in every phenomenon of consciousness we find the coexistence of ego and thing, it follows that the thing is not ideality but reality. What we find in the fact of perception is, on the one hand, the ego, and, on the other, the thing perceived. The phenomenon "consciousness of..." is not a general form of the mind. For this reason the phenomenological method should not be applied to the description of the phenomenon "consciousness," but to the description of the phenomenon "real human life," which is the coexistence of the ego with the things around it or with circumstance. It is therefore obvious that consciousness is a hypothesis, not a phenomenon, and this hypothesis has been inherited from Descartes.[31]

Nor is Heidegger sufficiently radical. In *Sein und Zeit* he does not restate the problem of being, and in fact does not speak at all of being. He merely distinguishes the different meanings of being. Nor has he stated the problem of being in his subsequent writings. Radicalism would have consisted in investigating what is the meaning of "is" when we ask "What is something?," before knowing what kind of thing or being we have before us. This is a question that has not been asked until now, and for this reason no one has seen with clarity what being is. Heidegger extends the term "being" to signify anything ultimate than man inquires about.[32]

Present radicalism requires a new mode of stating the problem, and must go "beneath the foundations themselves" and beyond the things that seemed to be most unquestionable and ultimate. In the order of reality we must ask, not "What things are there?" or "What or how they are?", but "Why is this 'are'?", "Why is there 'to be' in the universe?". In the order of knowledge we must ask, not for its foundation or its limits, as Plato, Aristotle, Descartes, and Kant asked, but for something previous to all that, namely, "Why do we occupy ourselves in trying to know?" In the order of truth we must ask, not for a new criterion of truth, but "What is truth as such?," "What are the proper characteristics of that necessity or interest of man which we call truth?"[33] A philosophy that starts from life as the radical reality answer these questions. The fact that philosophy is radical knowledge already implies that it is universal knowledge, whereas all other human perspectives are partial[34].

[31]*Ibid.*, pp. 112-114, note 1; cf. also "Apuntes sobre el pensamiento," *Obras completas*, V, pp. 540 ff.

[32]*Ibid.*, pp. 110-111.

[33]*Ibid.*, pp. 121-124.

[34]*Ibid.*, pp. 162-163.

If man, for Ortega, devotes himself to philosophy only because without his traditional beliefs he finds himself lost in life, it follows that for Ortega philosophy is primarily practical. The fact of being lost and not knowing what to do forces man to form an idea of things and of himself, and compels him to investigate what exists in reality. And all this is in order to be able, in view of the true character of the universe, to know how to act or behave. Practical knowledge is founded on theoretical knowledge. Neither security nor happiness of life is possible unless one is clear about the universe. Knowledge perfects activity, but, viceversa, activity impels and directs knowledge. For this reason when philosophy, after its initial steps, started its historical voyage in the Platonic academy, it was primarily as an ethics. Plato never ceased to be Socratic in this point. Since then philosophy has always been a science of what to do, a practical science.[35]

Ortega adds, however, that far from being or even aspiring to be a radical and universal knowledge, philosophy, every philosophy, is a permanent failure.[36] Never can a philosophical system be absolutely radical, for every subsequent system, if it be authentic philosophy, which he considers more radical than all previous philosophies, will also fail and be supplanted by a subsequent philosophy. Nor do the various philosophical system succeed in being really universal but are merely more or less partial views. In this connection Ortega observes that because philosophy is always a failure, it is the most profound and the most human activity, "for man is precisely a substantial failure, or to put it in a slightly different way, the substance of man is his inevitable and magnificent failure." He seemingly means that man is always a failure in the sense that he never succeeds in realizing the ideal, the project that he is.

Yet although philosophy is always a failure, it is also an achievement insofar as it is just philosophy. No matter how erroneous its doctrines may be, they are such in a radical and universal perspective, which of itself is truer than any other non-philosophical, partial, and limited perspective. Briefly, every past philosophy appears to us as a failure because subsequent philosophies have been more radical and more complete. It is precisely

[35]*Ibid.*, pp. 102-103.
[36]*Ibid.*, pp. 102 ff; "Prólogo a Historia de filosofía," pp. 417-418.

such lesser integrity or lesser degree of integration that is the failure of previous philosophies.[37]

To express it somewhat differently, at first view the history of philosophy appears as a defunct world of errors. But soon such errors acquire a positive aspect, for each subsequent philosophy profits from them by avoiding them. Finally, the so-called errors appear as partial truths. In the last analysis, a philosophy is said to be erroneous, not because it is not true, but because it is not sufficiently true. The previous philosopher stopped prematurely in the dialectical series of his thoughts; he did not continue thinking. His successor utilizes his doctrine, incorporates it in a new repertory of ideas and continues to advance. He does not follow indefinitely the road of his predecessor, but there comes a moment in which he must take a new road. Nevertheless, since he must keep in mind the previous road, it can be said that the new one is a continuation of the old but with a change in direction. "From this point of view the succession of philosophers appears as one philosopher who for 2500 years has been continuously living and thinking."[38]

Philosophy is distinct from particular sciences. It deals with ultimate, radical, and universal questions, whereas the sciences deal with penultimate and partial questions. In addition, philosophy is knowledge, whereas the sciences are not knowledge properly speaking. The sciences do not pretend to be knowledge in the full meaning of the term, but rather constructions for making technology possible. Philosophy, as has been stated, is always a failure, whereas the sciences would be meaningless if they did not at least partially attain their purpose.[39]

Finally, the tragic and less serious sides of philosophy should be pointed out. Philosophy has a tragic side because he who starts philosophizing has lost his faith in the universe he lives in; this universe ceases to be firm and becomes formless, insecure, problematic, fluid. To be on it is the contrary of standing, it is to fall, to be lost, to drown. Life is felt to be a deception. This is the tragic side of philosophy.

But it is false to define life as if in its root it would consist only in this tragic aspect. Heidegger is mistaken when he asserts

[37] *Idea de principio,* II, pp. 128-129; "Prólogo a Historia de la filosofía," pp. 417-418.

[38] *Origin of philosophy,* pp. 13-27.

[39] *Idea de principio,* II, pp. 126-127. See also *En torno a Galileo,* p. 16; *Ideas y creencias,* p. 404.

that philosophy consists in showing that life is nothingness. Life is, of course, a "possible death" and absolute danger, but it is not only death, for if so "a man would not live beyond the instant required to commit suicide." Even if we admit, with some reservations, that life is existing nothingness and living danger, it can only be such if it is also an acceptation of danger and the will to exist in spite of everything. Life is "danger and challenge to danger, despair and fiesta, anguish and sport." The pessimism of Kierkegaard, Unamuno, and Heidegger cannot be accepted.

Together with the tragic side of philosophy we must stress its less serious side. Philosophy invents or creates ideas—not beliefs—, and the ideas, whether philosophical or scientific, approach poetry. They are not serious things. Philosophy does not possess the pathetic character or tonality of religion but the humorous tonality of a game. Ideas persuade or convince us because they are true, and they are true because they realize the prerequisites that the theory imposes upon itself to be perfect in its own order. True, the philosopher creates ideas and certitudes in order to continue living, but this does not mean that when he philosophizes he commits himself. Philosophy is the opposite of engagement; it is theory and theory means permanent revocability. Philosophy does not consist in demonstrating truth by the sacrifice of ones' life, but, on the contrary, in demonstrating truth in order to live authentically. Existentialist philosophy is *a limine* impossible, it is a radical tergiversation.[40]

Universidad de Deusto
Bilbao, Spain

[40]*Idea de principio,* II, pp. 145-183. In this place Ortega stresses the subjective element of ideas. In other places, particularly when he tries to avoid idealism, he stresses their objectice aspect. One thing is clear. According to him philosophy does not consist in knowing the bare, primary reality, but in forming ideas of primary reality, which are the ersatz for broken beliefs. The ideas are not that by which we know reality, but that which we know, and they are interpretations.

4

SUBJECTIVITY, FACTS, AND VALUES

by

George J. Stack

In a variety of ways there has come about a confluence of philosophical concern focusing upon the question of subjectivity in science and upon the relationship between values and facts in scientific description and theory construction. From a number of diverse quarters there has emerged a reaction against positivism (in its extreme form) as well as against what might be called dogmatic empiricism. It seems to me that these particular questions lead to problems dealt with not only by philosophers of science, but by a number of recent and contemporary philosophers, especially those who approach philosophy from the perspective of existential phenomenology. In this analysis I will not be primarily concerned with defending or attacking subjectivity in scientific investigation; rather, I will be concerned with relating the phenomenological perspective of human experience to the question of the interaction between facts and values in scientific inquiry in general. I will focus my attention upon two basic problems: (1) what is the meaning of subjectivity in the context of scientific investigation? (2) how do values affect or infiltrate the judgements of, or interpretations of, facts? In regard to (1), I will try to show that the entire question of the place of subjectivity in science (as it is dealt with, for example, in Israel Scheffler's *Science and Subjectivity*) is too often approached from a pre-phenomenological point of view which makes the question of the relationship between subjectivity and objectivity difficult, if not impossible, to resolve. I will deal with the second question in terms of the relationship between "subjectivity" and value as well as in terms of the influence of various modes of value upon factual judgment and the interpretation of phenomena.

I. *Subjectivity and Science*

On the basis of discoveries in microphysics, the development of, or more accurately, recrudescence of fictionalist interpretations of scientific theories, instrumentalist approaches to the philosophy of science, criticisms of the assumptions of empiricism such as those of Feyerabend, phenomenological psychologies which have challenged behaviorism, and a general atmosphere (which I take to be healthy) of anti-reductionism, the question of subjectivity in the scientific enterprize has been raised both by those who oppose it and those who champion it. Usually, it is in the statement of what the problem is that predominantly pholosophical questions arise. While some contemporary physicists (such as E. P. Wigner and others) have been led to the extreme view that an individual person's consciousness is the only "absolute reality," most scientists and philosophers of science have merely expressed their puzzlement over the complex data discovered in quantum physics or have postponed (as Einstein once did) the discovery of a more traditional causality to a future time in which the dilemmas of quantum physics will be revolved by further research or theoretical reformation. As many others have observed, the contemporary physicist has come face to face with problems which are of a purely philosophical order and which can only be brought to a philosophical resolution. Werner Heisenberg has, for example, declared that the dualistic ontology of Descartes is no longer applicable to modern science, that the scientific observer no longer confronts nature as an objective observer, but as an agent in the interaction between man and nature. In the paradoxes of certain aspects of quantum physics an undeniable element of subjectivity has emerged in scientific inquiry which is a challenge to all forms of positivism.

The subjective-objective dichotomy which is basically derived from Descartes' dualistic conception of finite reality exemplified in the distinction between *res cogitans* and *res extensa* is the philosophical legacy which has led to the typical statements about the objectivity of scientific inquiry as opposed to the subjective states or acts of consciousness of individuals. The radical responses to this dualism–subjective and objective idealism, on the one hand, and epiphenomenalism and materialism, on the other hand—have led to a number of epistemological difficulties which still haunt contemporary philosophy. There has been, however, a tendency in twentieth century philosophy (not the only one to be sure) which has attempted to reconcile the claims of idealism and those of materialism and which has formulated what may be described as a materio–idealist ontology. While few of those who shared the belief that the radical separation of matter and mind should be overcome have followed Russell's early suggestion of a kind of neutral monism, the tendency has had champions in both the pragmatic movement in American philosophy (especially John Dewey) and the various forms of existential phenomenology. These currents in recent and contemporary philosophy have endeavored to steer a middle course between an implausible idealism and a dogmatic materialism. Neither for Dewey nor Heidegger is there any "problem" about the existence of the external world; their very approach to the question of the relation of human experience to "nature" (Dewey) or of *Dasein* to its world (Heidegger) precludes the emergence of the problem of the relationship between subject and object since the radical separation of the two is never presupposed or assumed *ab initio*. Of course, it is in the sophisticated phenomenological analyses of Edmund Husserl that the attempt to transcend the subjective–objective dualism is expressed in the most comprehensive manner. The very question of the possibility of subjectivity in science is considered a serious challenge to the integrity of science by philosophers like Scheffler precisely because the central problem is formulated in pre–phenomenological terms. While I will not hold that phenomenology completely obviates all of the problems of subjectivity related to epistemic clarification, I will try to show that phenomenological analyses of the role of subjectivity in human knowledge are illuminating analyses which still preserve what is of value in a Kantian understanding of the relationship between the "spontaneity of thought" and the "receptivity of sense." In order to defend this view, a brief explication of the problem of subjectivity in scientific observation or inquiry as stated by Scheffler is required.

For Scheffler, the ideal of objectivity in science is correlative to the application of reason to an understanding of the world. Against those who suggest that subjectivity cannot be overcome in determining the "objects" or intentions of scientific investigation, it is said that

> The reality . . . revealed under the methodological publicity of scientific method is . . . a reality in which we are ourselves but limited natural elements. Our wishes and perceptions have not

> made this reality, but have sprung up within it as functions of organic development in a small corner of the universe of nature.[1]

Now, aside from the fact that this putative factual remark incorporates a presumptive metaphysics (reminiscent of Dewey's metaphysical views in *Experience and Nature,* but typical of all naturalistic metaphysics), there is a misunderstanding here concerning what those who disclose a subjective element in scientific inquiry are claiming. Certainly, it is rare to find anyone simply claiming that man's "wishes" or "perceptions" create or produce the phenomena which are encountered in ordinary experience or scientific observations. Such an understanding of the way in which human consciousness or human values condition the phenomena under investigation in science is closer to some extreme form of philosophical idealism and bears little relationship to the views of those who proclaim that human consciousness as well as historically determined values affect one's understanding of observed phenomena or, more generally, the structure of nature. The attacks against objectivity in science are said, nevertheless, to be derived from three basic sources: (1) the claim that there is, in some striking instances, a subjective element in observation; (2) that an element of subjectivism in scientific inquiry is inevitable in terms of shifts of meanings conditioned by largescale theoretical reformations or revolutions (e.g., the shift from Newtonisn to Einstenian mechanics); and (3) that the history of science itself reveals alterations of theoretical viewpoints or culturally determined *Blicke* which serve to undermine the ideal of strict objectivity. These three bases for averring that subjectivity does play a role in the scientific enterprize reduce to two insofar as they can be characterized as observational subjectivity and theoretical subjectivity. The latter includes universally accepted theoretical models or paradigms as well as what W. O. Quine once called "cultural posits" or what might be called, after Heidegger, "ontological projections."

The problem of the infiltration of subjectivity into scientific observation has, as I have said, received amplification from the paradoxical discoveries association with quantum physics. Thus, as a case in point, one may refer to the problems of measurement in quantum theory, Simply put, it has been found that the observer

[1]Israel Scheffler, *Science and Subjectivity,* New York, 1967, p. 11.

has a clear effect upon quantum–level processes. For, it is interference effects which preclude the exact calculation of the effect of energy transfer in an observation, a process which is necessitated by the nature of the phenomenon under study. Put in symbolic terms, it may be said that if 0 is an object (or system) which is known by entities (I) which (a) interact with 0 and which also (b) interact with the observer or his apparatus (A), then—according to quantum measurement theory—0 and I cannot be separated since the physical properties of 0 are affected by I and 0 is affected by I. Information about 0 is acquired by virtue of an interaction with I and there is no information attained about 0 which is independent of the information yielding interaction. The constitutive role of the observer in such observational processes is clear.[2] While quantum measurement is paradigmatic of the emergence of a subjective element in natural science, all instances of scientific observation are characterized by similar, though less dramatic, difficulties.

Scheffler holds that the independence of the observed phenomenon is essential to the notion of scientific observation even though he does admit that there is no observation which is entirely independent of what he calls "conceptualization." However, the nature of the "given" or the presented phenomena cannot be said to be absolutely independent of "processes of interpretation." The phenomenon which is observed is not "unaltered" in the process of observation since "conceptual change" does affect what we describe in our observations. Although it is said that observation does provide "independent" control over belief, even though it is necessarily conditioned by the categories applied to it, by psychological set, and by the possibility of error,[3] it is assumed that subjectivistic analyses of observation have been obviated. To my mind, Scheffler's analysis of the claim that there are subjective elements in observation not only does not serve its ostensible purpose (to show that these claims are invalid), but provides evidence in defense of the claim he is attacking. I will briefly list the relevant assertions he makes concerning observation because they are directly relevant to points I will deal with subsequently. The following factors are said to influence or affect the process of observation:

[2]Richard Schlegel, *Completeness in Science* (New York: Appleton-Century-Crofts, 1967), pp. 190-191.

[3]I. Scheffler, *op. cit.*, p. 45.

(1) Processes of interpretation
(2) belief
(3) expectation
(4) set or mental attitude
(5) alteration by conceptualization (e.g., application of specific conceptual schema)
(6) logical constraint (e.g., the inability to apply contrary properties to the same phenomenon)
(7) cultural determinism
(8) the non-certainty of the "given"
(9) the ambiguity of 'fact' (e.g., the tendency to identify "facts" with either things or processes or with their descriptions)
(10) guiding hypotheses
(11) individuation and classification of phenomena
(12) the element of arbitrariness in the creation of new category schema
(13) selective orientation
(14) the interest of the observer (or, to use an expression that is suggested but not used, the intentionality of the observer)

While (6) is a controlling factor in observation which clearly conditions all observation which claims to be scientific, it is clear that the other factors which Scheffler admits affect observations are such as to put in question the very objectivity he assumes is present in scientific observation. Despite the rather extensive qualifications that are imposed upon objectivity in observation it is concluded that "hypotheses are controllable by observation even if observation be construed as fully categorized."[4] Furthermore, it is argued that there is an element of arbitrariness in the act of freely creating "new category schemes."[5] Despite this admission, it is said that this inevitable element of arbitrariness is not "inconsistent with control." Surely, however, one must at least consider the possibility that the freely created "constructs" of the scientist do condition and determine the nature and type of phenomena which a scientific inquiry will attend to as well as the phenomena that will be bracketed.

The "category systems" that Scheffler avers make no truth-claims clearly constitute the aim, limit, and scope of a given

[4]*Ibid.*, p. 42.
[5]*Ibid.*, p. 43.

scientific inquiry much in the same way that a chosen methodology (e.g., behaviorism in psychology) already constitutes what will or will not count as relevant data. Aside from this question of the constituting function of category systems (which, in effect, may be influenced or shaped by 1, 2, 3, 4, 5, 7, 10, 11, 12, 13, and 14 in my list of Scheffler's factors which condition observation), I think it is questionable whether, on the basis of the very factors which are said to influence scientific observation, there truly are purely arbitrary category schema or systems which do not entail at least some truth-claims. If, to take a hypothetical case, a scientist were to adopt the Kantian categorical system, then would it not be the case that the concept of "the given" or the conceptual understanding of phenomena would be constituted by, say, the acceptance of the category of substance? Or, to take a more recent case in point, would not the adoption of the category of "dialectic" in relation to an interpretation of social phenomena determine the understanding of such phenomena? While it is true, as Scheffler points out, that isolated categories *per se* can be neither true nor false, it seems to me that certain categorical systems do, indeed, entail some metaphysical or epistemological presuppositions which would affect the meaning of hypotheses which are formulated in terms of them. Thus, the very concepts of phlogiston or, for that matter, ether imply physical theories of a certain kind and certainly influenced the interpretation of empirical data until their usefulness and meaningfulness was either theoretically and/or experimentally undermined. Since scientific revolutions often involve a replacement of a theoretical system or ontological projection by another theoretical framework, it seems that the alteration by conceptualization (5) which Scheffler refers to as a factor influencing observation is an alteration of a categorical system. While the elements of a categorical schema or system (i.e., the categories themselves) are neither true nor false, the schema or system does influence hypothesis—formation and does determine, to some extent, the selectivity of relevant phenomena or data and the interpretation of such phenomena or data. This is especially the case in regard to the dominant metaphysical, ontological, or epistemological matrix which is adopted in scientific inquiry.

Without denying an inexpungeable element of objectivity in observational situations (e.g., the primitive facticity of the phenomenon observed), it is too much to claim that observation "is . . . critically independent of hypothesis."[6] For, any observation statement which is scientifically meaningful is based upon implicit theory or upon a theoretical framework which serves as the basis of an interpretation of a phenomenon. Thus, to cite a relatively simple case of scientific observation, the medical doctor observing an x–ray negative must be guided in his interpretation of the *meaning* of the pictures he is examining by some hypothetical assumptions. If observation, in such an instance, were entirely independent of hypothesis, the x–ray picture would be practically unintelligible. Furthermore, the very language used to describe or express a particular perceptual observation is itself characterized by some fundamental conceptualizations which may be assumed to embody what J. L. Austin has described as the distinctions which men have seen fit to make in the course of their experience and thought. In the most elementary empirical judgments (and, hence, *a fortiori,* in an observational statement) there is an inevitable interpretative element which is, in general, traceable to one or more of the general factors influencing the formulation of that judgment. To say, for example, that "The watch is on the table" implies that an interpretation of a visual phenomenon (that x) has taken place, that this entity is judged to be similar to other experienced phenomena identified as "watches," that this "watch" is in a particular spatial relationship to another entity or phenomenon (i.e., that something which is identified as belonging to the class to tables). Furthermore, the use of the definite articles "the" indicates that the observer is identifying the entities referred to as particular *unities* or he is using "the" to produce a "specifying or particularizing effect." A language in which the definite article is used is one which has been structured in such a way as to express references to individuals or particulars. Needless to say, the notion that there are individuals is surely a metaphysical notion, albeit a well–founded one.

Whether one agrees with the early Wittgenstein that natural languages are pervaded by a logical structure or with Nietzsche that languages reflect and preserve metaphysical or epistemic assumptions, it is clear that the historical development of language

[6]*Ibid.,* p. 45. In contrast to this view, it has recently been said that "...the description of every single fact [is] dependent on *some* theory [or hypothesis]." P. K. Feyerabend, "Problems of Empiricism," in *Beyond the Edge of Certainty,* ed. R. G. Colodny (Englewood Cliffs, N.J.,: Prentice-Hall, 1965), p. 175.

or its etvmological roots indicate that fundamental or primitive concepts or categories do condition our understanding of man and his world. The general tendency dominant in the philosophical or scientific use of language is for non-technical or quasi-technical terms to be adopted by philosophers or scientists in the earliest development of languages in evolving cultures, societies, and civilizations.

Thus, to cite only a few instances, the Greek word for cause (αιτια) had its origin in the forensic language of the ancient Greeks and retained, even in Aristotle's thought (insofar as he repeatedly illustrates the meaning of cause or the doctrine of four causes in terms of the model of human action), an anthropomorphic significance. Again, the significant philosophical term "potentiality" *(dunaton)* had developed from ordinary Greek language which expressed socially significant powers. *Dunaton* and *dunamis* originally meant physical power or prowess. Gradually these terms came to be used to refer to political or financial power. When Aristotle begins to write about "the category of potentiality" he does not yet use the words referring to such potentiality in a technical, metaphysical sense. Potentialities are described in the *Magna Moralia* as "authority, riches, strength, and beauty."[7] Eventually, Aristotle came to relate the metaphysical notion of potentiality to matter while, at the same time, retaining a conception of distinctive human potentialities (the rational potencies or *logon dunatai* of the *Metaphysics)* which was rooted in the pre-philosophical uses of the terms translated as potentiality. When Soren Kierkegaard was seeking a vocabulary by which to describe the dialectical "movements" of human becoming *(Vorden),* he seized upon the metaphysical language of Aristotle,[8] referring to man's self-becoming in terms of the dynamic movement of the self from potentiality to actuality.

In yet another important instance of linguistic development relevant to philosophical thought, it is interesting to note that Spinoza and Schopenhauer used the word *causa* to express either reason or cause. The philosophical encrustations which developed around this term surely led to the notion that causal relationships

[7]Aristotle, *Magna Moralia,* trans. G. C. Armstrong (London: Heinemann, 1962), 1183b28ff.

[8]Cp. George J. Stack, "Kierkegaard's Ironic Stage of Existence," *Laval Théologique et Philosophique,* XXV (Fall, 1969), pp. 193-207; George J. Stack, "Kierkegaard's Concept of Possibility," *Journal of Thought,* April, 1970, pp. 80-92.

are necessary in the sense that the relationship between cause and effect was construed as a relationship of logical entailment When Hume criticized this interpretation of casuality he not only brought objections to it terms of an empirical, psychologistic analysis, but he inaugurated a reformation of the use and *meaning* of cause.

Finally, to cite only one of many instances in which the metaphysical or epistemic notions embeded in natural languages affected intellectual history, one can point to Heidegger's analysis (in *Sein und Zeit)* of the pervasive influence which Descartes' categories *(res extensa, res cogitans)* had on the language and thought of Western man. The tendency to think of man as an object or as a quantitative energy system—in point of fact, all of the mechanomorphic conceptions of man—has its origin, on the one hand, in the influence of the model of physics on modern thought, and on the other hand, in Descartes' ontology of *res* or "things." In recent times, Paul Feyerabend has made an observation similar to that of Heidegger in his assertion that "even everyday languages, like languages of highly theoretical systems, have been introduced in order to give expression to some theory or point of view, and they therefore contain a well-developed and sometimes very abstract ontology."[9] Whereas one may question whether ordinary languages are deliberately "introduced" for the reason Feyerabend gives, there is sufficient evidence to indicate that, as a matter of fact, natural languages tend, over a period of time, to absorb and reflect some general metaphysical *Weltanschauung* or some of the theoretical concepts of the natural sciences, psychology, or the social sciences.

Although the question of the interrelationship of natural languages and philosophico-scientific language is a large one and one which calls for a great deal of empirical investigation, it is obvious, I believe, that languages or families of languages significantly affect the descriptive terminology and orientation of scientific observation. In this general sense, then, language or linguistic renovation ought to be one of the factors which, directly or indirectly, condition the formulation of observational statements. Although Scheffler allows for the possibility that a "language system" may determine the meaning of categories used in observational language he denies that this leads to a "subjectivism that appeals to meaning." It would

[9]P. K. Feyerabend, "Explanation, Reduction, and Empiricism," in H. Feigl and G. Maxwell, eds. *Minnesota Studies in the Philosophy of Science*, III (Minneapolis: University of Minnesota Press, 1962), p. 76.

seem, however, that there is a basis—in regard to the theoretical content of languages at particular historical periods—for undermining any claim that observational statements have only an objective reference or a strictly objective pole. To admit that language systems can condition the language of observation does not lead, as Scheffler avers, to subjectivism. Rather, it is simply an admission that there are extra-scientific world-orientations or cultural values which have a constituting function in scientific observation and inquiry. Again, because Scheffler formulates his question in terms of a dichotomy between subjective or objective understandings of science, he is led to exaggerate the effects of introducing factors which influence or constitute scientific investigations. The very oppositions which someone like Scheffler struggles with are precisely the oppositions which Husserl's phenomenology sought to overcome.

The implicit notion of subjectivity which is the *bête noir* of Scheffler is one which has its roots in the radical separation of consciousness and matter (as well as other consciousnesses) in Descartes *Meditations*. Although Descartes' *cogito ergo sum* seems to have been a conclusion which "demonstrated" the existence of a personal or individual consciousness, it is clear that Descartes did not, in fact, arrive at the existence of an I-consciousness. In the *Meditations* his general procedure seems to be to argue from a variety of mental acts or states of consciousness (e.g., perceiving, doubting, willing, imagining, etc.) to the existence of a consciousness that is the origin or cause of these acts or the being which undergoes such states. While the specific content of states of consciousness may be said to be individual or particular, there is no evidence, in Descartes' *Meditations,* that the apparently solipsistic consciousness he refers to is an *individual* consciousness. Descartes provided no criterion for the individuated characteristics of the self. Failing to draw out the implications of his argument for an existing finite consciousness, as Husserl has argued, he hesitated before the transcendental turn. In the various mental acts or states of being Descartes referred to is a common, fundamental activity —that of intentionality. Whether we attend to something actual or something ideal (in Husserl's terms, something "irreal") the intentional *nisus* of consciousness is revealed. Husserl's analysis of the phases or stages of intentionality, of the concrete process of thinking, of the "form of thinking" he held to be imbeded in all thinking, was directed at clarifying or elucidating a theory of reason which would disclose the basis of *radikale Besinnung.*

In addition, of course, he was concerned with a clarification of the Cartesian *cogito* which would retain the constituting subjective activity of consciousness while avoiding an untenable solipsism. The third general intention of Husserl was to transcend his own early psychologism (derived, basically, from the philosophy of Hume) and to overcome what he describes as "natural subjectivity." To my mind, it seems to be this last notion of subjectivity (i.e., Humean or psychologistic subjectivity) that Scheffler attempts to attack. Ironically, Hume himself did not turn his own psychologism (e.g., in his analysis of causality) upon his own conception of abstract relations of ideas; rather, it was the early Husserl who raised the question whether there might not be a psychological basis for the clarification of the logic of the deductive sciences. Against this view, Husserl argued (in the *Prolegomena zur reinen Logik* and in subsequent works) that psychologism was incapable of accounting for the objectivity of scientific theories and that it tended to relativize truth, to lead to the view that there is no "truth in itself."

The central element in Husserl's *Formale und transzendentale Logik* which is directly relevant to my attempt to criticize Scheffler's concept of subjectivism in science is the emphasis upon constituting subjectivity or the ineluctable transcendental subjectivity which is the constituting ground, as it were, of sense-investigation. Insofar as Husserl argues that all being fundamentally derives its "sense" or meaning from constituting consciousness, there is an underlying, inevitable, subjective pole in the discernment of the actual or the ideal, in the spontaneous and productive activity of consciousness. This subjective pole, however, is distinguishable from psychological (or, as Husserl prefers to say, psychic) factors such as belief, mood, or "set" which are admitted as possible conditioning factors influencing observation, interpretation, and judgment. Insofar as all judging is a function or performance *(Leistung)* which is a constituting subjectivity, there is an ineliminable cognitive activity which selects, organizes, classifies, and categorizes the phenomena encountered in observational experience. This is not to say that Husserl's phenomenology entails, as his critics repeatedly charge, a commitment to a subjectivistic, idealistic epistemology. Intended objectivities remain objectivities despite the fact that the *Sinn* of such objectivities is rooted in subjectively constituted judgments. As S. Bachelard has recently said in her study of *Formale und Transzendentale Logik,* the constitutive subjectivity of the transcendental ego does not *create* phenomena. Rather, it confers *Seins-sinn* ("being-sense") upon being. The world, as well as the phenomena encountered in it, remains transcendent to the transcendental ego as well as to its *cogitationes.*[10] For phenomenology, as Merleau-Ponty once said, the world is "already there"—*le monde est toujours «déjà là» avant la réflexion, comme une présence inaliénable.*[11] This "inalienable presence" of the phenomena of the world—the world of actuality—is also *déjà constituée* since it is, for the most part, intelligible, a spiritual realm in which man lives and moves. The intelligibility of factical phenomena is not a *datum* or a *factum;* there is no absolutely independent "given" which comprises the objects of empirical judgments. Human consciousness is capable of apprehending any number of diverse phenomena, ideal or actual, which are intelligible precisely because of the spontaneous, constitutive activity of consciousness. This understanding of the relationship between human consciousness and the world does not, however, commit one to the kind of psychologistic subjectivism which is properly attacked by philosophers such as Scheffler. Husserl would have agreed with Scheffler that "natural human subjectivity" must be transcended in order to attain to an understanding of the "things themselves."

Because of the interaction of the observer and the observed, because of the causal factors (already cited) which affect observation, because of the basic subjective, constituting activity of consciousness there can be no absolute or perfect objectivity in scientific observation or observation statements. Of course, as we move from the human sciences to the purely physical sciences we have a much greater approximation of an ideal scientific objectivity. The notion of objectivity which is often sought by philosophers of science is a kind of Kantian ideal of reason which is valid and meaningful, but which is clearly only approximated in scientific observation or observational judgment. As Husserl has pointed out, the model of a more or less pure objectivity in human knowledge is found in logic. However, even in an analysis of logic which is purged of psychologistic elements there is a cognitively subjective pole in logical judgment since jugmental activities produce categorial ob-

[10]Suzanne Bachelard, *A Study of Husserl's Formal and Transcendental Logic* (Evanston, Ill.: Northwestern University Press, 1968), p. 162.

[11]M. Merleau-Ponty, *Phénoménologie de la perception* (Paris: Gallimard, 1945), p. i.

jectivities which are derived from intentional operations and require syntheses. Objects of judgment *(urteilmässig)* are objects for an intentional consciousness which is capable of achieving intentional shifts and, hence, of attending to various aspects of, say, an observational situation. The pure objectivity which philosophers such as Scheffler seek would require a return to "pure experience." But this, as Husserl argues in his *Formale und Transzendentale Logik,* would require that one exclude *(ausschalten)* all of the idealizations (or idealities) which impregnate the concretely existing world. If it were possible to achieve this return to pre-predicative, pre-categorical experience (as Husserl suggests is possible), one may wonder whether such experience would be intelligible or meaningful. Surely, in the case of protocol statements or observational statements such antepredicative experience would contribute little to our capacity to interpret or understand such phenomena. If, as Husserl avers, the ideal formations of logic are "essentially products of the correlative structures of productive cognitive life,"[12] then this is also the case, *a fortiori,* in observational judgment.

If we can accept the general principles of the phenomenological analysis of intentional acts of consciousness (especially in the case of the acts of judgment which are paradigmatic of all knowledge), then the question of objectivity or subjectivity in science as it is raised by Scheffler is by-passed. Scientific knowledge is neither purely subjective nor purely objective since all knowledge has a cognitively subjective pole or constitutive basis as well as an objective pole. The "states-of-affairs" *(Sachverhalte)* which are known or reported in observational judgments are objectivities which are, nevertheless, constituted in their intelligibility by the mediation of consciousness as the subjective pole of cognition. The "thereness" of the facticity of observed data is never denied by a phenomenological approach to empirical observation. The object of knowledge in such instances is that which is recognized as a result of the synthesis of "receptive experience" and "predicative spontaneity." To my mind, this Kantian notion is as valid as it was when Kant first formulated it in his *Kritik der reinen Vernunft.* There is nothing in Scheffler's *Science and Subjectivity* (or in recent, related studies) which obviates this basic epistemic principle. The very question of the relationship between facts and factual observation

[12]Edmund Husserl, *Formale und transzendentale Logik* (Halle: Niemeyer, 1929), p. 263.

statements (which is discussed by Scheffler)[13] is one which relates us back to the consideration of the variety of factors which condition the expression of observational statements as well as to Husserl's emphasis upon what he calls the subjective a-priority which constitutes all judgments. In order to understand what an observed phenomenon is, judgment is essential. And judgment, as I shall argue, requires an interpretation of phenomena.

It is at this point that there is a confluence of all of the factors previously considered in relation to the cognitively subjective and psychologistically subjective influences on scientific investigation in general. Aside from the determinations already considered, there is the need to recognize that there are extra-observational, extra-scientific valuations which are intimately associated with the factual and theoretical aspects of scientific inquiry. It is to this general question of value-determinations which influence the formulation of empirical judgments that I will now turn my attention. To the constitutive activity of consciousness, the categorical, theoretical, and linguistic factors which can influence observational judgment (as well as the various psychologistic factors which are generally acknowledged as relevant to the observational situation) must be added the valuational factors which may also play a constitutive role in the judgment of, and interpretation of, empirical states-of-affairs.

II. *Values and Scientific Facts*

The development of modern science has generally produced what has become a universal empirical ontology which is the dominant world-orientation of the contemporary world. Aside from the two unquestioned assumptions of empiricism which have been isolated by W. O. Quine (*viz.*, reductionism and the bifurcation between analytic and synthetic truths which, of course, has its historical roots in Leibnitz, Hume, and Kant), there is a third presupposition of empiricism which is not necessarily shared by all empiricists, but which is a pervasive characteristic of what I have called the empirical ontology. That is, the assumption that all factual statements are value free or are entirely independent of values or valuations. This assumption is questionable and unjustifiable for a number of reasons. The chief reason is that factual assertions

[13]Scheffler, *op. cit.*, p. 100 ff.

or, more properly, factual judgments are granted a putative epistemic neutrality which, in general, is unwarranted. Although the question of the relationship between facts and values is often examined from the standpoint of ethics or social criticism (i.e., the responsibility of the scientist to society or human welfare), I will be concerned, basically, with non-ethical values in attempting to show the way in which general or specific valuations infiltrate factual judgments. While there may be some non-controversial instances in which the value-laden character of factual assertions is by no means obvious, I do not think that such counterexamples nullify the particular claims that are put forward in my explication of the influence of values upon basic features of scientific inquiry.

Before turning to a discussion of the various ways in which values infiltrate factual assertions, there are some fundamental questions which should be dealt with concerning the nature and meaning of facts. Although many would generally agree that there are facts, there is some controversy concerning the precise nature of facts themselves. A provisional answer to the question, What is a fact? is a necessary propaedeutic to an examination of the relationship between values and facts. Clearly, the term "fact" is itself somewhat ambiguous.

The word "fact" seems to have its pre-technical roots in social existence or public action insofar as *factum* means a "deed" or "that which is done." *Ab initio,* the word *factum* seems to be rooted in the context of historical occurrences in the sense that it refers to what *has* happened or taken place. The word *factum* is ultimately derived from the verb form *factum est,* signifying an accomplished feat. The Italian *fatto* and the French *fait* (*fait:* action, *chose faite*) all indicate the sense of activity or accomplishment.

The use of "fact" as a primary category of actuality is, generally speaking, a nineteenth century phenomenon. A notion of fact as an objective, independent, hard datum was held by 19th century scientists who tended to assume that facts had a meaning in themselves, wholly independent of the observer and of the constructive aspect of scientific understanding. The tendency to treat facts as if they were intelligible entities in themselves eventually led to the the basic ambiguity of the term "fact." For, the question may be raised whether facts are occurrences or events which actually happen or whether they are statements which express, "picture," or describe actual states-of-affairs.

While there are those philosophers who maintain that facts

simply are and are not, unlike propositions, either true or false, there are those who hold that facts are propositions of a particular kind. Traditionally, facts have usually been construed as the phenomena or objective data which statements or propositions having empirical reference describe. In this sense of the term, facts are identified with that which makes an empirical proposition true. Of course, those philosophers (like the Wittgenstein of the *Tractatus-Logico-Philosophicus*) who claimed that propositions of a certain kind "picture" facts presupposed a correspondence theory of truth which was itself ultimately undermined by the epistemological structure which was constructed upon this assumption. That is, the assertion that "language pictures the totality of facts," is clearly neither a tautology nor an analytic truth nor an empirical proposition in the natural sciences. Hence, in terms of the theory of truth that emerges in the *Tractatus,* the nature of the truth-claim of this basic presupposition is indeterminable. What the self-negating conclusion of the *Tractatus* indicates—among other things—is the ambiguity of the relationship between what Husserl called the "ideality" of language and empirical facticity or actuality. It is perhaps such a difficulty which led Otto Neurath to the view that

> It is always science as a system of statements which is at issue. *Statements are compared with statements,* not with "experiences," "the world," or anything else . . . these meaningless duplications belong to a more or less refined metaphysics . . . we confine ourselves always to the sphere of linguistic thought.[14]

Such a conception of empirical science is paradoxical since an appraisal of a "comprehensive set of statements" in relation to previously coordinated statements leads to the abandonment of any factual reference and to a coherence conception of scientific truth in which any so-called "coherent totality" is as plausible as any other. While one may admit that the determination of the relationship between statements and empirical immediacy is a difficult question, the denial that scientific statements have any relationship to empirical actuality implies the negation of any claim to have knowledge *about* any actual, temporal state of affairs. Furthermore, if Otto Neurath's conception of scientific assertions were adopted, there would be no discernible difference between a self-consistent

[14]Otto Neurath, "Soziologie im Physikalismus," *Erkenntnis,* II (1931-1932) p. 291.

logical system and a "coherent totality" of *soi-disant* empirical statements. As Scheffler has pointed out, one can abandon claims to apodictic certainty in science without necessarily abandoning what he appropriately describes as the "referential import of science."[15]

The nature of this basic difficulty has been clearly expressed by Moritz Schlick in his comments upon the relationship between judgment and that to which the judgment refers. He argues that

> the judgment is something completely different from that which is judged . . . it is not like that which is judged . . . For the concepts occurring in the judgment are certainly not of the same nature as the real objects which they designate, and the relations among concepts are not like the relations of things.[16]

This distinction between the factual judgment and the phenomena or facts about which the judgment is made seems to be a valid one in terms of the preservation of an extra-linguistic reference to entities which are encountered in perceptual, experiential immediacy. In the *Lebenswelt* of man it is the extra-linguistic facticities which lie at the basis of what comes to be formulated in empirical judgments or as empirical knowledge. As Husserl has put it in *Formale und Transzendentale Logik,* "experience is the primal instituting of the being-for-us of objects."[17] However, there is a way in which the lacuna between judgments and that which is judged can be bridged: that is, by virtue of the act of interpretation. For the moment, however, I must continue to focus attention upon the attempt to clarify the meaning of fact in the light of Moritz Schlick's statement concerning the distinction between judgments and extra-judgmental referents.

There is a sense in which a perceived phenomenon or a field of phenomena is not, as such, a fact. For, in order to judge that, for example, my automobile is in my driveway, I must initially perceive a set of phenomena or I must perceive the presence of entities in specific spatial relationships. While many might say that the fact in such an instance is discovered in the perceptual process, one may question whether this is the case. It would seem to be the case that when we perceive we rapidly interpret the perceptual data

[15]Scheffler, op. cit., p. 115.
[16]Moritz Schlick, *Allgemeine Erkenntnislehre* (Berlin: Springer, 1929) p. 56.
[17]E. Husserl, *op. cit.,* p. 164.

we are aware of, tending to fill in the aspects of the phenomenon not actually perceived in imagination. Thus, for example, only perceiving an aspect of my automobile, I assume or imagine that the unperceived features of the automobile are actually *there* and are possible objects of perception. In the judgment that the automobile parked in my driveway is *my* automobile, I am, of course, relying on my memory of having parked it there previously, my memory of the physical characteristics of the automobile, etc. But, in addition, I am assuming, on the basis of only some visual sensory data, that *this* automobile is my own. This judgment in itself indicates the interpretive element which appears to be simultaneous with our perceptual experiences. To be sure, in our ordinary perceptual experience we are usually no longer aware of this rather rapid process of interpretation.

That the interpretive process I believe accompanies or pervades perceptual experience becomes so habitual that, in time, we are no longer aware that we are involved in it can be illustrated in instances when we are perceiving quite unfamiliar phenomena or ambiguous perceptual stimuli. Again, familiar objects may not be immediately recognized in unusual or atypical surroundings.

It is in tactile perception, perhaps, where we can discern this interpretative aspect of perception most clearly. For, the immediate touch sensation is not, say "hot," "cold," or "warm." To say, for example, "this object is warm," requires an interpretative judgment about what is immediately perceived, an interpretation of the primitive tactile datum which is a particular kind of touch sensation. The categorical, conceptual identification of such touch sensations seems to require an interpretative understanding of what is experienced. The difficulty (which Berkeley first discovered) that individuals who have acquired sight (after a reasonably long period of blindness) have in relating touch sensations to visual perception at least suggests that perception involves the synthesis of the "information" acquired by means of the various modalities of sense, a synthesizing process which seems to be characterized by a complex interrelationship among memory, imagination, and an intentional, cognitive act of interpretation.

In order for the objective datum or phenomenon to be described as a fact, it must be "made" intelligible. That is to say, it must be an object of an intentional judgment and, hence, subsumed under what Husserl describes as a categorical ideality. An event or occurrence (say, a flash of lightning) is not in itself intelligible;

its intelligibility seems to lie in the logical form of the description of it. Although it makes sense to say that the statement "There is a flash of lightning" is true or false, it does not make sense to say that the flash of lightning in itself is true or false.

The general problem of determining what facts are is not only a problem of terminology which, presumably, could be resolved by stipulations. For, if we are to assume that only certain types of propositions are facts, then the question arises concerning how we ought to describe the data or phenomena which these facts "picture," refer to, or describe. Whereas there are uses of "fact" which do not refer to concrete phenomena which are encountered in perception (e.g., it is a fact that the proposition "a white swan is white" is necessarily true), but to proposition or statements, the more typical use of the term has reference to some state of affairs in the world. Needless to say, the actual states of affairs continue to be whether they are designated as facts or not. While actual events or ocurrences may not be, strictly speaking, intelligible in themselves, they have an undeniable facticity.

One of the consequences of identifying facts as a certain class of propositions (e.g., contingent or empirical propositions) is the implication that all such propositions are true or, at least, appear to entail a truth claim. Certainly, there is a sense in which the description of an assertion as factual is an honorific designation. Now, when we say that P is a fact, the obvious implication is that P is true. In describing a statement as factual we say, by implication, that it is true, is a verified or confirmed "fact." Hence, we are often led to speak about positive fact–statements and negative fact–statements rather than saying that P is true *because* it describes a state of affairs in the world.

While it is true that there is an overlap of so–called negative facts and false statements or false empirical propositions, there is a sense in which there is a logical significance to Wittgenstein's conception of "negative facts" *(negative Tatsachen).* In order to refer to the non–existence of a state–of–affairs we may be led to formulate a notion of negative fact. However, there is a sense in which the very notion of negative facts is paradoxical. For, the assertion of a statement having the form "It is not the case that . . ." is misleading insofar as it looks as if a possitive assertion about something were being made. If we examine the statement, say, that "Lyndon B. Johnson is the President of the United States," we see that it is simply a false empirical statement. On the other hand, the statement that "It is not the case that Lyndon B. Johnson is the President of the United States" is a straightforward true statement. The meaningfulness of any so-called negative fact [e.g., —(p)] is clearly derived by virtue of an implicit reference to some positive fact or positive facts. As Raphael Demos once put it,

> There are no negative facts . . . insofar as a negative proposition is asserted of a fact at all, the term of reference must be the world of positive facts.[18]

In a sense, every assertion of a positive fact entails a set of negations which are, as Sartre pointed out in *L'Etre et le néant,* implicity understood in the assertion of such a proposition. However, the purely logical point that Wittgenstein makes has a certain validity since we can think or imagine that is not the case—i.e., a *possible,* but non-existent state--of-affairs—and we can inscribe or utter such statements and, hence, have an implicit understanding of the meaning of such statements. The difficulty with such a view, on the other hand, is that it seems to suggest a reference to negative facts which "exist" as positive facts do. Wittgenstein's notion involves the claim that a negative fact is not something conceived of as existing in itself. Obviously, there is no negative fact which has the property of negativity. Recently, Wittgenstein's notion of negative fact has been defined in the following way:

> a negative fact is the non-existence of a state of affairs, which non-existence is the one and only one fact which negates (i.e., contradicts) that state of affairs.[19]

This definition is based upon Wittgenstein's analogy illustrating the meaning of negative fact. Thus, Wittgenstein avers that "to the fact that a point is black there corresponds *[entspricht]* a positive fact, and to the fact that a point is white (not black), a negative fact."[20] This particular illustration is odd since a fact is described by Wittgenstein as "the existence of states of affairs" *[Was der Fall ist, die Tatsache, ist das Bestehen von Sachverhalten.]* And a negative fact is generally described as having reference

[18]Raphael Demos, "A Discussion for a Certain Type of Negative Proposition," *Mind,* XXVI, (January, 1917), p. 189.

[19]James C. Morrison, *Meaning and Truth in Wittgenstein's Tractatus."* (Paris and the Hague: Mouton, 1968), p. 108.

[20]Ludwig Wittgenstein, *Tractatus Logico-Philosophicus,* trans. D. F. Pears and B. F. McGuinness (London: Routledge, 1961), p. 47.

to a non–existent state of affairs. Strictly speaking, then, there are a multiplicity of possible negative facts. Thus, if we assume the truth of the statement, "this point is black," there are any number of negative facts that can be asserted (the statement, "This point is white," is a false statement and, in a sense, is one possible negative fact). From the assertion that "It is not the case that this point is white," we certainly cannot infer that it is black, green, blue, yellow, etc. However, from the fact that a given point is black, I can infer that it is not non–black. All such negative statements may be legitimately described as negative facts. Wittgenstein's notion of negative facts is idiosyncratic and, in some respects, questionable in his own terms.

At one point in the *Tractatus* he remarks that it is possible to "express" a negative proposition by means of a negative fact (note the suggestion here that there is a distinction between negative *statements* and negative *facts*). As an illustration he gives the following: "suppose that 'a' does not stand in a certain relation to 'b'; then this might be used to say that aRb was not the case."[21] Clearly, the meaningfulness of such an assertion can only be determined in relation to a presumed positive fact (even though the elements of such a proposition are understood independent of the positive or negative nature of the fact). The question which Wittgenstein raises in his *Notebooks,* "Is the positive fact primary, the negative secondary . . .?"[22] is one which he himself had answered already in the *Tractatus.* For, he averred that "the negative proposition is constructed by an indirect use of the positive."[23]

Insofar as Wittgenstein intented to show that all positive statements about a thing, object, process, or state–of–affairs do, in a manner of speaking, entail negative statements, the logical category of *negative Tatsachen* is useful and meaningful. However, from the standpoint of an empirical analysis of facts, it is clearly misleading to speak of negative facts (which tend to suggest a kind of state–of–affairs which, in some paradoxical sense, may be said to "be") and it is certainly questionable to argue that a positive, elementary statement has one and only one "corresponding" neg-

[21]*Ibid.,* p. 103.

[22]Ludwig Wittgenstein, *Notebooks 1914-1916,* ed. by G. E. Anscombe and G. H. von Wright (Oxford: Blackwell, 1961), pp. 32e.-33e.

[23]Ludwig Wittgenstein, *Tractatus Logico-Philosophicus,* p. 103: "...der negative Satz indirekt durch den positiven gebildet."

ative fact. Although, from a logical point of view, it may be the case that an elementary proposition may have only one negation, a positive empirical statement implies any number of negative facts which are implicity understood if one understands the meaning of the original, positive statement. To my mind, Wittgenstein's logical analysis of facts (which are sometimes referred to as propositions and sometimes as actual states of affairs) is determined by his *a priori* assumption that "logic pervades the world," even though he occasionally indicates his desire to talk about "empirical reality" *(Die empirische Realität),* to refer to non-propositional actualities as "facts".

The ambiguity of the term "fact" continues to be present in Wittgenstein's *Tractatus* despite the fact that he intended to provide a purely logical analysis of the structure of propositions in general as well as of factual statements. This is clear in Wittgenstein's distinction between *Tatsache* (that which is the case as expressed linguistically) and *Sachverhalten* (which is referred to as an *existent* fact),[24] between the factual proposition and the state-of-affairs it presumably corresponds to or "pictures". What must be borne in mind, however, is that the correspondence theory of truth which Wittgenstein brings to a kind of precise formulation is itself, as Heidegger has argued in *Sein und Zeit,* based upon the primordial understanding of Dasein's Being-in-the--world. As Heidegger has put it (in his discussion of the correspondence theory of truth),

> Das Aussagen ist ein Sein zum seienden Ding selbst . . . Zur Bewährung kommt, dass das aussagende Sein zum Ausgesagten ein Aufzeigen des Seienden ist, *dass* es das Seiende, zu dem es ist, *entdeckt.* Augewiesen wird das Entdeckend-sein des Aussage . . . *Wahrsein (Wahrheit)* der Aussage muss verstanden werden als *entdeckendsein.* Wahrheit hat also gar nicht die Struktur einer Übereinstimmung zwischen Erkennen und Gegenstand im Sinne einer Angleichung eines Seienden (Subjekt) an ein anderes (Objekt).
>
> Das Wahrsein als Entdeckend-sein ist wiederum ontologisch nur möglich auf dem Grunde des In-der-Welt-seins.[25]

In Wittgenstein's language—in the *Philosophical Investigations*—there is a *Lebensform* which is the primal basis for language-use,

[24]J. C. Morrison, *op. cit.*, p. 20.
[25]Martin Heidegger, *Sein und Zeit* (Tübingen: Niemeyer, 1963), p. 218.

for the expressions having reference to immediate actualities which are encountered in human experience. The distinction between factual statements or judgments and the phenomenal facticities they refer to can be retained without assuming a *radical* bifurcation between the two. However, the relationship between factual propositions and facticities should be understood as mediated by at least an element of interpretation.

There are good reasons, as we have seen, for retaining the distinction between fact–statements (positive, empirical statements) and the facts they may be said to "report" or describe. If we desire to support the notion that facts are contingent statements or propositions, it may be possible to refer to the objective data or states–of–affairs by using the terms *factum* or *facta*. Thus, we could describe *facta* as the data, phenomena, occurrences, or collections of objects which are referred to in factual statements or by F–propositions (fact–claiming statements as distinct from the truth–claims of tautologies or analytic statements). *Facta* are the concrete actualities which we encounter or discover in immediate experience or in the *Lebenswelt*. Having preserved this necessary distinction between F–propositions and *facta,* we can now focus our attention on the question of the valuational component in factual judgments and in the process of selecting and in the designation of facts.

First of all, the most general question that we may raise is why we assume there are facts at all. Correlative to this question is the problem of the ways in which *facta* are construed. In general, the assumption of the existence of objective, public facts which can be discerned by any rational man by virtue of perceptual judgment is itself possible in terms of a cultural perspective which fosters, prizes, or values factual knowledge. Historically, it would seem, factual explanations of a variety of phenomena had been preceded by mythical or religious explanations of the same or similar phenomena. Gradually, more impersonal, non–mythic accounts of natural phenomena tended to replace the previous modes of explanation or interpretations of the nature and meaning of facts. In the earliest of the pre–Socratic philosophers—Thales—we can discern the odd intermingling of poetry, animism, and science. Because of the powers in things, they were considered to be ensouled or "full of gods". Most mythopoetic forms of thought or expression retain this general notion of the marvelous character of ordinary events, what might be called the mystical nature of facts.

To simplify what is an extremely complex development, it is clear that the factual orientation of Western man has historical roots which have already (albeit partially) been traced. It would seem as if man, at many points in history, has been faced with the choice of the paradigmatic model by which he would describe and interpret natural phenomena (including the phenomena encountered in his social existence). Strictly speaking, of course, this "choice" is, in a sense, metaphorical since we cannot assume that any individual or group suddenly decided upon the model by which factual phenomena or events in general would be understood. In Lucretius' *De rerum natura,* for example, we can sense the tension between the lure of the mythical understanding of events and human destiny and the liberating explanations of Epicurus in the underlying sadness this new wisdom brings. Changes in generally accepted cultural perspectives seem to come about gradually even though the consequences of these changes bring about social upheavals which are often sudden and explosive. The same is true, *mutatis mutandis*, of shifts in the basis for an understanding of the nature, meaning, and significance of facts. Indeed, the emergence of a dominant cognitive, psychological, and cultural perspective tends to determine what will or will not count as fact, what facts will be selectively emphasized or attended to, and what the chief interpretations of *facta* will be. These general world-orientations are formulated in what develops into a complex synthesis of general modes of thought, shared sentiments, systems of belief and what may be described as a system of interrelated cultural values which are usually coeval with a general spiritual *nisus*.

If such generalizations seem to claim too much, I believe there are sufficient historical instances which tend to support such claims. Thus, for example, there are instances in which the importance or usefulness of certain discoveries was not recognized or was ignored, for the most part, because they were in conflict with, or incongruous with, dominant cultural "sets" or values.

The ancient Greeks, for example, had an unusual talent for technological development which they chose not to bring to fruition. Thus, they discovered a primitive steamboat, but used it only for their amusement, never following through in its development. The *ethos* of a people at a specific historical stage seems to preclude the acceptance of certain factual information, insights, or techniques. In such instancies certain facts are clearly recognized, but are not understood as having significance or value for the historical peoples who have discovered them or to whom they have been presented. It may be said that, in such cases, an overriding valuational orientation prohibits the appropriate implementation of certain facts.

In the sciences there are countless cases of entrenched cultural–intellectual "sets" which prohibited or inhibited the acceptance of new theoretical or factual discoveries. Thus, for example, the Swedish chemist and physicist Arrhenius encountered opposition in regard to his theory of ionization despite the impressive amount of empirical data he had accrued. In recent times, the physical theory of determinism had been flatly denied and vitriolically attacked by physicists who could not accept or understand quantum physics or the notion of the apparent acausality in the "behavior" of sub–atomic particles. While there may be good reasons for questioning or even rejecting new paradigms in the sciences, it is often the case that certain general, pervasive, cultural values lie at the basis of a world–orientation which precludes the acceptance of, or absorbtion of, certain facts.

In general, the choice of specific phenomena out of the panorama of possible phenomena as significant facts already suggests the influence of a particular value–orientation. The very valuation of *facta* or factual information by Western man was not a necessary stage in the development of man or of human culture. This is not to say, of course, that it has not proved to be a dramatically useful value–orientation, one that has transformed, for good and ill, the human environment. The point is, however, that this impressive empirical ontology is one of the alternative ways in which man could have chosen to understand and interpret nature or himself. In this general sense, then, it may be said that a factual orientation towards nature, the world, or man is an expression of a more or less universal value–orientation. As man's historically determined conceptions of nature have changed, so, too, have his conceptions of his relationship to nature, as well as his conceptions of himself, changed.

What Max Weber once said about scientific truth as such is equally applicable to a general fact orientation. "The belief in the value of scientific truth is the product of certain cultures and is not a product of man's original nature."[26] Although I think there is no necessity in referring to man's ostensible "original" nature, Weber's basic point is quite valid. For, there is clearly no necessity in man's "choice" or "decision" to embrace scientific truth as the ultimate paradigm of truth. As Martin Heidegger has pointed out, the *Dingontologie* which is traceable to the ontology of Descartes is, *mutatis mutandis,* still the generally accepted *Weltontologie* of the Western World,[27] one which entails the reduction of all phenomena, even man, to the status of "things" or "objects". Hence, the empirical ontology we have referred to has its roots in philosophical ontological projections which came to be valued as dominant world-orientations and which tended to reinforce the acceptance of the scientific paradigm of truth. Although Heidegger would deny that the general acceptance of a *Weltontologie* is itself an expression of cultural values, I tend to think that the persistence of the conversation and preservation of such general theories of reality suggests that they do have value-laden components. At any rate, since the accumulation of objective factual data is intimately related to the search for scientific truth, the valuation of facts seems to be, in some sense, culturally conditioned. If these suggestions have validity, it may be said that facts are valuations insofar as *facta* are conceived of as being "worth something" or as having value. This is not to hold that facts *are* values or that the terms "fact" and "value" are fused; rather, the appreciation of the significance of facts is a fundamental value within the matrix of a purely scientific *Weltanschauung* or within a framework in which scientific truth is considered the only meaningful mode of truth. Even if one contested this general claim about the valuational basis of a fact orientation, there are more specific reasons for arguing that facts are infiltrated by values or are value-laden in at least some respects.

Although the tendency to rely upon "hard data" in empirical sciences is usually unchecked or unexamined, it has sometimes been indicated that values play an important part in science, specifically as "determinants of the *meanings* which are seen in the events with which it [science] deals."[28] Of course, the determi-

[26]Max Weber, *The Methodology of the Social Sciences,* trans. E. A. Shils and H. A. Finch (Glencoe, Ill.: Free Press, 1949), p. 110.

[27]M. Heidegger, *op. cit.* p. 100.

[28]Abraham Kaplan, *The Conduct of Inquiry* (San Francisco, Calif.: Chandler, 1964), p. 382.

nation of the meaning of facts is basically a hermeneutic problem insofar as a factual judgment may be construed as an interpretative act. Isolated empirical phenomena are not significant in themselves —they must be related to a theoretical framework or to other factual assertions. The interpretative element in the determination of the meaning of observed *facta* is present in this process of relating this judgment to a matrix in which its meaning may be clarified. The objective data are usually related to general evaluative concepts which make these facts "worth knowing." In one sense, surely, the significance of such factual data is derived from generally accepted evaluative concepts.[29]

In order to determine the meaning of a fact or in order to know how to construe facts, we must assume some antecedantly accepted criterion of value or some valued theoretical matrix. If, for example, the language of factual statement or judgement is that of physical-objects statements, this does not mean that a judment expressed in such language is value-free or entirely independent of cultural "sets" universally accepted at a particular time. As W. O. Quine has put it,

> Physical objects are conceptually imported into the [knowing, judgmental] situation as convenient intermediaries—not by definition in terms of experience, but simply as irreducible [cultural] posits.[30]

What W. O. Quine has referred to as "cultural posits" are surely tantamount to cultural values which affect our interpretation of, and understanding of, a variety of phenomena. What is significant in this regard is that facts are construed in terms of conceptual schema which are themselves valuational. Thus, for example, if a philosopher or scientist prefers or chooses to conceive of (and describe) physical phenomena in terms of the categories of "processes," "interactions," "reciprocal interrelationships," or "events," this selected cognitive framework will obviously determine how he conceives of *facta*.

If we raise the question concerning why a specific conceptual schema is accepted, the usual answer is that this "new" schema is "better than" or "more comprehensive than" previous cognitive

[29]Max Weber, *op. cit.*, p. 111.

[30]W. O. Quine, *From a Logical Point of View* (New York: Harper, 1963), p. 44.

systems of description and explanation. Or it may be said that such a conceptual schema is pragmatically valuable, heuristically valuable, or is a more effective conceptual schema. In the sciences it is usually said that explanation E' replaces explanation E because it is "more consistent with the facts." There is, however, a certain circularity in this claim. For, it is assumed that a set or collection of *facta* which are described in a newly adopted terminology are more accurately described or are better explained by virtue of this more recent cognitive framework. The assumption that E' is more accurate because it more effectively or efficiently deals with the phenomena in question is itself based upon a choice made between E and E' which is surely not only made in terms of the data or *facta* to be explained. Hence, it is reasonable to assume that the evaluation of the various merits of E' over E has taken place. That is to say, some kind of value judgment has been made implicitly or explicitly. It is clear from this sketch of the replacement of one explanatory structure by another that the *facta* or objective data appealed to are not neutral data, but are presumably reinterpreted in the light of an emergent value. Typically, I believe, this emergent value is what Quine has called a cultural posit or what I would describe as a thetic projection of a cultural value. This is not to say that projected cultural values are the only factors determining the selection of explanatory systems (or descriptive terminology). Rather, I am simply stating a weaker thesis—i.e., that cultural values are relevant determining factors in the selection of recently proposed descriptive terminology, categorical schema, or explanatory systems. (In terms of the determinants affecting the process of observation which are discussed in relation to Scheffler's concept of scientific objectivity, I am arguing that it is often the case that there is an interrelationship among (4) set or mental attitude, (5) alteration by conceptualization, (7) cultural determinism, (12) the element of arbitrariness in the creation of new category schema, and (13) selective orientation).

To return to a discussion of the descriptive categories which function as determinants in empirical, judgmental situations, it is clear that an understanding of perceived phenomena "as" physical objects, "as" things, "as" processes, "as" events, "as" occurrences, etc., already presupposes that a value interpretation has taken place. Whereas Heidegger would say that a presupposed or historically derived ontology conditions our understanding of ontic or factual phenomena, I would maintain that culturally determined values (even if they are only, for example, those of the sub-culture of the scientific community) condition interpretation and, hence, our understanding of factual phenomena.

In order to understand a phenomenon *as* something, as Heidegger has pointed out, *Das "Als" macht die Struktur der Ausdrücklichkeit eines Verstandenen aus; es konstituiert die Auslegung.*[31] Although Heidegger tends to deny that values, cultural or otherwise, lie at the basis of ontologies (in this regard he refers only to the attribution of *Wertprädikaten* to ontic entities and never truly considers the possibility that cultural values might influence the formulation of a *Weltontologie* or that a philosophical ontology might become a significant cultural value itself as it becomes embeded in the language and thought of a people or a civilization), he quite accurately suggests that how we interpret the phenomena of the world determine our understanding of our relationship towards nature or "the world".

If, for example, the natural world is conceived of as a system of "things" which are in "opposition" to each other (the term *Gegenstand,* for example, preserves this notion insofar as something is said to *gegen-stehen*: "to stand against" or "to stand opposed to" something else) or which are related to each other in terms of mechanistic causation, then, as Heidegger has argued, this *Dingontologie* is turned back upon man (or *Dasein*) and a distorted conception of man and his world is perpetuated. What may be called the "thingification" *(Verdinglichung)* of nature was a theoretical precondition for the emergence of a technological orientation towards nature. Although Heidegger's conception of the detrimental effects of "metaphysics" on the Western mind is an extravagant claim (which it would be difficult to demonstrate or refute), his analysis of the radical reformulation of man's understanding of nature as a whole or ontic phenomena in particular and its consequent effects upon how one conceives of the "world" and man himself is profound. Even if one does not accept all of the details of Heidegger's phenomenology of the world, one can still agree with his general view that man could have understood and interpreted ontic phenomena or beings in ways quite different from the way in which he has come to understand and interpret such phenomena. In this regard, Heidegger's phenomenological analysis of the being of *Dasein* and *die Welt* is itself an important ontolo-

[31]Martin Heidegger, *op. cit.*, p. 149.

gical reformation which is directed against an ontology of things which, in many ways, has been incorporated into what I have described as the empirical ontology which pervades so much of contemporary thought.

Although it is often admitted that value judgments or valuations cannot entirely be extracted from historical narration or historical reconstruction, it is thought that valuations do not enter into the protocol statements of the scientific observer. As I have already argued, this assumption is quite questionable. For, it has been said that observation statements or protocol statements necessarily involve *interpretations* of the *facta* observed.[32] Now, it would seem to be the case that interpretations are themselves selected from a number of possible alternatives and reveal a particular theoretical preference or valuation. If, for example, it is maintained that a theory or hypothesis is adopted in terms of, say, a criterion of "epistemic utility," it is clear that this is itself an expression of value. For, if one avers that one should appeal to "epistemic utility" as the basis for choosing one theory or hypothesis over competing theories or hypotheses, the guiding principle which is implicitly appealed to is, "Whenever possible, decide among competing theories or hypotheses on the basis of the epistemic utility of a given theory or hypothesis." Such a principle is clearly a recommendation which is posited not in terms of the *facta* to be explained, but in terms of an extra-scientific criterion of value—i.e., epistemic utility. While there may be sound reasons for choosing this or that theory or hypothesis in terms of its epistemological usefulness, it is simply false to maintain that this criterion of selection is value-neutral.

Obviously, there are any number of instances in the history of the sciences in which specific, identifiable valuations intervene in theoretical analyses or in theory construction. Thus, for example, when the Japanese physicist Yukawa postulated the "existence" of neutral mesons or nutrettos he did so primarily in terms of an assumption of the symmetrical structure of nuclear fields. This is basically an aesthetic consideration, one which clearly illustrates the influence which non-factual, valuational considerations have on certain theoretical preferences.[33] Certainly, there are no *a priori* or

[32]Rudolf Carnap, *Erkenntnis,* 2 (1932), p. 107.

[33]Louis de Broglie, *Physics and Microphysics* (New York: Harper, 1960), p. 37.

empirical grounds for assuming that nuclear fields are necessarily symmetrical rather than asymmetrical. Of course, there are cultural and even anthropomorphic factors which would lead an investigator to value or prefer (on aesthetic grounds) a theoretical conception which would preserve the notion of structure as harmonious, balanced, or symmetrical. Indeed, the more recent postulation of anti–matter in theoretical physics is, in a sense, testimony to the psychological force of the tendency to seek an ideal symmetry in natural phenomena.

On a more general level, I think it can be argued that the conventionalism of Henri Poincaré reveals the importance of valuational preferences upon the choice or selection of useful or viable hypotheses. When an investigator is attempting to discover which hypothesis, amongst available hypotheses, best explains a given body of facts, he is obviously confronted with a problem of choice. This kind of choice, Poincaré has suggested, should be guided primarily by considerations of simplicity.[34] Clearly, such a principle of simplicity is not justified by an appeal to *facta* or objective phenomena. A cursory examination of this principle—"The best hypothesis is the simplest one."—indicates that it is not a tautology not an analytic or *a priori* truth and not an empirical assertion. As a procedural recommendation, it obviously has the form of a value judgment.

In continuity with an implicit assumption of the validity of Poincaré's conventionalism, it has recently been said that the selection of the simplest of two or more theories can be justified in terms of the criteria of "beauty" and "convenience."[35] Now, without involving ourselves with the complex question of the degree of probability of confirmation which a simpler theory may possess (which is clearly a purely cognitive non–valuational question), it is apparent that the above bases for justifying a preference for a simpler theory (or hypothesis) are grounded in valuational preferences which are clearly extrascientific and which are quite similar to those which determine or, in some cases, influence the interpretation of factual phenomena.

Since factual data or *facta* do not seem to be intelligible in them-

[34]Henri Poincare, *Science and Hypothesis* (New York: Dover, 1952), p. 146.

[35]W. O. Quine, "On Simple Theories of a Complex World," in *Probability, Confirmation, and Simplicity,* ed. M. H. Foster and M. L. Martin (New York: Odyssey, 1966).

selves, and since the meaning of such *facta* is relational (i.e., is dependent upon what Husserl called "fulfilled meaning" which provides the fulfilled judgment which is the intentional object of consciousness), it is not the case that there are uninterpreted factual phenomena. In this sense, pure description is a myth or, at best, a Kantian "ideal of reason" which may be approximated, but never actually attained in any factual judgment. Obviously, the very factual phenomena attended to are selected from a variety of possible phenomena. This process of selectivity, we may safely assume, is, to some extent, guided by, or influenced by, various implicit or explicit criteria which are value-laden.

When a scientist appeals to the heuristic value of a theory or hypothesis or to its pragmatic value, he has indicated that his inquiry is by no means entirely value-free. The values affecting his selection of a theory or hypothesis may be subjective, may be conditioned by generally accepted beliefs or opinions of the scientific community at a specific historical moment, or they may be expressions of uncritically accepted, unanalyzed cultural values. What applies to theories or hypotheses applies, with equal justification, to the recognition of facts. For, as has recently been said, "what we are prepared to recognize as fact depends to a large extent on the values we hold."[36] And it is precisely such values which are the unexamined presuppositions of scientific inquiry and of the ordinary interpretation of *facta.* What is often described as, and accepted as, "brute" facticity is often a veiled value-interpretation of what is an ostensibly neutral factual phenomena. Such an understanding of factual phenomena is, *a fortiori,* applicable in those instances in which the scientific investigator proclaims an interest in the "relevant facts" pertaining to his sphere of inquiry. For, the very criterion of relevance requires the positing of, or acceptance of, a metempirical basis of selectivity which, again, is surely affected by the values consciously or unconsciously adopted by the investigator.

Generally speaking, the description of natural phenomena or *facta* is not possible without the assumption of, or reference to, some theoretical structure. Even the most ordinary singular statements are invariably "*interpretations of the 'facts' in the light of*

[36]Peter Caws, *Science and the Theory of Value* (New York: Random House, 1967), p. 63.

theories."[37] Now, the theories which determine the interpretation of facts are, in the most general sense, historically conditioned. And the most significant historical phenomena, of course, are related to the general theoretical matrices which are generally accepted or propounded by the leaders in a scientific discipline in which a specific theory is relevant. Thus, for example, the construction of the model for the structure of deoxyribonucleic acid by Watson and Crick was possible in terms of the framework of studies which already has been done by Linus Pauling (and other biochemists) as well as the empirical data acquired by crystallographers. Quite often, as has recently been argued, more or less dramatic changes in theoretical explanations tend to carry in their wake ontological reformations and even changes in the basic meaning of the terms used. Thus, Paul Feyerabend has argued that

> What happens when transition is made from a restricted theory T' to a wider theory T (which is capable of covering all the phenomena which have been covered by T') is something much more radical than incorporation of the *unchanged* theory T' into the wider context of T. What happens is rather a *complete replacement* of the ontology of T' by the ontology of T, and a corresponding change in the meanings of all descriptive terms of T' (provided these terms are still employed).[38]

Of course, this kind of ontological shift would naturally affect the interpretation of "relevant" facts. Indeed, as Feyerabend has argued, "experimental evidence does not consist of facts pure and simple, but of facts analyzed, modeled, and manufactured according to some theory."[39] While it may be an overstatement to say that *facta* are "manufactured," it is clear that their meaning and/or their interpretation is theory-referential.

It is interesting to note that Heidegger's view that the scientist is engaged in the projection of nature in his theoretical formulations is not far removed from the views of philosophers of science such as Feyerabend. In his discussion in *Sein und Zeit* concerning the rise of mathematical physics Heidegger argues that what was decisive was not a high regard for observed "facts," but rather for the way in which nature or natural processes were "mathematically

[37]Karl Popper, *The Logic of Scientific Discovery* (New York: Harper, 1961), p. 423.

[38]Paul Feyerabend, *op. cit.*, p. 59.

[39]*Ibid.*, pp. 50-51.

projected" *(mathematischen Entwurf der Natur selbst).* Clearly, the projected conception of nature (in mathematical terms) determines the kinds of facts which are considered relevant. As Heidegger puts it,

> Erst "im Licht" einer dergestalt entworfenen Natur kann so etwas wie eine "Tatsache" gafunden und für einen aus dem Entwurf regulativ umgrenzten Versuch angesetzt werden. Die Begründung der "Tatsachen wissenschaft" wurde nur dadurch möglich, dass die Forscher verstanden: es gibt grundsätzlich keine "blossen Tatsachen."[40]

The totality of such projection as characterizes mathematical physics is described by Heidegger as *Thematisierung* or objectification. What is understood as, or identified as, subject to mathematical interpretation is no longer a neutral datum, but is already constituted by the theoretical framework already adopted. The entities taken as the "theme" of a particular scientific projection are, as Heidegger expresses it, discovered by virtue of a previous projection of their state of being.

In terms of my general argument concerning the value-laden character of certain aspects of scientific investigation, it may be said that the choice or selection of a given theoretical framework or "projection" presupposes a valuational preference for such a framework over other alternative modes of interpretation or explanation. The understanding of what is "there" or what is the case presupposes an implicit or explicit ontological commitment, a commitment which itself cannot be justified in terms of, or by reference to, the facts or factual data which are "discovered" on the basis of its prior assumption.

There is no basis for the assumption that the interpretation of a datum or a collection of *facta* is purely presuppositionless. While the referential matrix guiding interpretation may be composed of well-founded theoretical notions, it is also possible that some extra-scientific values infiltrate the selection of a given referential matrix or are incorporated into such a matrix. Although Heidegger would tend to deny that cultural values lie at the basis of some interpretations of *facta*, I believe that such a notion is not entirely inconsistent with his view that

[40]Martin Heidegger, *op. cit.*, p. 362.

> Die Auslegung von Etwas als Etwas wird wesenhaft durch Vorhabe, Vorsicht und Vorgriff fundiert. Auslegung ist nie ein voraussetzungsloses Erfassen eines Vorgegebenen. Wenn sich die besondere Konkretion der Auslegung . . . gern auf das beruft, was "dasteht," so ist das, was zunächst "dasteht," nichts anderes als die selbstverständliche, undiskutierte Vormeinung des Auslegers, die notwendig in jedem Auslegungsansatz liegt als das, was mit Auslegung überhaupt shon "gesetzt," das heisst in Vorhabe, Vorsicht, Vorgriff vorgegeben ist.[41]

The question is, what is the source of such an "undiscussed assumption" *(undiskutierte Vormeinung)?* If it is said to be a theory of some kind, then perhaps that theory can be shown to have been selected or chosen on the basis of some criterion or criteria which, in turn, can be traced to a fundamental belief (e.g., in the uniformity of nature) which is itself based upon a value-preference. Thus, it has been argued that the adoption of the maxim of the uniformity of nature, or the view that ". . . things similar in some respects tend to prove similar in others," is to adopt a vague notion of similarity which is itself "relative to the structure of one's conceptual scheme or quality space."[42] It may be said, then, that such phenomena are ultimately rooted in the value system or valuational predilections of an individual (or, usually, the value systems of a culture or of a scientific community). Primitive assumptions or presuppositions are very much like basic beliefs which we hold without any absolute justification, but which are preferences which we find it difficult to abandon. This is not to say that such presuppositions are without pragmatic or heuristic significance. Thus, to cite an earlier illustration, sub-atomic fields may or may not be symmetrical in actuality, but theoretical physicists tend to have a preferential disposition to believe that, in fact, they are symmetrical. As Poincaré once expressed it, "scientists think that certain facts are more interesting than others because they complete an unfinished harmony."[43] This general quest for "harmony" or "symmetry" is so pervaisve that it could be characterized as the basic valuational project of the scientist. Indeed, so entrenched are such general valuational projects that scientists confronted with emerging evidence that historically valuable principles do not apply or

[41]*Ibid.*, p. 150.

[42]W. O. Quine, "On Simple Theories of a Complex World," in *op. cit.*, p. 250.

[43]Henri Poincaré, *The Value of Science* (New York: Dover, 1958), p. 152.

seem to apply to specific factual data, are unwilling or unable to abandon such principles, even in a limited domain of phenomena. Thus, for example, when Max Planck encountered indeterminacy in quantum physics, he firmly believed that the quantum hypothesis would eventually result in a "more exact formulation of the law of causality."[44] The persistent desire to preserve a conceptual model or paradigm of explanation in the face of sufficient contrary evidence suggest an unwillingness to part with a valued ontological projection.

Although many philosophers of science and some social scientists are willing to admit the inevitability of the intrusion of value judgments in the social sciences, most philosophers of science exclude such judgments from the methodology, theory-construction, and interpretations of the physical sciences. Thus, for example, Karl Popper has maintained that

> where predilections and interests have such influence on the content of scientific theories and predictions, it must become highly doubtful whether bias can be determined and avoided. Thus we need not be surprised to find that there is very little in the social sciencies that resembles the objective and ideal quest for truth which we meet in physics.[45]

In his *Reason and Nature* M. R. Cohen made a similar observation,[46] suggesting that the social sciences abandon their value-free posture. Generally speaking, Cohen's advice has been taken by a number of sociologists in recent times. Thus, for example, Gunnar Myrdal has argued that

> The process of selecting a problem and basic hypothesis, of limiting the scope of study, and of defining and classifying data relevant to such a setting of the problem, involve a choice on the part of the investigator. The choice is made from an indefinite number of possibilities. The same is true when inferences are drawn from organized data . . . Scientific conventions usually give guidance. But, first, convention itself is a valuation, hidden in tacit preconceptions which are not discussed or even known.[47]

[44]Max Planck, *Where is Science Going?* (New York: Norton, 1933), pp. 143-155.

[45]Karl Popper, *The Poverty of Historicism* (New York: Harper, 1964), p. 16.

[46]M. R. Cohen, *Reason and Nature* (New York: Free Press, 1953), p. 349.

[47]Gunnar Myrdal, *Value in Social Theory* (New York: Harper, 1959), pp. 153-154.

Many contemporary social scientists speak openly about what Gouldner called "the myth of a value-free sociology." Indeed, in the writings of classical sociologists such Max Weber one can find anticipations of this current tendency to admit the valuational basis of sociological research, despite the fact that Weber himself was, for the most part, a proponent of the value-free image of sociology. In regard to the limited area of scientific investigation, it is held that.

> Only a small portion of existing concrete reality is colored by our value-conditioned interests and it alone is significant to us. It is significant because it reveals relationships which are important to us due to their connection with our values . . . We cannot discover . . . what is meaningful to us by means of a "presuppositionless" investigation of empirical data. Rather perception of its meaningfulness to us is the presupposition of its becoming an *object* of investigation.[48]

Such admissions, of course, do not involve the abandonment of the ideal of scientific objectivity; rather, they simply indicate the valuational component in scientific inquiry. Now, it would seem that there is some evidence that the physical sciences are also affected by valuation considerations as well. Even if one grants that some of the valuations of the physical scientist are cognitive values which are intimately related to existing knowledge in a particular sphere of inquiry, it is also the case that aesthetic and cultural values also play a role in the theoretical formulations and hypothesis selection of the physical scientist.

There is some evidence to suggest that certain epistemic preferences reveal a commitment to extrascientific (often metaphysical) values. Thus, for example, it has been reported that Heisenberg, in order to eliminate references to unobservable quantities, adopted a phenomenological orientation which would eliminate from physical theory whatever does not strictly correspond to observable entities or phenomena.[49] It is clear, I believe, that such a proposal reflects a valuational preference which is not adopted purely in terms of the data to be interpreted or even in terms of the theoretical matrix of quantum mechanics itself. Rather, it is somewhat analogous to the decision to adopt a behavioristic method in psy-

[48]Max Weber, *op. cit.*, pp. 72, 76.

[49]Louis de Broglie, *The Revolution in Physics* (New York: Noonday, 1953), p. 189.

chology (rather than a phenomenological or psychoanalytical approach) in order to understand, describe and explain human behavior. Clearly, in such instances one cannot appeal to the "facts themselves" in order to determine what interpretation of these facts or what methodological procedure is to be adopted since the interpretation or method itself determines what will or will not count as facts, how these facts are to be construed and what the "relevant" facts are. Such holistic, metaphysical values are often the basis for what may be called the *nisus* of scientific investigation whether they are implicitly assumed or explicitly avowed.

Values, then, in the broadest sense of the term, do indeed enter into the "ideal objectivity" of the physical sciences. What is interesting about this is that it is readly admitted by physical scientists themselves, despite the insistent denials that this is the case by philosophers of science.[50] It is surely the case that there are a number of non-factual criteria or extrascientific criteria which enter into the selection of theories or hypotheses, criteria which are quite often reflections of dominant metaphysical, methodological, aesthetic, linguistic, personal, or symbolic values. Under the rubric of "symbolic values" I would include preferred symbolic formulae as well as generally accepted models or schemata (e.g., the geocentric image of the solar system which dominated cosmology and astronomy for such a long period of time or the image of matter as comprised of indivisible atomic elements conceived of as the building bricks of the physical world, etc.). Quite often, it would seem, extrascientific valuations involve the choice of a method of description or explanation which is not an exact "fit" with the relevant factual phenomena under investigation. Thus, for example, Pierre Duhem was self-consciously aware of the nature of theoretical or hypothetical selection in science and indicated that it is often the case that valued symbolic formulae do not accurately describe—and, *a fortiori,* do not "picture"—the concrete fact *(factum)* which such formulae ostensibly represent. He maintained that there cannot be complete parity between an abstract symbol and the concrete fact (or "practical fact") which it was designed to represent or express. The theoretical formulae which the physicist appeals to in order to "express" the concrete facts or *facta* observed in experimentation cannot be the exact equivalent of

[50]Cf. Erwin C. Schrödinger, *Science, Theory, and Man* (New York: Dover, 1957) Chapter IV, p. 37.

these facts.[51] To be sure, considerations of "simplicity," "neatness," or "aesthetic uniformity" may be the non-factual or extra-scientific criteria which are appealed to in order to "justify" the abandonment of an exact correspondence between concrete facts and theoretical description. However, it is clear that the acceptance of specific extra-scientific criteria on the basis of implicit or explicit value preferences can, and, in fact, often does determine (a) what facts are relevant and (b) what factual data will be selectively ignored or bracketed in order that the non-factual criteria may be satisfied. In such typical cases, the significance of valuations for the "structure" of scientific description or explanation cannot be ignored. The factual data or *facta* which are attended to are not treated as if they were purely neutral data, but are shaped and determined by theoretical preferences or, in Duhem's terms, "symbolic formulae" which are, in turn, conditioned by or, at least, influenced by extra-scientific or non-factual criteria. If it is granted that various kinds of valuations infiltrate theory-construction, theory-selection, and theory-application (to a set of *facta*) then what Mario Bunge has recently said about the relationship of theory to facts lends support to my general contention about the value-laden character of the scientific enterprize. Bunge attacks the assumption of many philosophers of science that "experience [or observation of facts] is the basis of theory." He argues that

> According to the official philosophy of science, agreement with fact is not only necessary but also sufficient for the acceptance of a scientific theory, because scientific theories are just data summaries or, at worst, codifications of data and slight extrapolations from them. In accordance with this view, if a theoretical prediction conflicts with an empirical datum it is the former, not the latter, which has to go . . . for experience is the highest court of appeal. This view is methodologically, philosophically and historically untenable: first, because it is standard scientific practice to reject data when they conflict with established theories; second, because data are anything but given: they are produced and interpreted with the help of theories; third, because most theories do not concern observations and measurements . . . but . . . rather idealized models of [things]; fourth, because . . . testable propositions seldom if ever follow from the assumption of a single theory but . . . are entailed by

[51]Pierre Duhem, *The Aim and Structure of Physical Theory* (New York: Atheneum, 1962), p. 151.

> the theory in conjunction with additional assumptions and . . . bits of information other than those serving to check the theory . . .[52]

Needless to say, such a view is compatible with my discussion of the valuational basis of general theoretical matrices and is also relevant to the kind of arguments I brought to bear upon Scheffler's conception of observation and scientific objectivity. That there is a confluence of the questions of the nature of facts, of observation, of theoretical preference, of the meaning of scientific objectivity and of various modes of valuation is not surprising since it has been one of my intentions to uncover precisely this interrelationship in the activity of scientific investigation.

Although I believe that I have sufficiently indicated the value-laden character of various aspects of scientific inquiry, I would like to touch upon the question in relation to yet another of the social or human sciences—that is, history. It has often been said that accounts or reconstructions of historical events are notoriously value-laden. Specific historical events are selected and designated as "important" or they are ignored or discarded as "insignificant" or "unimportant". This is one of the many valuational factors which influence the historian's reconstruction of the past or his description of the present. Clearly, the personal as well as the general, cultural values of the historian deeply influence his judgments and descriptions of historical events. What M. R. Cohen has said about the historian's craft is instructive in this regard. For, he has pointed out that

> the historian has to supplement the facts before him with hypothetical ones—in which process he is obviously dependent on his general philosophy of life or schema of relative value . . . he must select from the great mass of facts those which he considers most important, which again involves a process of valuation—since importance is distinctly a category of value.[53]

Aside from the valuational category of importance, there are other significant instances of valuational preferences in historical explanation—i.e., in the selection of the causal factors which are consid-

[52]Mario Bunge, "Theory Meets Experience," in *Mind, Science, and History,* ed. H. Kiefer and M. Munitz (Albany, N.Y.: SUNY Press, 1970, Vol. II, pp. 139-140.

[53]M. R. Cohen, *op. cit.,* p. 381.

ered to be historically "relevant" or fundamental. Whether the historian emphasizes "cultural", "political," "military," "geographical," "climatic," "philosophical," or "economic" factors will clearly influence his interpretation, description, and evaluation of the *facta* which he selects, classifies, and organizes. Again, a subjective or culturally determined preference for mechanistic, teological, or evolutionary accounts of historical developments will again determine what *facta* the historian thinks are relevant or what events are significant. Such general, theoretical valuational preferences in historical explanation are ineluctable. Indeed, cultural values or culturally determined *Weltanschauungen* not only influence the writing of history, but also determine whether historical explanations will or will not be valued as such. In many respects, there is a close relationship between the sense of history and attention to factual data. Despite a growing psychological atmosphere in which there is a turning away from the past and "tradition," those who are concerned with the cultural and spiritual life of man still tend to believe that in order to understand something one must first understand its history.

The valuation, in the Western world, of the importance of history is not universally shared by all peoples. India, by the admission of its own philosophers and scholars, has been, for the most part, an ahistorical nation. The significance of the concatenation of events and their interrelationship in the human world has simply not been recognized, has not been the focus of precise attention. Even in the dating of documents important in the cultural development of India there is a startling imprecision. There is a sense in which it is true that, as has recently been said,

> the cultures of the East . . . belittle man as individual man. Under this runs an indifference to the world of the senses, of which the indifference to experienced fact is one fact . . . these cultures of the East . . . lack the language and the very habit of fact.[54]

This "habit of fact," as I have already suggested, is perhaps the most universally shared value in the Western world, the universal determination of any possible act of understanding, the ultimate basis for the interpretation of natural and social phenomena. It is

[54]J. Bronowski, *Science and Human Values* (New York: Messner, 1956), p. 43.

obviously a value which cannot be justified by a reference to "objective data," but it can only be justified in terms of some pragmatic or teleological value. That *facta* are recognized as, or considered as, of worth or value indicates the most universal and pervasive way in which values infiltrate any attempt to achieve a purely neutral understanding of, or description of, various phenomena. Even if one adopts a factual orientation towards the world or towards human actions (or human being), the scientific description and selection of *facta* is not possible, as we have seen, without some appeal to non-factual or extra-scientific values of some kind.

In general, when we are considering what will count as relevant data we cannot solely rely upon the historical development of science or the alleged neutrality of facts. Rather, as has recently been argued, we must reconstrue the conception of data in such a way as to incorporate "the prospective aspect of the world presently appredended as value."[55] This is not to say that a factual orientation is not a fruitful one or one that should in any sense be abandoned lightly nor is it to say that the scientific ideal of objectivity be rejected out of hand. Rather, it does mean that the radical bifurcation of facts and values perpetrated by some philosophers of science and commentators on science is illicit, a dogma that is held without justification. To be sure, the conceptual distinction between facts (or *facta*) and values ought not to be collapsed. However, we should simply be aware of the influence of values upon factual judgments and admit that, in a non-trivial sense, the value-laden character of theory-selection, theory-construction, and the interpretation of *facta* is part and parcel of the scientific or empirical enterprize. While admitting that *facta* or factual phenomena can be distinguished from various kinds of value, values expressed or made manifest in the various modalities I have indicated cannot be entirely divorced from our understanding of, our description of, or our interpretation of factual phenomena. The intelligibility of phenomena is not "given;" hence, there is an ineluctable hermeneutic element not only in philosophy, but in science as well. Insofar as interpretation is necessary for understanding or the discernment of the intelligibility of something, human knowledge cannot be adequately accounted for without making reference to the admission of value in human experience and thought. Facts are not, of course, identical to values; rather, the

[55]Peter Caws, *op. cit.*, p. 75.

relationship between facts and values is a kind of subtle interaction which, ironically, is not unlike the interaction between the "subjective" aspect (in Husserl's sense) of human thought and the "raw data" which are encountered in observation and perception.

The presumed epistemic neutrality of scientific fact may be described as a Kantian ideal of reason to which the actual practice of scientific inquiry bears an asymptotic relationship. The radical separation of fact and value which has been propounded by some dogmatic empiricists is clearly an exaggeration, an exaggeration which neglects the obvious influence of valuations of different kinds upon a generalized factual orientation, theory and hypothesis-selection, the determination of relevant facts, the selectivity of factual data, and the conferred distinction placed upon certain facts. The judgment that something is a "relevant," "important" fact is one which usually requires at least some interpretation of the *facta* in question. And, as I have suggested, all interpretation is, as Nietzsche once pointed out, basically value-interpretation. To be sure, we need not abandon the valid and useful distinction between *facta* and values; but, on the other hand, we should not allow ourselves to assume that facts and values are not, in any sense, interrelated, that facts are not to some extent, value-laden. For, to do so may lead us to embrace an empirical dogmatism which is clearly as presumptuous as the aprioristic dogmatism which the empirical orientation sought to avoid.

State University of New York at Brockport

5

UNITY, SUCCESSION, AND PERSONAL IDENTITY IN HUME

by
John Driscoll

Hume's discussion of personal identity in the *Treatise* is, by his own account, the most perplexing part of a generally quite perplexing book: ". . . upon a more strict review of the section concerning *personal identity,* I find myself involv'd in such a labyrinth, that, I must confess, I neither know how to correct my former opinions, nor how to render them consistent." (T 633)[1]

There are undoubtedly many significant deficiencies and some outright mistakes both in the particulars of Hume's treatment of personal identity and in the general principles which that treatment presupposes from earlier parts of the *Treatise:* all this must be admitted at the outset. However this article will make no attempt to identify these problems. They have been examined time and again elsewhere, perhaps to the point of obscuring the genuine accomplishments of Hume's investigation of personal identity. Instead, employing without criticism the impressions, ideas, relations, *minima indivisibilia* and all the other items of Hume's conceptual inventory—problematic as they may be—and departing from Hume's express statements only to make a few necessary distinctions, this article will attempt the modest task of suggesting that there is rather more consistency in Hume's treatment of personal identity than his own remarks may lead us to believe.

The first obstacle that stands in the way of finding a consistent interpretation of Hume's treatment of personal identity, odd as this may seem, is the problem of establishing exactly why Hume himself found it inconsistent. He tells us that

[1] *A Treatise of Human Nature,* ed. L. A. Selby-Bigge (Oxford: Clarendon Press, 1888): references to the *Treatise* will be made in the text by a "T" followed by the page number of the Selby-Bigge edition.

> . . . there are two principles, which I cannot render consistent; nor is it in my power to renounce either of them, viz. that all our distinct perceptions are distinct existences, and that the mind never perceives any real connexion among distinct existences. (T 636; italics omitted)

However, as one writer has acutely observed, the two principles are not inconsistent with each other.[2] It is quite possible both to conceive and to imagine a set of distinctly existing perceptions without any "real" connection between them. What, then, is the rub? As it will turn out, simply identifying the precise inconsistency will be the better part of solving it.

The first part of the article will examine the role of the imagination in Hume's discussion of personal identity. The second part will trace the problem of identity back to the more fundamental notions of unity and succession. The third will try to use these notions to find the inconsistency and to suggest a few distinctions on the basis of which it might be eliminated.

1. *Identity and the Imagination*

Hume's treatment of personal identity in *Treatise* I iv 6 has two parts: a short and simple proof that we have no idea of personal identity and a long and detailed explanation of why we think we do. The proof runs as follows:

> It must be some one impression, that gives rise to every real, idea . . . If any impression gives rise to the idea of self, that impression must continue invariably the same, thro' the whole course of our lives; since self is suppos'd to exist after that manner. But there is no impression constant and invariable. (T 251)

The first line is simply a restatement of the thesis of the *Treatise:* "That all our simple ideas in their first appearance are deriv'd from simple impressions, which are correspondent to them, and which they exactly represent." (T 4) If ideas must *exactly* represent the corresponding impressions, then *if* the supposed idea of personal identity or self implied invariable continuity, it follows that there would have to be an invariable impression of self—which in

[2]Robert Fendel Anderson, *Hume's First Principles* (University of Nebraska Press, 1966), p. 34.

fact there is not. (T 252) But why need the supposed idea of personal identity imply invariable continuity? In the second part of his treatment of personal identity Hume repeats that we call an object "the same" or "identical" if it "remains invariable and uninterrupted thro' a *suppos'd* variation of time" (T 253: emphasis added); however it is only in *Treatise* I iv 2, an interesting passage which we will have occasion to turn to below, that he explains his definition and the occurrence within it of the suspicious "suppos'd variation of time."

There being no idea or impression of personal identity, the "self" is "nothing but a bundle or collection of different perceptions, which succeed each other with an inconceivable rapidity . . ." (T 252) We mistakenly attribute an identity to this *succession* of diverse perceptions, Hume explains, for the same reason that we mistakenly attribute identities to plants, animals and other constantly changing physical objects: "the action of the imagination" is "almost the same to the feeling" as when we consider an invariable and uninterrupted object that is properly called identical.

Since Hume provides examples of several different senses of "sameness" or "identity" ranging from the valid to what he considers the utterly mistaken, it will be helpful for clarity's sake to put them into some kind of order. (1) By the definition of identity, as we have seen, only an "object"—this is Hume's word: it is presumably meant to be neutral between perceptions and external objects—which is both invariable and uninterrupted through a "supposed" variation in time is what Hume calls a "perfect identity." (T 255) Such an object might also be called a "numerical identity" as opposed to (2) the "specific identity" of, for example, two notes of invariant pitch and loudness separated by an interruption. (T 258) On the other hand, (3) if there is a variation in the object without a corresponding break or interruption in our thought—whether because the variation is imperceptible by relation to the whole or because it occurs gradually—"the passage of the thought from the object before the change to the object after it, is so smooth and easy, that we scarce perceive the transition, and are apt to imagine, that 'tis nothing but a continu'd survey of the same object" (T 256); this Hume calls "imperfect identity."[3]

[3]"...it must be the uninterrupted progress of the thought, which constitutes the imperfect identity." (T 256) It is interesting that Selby-Bigge conjectures

Finally, (4) when one object is succeeded by a second different object related to it by resemblance or causality (cf. T 260-261) in such a way that the "relation facilitates the transition of the mind" from the one to the other and "renders its passage as smooth as if it contemplated one continu'd object", we mistakenly substitute the notion of identity for that of a succession of related but diverse objects. (T 254) When reflection reveals that the resemblance hides a real variation and interruption, we attempt to justify our mistake by means of a fiction either of something invariable and uninterrupted (e.g., substance) or of something mysterious and inexplicable (e.g., soul) underlying the variable and interrupted objects. (T 255) Since it fits into this fourth class, "The identity, which we ascribe to the mind of man, is only a fictious one . . . ." (T 259)

Hume's explanation of our "propension to ascribe an identity to [our] successive perceptions" is clearly parallel to his explanations of causality and of the supposed continued existence of bodies earlier in the *Treatise:* all three cases are explained by the operation of the imagination. On the basis of the qualities of resemblance, contiguity in space or time (succession), and causality, the imagination is free to *unite* any two ideas, although the resulting conjunction is not to be regarded as an inseparable connexion since the imagination is also free to separate any two ideas. (T 10) Rather, "we are only to regard it as a gentle force, which commonly prevails . . ." (T 10)—and often leads us into "errors, absurdities, and obscurities" as well. (T 267) One such error occurs in the philosophical account of causality as necessary connexion when "the idea of necessity" arises from "that propensity, which custom produces, to pass from an object to the idea of its usual attendant." (T 165) It is this same mistaken transition or passage of the imagination which first leads us to think of the continued existence of body or of personal identity—although in the case of causal necessity the transition is from the impression of an object to the idea of a different object constantly conjoined with it, while in the case of the continued existence of unchanging bodies it is from one perception to another only specifically identical with

"perfect?" in the margin as a more plausible reading than "imperfect" here. The conjecture is understandable, since perfect identity is itself recognized by the uninterrupted progress of thought (as will become clearer when we consider *Treatise* I iv 2 below). However on the basis of the ordered senses of identity the "imperfect" actually found in the text makes equally good sense.

it (i.e., invariable but interrupted: T 202) and in the case of personal identity from one perception to a succeeding perception which distinctly varies from it. If reason reflects on the interruption in the former case or the variation in the latter so that the imagination is no longer able to make its easy transition from one perception to the other, the imagination has a "propension to *unite* these broken appearances by the *fiction* of a continu'd existence . . ." (T 205; emphasis added)—whether of body or self—in order to justify its original mistake. In both cases, of course, its original mistake lay in considering identical something not *both* invariable and uninterrupted.

2. *Identity, Unity and Succession*

But why need an object continue "invariable and uninterrupted thro' a suppos'd variation of time" (T 253) in order to be properly called identical? Terence Penelhum presses Hume on this point, arguing that this is not the way we use the word.[4] However the question at hand is not whether Hume's theory of personal identity is faithful to ordinary language but whether it is consistent with itself. Let us therefore examine Hume's theoretical justification for his redefinition of "identical" in *Treatise* I iv 2 (an important passage which, it is interesting to note, Penelhum never mentions).

In *Treatise* I iv 6 the precise definition of identity leads to the conclusion that the idea of personal identity can result from no corresponding impression but is instead a fiction produced by the imagination. In *Treatise* I iv 2 the elaboration of the definition of identity in terms of unity, number, succession, and time leads to the conclusion that identity as such—even "perfect" numerical identity— is itself produced by a fiction of the imagination! This is, of course, the import of the suspicious "suppos'd" in the definition of identity as uninterrupted invariability through a "suppos'd variation of time":

> I have already observ'd, that time, in a strict sense, implies succession, and that when we apply its idea to any unchangeable object, 'tis only by a fiction of the imagination, by which the unchangeable object is suppos'd to participate of the changes of

[4]Terence Penelhum, "Hume on Personal Identity," in *Hume: A Collection of Critical Essays*, ed. V. C. Chappell (Garden City: Anchor, 1966), pp. 224 and 227.

> the co-existent objects, and in particular of that of our perceptions. (T 200, 201)

To say that an object is identical with itself would "mean nothing", Hume points out: ". . . the view of any *one* object is not sufficient to convey the idea of identity," since "*one* single object conveys the idea of *unity,* not that of identity." (T 200; emphasis added) Instead we have to imagine a variation in time so that the object at t_1 is the same as but not one with the object at t_2. In order to do this, Hume suggests, our imagination would have to make up one or the other of the following fictions.

We might survey both points of time "at the very same instant; in which case they give us the idea of number, both by themselves and by the object; which must be multiply'd, in order to be conceiv'd at once, as existent in these two different points of time." (T 201) To be understood, this first suggestion requires a bit of elaboration. Implicit in it is Hume's thesis that a duration or lapse of time such as that between t_1 and t_2 cannot be conceived without the more fundamental conception of "*different* ideas, or impressions, or objects dispos'd in a certain manner, that is, *succeeding* each other." (T 37; cf. T 35) It is only this difference in succeeding objects implicit in the distinction between t_1 and t_2 which allows us to form a notion of identity such that the object at t_1 and t_2 is identical with itself but not simply one. Hume's proof is that if we imagine t_2 folded back into t_1 (i.e. imagine the implied difference between them destroyed) we would then have to imagine the object multiplied into two different objects in order to prevent the identity from becoming simple unity.

The second way in which we may arrive at the notion of identity is to "trace the succession of time by a like succession of ideas, and conceiving first one moment, along with the object then existent, imagine afterwards a change in the time without any variation or interruption in the object; in which case it gives us the idea of unity." (T 201; italics omitted) Hume's point is that we cannot even get to a t_2 from t_1 until the object perceived at t_1 has been *perceivably* succeeded by a "changed" object (T 35), where "changed" presumably means different or distinct in the case of an individual perception and increased or decreased by a part in the case of an external object. (T 6 & 255) As suggested by Hume's definition of identity as uninterrupted invariance "thro' a suppos'd variation of time" (T 235), this "perceivable succession of changeable objects" (T 35) is then superimposed on the unity of the unchangeable, invariant and uninterrupted object in the form of the t_1-t_2 distintion. Accordingly it is only "a fiction of the imagination, by which the unchangeable object is suppos'd to participate of the changes of the co-existent objects . . ." (T 201) The presumption is carried over from Hume's discussion of time that "since the idea of duration cannot be deriv'd from [an unchangeable] object, it can never in any propriety or exactness be apply'd to it . . . ." (T 37)

It is not the purpose of this paper to discuss Hume's view of time—except to suggest that time itself as well as identity can be traced back to the more fundamental notions of unity and succession. Hume says that, " 'Tis a property inseparable from time, and which in a manner constitutes its essence, that each of its parts *succeeds* another . . . ." (T 31; emphasis added) However Hume does not precisely say that time is to be defined as a succession of distinct objects or perceptions; the relation is more like material concomitance: ". . . time cannot make its appearance to the mind, either alone, or attended with a steady unchangeable object, but is *always* discover'd by some perceivable succession of changeable objects." (T 35; italics altered) Why, then, cannot every instance of "time" in Hume's text, cases of obvious Fregean difficulty duly excepted, be replaced by "perceivable succession of changeable objects"? (If this procedure were followed, some of the most troublesome statements in the text would be rendered innocuous: e.g. " 'Tis certain then, that time, as it exists, must be composed of indivisible moments." (T 31) If this were written, "It is certain that every perceivable succession of changeable objects must be composed of indivisible moments," it would follow directly from Hume's variously stated principle that, for example, every color shade must produce a distinct idea. (T 6) The statement might still be proved wrong, but it would no longer be patently false. Statements like this are highly exceptionable only because of Hume's failure—apparently motivated by his parallel treatment of space—to distinguish between perceptual succession and clock time or the theoretical time of Newtonian physics.) In any case "time" may be replaced by a phrase such as "succession of distinct perceptions" throughtout the discussion of identity just completed. Identity would then be defined simply as the fictional superposition of the invariable and uninterrupted *unity* of a single perception and the *multiplicity* of a succession of distinct and varying perceptions. Such a definition would stress even more clearly than a definition in terms of time—itself then equated with perceptual succession—Hume's primary thesis that identity is a fictional "medium betwixt unity and number; or more properly speaking, is either of them, according to the view, in which we take it . . ." (T 201)

Just as personal identity was found to be a product of the imagination by an argument based on the precise notion of identity, so now identity itself is found to be a fiction of the imagination by an argument based on the incompatibility of *unity* and *succession.* The incompatibility is based on Hume's position (a) that a perceived succession must consist of distinct, non-coexistent, indivisible parts (T 31, 35–36) and (b) that unity is a real *idea* copied from a corresponding impression of "one single object". (T 72, 200) It is difficult to fault Hume on the first position, since, even if non-coexistence and indivisibility are excepted as questionable, it remains impossible to conceive of a succession of less than two distinct elements. On the other hand, although several succeeding elements might be considered a unity if unity were taken vaguely as a notion (even as succession itself is taken vaguely as the manner in which perceptions appear to the mind —T 36), it is the cornerstone of Hume's distinction of arithmetic and algebra from geometry that the former are exact studies insofar as they involve the one-to-one correspondence of "unites" which are "copy'd from our impressions." (T 71-72) ("When two numbers are so combin'd, as that the one has always an unite answering to every unite of the other, we pronounce them equal . . ."—T 71) Thus, for the moment at least, unity and succession must be taken as incompatible for Hume.

3. *Unity, Succession and Hume's Problem of Consistency*

It is this incompatibility between unity and succession which makes Hume's treatment of personal identity inconsistent.

In the latter part of *Treatise* I iv 6, after completing his long treatment of the problem of attributing identity to any changing object, Hume turns directly to that identity "which we ascribe to the mind of man." (T 259) He notes that all distinct perceptions which enter into the "composition" of the mind are distinct existences, separable one from one another. However:

> . . . as, notwithstanding this distinction and separability, we suppose the whole train of perceptions to be *united* by identity, a question naturally arises concerning this relation of identity; whether it be something that *really binds* our several perceptions together, or only associates their ideas in the imagination. (T 259; emphasis added)

The answer is easy to find, says Hume: "The understanding *never* observes any *real* connexion among objects" but merely makes an easy transition between ideas when relations of resemblance, contiguity and causation—its own "uniting principles"—are present. (T 259, 260; emphasis added) There are three different statements here, only two of which can be held consistently at any one time:

(1) The train of perceptions is *united* by identity,
(2) Every perception is distinct and separable from every other, and
(3) The understanding never *really binds* our perceptions together nor observes any *real* connexion among objects.

Accordingly in *Treatise* I iv 6 Hume rejects (1). When in the Appendix to the *Treatise* he says that (2) and (3) are inconsistent, he must mean not that they are inconsistent with each other (for, as we have seen, there is nothing contradictory in their joint assertion taken by itself), but that they are together inconsistent with (1). All three cannot be asserted together since identity (1) is a product of the imagination whose "general and more established properties", the understanding (T 267), can neither establish nor find a *real* unity or connexion among perceptions (3) which are distinct existences (2).

Assuming that (2) cannot be dropped or significantly altered without a major reconstruction of Hume's entire philosophy,[5] let us focus our attention on (1) and (3), for it is here Hume suspects the problem may lie: "When I proceed to explain the principle of connexion, which binds [our perceptions] together, and makes us

[5]For a discussion of Hume's actual mistake on this point, cf. John Laird, *Hume's Philosophy of Human Nature* (London: Methuen, 1932), pp. 82-83. Laird concludes that "despite Hume, there is no absurdity in believing in the existence of inseparable companions which are intellectually, not impressionalistically or pictorially, separable; and Hume begged the question by asserting, in effect, that imaginative or sensorial separation was the only kind of distinction men could draw even in their thoughts."

attribute to them a real simplicity and identity; I am sensible, that my account is very defective . . ." (T 635) In (1) Hume mentions the supposition that the succession of perceptions is *united* by *identity*. First of all, what sense can be given to the verb "to unite" (Admittedly, Hume may be using the word in the "vulgar" sense) if unity is to be defined *only* as an idea drawn from a single corresponding impression? Secondly, what of the possibility that our succeeding perceptions are not bound together *only* by identity or some such product of the imagination and understanding but that —subject to the reply given to the first question—the succeeding perceptions are already a unity in another sense *antecedent* to the operations of the imagination and understanding?

These two mutually dependent questions are suggested by a short passage in *Treatise* I iii 14 ("Of the Idea of Neccessary Connexion") in which Hume allows for (a) a succession of subjects in nature "independent of, and antecedent to the operations of the understanding" with a uniting principle unknown to us except through the experience of relations and the passage of the imagination, and (b) a corresponding succession and unknown uniting principle among our internal perceptions:

> As to what may be said, that the operations of nature are independent of our thought and reasoning, I allow it; and accordingly have observ'd, that objects bear to each other the relations of *contiguity* and *succession;* that like objects may be observ'd in several instances to have like relations; and that all this is *independent* of, and *antecedent* to the operations of the understanding. But if we go any farther and ascribe a power or necessary connexion to these objects; this is what we can never observe in them, but must draw the idea of it from what we feel internally in contemplating them . . .
> The *uniting* principle among our internal perceptions is as unintelligible as that among external objects, and is not known to us any other way than by experience. Now the nature and effects of experience have been already sufficiently examin'd and explain'd. It never gives us any insight into the *internal structure* or operating principle of objects, but only accustoms the mind to pass from one to another. (T 168, 169; italics added)

The import of the passage depends on the interpretation of "uniting principle."

Let us begin with the uniting principle among external objects.

Hume cannot here be referring to the "uniting principle among ideas" (T 10) or the "uniting principle in the ideal world" (T 260), viz. the relations of resemblance, contiguity in space and time (succession) and causation, since these are the very qualities *of* experience which allow the imagination to pass from one perception to another—not the "internal structure or operating principle of objects" *into* which experience "never gives us any insight." Although experience tells us nothing about the principle that unites external objects, we apparently do know that they *are united* (Why else even postulate a principle which, were it known, would explain their unity?) in the relations of contiguity and succession "independent of and antecedent to the operations of the understanding", i.e. antecedent to the sort of mistaken and fictitious unity supposed in identity and other products of the imagination and understanding.

Similarly, the uniting principle of our internal perceptions is unknown, but we apparently *do* know that they are united into a *succession which is itself a unity* in some sense in which "unity" is not an idea derived from a single impression, for single impressions can only appear within the succession. Let us label this new sense *unity*$_2$ to distinguish it from the idea of unity (*unity*$_1$) derived from a single impression as used above (pp. 125-127).

Not only is it necessary to distinguish two senses of "unity", however; it is also necessary to distinguish two senses of "succession". For example, when Hume speaks, as he frequently does, of the "determination to pass from one perception to another" (T 635, e.g.), the word "another" may be taken in two entirely different ways, one of which applies to a determination of the imagination while the other applies to a determination *tout simple*. For example, the imagination may be determined to pass from an impression of a river at one moment to an impression of it at a second moment because of the very strong resemblance of the impressions. (T 258) However if a duck happens to swim by, the first river-impression may be succeeded not by a second river-impression but by a duck-impression because of the relation of contiguity. On the other hand it is *not* possible for the first river-impression to be succeeded by *no* perception unless the river watcher dies on the spot (in which case the whole issue becomes theological). Although Hume may be right in saying that *during* a dreamless sleep one "may truly be said not to exist" (T 252), this does not mean that sleep is a "gap" in the *succession* of perceptions, for our last waking perception at night is followed by our first waking perception of the morning—whether this be an impression of an alarm ringing or an idea of having slept or of having dreamt. (Of course this view of sleep and dreaming is not uncontroversial, but it is certainly quite plausible.) Thus the "another" may mean the particular perception to which the imagination *happens* to be determined to pass, or it may mean any possible perception at all—without which the succession ceases to be a succession. Thus we may distinguish the particular contingent *succession*$_1$ (a, b, c, . . ., z) which happens to be produced by the imagination in a given case from the *succession*$_2$ (x_1, x_2, x_3, . . ., x_n) which is simply the *manner* in which the particular perceptions appear, viz. as succeeding one another. (Cf. T 37)

The two senses of unity are obviously correlated with the two senses of succession. Unity$_1$ is the reason why no real connexion can occur in the succession$_1$ produced by the imagination, for unity$_1$ is an idea which derives from and applies to the particular impressions which are distinct existences and which the imagination is free to separate as well as to unite. Unity$_2$ is the unity *of* a succession—but it could never unify a succession$_1$ since the very imagination which produces the fictional unity (called "identity") of succession$_1$ is equally free not to produce that unity. There can be no "real" unity, no "real" connexion, in a succession$_1$. (T 169) Nor, on the other hand, can a succession$_2$ be a unity$_1$, since it is not possible for a succession of any kind to be produced by a *single* impression. A unity$_2$ can be the unity only of a succesion$_2$.

What is this unity$_2$ of the succession$_2$? It is at least possible to say what it is not. It obviously has no existence of its own above and beyond the particular cases of succession$_1$ of which it is the formal law; it has no content of its own above and beyond the perceptions, each of which is a unity$_1$, that contingently make up the particular cases of succession$_1$. It is not the cause of the operations of the imagination, although if one were to deny its possibility one would thereby deny the possibility that the imagination can unite or even separate two perceptions. It is not time, as we have seen—at least not time in the usual non-Humean sense that includes clock-time and the theoretical time of physics. It is not dependent on the succession of objects in nature for even a particular succession$_1$ is not so dependent.[6] Nor is it to be equat-

[6]Locke is instructive here: "But wherever a man is, with all things at

ed with memory. In what is obviously a refutation of Locke's theory of personal identity as based on memory,[7] Hume asks whether the perceptions of a day ten or twenty ago are to be excluded from the succession that we (erroneously) come to call personal identity simply because they are forgotten: ". . . therefore, memory does not so much *produce* as *discover* personal identity, by shewing us the relation of cause and effect among our different perceptions." (T 262)

However although the $unity_2$ of the $succession_2$ is neither memory nor time nor a product of the understanding nor a $unity_1$ nor a $succession_1$, it is compatible with all of them. In fact, with the probable exception of $unity_1$, none of these would be possible without it. Thus there is no inconsistency in asserting together:

(1) The *$succession_2$* of perceptions is a *$unity_2$*,
(2) Every perception is a distinct and separable existence: i.e. a *$unity_1$*, and
(3) The understanding never really binds our perceptions together nor observes any real connexion among objects: i.e. the operation of the understanding never results in a *$unity_1$*.

Hume, of course, did not make any explicit distinction between $unity_1$ and $unity_2$ or between $succession_1$ and $succession_2$, although one passage at least suggests such a distinction, as we have seen above. However the point is that the distinction is perfectly consistent with Hume's philosophy except insofar as Hume admits his philosophy to be inconsistent, and Hume admits his philosophy to be inconsistent only on a point where the distinction would render it consistent: "But all my hopes vanish, when I came to explain the principles, that unite [read: $unite_1$, as is very clear from the context] our succesive [read: $successive_1$] perceptions in our thought or consciousness." (T 635-36) There can be no $unity_1$ of a $succession_1$. But there *can* be a $unity_2$ of a $succession_2$—although it cannot be "explained."

---

rest about him, without perceiving any motion at all,—if during this hour of quiet he has been thinking, he will perceive the various ideas of his own thoughts in his own mind, appearing one after another, and thereby observe and find *succession* where he could observe no motion. *(An Essay Concerning Human Understanding,* II xiv; emphasis added)

[7] *Ibid.,* II xxvii.

Kant called it the "transcendental unity of apperception",—although by doing so he did not so much explain something which Hume failed to find as acknowledge that Hume had found something that cannot be explained.

University of Michigan

6

THE ONTOLOGICAL ARGUMENT: PROPONENTS AND OPPONENTS

by

Bernardino M. Bonansea, O.F.M.

Few topics in the field of philosophy are so fascinating as St. Anselm's ontological argument. Although the subject of endless discussion, the argument continues to draw the attention of philosophers of different persuasions. New interpretations have superseded those of the past and new insights into the controversy have been revealed which point out, among other things, the difficulty and complexity of the issue. It is no longer permissible to dismiss the argument merely on the grounds that great minds like Aquinas and Kant have disposed of it once and forever. The issue is not quite that simple. While it is still possible to reject the argument as a cogent theistic proof, this can be done only with due reservation as to the real intention of its author. This in turn must be determined in the light of the general context in which the argument is presented and the philosophical and theological background of Anselm's thought. Once this is done, it will appear that the *ratio Anselmi* cannot be considered as a mere play upon words, as it has sometimes been labeled, and that many of the attacks upon it are either unjustified or groundless.

An objective study of the Anselmian argument throughout the history of philosophy may reveal that while undue credit has been given to certain modern and contemporary thinkers for their role in the controversy about it, the actual contribution of philosophers who long preceded them on the academic arena has often been neglected or even completely ignored. Yet it is perhaps in the writings of these forgotten masters, who both historically and intellectually are closer to the "father of scholasticism" than their later contenders, that one may find a clue to a better appreciation of the celebrated argument. One such master is John Duns Scotus, whose contribution to the understanding of the *ratio Anselmi* was the subject of our previous study.[1] We wish now to move a step further and submit the Anselmian proof to a more detailed analysis by developing certain points that were only summarily mentioned in that study and by evaluating some of the criticisms of which the proof has been the object.

To avoid misunderstanding, a distinction must be made at the very outset between two different issues: first, the nature and scope of the argument in the mind of its author, and second, the value of the argument as an attempt to prove the existence of God. The first issue must be solved in terms of the argument's original text as contained in the *Proslogion* and set in relation to Anselm's other writings where his philosophical, and especially his epistemological, doctrines are more clearly stated. The solution of the second issue rests to a great extent on the critic's conviction as regards the possibility, ways, and means of attaining to any knowledge of a Supreme Being by unaided reason. The failure to make such a distinction has contributed to much of the confusion in appraisals of the Anselmian proof. In this study the two issues will be kept separate.

I. *Anselm and Gaunilo*

What was Anselm's precise intention in setting forth his famous and much debated argument? To judge from the trouble he went to in reaching its final formulation and the enormous importance he attached to his discovery, it would seem that he was quite certain that he had arrived at a solution of the problem that had beset him for so long a time, namely, to find a single argument which would of itself suffice to demonstrate that God truly exists.[2] This is undoubtedly the impression one gets from reading the

[1]Cf. "Duns Scotus and St. Anselm's Ontological Argument," in *Studies in Philosophy and the History of Philosophy,* ed. John K. Ryan, IV (Washington, D.C.: The Catholic University of America Press, 1969), 128-41.

[2]See preface to *Sancti Anselmi Proslogion seu Alloquium de Dei existentia,* in *Patrologia Latina,* Vol. 158, col. 223. (The *Patrologia Latina* will henceforth be referred to as PL followed by volume number and column). For the reader's convenience, reference will also be given to the English translation of the *Proslogion* and other Anselmian works in *St. Anselm: Basic Writings,* trans. S. W. Deane (2d ed.; La Salle, Ill.: Open Court Publishing Company, 1962). For the above passage see *ibid.*, p. 1.

preface to the *Proslogion* written by Anselm himself and the historical account of the argument transmitted to us by his disciple Eadmer.

If such was Anselm's conviction, we must carefully analyze his claim and see what it really amounts to in terms of his own thinking and the general context of the argument. The reader of the *Proslogion* is immediately struck by the close relationship between faith and reason that runs through the entire work. Hence it is only natural to ask what role, if any, does faith play in Anselm's approach to God, and especially in the argument under consideration.

To state the problem more clearly, is the argument strictly philosophical, and hence completely independent of the data of revelation, or is it merely a "discourse on the existence of God" —this is the subtitle of the treatise—as known to us by faith? If it is held that the argument is purely philosophical, we may ask further, is Anselm's really an a priori demonstration arguing from the concept of God to his existence, or is there any way to justify his reasoning and avoid at the same time what has been termed an illicit transition from the logical to the real order? If, on the other hand, the *ratio Anselmi* is only a reflection on a doctrine known by revelation, can we still speak of it as a rational argument for the existence of God? These are vital questions that have been raised by critics in their attempt to penetrate into the mind of Anselm and discover what was his real intention in the writing of the *Proslogion*.

There can be no doubt that Anselm approached the problem of God's existence from the point of view of a believer who tries to understand the meaning of his own belief. This he tells us explicitly in the preface to his work.[3] The fact that the original title of the *Proslogion* was *Fides quaerens intellectum* (Faith Seeking Understanding) is a confirmation of this point. Likewise, there seems to be no doubt that Anselm was convinced that faith is a necessary requirement for understanding the full import of his argument.[4]

[3]Preface to the *Proslogion,* PL 158, 224; *Basic Writings,* p. 2: "I have written the following treatise, in the person of one who strives to lift his mind to the contemplation of God, and seeks to understand what he believes."

[4]*Proslogion,* chap. I; PL 158, 227; *Basic Writings,* p. 7: "For this also I believe, that unless I believed, I should not understand." See also *Proslogion,* chap. IV; PL 158, 229; *Basic Writings,* p. 10.

Having granted that much, it remains to be seen whether in Anselmian terms a rational demonstration of God's existence is still possible. Despite all arguments to the contrary, it is this writer's contention that faith does not affect or weaken the value of a demonstration as long as this is kept within the limits of man's reasoning ability. And this, we believe, is precisely the case with the Anselmian proof. Indeed, Anselm does not take as starting point of his demonstration the existence of God as known by faith, in which case he would simply beg the question. What he assumes as a major premise of his reasoning is the idea of God as "that than which nothing greater can be conceived." This, he says, is what we believe about God. Then he goes on to work on such idea, which the human mind can perfectly understand even apart from revelation, and tries to show by the principle of contradiction that it is impossible to grasp its full ideological content and deny at the same time the existence of the being for which the idea stands. The reasoning may fail to convince an unbeliever, or even a believer for that matter, but there is nothing in it that would seem to demand faith as its necessary element. To state it another way, faith may be required as a necessary condition for the conviction of the value of Anselm's reasoning, but not for the value of the reasoning itself.

To further clarify our point, we cannot see any inconsistency in seeking to prove by reason a doctrine that is already held to be true by a superior source of knowledge such as revelation, just as we cannot see how one can disprove Anselm's claim that faith may help towards, or even be required for, convincing a person of the value ot his reasoning about God. The value of an argument and conviction of its value, especially when the argument in question concerns the existence of a being that transcends all empirical evidence, are two different things.[5]

If our understanding of the problem is correct, then the alternate interpretation of the *ratio Anselmi* as a mere reflection on the doctrine of God's existence known by revelation must *ipso facto* be ruled out as incompatible with a strict rational demonstration. The question then arises: What kind of demonstra-

[5]For a development of this point see the present writer's study, "The Theistic Proof and Some Contemporary Philosophical Trends," *Akten des XIV. Internationalen Kongresses für Philosophie, Wien, 2-9 Sept., 1968,* VI (Vienna: Herder, 1971), 173-80.

tion is it? If the starting point of Anselm's reasoning is merely a concept of the being whose existence it purports to prove, no matter what the source of that concept, how is Anselm able to move from a concept to the existence of the being so conceived? This is unquestionably the major difficulty Anselm had to face in defending the value of his argument.

As is well known, Gaunilo, a monk of the abbey of Marmoutiers near Tours, was the first to attack Anselm's argument "on behalf of the fool." Gaunilo's observations deserve special consideration because they anticipate most of the objections subsequently raised against the argument and also because they offered Anselm an opportunity to clarify certain points of the *Proslogion* that had either been left obscure or had not been fully developed.

Gaunilo's objections may be summarized as follows. The notion of a being than which no greater can be conceived is not different from the notion of a fictional being or a being whose existence has not been ascertained. To hold the contrary, one must show that the being in question is of such a nature that it cannot be understood without grasping at the same time its actual existence. But if this were the case, then there would be no difference between having an object in the mind prior to its actual existence, such as the idea of a painting in its potential state, and understanding the object in its concrete reality, such as the idea of a painting once it has been completed. Besides, if the existence of that being is so evident that its nonexistence cannot even be entertained in thought, why should one bother himself with proving it? Would it not be enough to thing of that being to know that it really exists? But obviously this is not the case, for despite their idea of God there are still those who persist in denying his existence.

To support his point, Gaunilo brings forth his example of the "lost island," i.e., an island "more excellent than any other lands" and such than no better can be conceived. Yet, he says, despite the fact that we can form a clear concept of it, it does not follow that the island in question is actually existent. As a matter of fact, the island has never existed except in the imagination of men. Similarly, Gaunilo argues, I can very well form the concept of a being greater than any other being, and still doubt whether this being is anything but a fiction of my mind. Briefly, Gaunilo wants to say that existence is not something that can be inferred from a mere concept in the mind, whether it is the concept of God or of any other being. To think otherwise is to make an illicit transition from the ideal order to the order of reality.[6]

To judge from the nature and length of Anselm's refutation of Gaunilo's objections, he made a serious effort to correct certain ideas about his argument that had led his critic to a wrong interpretation of it. As a result, his *Reply* to Gaunilo, made up of ten chapters, is extremely enlightening and is indispensable for an objective evaluation of the whole issue. His answer is as follows.

In the first place, Anselm sharply criticizes Gaunilo's comparison ot the notion of God with the notion of a purely fictional being or "a being that is altogether inconceivable in terms of reality." If the two notions were alike, then either God would not be a being than which a greater is inconceivable, or he vould not be able to be conceived at all. Now both of these suppositions are false, and to this effect he appeals to Gaunilo's faith and conscience. Hence, since the being in question is conceivable, it must also exist in reality. If not—and here Anselm gives a new turn to his argument—it would be possible for it to have a beginning and this would make it a different kind of being. It is indeed greater to exist without a beginning than to come into existence at a particular moment of time. (As far as Anselm's reasoning is concerned, an eternally contingent being seems to be out of question). Likewise, a being than which a greater is inconceivable cannot exist only at any particular place or time; it must exist as a whole everywhere and always. The reason is that whatever exists only temporarily or at a particular place can be conceived as nonexisting at all, which again is in direct contradiction to a being whose nonexistence is inconceivable.

A further observation of the greatest importance for a proper grasp of the Anselmian proof is that if the being under discussion is in the understanding, as it certainly is whenever I grasp its meaning, it is possible to think of it as existing also in reality. But as soon as this possibility is realized, it will be seen that the inference from possibility to actuality is demanded by the logic of reasoning. In fact, how could a being than which a greater is not conceivable exist only in the understanding if I can think of it as existing also in reality—which is undoubtedly greater than to exist in the understanding alone—and at the same time remove such

[6]Cf. *Liber pro insipiente adversus S. Anselmi in Proslogio ratiocinationem*, PL 158, 241-48; *Basic Writings*, pp. 145-53.

a reality from it? Would not that be a contradictory notion, since on the one hand I form the concept of a greatest conceivable, and therefore possible, being, and on the other hand I remove from it one of the essential features of its greatness, i.e., existence?

It must be noted that it is no question here of mere conceptual existence, in which case the argument would be self-defeating; it is a question of actual, real existence, which, in Anselm's thinking, is a perfection that has to be included in the notion of the greatest conceivable being. It is possible to disagree with Anselm's viewpoint, but it cannot be denied that that is his position, as the following text clearly indicates: "What more consistent inference, then, can be made than this: that if a being than which a greater cannot be conceived is in the understanding alone, it is not that than which a greater cannot be conceived?"[7]

On the basis of the foregoing observations, it will be easy for Anselm to dismiss Gaunilo's analogy of the "lost island." The analogy simply does not apply to his own reasoning. First, because there cannot be such thing as an island than which no greater can be conceived, since no matter how excellent the island may be, it is always possible to think of a better one. Secondly, an island, by its very nature, is a limited reality and hence only relatively perfect, whereas Anselm's being must possess all perfections to the ultimate possible degree. Thirdly, an island, like any other creature, is a contingent being or such that it is indifferent for it to exist or not to exist. In other words, one can think of it as nonexisting without any contradiction, which is precisely the opposite of the kind of being Anselm had in mind in the formulation of his argument. It is because of these contrasts between the two kinds of being, which were no doubt in the back of Anselm's mind, even though he did not spell them out in exactly the way we have done, that he can challenge Gaunilo in the following terms: "I promise confidently that if any man shall devise anything either in reality or in concept alone to which he can adapt the sequence of my reasoning, I will discover that thing, and will give him his lost island, not to be lost again."[8]

Having clarified the problem of the supposed island, Anselm turns to Gaunilo's final remark, which at first sight may appear

[7]Cf. *Liber apologeticus contra Gaunilonem respondentem pro insipiente,* chap. II, PL 158, 252; *Basic Writings,* p. 158.

[8]*Liber apologeticus,* chap. III, PL 158, 252; *Basic Writings,* p. 158.

to be a purely semantic subtlety but in truth is something much more significant. Referring to Anselm's oft-repeated statement that the nonexistence of the being in question is inconceivable, Gaunilo had suggested that a better term for it would be "unintelligible." For, he added, just as unreal things are unintelligible yet their existence is conceivable, so is with God whose nonexistence or even the possibility of his nonexistence is unintelligible and yet it can be conceived, as is the case with the fool. Anselm takes issue with Gaunilo's observation on the grounds that no comparison is possible between the nonexistence of God and the nonexistence of unreal things, even as far as our thinking is concerned. While there is no contradiction in thinking of the nonexistence of unreal things—indeed, that is the only way we think of them—it is impossible to think of the nonexistence, or even the possibility of nonexistence, of God. Furthermore, if the nonexistence of God is only said to be unintelligible, there would be no difference between God and creatures, since all existing beings are intelligible to the extent that they exist.

To understand the logic of Anselm's reasoning, one must keep in mind the distinction between conceiving *(cogitare)* and understanding *(intelligere),* a distinction that was accepted by him as well as by Gaunilo. Whereas conceiving may refer to both existing and nonexisting beings, although not at the same time and in the same respect, understanding can only be in terms of actually existing beings, both material and spiritual. It is precisely because God is such a unique being to which existence is due that, in Anselm's view, our mind is unable even to think of him as nonexisting. That will explain his statement that while "nothing, so long as it is known to exist, can be conceived not to exist," and "whatever exists, except that being than which a greater cannot be conceived, can be conceived not to exist, even when it is known to exist, . . . of God alone it can be said that it is impossible to conceive his nonexistence."[9]

With this last remark one might think that Anselm had refuted all the objections that Gaunilo had marshaled against his argument; but that is not the case. Going once more through the script of his objector, he discovers more weak spots, inconsistencies, and even misrepresentations which he feels must be brought into the open and thus further reveal some of the peculiarities of the argument.

[9] *Liber apologeticus,* chap. IV, PL 158, 254; *Basic Writings,* p. 161.

One first point he finds necessary to clarify is the notion of the being whose existence he is attempting to prove. To this effect he accuses Gaunilo—and rightly so—of having misquoted him by having him say that he wanted to demonstrate the existence of God merely from the notion of a being greater than all other beings. "Nowhere in all my writings," he asserts emphatically, "is such a demonstration found. For the real existence of a being which is said to be *greater than all other beings* cannot be demonstrated in the same way as the real existence of one that is said to be *a being than which a greater cannot be conceived*."[10] In fact, it is not altogether clear, and certainly not so on the strength of Anselm's reasoning, that a supreme being must exist merely because it is greater than all other beings, since it is always possible, at least in theory, to think of its nonexistence without contradiction. This very possibility would seem to make it inferior to a being whose nonexistence is absolutely inconceivable.

But the main point at issue is not so much the difference between the two kinds of being under discussion, but rather the question as to whether or not an argument for their existence can be made from their concept. It is Anselm's contention that while a cogent argument for the existence of God can be built on the idea of a being than which no greater is conceivable, no such argument is possible in the case of a being that is simply greater than all other beings. In point of fact, he adds, it is not difficult to see that the former will also be the latter; the reverse position, however, need not necessarily be true.[11]

In his analysis of the argument in the *Proslogion,* Gaunilo not only finds fault with Anselm's reasoning; he also questions the value of its premise, namely, the idea of the greatest conceivable being, since, in his view, there is no way of forming such an idea either from the being itself or from any other being. This is obviously a very serious objection which Anselm cannot let go unheeded, for, if it were proved valid, his whole argument would crumble. His answer is swift and to the point, if we care to place it within the perspective of Platonic–Augustinian thought common at his time.

Granting the Platonic principle that a limited good is only

[10]*Liber apologeticus,* chap. V, PL 158, 254; *Basic Writings,* pp. 161-62.

[11]See the whole chapter V of *Liber apologeticus,* PL 158, 254-56; *Basic Writings,* 161-64.

conceivable in terms of a supreme good in which it participates, Anselm argues that from the limited goods of our experience and by ascending from the lesser to the greater good, one can form a sufficiently valid notion of a being than which a greater is inconceivable. "So easily, then, can the fool who does not accept sacred authority be refuted, if he denies that a notion may be formed from other objects of a being than which a greater is inconceivable."[12] As for a Christian, Anselm simply reminds his objector of St. Paul's statement in Romans, I, 20, that the invisible things of God can be understood from the things he has made, including his eternal power and divinity.[13]

But even if it were true, Anselm goes on to say, that we cannot conceive or understand a being than which a greater is inconceivable, it will nevertheless be possible for anyone to understand at least the meaning of such an expression. Just as we understand the meaning of the term ineffable, even though we may not grasp what is said to be ineffable, so we understand what is meant by the term inconceivable, although that to which the word applies is not conceivable. In other words, Anselm wants to say that the value of his argument does not depend on the actual understanding of the being under discussion, but simply on the understanding of what a being than which a greater cannot be conceived is meant to be. This, he suggests, can be understood by everyone, including him who denies the existence of that being, for "whoever . . . makes this denial, understands and conceives of that than which a greater is inconceivable."[14]

Having made this concession, Anselm is still convinced that it is possible for everyone both to conceive and to understand a being than which a greater is inconceivable, and not merely the logical content, as it were, of such an expression. It is likewise possible for everyone to understand that the being so conceived must exist, "for anything whose nonexistence is possible, is not that which he conceives."[15]

Anselm is obviously satisfied with his refutation of Gaunilo's objections, none of which, he insists, carries such weight as to invalidate the cogency of his argument. Hence he feels justified in

[12]*Liber apologeticus*, chap. VIII, PL 158, 258; *Basic Writings*, p. 168.
[13]*Liber apologeticus, loc. cit.; Basic Writings, loc. cit.*
[14]*Liber apologeticus*, chap. IX, PL 158, 259; *Basic Writings*, p. 169.
[15]*Liber apologeticus, loc. cit.; Basic Writings, loc. cit.*

making a final statement which reaffirms his conviction and summarizes the entire argument: "So great force does the signification of this reasoning contain in itself, that this being which is the subject of discussion, is of necessity, from the very fact that it is understood or conceived, proved also to exist in reality, and to be whatever we should believe of the divine substance."[16] This statement makes it clear, in case there is still doubt about Anselm's contention, that the existence of God, along with all other attributes ascribed to him on the basis of revelation, can be proved from the very fact that we understand not only the meaning or logical content, but the full dimension, that is, the ideological as well as the ontological content of the notion of "that than which no greater can be conceived."

The argument, it is worth repeating, is not so much an attempt to prove God's existence from the idea that we have of a supremely conceivable being in the abstract or logical order, as though it were enough to have such an idea to know for sure that God exists. Rather, Anselm's purpose is to show that one cannot possibly think of a being than which a greater cannot be conceived without admitting at the same time that such a concept, or better, such a notion —for it is not merely a concept—includes necessarily, if it is to have any value, the existence of the being in question. In other words, according to Anselm's reasoning, we do not arrive at God from the idea of him as a purely mental construct, but we cannot have an idea of him that does not include his existence, or to be precise, his real existence. This may appear to be a subtle distinction, but it is not. It is a distinction that must be made for a proper understanding of the argument in light of the ideological realism that Anselm shared with the entire Augustinian tradition, as pointed out in our previous study.[17]

It will perhaps be objected that if this observation is correct, one can no longer speak of the *ratio Anselmi* as a demonstration a priori in the strict sense of the term. We are inclined to agree with such a view and suggest that demonstration *a simultaneo* is a better term for it. We would further suggest that "argumentation" is also a better translation of the Anselmian term *ratio* and more in keeping with the general character of the *Proslogion* as "a discourse on the existence of God."

[16]*Liber apologeticus,* chap. X, PL 158, 260; *Basic Writings,* p. 170.
[17]"Duns Scotus and St. Anselm's Ontological Argument," *art. cit.,* pp. 133-34.

II. *Bonaventure and Aquinas*

It would be a long and perhaps fruitless task to analyze all the aspects of the problem that the controversy between Anselm and Gaunilo has aroused in the history of philosophy. However, it is important to consider the reactions of various philosophers both to Anselm's argument and to his debate with Gaunilo and to evaluate them on the basis of our understanding of the problem at issue.

The first major figures in the history of the argument are St. Bonaventure and St. Thomas Aquinas, the representatives of the two largest schools of thought in the thirteenth century. Their attitude toward the *ratio Anselmi* is of primary importance because of the enormous influence it exerted on later philosophers, especially within scholastic circles.

Bonaventure discusses the Anselmian argument in his *Commentary on the Sentences* of Peter Lombard and the opuscule *De mysterio Trinitatis.*[18] The two treatments move along the same line, but whereas in the first work the *ratio Anselmi* is introduced at the beginning of the question, "Whether the existence of God is so true that its nonexistence cannot be conceived," in the second Anselm's proof is incorporated into a more extensive article dealing with the general question, "Whether truth is a property of the divine being." In fact, the proof is but an application of the answer to the question at issue. Once it has been established that truth is an absolute property of God, it is only logical to ask whether God's existence shares in the same degree of truth as the divine nature with which it is to be identified. Clearly, then, Bonaventure's approach to Anselm's argument is from the point of view of the divine nature itself rather than from the viewpoint of our knowledge of it.

In his answer to the question whether the existence of God is indubitably true, Bonaventure appeals both to the author of the *Proslogion,* whose reasoning he completely endorses,[19] and to St. Augustine's notion of divine truth as the source and foundation of all other truths, including the truth of the statement that God

[18]Cf. St. Bonaventure, *Opera Omnia* (Quaracchi: Typographia S. Bonaventurae, 1882-1902), Vol. I, *In I Sent.,* d. VIII, Pt. I, a. 1, q. 2, pp. 153-55; Vol. V, *De mysterio Trinitatis,* q. 1, a. 1, pp. 45-51.

[19]*De myst. Trin.,* Nos. 21-24, p. 47.

exists.[20] Likewise, in accordance with Aristotle's principle that the more basic and universal a truth is the better it is known,[21] Bonaventure argues that the truth of God's existence is most certain and evident because it is the first of all truths, both in itself and in our understanding. Its evidence is such that it excludes even the possibility of its denial.[22] In concluding his series of arguments in favor of the absolute necessity of God's existence from the idea we have of him, Bonaventure writes: "If God is God, God exists. The antecedent is so true that its contradictory is unthinkable. Therefore, the existence of God is indubitably true."[23] In a parallel conclusion in the *Commentary* he writes: "God, or the supreme truth, is being itself, [and such] than which no better can be conceived. Hence, since the predicate is included in the subject, [God] cannot not exist, nor can he be conceived as nonexistent."[24]

Evidently Bonaventure's reasoning, even more than Anselm's, rests on the assumption that we already have a notion of God either from revelation[25] or from some other source, such as reason or experience. Just as we can argue from creatures to their creator on the basis of the principle of causality,[26] so we can know the privations and limitations of the beings of our experience only through the knowledge of the opposite perfections. This means that "our mind experiences necessarily within itself some sort of light through which it knows the first being."[27] Furthermore, Bonaventure shares Augustine's view that the human soul, by being present to itself, knows itself directly, and since God is present to the soul even better than the soul is to itself, then the knowledge of God is inserted, as it were, into our soul.[28]

To the objection that many people, including the fool described by the Psalmist, are not aware of the knowledge in question, Bonaventure answers with Anselm that such ignorance is not due to the fact that God is not knowable or that our mind has no ability to know him, but rather to the knower's lack of reflection on what

[20]*Ibid.*, Nos. 25-26, p. 47.
[21]Cf. Aristotle, *Posterior Analytics,* Bk. I, chap. 2.
[22]*De myst. Trin.*, q. 1, a. 1, No. 27, p. 48.
[23]*Ibid.*, No. 29, p. 48.
[24]*In I Sent.*, d. VIII, Pt. I, a. 1, q. 2, *Conclusio*, p. 155.
[25]*De myst. Trin.*, q. 1, a. 1, No. 21, p. 47.
[26]*Opera Omnia,* Vol. V, *In Hexaëmeron,* V, No. 29, p. 359.
[27]*Ibid.*, No. 30, p. 359.
[28]*De myst. Trin.*, q. 1, a. 1, No. 10, p. 46. See also No. 1, p. 45.

the term God really means.[29] As for the kind of knowledge of God man can attain in this life, Bonaventure agrees with most of the schoolmen that it is neither perfect or comprehensive, since such knowledge belongs to God alone, nor clear and distinct, such as that of the blessed in heaven. It is only partial and confused knowledge, inasmuch as God is known to be the first being from whom all other beings derive their existence.[30]

With Bonaventure, as with Anselm, there is no question of an illicit transition from the idea of God to God's existence, the objection commonly raised against the ontological argument. As Gilson puts it, "the idea is for him [Bonaventure] simply the mode whereby the being is present in his thought: there is therefore no real gap to be bridged between the idea of God whose existence is necessary, and this same God necessarily existing."[31] On the other hand, Bonaventure does not simply accept Anselm's reasoning without bringing into it new insights that are no doubt in keeping with the general context of the *Proslogion,* but nevertheless have not been made explicit by its author. To quote once more from Gilson:

> With St. Bonaventure the truths presupposed in St. Anselm's argument come into the foreground and, shown in their full evidence, in some sense absorb the proof. If, in fact, the line of argument of the *Proslogion* draws its value from the profound contacts that our idea of God maintains with its object, it is rather the realization of this action of God in our thought that constitutes the proof of His existence, and not the analytical working out of the consequences involved in the notion we have of Him.[32]

To turn from Bonaventure to Aquinas is to see a totally new picture, that is, a completely different interpretation of the *ratio Anselmi.* This difference of approach should not surprise anyone who is acquainted with the relative degree of freedom with which the thirteenth-century schoolmen moved within the area of philo-

[29] *Ibid., Conclusio,* Nos. 1, 2, 3, p. 50.

[30] *Ibid., Conclusio,* No. 13, p. 51.

[31] Etienne Gilson, *The Philosophy of St. Bonaventure,* trans. Dom Illtyd Trethowan (London: Sheed and Ward, 1940), p. 129.

[32] *Ibid.,* pp. 129-30. For St. Bonaventure's teaching on man's knowledge of God and the arguments for God's existence see P. León Veuthey, O.F.M. Conv., "Le problème de l'existence de Dieu chez S. Bonaventure," *Antonianum,* XXVIII (1953), 19-38.

sophy and the conflict they were gradually drawn into by the introduction of Aristotle's thought into what was predominantly a Platonic–Augustinian tradition. Thus, although Bonaventure made extensive use of Aristotle's works, he adhered basically to the Augustinian tradition which he saw as being more in keeping with Christian thought and his own theological speculation. On the other hand, Aquinas had no strong tradition behind him in his own Order, was more directly exposed to Aristotle's profound and ingenious metaphysical thinking, and went all the way in an attempt to absorb Aristotelian philosophy into his own synthesis. His attitude toward the Anselmian argument is a case in point.

Aquinas discusses the *ratio Anselmi* in several of his works but with no appreciable difference of approach.[33] In both the *Summa theologiae* and the *Summa contra gentiles* he fails to name the author of the argument, while in the second work he speaks of not just one but several authors as defenders of the argument under discussion.[34] This has led historians to suspect that in his polemic Thomas had in mind not so much Anselm himself as certain contemporary philosophers and theologians, especially Bonaventure.[35] Whoever may have been his objects of criticism, neither Anselm nor Bonaventure or any other upholder of the argument had presented the problem in quite the same terms as Thomas does, namely, "Whether the existence of God is self-evident."[36] As a matter of fact, none of those authors would have subscribed to the view that the existence of God is self-evident. They all thought of this as a demonstrable truth and as such the opposite of what a self-evident proposition is.[37] Anselm and Bona-

[33]The principal texts where Aquinas discusses the *ratio Anselmi* are: *In I Sent.,* d. 3, q. 1, a. 2, ed. Mandonnet (Paris: Lethielleux, 1929), 93-95; *Summa contra gentiles,* Bk. I, chaps. 10-11; *Summa theologiae,* I, q. 2, a. 1; *De veritate,* q. 10, a. 12; *In Boethii de Trinitate,* q. 1, a. 3, obj. 6 and ad 6, ed. Decker (Leiden: Brill, 1955), pp. 70, 73-74.

[34]Anselm's name is mentioned by Aquinas in *In I Sent.,* d. 3, q. 1, a. 2, obj. 4 and ad 4, pp. 93 and 95; *De veritate, loc. cit.;* and *In Boethii de Trinitate, loc. cit.*

[35]Cf. Anton C. Pegis, "St. Anselm and the Argument of 'Proslogion,'" *Mediaeval Studies,* XXVIII (1966), 262 ff.; Etienne Gilson, *The Christian Philosophy of St. Thomas Aquinas,* trans. L. K. Shook, C.S.B. (New York: Random House, 1956), p. 48.

[36]See, for example, *Sum. theol.,* I, q. 2, a. 1: "Utrum Deum esse sit per se notum"; *Cont. gent.,* I, 1: "De opinione dicentium quod Deum esse demonstrari non potest cum sit per se notum."

[37]Cf. Pegis, *art. cit.,* pp. 262 ff. for a discussion of this point.

venture, as we have seen, devote a considerable amount of space to the demonstration of the existence of a being than which no greater can be conceived. In addition, both of them have recourse to the traditional theistic arguments which were later so well synthesized by Thomas in his well-known five ways.

Having stated the problem in these terms, Aquinas goes on to describe a self-evident proposition as that which is known immediately upon the knowledge of its terms, such as the proposition that a whole is greater than a part. Now the proposition "God exists," Aquinas writes, is held by some philosophers to be such a proposition, for once we understand the meaning of the two terms we see immediately that existence is of the very nature of God. Hence they hold that it is self-evident that God exists.[38]

In refutation of the argument Thomas states, first, that a distinction must be made between a proposition that is self-evident in itself and one that is self-evident to us. The proposition "God exists" is self-evident in the former sense, since the subject and the predicate are identical, but not in the latter sense, for it is not evident to us that God is his own existence. This truth must be demonstrated and that can only be done starting from the objects of our experience, which are more evident to us.[39] Moreover, referring specifically to Anselm's notion of a being than which no greater can be conceived, Aquinas argues that such is not the meaning conveyed to everyone as soon as he hears the word God. Indeed, some people have an entirely different notion of God, a statement with which Anselm would perfectly agree. But even if the word God were generally recognized to mean a being than which no greater can be conceived, Aquinas stresses that it would still be uncertain whether such a being exists in reality or whether it is but a concept of our mind. It remains to be proved therefore, especially to an unbeliever, that such a being does actually exist. Finally, Anselm's reasoning that if God can be thought not to be then it is possible to think of something greater than God, is not valid. For the possibility of thinking of God as nonexistent is not due to the imperfection or uncertainty of the divine being but rather to the weakness of our mind which cannot behold God himself and can argue to him only from the effects of his creation.[40]

[38]Cf. *Sum. theol.*, I, q. 2, a. 1, obj. 2 and *Respondeo; Cont. gent.*, I, 10, No. 1.

[39]*Sum. theol.*, I, q. 2, a. 1, *Respondeo; Cont. gent.*, I, 11.

[40]*Sum. theol.*, I, q. 2, a. 1, ad 2; *Cont. gent.*, I, 11.

Such is Aquinas' position on the *ratio Anselmi.* In all fairness it must be said that, apart from his initial misrepresentation of the problem as seen above, his objections to the argument are strong and quite consistent with his Aristotelian background. If ideas have no value-content except insofar as they reflect a concrete material object or are derived from it through the process of abstraction, it is useless to try to construct an argument for the existence of a being merely from the idea we have of it in our mind, be it the idea of the greatest conceivable being. From the Aristotelian viewpoint the idea in question has no ontological value and any attempt to build a theistic argument on it is doomed to fail. It falls short of bridging the gap between mind and reality, and it incurs the charge, so often leveled against the Anselmian proof, of being an illicit transition from the ideal to the real order.

Aquinas was therefore right in refuting the Anselmian argument on Aristotelian premises, and so are his followers who for centuries have been repeating the same objections with no appreciable effort to place the argument within its proper historical and ideological context. But the question is: Is the Aristotelian epistemology the only valid one? Is it true that the formal and proper object of our intellect, even in this life, is only a material quiddity and that sense experience and abstraction are the only valid process of acquiring knowledge? These are fundamental issues that have received different solutions in the course of history and none of them seems to be completely satisfactory. Hence the value of Aquinas' criticism of the *ratio Anselmi* is conditioned upon the acceptance of the Aristotelian theory as the only valid cognitive theory. Once this is questioned—and there is an entire school of thought from Plato to Augustine, from Anselm to Bonaventure, and from Duns Scotus to many present-day thinkers who question it—then the criticism itself becomes questionable.

Whatever side one may take in the controversy, it seems clear that Aquinas did not give Anselm the credit he deserves for his discovery. Stated more bluntly, he did not show himself to be completely objective in his presentation of Anselm's view. However, the truth of the matter is that this lack of objectivity in the presentation of opposite views is not something peculiar to Aquinas or to his treatment of the ontological argument. It is rather a common attitude among medieval schoolmen whenever in their writings they want to make a particular point of doctrine.

A notable exception in the case under consideration is John Duns Scotus, who was neither an all–out Aristotelian nor a complete Augustinian, although he had great esteem for both Aristotle and Augustine. From his vantage point as an impartial critic, he did not accept the argument as a cogent demonstration of God's existence, thus agreeing with Aquinas, but at the same time he showed a keen interest in the argument, which is not so evident in Aquinas. Scotus showed that a being than which no greater can be conceived is possible because its concept implies no contradiction, and if possible it must exist, or else it could never exist since it is of its nature to be a self–existing being. He thus provided the *ratio Anselmi* with a more solid and credible basis and transformed it into what might be called a confirmatory argument for God's existence rather than an absolutely convincing proof, as it was meant to be by its author. Since Scotus' position has already been the object of particular study by the writer, we refer the reader to it.

In the period immediately following the Middle Ages no important contribution to the understanding of the argument was made. We therefore pass to the consideration of the Anselmian proof in modern times.

III. *Descartes, Leibniz, and Kant*

The name of René Descartes is so closely associated with the ontological argument that in some cases his version of it has been given preference over its original formulation by St. Anselm. A conspicuous example of this is Kant who, as we shall see, ignores completely the *Proslogion* and attributes the argument to Descartes, even though he presents it in a form more similar to that of Leibniz. It is to these three representatives of modern philosophy that we direct our attention for their view of the argument.

Descartes discusses the ontological argument in his *Discourse on Method,* the *Meditations on First Philosophy,* and *The Principles of Philosophy,* as well as in his *Replies* to the objections to his works raised by some contemporary philosophers and theologians. Surprisingly enough, throughout the discussion Descartes never mentions the name of Anselm and there is some evidence to the effect that he was not even acquainted with the *Proslogion* at the time he wrote. In his answer to Père Mersenne, who had pointed out the affinity of his argument with the one presented by Anselm, Descartes says simply that he will read Anselm at the first opportunity.[41] Since this letter was written in December 1640, that is, long after he had finished writing his *Discourse* and his *Meditations,* the question has been asked by historians of philosophy as to the immediate source of his argument. In Gilson's view, Descartes knew the argument only through the criticism of Thomas Aquinas whom he had studied at the Jesuit college of La Flèche. The fact that he shares Aquinas' criticism against his supposed objector concerning the non-self-evidence of the proposition *God exists* and the impossibility of arguing to God merely from his verbal definition—two propositions Anselm himself would have readily accepted—seems to support the view that Descartes had not read Anselm's *Proslogion,* or if he had, he completely ignored it.[42]

Be that as it may, there seems to be little doubt that in his formulation of the argument Descartes depends on Anselm, whether directly or indirectly. The substance of his reasoning as it appears in his *Fifth Meditation* where the argument is more fully developed, may be summarized.

Everything of which I have a clear and distinct idea is true, and whatever is true is real, for I cannot have the idea of a pure negation. This is most certain in the realm of mathematics which deals with shapes and numbers. For instance, I have the idea of

[41]Cf. *Oeuvres philosophiques de Descartes,* ed. Ferdinand Alquié, II (Paris: Garnier, 1967), 290: "Je verrai saint Anselme à la première occasion."

[42]For the relationship between Descartes and Anselm see Etienne Gilson, *Études sur le rôle de la pensée médiévale dans la formation du système cartésien* (Paris: Vrin, 1930), chap. IV, "Descartes et Sant Anselme," pp. 215-23. Gilson admits that some authors, among whom he mentions Alexandre Koyré, defend the thesis that Descartes had read Anselm's *Proslogion* before writing his own *Meditations.* If this view is correct, Gilson remarks, then it becomes more difficult to explain Descartes' misunderstandings about Anselm's thought. *Ibid,* p. 222, n. 1. Descartes' apparent disregard for the contributions of the past has been pointed out by Leibniz, who mentions the ontological argument specifically: "Argumentum pro existentia Dei ab ipsa eius notione sumtum, primus quantum constat, invenit proposuitque Anselmus Cantuariensis Archiepiscopus libro contra insipientem qui extat. Et passim examinatur a Scholasticae Theologiae scriptoribus, ipsoque Aquinate, unde videtur hausisse Cartesius, eius studii non expers, *postquam apud Jesuitas Flexiae literas hausit.*" (This last sentence is an additional note by Leibniz himself). Cf. *Die philosophischen Schriften von Gottfried Wilhelm Leibniz,* ed. C. I. Gerhardt, IV (Hildesheim: Olms, 1960), 358.

a triangle and by analyzing its nature I see clearly that its three angles are equal to two right angles. This is true even if no triangle had ever been anywhere in the world except as a figure in my imagination or a thought in my mind. The idea of triangle and whatever belongs to it is therefore the idea of something and not of nothing. Nor can it be said that it is merely a product of my mind, for a triangle is and remains what it is whether I think of it or not.

Now, just as I have the idea of a triangle, so I have also in my mind a clear and distinct idea of God as a supremely perfect being in which [actual] existence is seen to belong to its nature not otherwise than it belongs to the nature of a triangle to be equal to two right angles. Hence the existence of God is no less certain to me than any truth in the mathematical order.[43] "It is at least as certain that God, who is a being so perfect, is, or exists, as any demonstration of geometry can possibly be."[44]

Descartes acknowledges that this truth is not immediately evident, so that it is possible for us to think of God as nonexistent. However, he insists that on closer study it becomes manifest that it is no more possible to separate existence from essence in God than it is to deny the equality of three angles to two right angles in a triangle. Therefore, since existence is a perfection and the idea of God is the idea of a most perfect being, to think of God as nonexistent is just as impossible as to think of a mountain without a valley.[45]

In anticipation of the objection that although I cannot think of God as nonexistent, any more than I can think of a mountain without a valley, still it does not follow that either God or a mountain exists in actual reality, Descartes—in the same fashion as Anselm before him in regard to the analogy of the perfect island—answers that the objection rests on a fallacy. Because I cannot think of a mountain without a valley it does not indeed follow that either mountain or valley exists, since existence is not part of their concepts. On the contrary, in the case of God existence is included in the very concept of him in such a way that

[43]Cf. *Meditations on the First Philosophy*, in *The Philosophical Works of Descartes*, ed. E. S. Haldane and G. R. T. Ross (New York: Dover, 1955), Vol. I, pp. 180-81.

[44]*Discourse on Method, ibid.*, p. 104. See also Proposition I in *Arguments Demonstrating the Existence of God, ibid.*, Vol. II, p. 57.

[45]*Meditations, ibid.*, Vol. I, p. 181.

it becomes impossible for me to think of him as nonexistent. It is not a necessity brought about by my thought, but rather a necessity imposed on me by the object of my thought, that is, the necessity of God's existence.[46]

As for the other objection, which was to be raised later by Kant, that his reasoning rests on the presupposition that God possesses all perfections and that existence is itself one of these perfections, Descartes insists that there is no presupposition involved in his argument. Indeed, one does not have to think of God at all, but as soon as he conceives the idea of a supremely perfect being, he cannot but include in it all perfections, one of which is of course the perfection of existence.[47]

It would be interesting at this point to analyze, in addition to Descartes' self-raised objections, all other objections marshaled by philosophers and theologians against the argument and forwarded to him after the manuscript of the *Meditations* had been circulated among them by Père Mersenne: objections that were later published by Descartes along with his own reply. However, such analysis, useful as it may be, would carry us beyond the limits of this survey. We shall instead confine ourselves to consider certain points that emerged from the discussion and which may serve to throw further light on Descartes' understanding of the argument.

Thus, in his answer to Caterus, Descartes stresses the distinction between possible and necessary existence and affirms that possible existence is contained in the idea of everything that is clearly and distinctly conceived, but not so necessary existence, which is peculiar to the idea of God.[48]

Likewise, in reply to an unidentified group of philosophers and theologians who took exception to his conclusion that God's existence can be inferred from the clear and distinct idea we have of his nature and suggested that the only conclusion to be derived from that idea is that existence belongs to divine nature but not that such nature exists unless we otherwise know that to be a fact, Descartes says that they have completely misunderstood his argument. If their suggestion were followed, the major premise should

[46]*Ibid.*, pp. 181-82.

[47]*Ibid.*, p. 182.

[48]Cf. *A Reply by the Author to the First Set of Objections, ibid.*, Vol. II, p. 20.

then be worded like this: "That which we clearly understand to belong to the nature of anything, can truthfully be asserted to belong to its nature," which is a pure tautology. Instead of this, Descartes insists that the major premise of his argument is: "That which we clearly understand to belong to the nature of anything can truly be affirmed of that thing," and not merely of that nature. Hence he feels justified in clinging to the original conclusion of his argument that the existence of God can be truly affirmed from the clear and distinct idea we have of him. Even if our idea of God is not adequate, as the same group of objectors hold, it is nevertheless sufficiently clear, Descartes retorts, to give us assurance that God's nature is possible, or not contradictory, and that necessary existence belongs to him.[49]

In the same vein, Descartes rebuts Gassendi's objection that existence is neither a property nor a perfection of an essence, not even in the case of God. Descartes argues that if by property is meant an attribute or perfection that can be predicated of a thing, then necessary existence in God is a true property in the strict sense of the term and such that it belongs to him exclusively, just as omnipotence and other divine attributes do.[50] Then, somewhat annoyed by Gassendi's remark that his argument does not prove anything, since it assumes what has to be proved, namely, that existence is a perfection included in the idea of a supreme being, Descartes concludes: "I pass over the rest, because, though saying that I explain nothing, you yourself explain nothing and prove nothing, save only that you are able to prove nothing."[51]

If we compare the Cartesian formulation of the ontological argument with that of Anselm, the striking similarity between the two is evident. Although the starting point is somewhat different, in the sense that for Anselm it is the idea of a supremely conceivable being, whereas for Descartes it is the idea of a supremely perfect being, nevertheless in each case it is an idea that is forced upon our mind by the very nature of the being under consideration, and not merely a product of our mind. It is a unique kind of idea for it represents a unique kind of being, i.e., a being that admits of no comparison with any other being, whether existent, possible, or fictitious. The conclusion of both arguments is like-

[49]Cf. *Reply to the Second Set of Objections, ibid.*, pp. 45-47.
[50]Cf. *The Author's Reply to the Fifth Set of Objections, ibid.*, p. 228.
[51]*Ibid.*, p. 229.

wise the same, namely, the existence of God. Again, in both instances the means of reaching this conclusion is the analysis of the value-content of the idea.

Yet, despite the similarity in the general structure of the arguments, there are important differences at the basis of the two formulations which make them quite apart from each other. Thus Anselm, the theologian, presupposes that we already believe in God and his argument is but an attempt to rationally justify such a belief. Descartes, the mathematician, by accepting the principle of clear and distinct ideas as a criterion of truth, tries to prove the existence of God from the analysis of the idea of a supremely perfect being which, in accord with his innatism, is clearly and distinctly present to our mind even prior to any contact with outside reality. It is precisely because of his innatism and his proposed criterion of truth based upon it that Descartes' version of the ontological argument, despite certain strong points, becomes more vulnerable than Anselm's original statement of it to the attacks of the critics.

Another chief proponent of the ontological argument in modern times is Gottfried Wilhelm Leibniz, whose system is in many respects compatible with the way of thinking developed by both Anselm and Descartes, but especially the latter. A high-ranking mathematician like Descartes, Leibniz attempts to construct a system of philosophy on a purely rational basis and by the use of a rigorous mathematical method. He admits the theory of innate ideas and innate truths, among which he includes the idea of God and the truth of his existence;[52] he teaches that existence is a perfection and a predicate; [53] and he shares the view that ideas have an ontological value of their own. Despite these similarities and his favorable attitude toward the Cartesian form of the ontological argument—he never directly mentions the *ratio Anselmi*—Leibniz takes issue with Descartes' reasoning and terms it

[52]Cf. *New Essays on the Human Understanding,* in *Leibniz: Selections,* ed. P. Wiener (New York: Charles Scribner's Sons, 1951), p. 471.

[53]For Leibniz' teaching on existence as a perfection cf. Gerhardt, *Die philosophischen Schriften von G. W. Leibniz,* Vol. IV, pp. 401-402, or *On the Cartesian Demonstration of the Existence of God,* in *The Philosophical Works of Leibnitz,* trans. George M. Duncan (New Haven: Tuttle, Morehouse and Taylor, 1890), p. 135. Leibniz speaks of existence as a predicate in *New Essays,* Bk. IV, chap. I, par. 7. See *Selections,* p. 461.

an imperfect demonstration of God's existence. The reason is that the argument assumes as true something that is not mathematically evident, namely, that the idea of a supremely perfect being implies no contradiction and is therefore the idea of a possible being. Until this assumption is justified, the argument —which is not a paralogism, as some scholastics, including Thomas Aquinas, maintained—is not convincing.[54] The most that can be drawn out of the argument is that, if God is possible, it follows that he exists.[55]

Elaborating further on this point, Leibniz remarks that it is not uncommon to fall into error by drawing conclusions from ideas whose truth has not been previously established. There are indeed true and false ideas, depending on whether or not the thing in question is possible. Thus we are likely to speak in terms of the fastest possible motion or the highest possible number, and at first glance we seem to have a fairly good idea of what we are talking. But on closer study we realize that there can be no such thing as a fastest motion or a highest number, simply because their notions involve an absurdity. In fact, one can always think without contradiction of a faster motion or a higher number than the preceding ones, since motion and number are of their very nature limited quantities.

Applying this line of reasoning to the argument for the existence of God based on the idea of a most perfect being, Leibniz says that, to make it a valid and cogent proof, it has first to be shown that the idea in question is a true idea or such that it involves no contradiction.[56] Leibniz proposes a way to show this.

A most perfect being is that which possesses all perfections, i.e., those simple qualities which are positive and absolute inasmuch as they express what they do without any limitation whatsoever. Now, there is nothing in the nature of such qualities that

[54]*New Essays*, in *Selections*, p. 472. As pointed out in connection with his reply to the second set of *Objections*, Descartes had actually tried to show that God is possible because the idea that we have of him implies no contradiction (cf. text referred to in n. 49 above). However, this reflection is somewhat incidental and is not found in Descartes' original presentation of the argument to which Leibniz refers.

[55]See *Meditations on Knowledge, Truth and Ideas*, in *Gottfried Wilhelm Leibniz: Philosophical Papers and Letters*, trans. Leroy M. Loemker (Chicago: University of Chicago Press, 1956), Vol. I, p. 451

[56]*Ibid.* See also *Discourse on Metaphysics*, in *Selections*, p. 324.

would make them incompatible with one another, since they are simple realities that cannot be resolved into, or defined by, any other reality short of losing their characteristic of absolute simplicity. On the other hand, there is no evidence that such perfections are not compatible with one another. Hence a being that embodies all such perfections is possible because it is conceivable, and if it is possible, it must exist, since existence is supposedly one of its perfections.[57]

The same argument is presented in a slightly different way in the *Monadology*. Whatever reality there is in essences, whether they are actual or only possible, it must be grounded in an actually existing being. This being must be necessary, that is, one in which essence includes existence, or else it could not be the source of all other essences and possibilities. Hence this being, which we call God, has the unique prerogative that it must exist if it is possible. And since nothing can hinder the possibility of that which is the source of all possibilities and is therefore infinitely perfect, the existence of God is thus established a priori.[58]

Leibniz' arguments can perhaps be reduced to the following syllogism. It is possible for a necessary being to exist, for its notion implies no contradiction. But if a necessary being is possible, it must exist, for existence is part of its nature. Therefore a necessary being, i.e., God, exists.

This, then, is Leibniz' version of the ontological argument, and he presents it both as an improvement upon the Cartesian proof and as an original contribution to the solution of the problem at hand. Was he justified in his claims? As for his first contention, Koyré seems to disagree on the grounds that by reducing the argument to the analytic proposition "The necessary being exists," Leibniz deprives the Cartesian proof of its ontological foundation and makes it an easy target for Kant's criticism. "In truth," says Koyré, "it is in its analytic character that lies its weakness. He [Leibniz] failed to see that the idea of perfection constituted a necessary foundation of the argument and

[57]The substance of this argument is contained in a paper entitled "Quod Ens perfectissimum existit," which Leibniz showed to Spinoza at The Hague in November, 1676. See Gerhardt, *op. cit.*, Vol. VII, pp. 261-62. See also *New Essays Concerning Human Understanding by Gottfried Wilhelm Leibnitz*, trans. Alfred G. Langley (3d ed.; Chicago: Open Court, 1949), Appendix X, pp. 714-15.

[58]Cf. *Monadology*, Nos. 44-45, in *Selections*, pp. 541-42.

that by eliminating it he deprived the demonstration of all its strength."[59] On the other hand, Hartshorne praises Leibniz for his attempt "to establish the logical possibility of the theistic concept," but observes at the same time that his failure to distinguish between existence and necessary existence as a perfection of an essence "betrays the persistent influence of Anselm's initial blunder."[60] The opponents of the ontological argument in any of its forms would of course blame Leibniz for confusing the logical or ideal order with the order of reality and for equating negative possibility, i.e., mere absence of evident contradiction, with positive possibility, which in the case of God can only be known through a clear and distinct idea of the divine essence or as a result of arguments a posteriori. Clearly, then, the value of Leibniz' version of the ontological argument, not otherwise than that of Descartes' version, rests on whatever strength and validity their rationalistic tenets may have, as we have previously indicated.

With regard to Leibniz' second contention, namely, that his version of the argument represents an original contribution to the understanding of the issue at hand, it is clear that historical evidence is against it, although Leibniz may not have known this. Duns Scotus, as shown in our previous study of the subject, had long before preceded Leibniz in pointing out the need to strengthen the Anselmian proof by showing, first, the noncontradiction, and hence the possibility, of a being than which no greater can be conceived, and secondly, the necessity for such a being to exist. Moreover, because Scotus had a more realistic approach to philosophy, he was able to prove these two points much more effectively than Leibniz did. The difference between the Leibnizian and the Scotistic versions of the argument is due mainly to the different philosophical background of their authors, but with an added qualification. Whereas Leibniz thought of his asserted newly revised argument as a strict demonstration of God's existence, Scotus was much more cautious and said that his "coloration" of the argument made it more acceptable but refrained from labeling it a strict philosophical demonstration. It is regrettable that while historians of philosophy, today even more than in the past, devote considerable study to

[59]Alexandre Koyré, *L'idée de Dieu dans la philosophie de St. Anselme* (Paris: Leroux, 1923), p. 232.

[60]Charles Hartshorne, *Anselm's Discovery: A Re-examination of the Ontological proof for God's Existence* (La Salle, Ill.: Open Court, 1965), p. 178.

Leibniz' rendition of the argument, they give only a passing reference to Scotus' interpretation of the *ratio Anselmi,* which is not only original but also more objective and better balanced.

Any treatment of the *ratio Anselmi* must include the name and doctrine of Immanuel Kant, who is responsible for the coining and popularization of the term ontological argument[61] and who, more than anybody else, has influenced the course of the entire philosophical movement after him. Kant has set a pattern for most of the criticism of the argument in modern and contemporary times, even though few of the argument's opponents would be willing to subscribe to those very fundamental positions of the *Critique of Pure Reason* which have determined its author's rejection of the argument. It is necessary therefore to place Kant's criticism within its literary and historical context in order to get a full understanding of his position on what appeared to be then, perhaps even more than now, a very controversial issue.

Kant discusses the ontological argument in Chapter III, Section IV of his Transcendental Dialectic. The chapter carries the title: "Of the Impossibility of an Ontological Proof of the Existence of God." In the course of his discussion he never mentions Anselm's name or his *Proslogion* and only toward the end of it he speaks of "the famous ontological argument of Descartes" after a somewhat casual reference to "the celebrated Leibniz." The study of the text of the *Critique* and its immediate sources seems to indicate that Kant did not know that Anselm was the true author of the argument, which he attributes to Descartes but presents in the form given to it by Leibniz. Actually, Kant does not even present Leibniz' own version of the argument but only its reformulation by Christian Wolff as found in Baumgarten's *Metaphysica* and Eberhard's *Vorbereitung zur natürlichen Theologie,* a teacher's manual.[62] Needless to say, Gaunilo seems to have been completely unknown to Kant, despite the fact that Gaunilo had anticipated many centuries before most of the objections made by Kant and others against the Anselmian proof. One ought not to be surprised, however, at this obvious disregard for basic rules of scholarship in a man who, even more than Descartes,

[61]Cf. Dieter Henrich, *Der Ontologische Gottesbeweis* (Tübingen: Mohr, 1960), p. 1, n. 1.

[62]Cf. Koyré, *op. cit.,* p. 231; James Collins, *The Emergence of Philosophy of Religion* (New Haven: Yale University Press, 1967), p. 102, n. 10.

attempted to revolutionize the whole course of philosophy by setting it on a new foundation and giving it an entirely new direction. His ambitious work, *Prolegomena to Any Future Metaphysics,* is an anticipation of the revolutionary plan that culminated in his three *Critiques.* It is within this plan that his criticism of the ontological argument must be studied and evaluated.

Kant states categorically that there are and there can only be three ways by which speculative reason can prove the existence of God. Two of these ways take their start from sensible experience and are called the physico-theological and cosmological arguments, while the third way proceeds from mere mental concepts and is therefore entirely a priori. This he calls the ontological argument, that is, an attempt to prove the existence of God from the concept we have of a most perfect or most real being *(ens perfectissimum* or *ens realissimum),* or simply from the idea of a necessary being.

Kant recognizes that men at all times have tried to prove the existence of an absolutely necessary being, but he claims that seldom have they made an effort to understand whether or not that idea makes any sense at all. He does not question the possibility of a verbal definition of the concept but rather raises doubts as to the content or reality underlying that concept. He maintains that the stereotyped examples taken from geometry, such as the absolute necessity that a triangle have three angles, are deceitful, for such necessity refers to judgments alone. It is a pure logical necessity which has no bearing on the reality of things, let alone on their existence.

In propositions of that nature, which Kant calls identical propositions, it is of course contradictory to reject the predicate while retaining the subject, because the predicate necessarily belongs to the subject. Thus it is contradictory to accept a triangle and reject its three angles; but there is no contradiction in rejecting both the triangle and its three angles. The same principle holds true, Kant argues, for the concept of an absolutely necessary being. One can simply dismiss its notion altogether by removing the existence of that being along with all its predicates, and if this is done no question of contradiction will ever arise.

At this point Kant realizes that his opponents, such as Descartes and Leibniz—and to them we must add Anselm—would not be impressed by this line of reasoning and that at best it would appear naive to them. Indeed, the concept of a necessary being, or of a most real being for that matter, is precisely such that one cannot remove the existence of its object without contradicting himself. The analogy of the triangle, they would suggest, is besides the point, for existence is not of the nature of a triangle. In the case of a necessary being, however, existence is so much part of its nature that one cannot, not even mentally, separate the one from the other.

Kant's answer to this objection is in accord with his preconceived theory that every proposition involving existence is synthetical, i.e., it must be based on experience, and this in the case at hand is completely lacking. To attempt to derive existence from a mere concept, be it the concept of a necessary being, is to commit a tautology. This holds true, Kant remarks, even in the case of a possible being, which becomes an empty concept unless it rests on principles of possible experience. Briefly, it is wrong to argue directly from the logical possibility of concepts to the real possibility of things.

This last observation leads Kant to discuss the distinction between logical predicate and real predicate. A logical predicate is one that abstracts from the content of the concept, for logic has no bearing on the reality of things. A real predicate, on the other hand, is one that determines a thing by adding something to its concept. Now being or existence, Kant continues, is not a real predicate, for it adds nothing that is not already contained in the concept of the subject. It is merely the positing of a thing, or of certain determinations, as existing in themselves.[63] Thus, when I say "God is," or "There is a God," I only posit the subject (God) with all its predicates, such as omnipotence and omniscience, as an object in relation to my concept. On this score, any distinction between the real and the possible disappears, since both are on the same conceptual level. "A hundred real dollars"—Kant uses the term thalers—"do not contain a penny more than a hundred possible dollars."

Needless to say, Kant observes, my financial position is affected quite differently by a hundred real dollars than it is by the same amount of merely possible dollars, but this is due to the

[63]For a detailed analysis of Kant's notion of logical and real predicates and their application to the problem under discussion see S. Morris Engel, "Kant's Refutation of the Ontological Argument," in *Kant: A Collection of Critical Essays,* ed. Robert P. Wolff ("Anchor Books"; Garden City, N.Y.: Doubleday, 1967), pp. 189-208.

fact that in the former case the object has been added to my concept synthetically. This, Kant suggests, is possible when the object in question can be known experimentally; but in the case of a supreme being no such knowledge is possible. Our only way of thinking of its existence is through a purely a priory form or category of the understanding which does not allow us to distinguish between actual and possible existence.

Hence, Kant concludes, even though the concept of a supreme being is in many respects a very useful concept, it in no way helps us to attain to the knowledge of God's existence, or even the possibility of his existence. "The attempt to establish the existence of a supreme being by means of the famous ontological argument of Descartes is therefore merely so much labor and effort lost.[64]

At first glance this appears to be a devastating analysis of the ontological argument: an analysis that has far-reaching consequences, inasmuch as it is to this form of argument that Kant will ultimately reduce what he believes to be the only two other possible proofs of God's existence, namely, the cosmological and the physico-theological arguments.[65] As we go through Kant's systematic and unrelenting demolition of all the structures on which the argument has been so carefully built by its authors, we may get the impression that the argument would never be able to survive the severe blow administered to it by the author of the *Critique*. But history has proved that this is not true. In the words of a recent author, "the [ontological] argument is like an eel: now you think that you have it in a conclusive form, and it slips away: now you think that you have killed it, and lo it lives again. The eel has wriggled for centuries, and will go on wriggling, for all the handling of Descartes and Leibniz, Kant, and you and me."[66]

Despite Kant's vigorous attacks, the argument is as alive today as it was at his time. The growing literature on the subject is sufficient evidence of this. However, this fact does not dispense

[64]Cf. *Immanuel Kant's Critique of Pure Reason,* trans. Norman K. Smith (Reprint; London: Macmillan, 1933), p. 507. For Kant's discussion of the ontological argument as presented in our paper see *ibid.*, pp. 499-507.

[65]*Ibid.*, p. 524: "Thus the physico-theological proof of the existence of an original or supreme being rests upon the cosmological proof, and the cosmological upon the ontological."

[66]Joseph Rickaby, S. J., *Studies on God and His Creatures* (London-New York: Longmans, Green and Co., 1924), pp. 63-64.

us from taking a closer look at Kant's criticism in order to see whether he really accomplished what he hoped to do.

Simply stated, Kant's position is that it is impossible to infer God's existence merely from the concept we have of him as of a most perfect or necessary being, because existence is not a perfection or predicate contained in that concept. Taken at its face value, Kant's reasoning is not much different from that of Gaunilo or Aquinas, and even his analogy of the hundred dollars is very similar to, although less pertinent than, Gaunilo's celebrated example of the most beautiful island. But if we analyze carefully Kant's criticism, we will see that it is much more destructive than it may first appear to be. At the root of the whole problem is Kant's epistemological theory that makes it impossible for speculative reason to attain to any knowledge that is not confined to sensible appearances of the objects of our experience. On such assumption it is pointless to speak of a proof for the existence of God, who by his very nature transcends all sense experience, whether such proof be based on the concept we have of him or be grounded in the reality of the material world, for even this reality cannot be reached by our reason. There is no way, in Kan't system, to attain to the knowledge of things in themselves or noumena; all we know is their appearances or phenomena.

Kant, it must be admitted, does not completely eliminate existence from his critical philosophy, but he reduces it to one of those a priori forms of the understanding—the power of thinking or judging as distinct from both pure and practical reason—by means of which the data of our sensible experience are synthesized. Consequently, for him existence is no longer a mode of an essence, as it is for rationalists such as Leibniz and Wolff, but a modality of judgment expressing the relationship of the object of sense intuition, the phenomenon, to our cognitive faculty. "The categories of modality," Kant writes in this connection, "have the peculiarity that, in determining an object, they do not in the least enlarge the concept to which they are attached as predicates. They only express the relation of the concept to the faculty of knowledge."[67]

As can be seen, Kant's attack on the ontological argument is part of a major systematic attack on the whole of natural theology and metaphysics, precisely as he had planned in his *Prolegomena*

[67]Cf. *Critique of Pure Reason, op. cit.*, p. 239.

to Any Future Metaphysics. In its introduction he writes: "My purpose is to persuade all those who think metaphysics worth studying that it is absolutely necessary to pause for a moment and, regarding all that has been done as though undone, to propose first the preliminary question, 'Whether such a thing as metaphysics be even possible at all.' "[68] His answer, as we know, will be a categorical "No." It is true that the metaphysics he had in mind is primarily the metaphysics of Leibniz and Wolff which is concerned with essences and the possibles rather than with actually existing things; but there is no doubt that in his mind even traditional metaphysics had lost all right to existence. It is in this broader context that Kant's attack on the ontological argument must be seen. Yet, despite Kant's negative attitude toward the ontological argument and metaphysics, it remains to his credit that he admitted in his precritical period the value of the theistic proof based on the possibles[69] and acknowledged in his *Critique of Pure Reason* the value of the idea of God, whose existence, together with freedom of the will and immortality of the soul, became for him postulates of practical reason.

IV. *Koyré, Barth, and Gilson*

While Kant has set a pattern of criticism of the ontological argument that has been adopted in various degrees by many subsequent thinkers both within and outside the Kantian tradition, there have been philosophers who accepted the argument and adapted

[68] Immanuel Kant, *Prolegomena to Any Future Metaphysics,* ed. Lewis White Beck (Indianapolis-New York: Bobbs-Merrill, 1950), p. 3.

[69] Cf. *Der einzig mögliche Beweisgrund zu einer Demonstration des Daseins Gottes,* in *Immanuel Kant: Werke in sechs Bänden,* ed. Wilhelm Weischedel, I (Wiesbaden: Insel, 1960), 617-738. Hartshorne writes in this connection: "In spite of his negative attitude toward theoretical theism, Kant, in the essay *Der einzig mögliche Beweisgrund des Daseins Gottes,* makes a contribution to theism which should never again be lost and which is not invalidated by anything himself later said." *Anselm's Discovery, op. cit.,* p. 211. It must be said, however, that Leibniz had already anticipated Kant's reasoning in his *Monadology.* See text referred to in n. 58 above. For a discussion of the theistic argument from the possible see this writer's study, "The Ideological Argument for God's Existence," *Studies in Philosophy and the History of Philosophy,* I (1961), 1-34.

it to their own particular system, such as Hegel[70] and Maurice Blondel.[71] A study of these variations of the argument would carry us too far and besides it would contribute little, if anything, to the understanding of the issues connected with the original Anselmian proof. We therefore pass them by and take up certain more recent interpretations of the argument with a view to broadening our perspective of it.

A penetrating analysis of Anselm's proof within the general context and historical background of his entire philosophical and theological thought has been made by Alexandre Koyré, whose work, *L'idée de Dieu dans la philosophie de St. Anselme,* has been widely acclaimed by the experts. Convinced that the argument of the *Proslogion* "which alone would have assured the immortality of its author" is but the conclusion and crowning of Anselm's entire theodicy,[72] Koyré discusses it only in the last two chapters of his volume, while in Appendix I he examines the psychological interpretation of the argument given by Dom Beda Adloch[73] and in Appendix II he makes a comparative study of Kant's criticism with Gaunilo's objections to the argument.[74]

In Koyre's view the *Proslogion* is an apologetic work concerned chiefly with the existence of God, which Anselm attempts to prove indirectly by showing against the fool of the Psalmist the logical impossibility of denying it. The basis of the demonstration

[70]For Hegel's formulation of the ontological argument see *Beweise für das Dasein Gottes,* Appendix to his *Vorlesungen über die Philosophie der Religion,* ed. Philipp Marheineke, II (Berlin: Duncker und Humblot, 1832), 466-83, trans. by E. B. Speirs and J. B. Sanderson as *Lectures on the Philosophy of Religion by Georg Wilhelm Friedrich Hegel,* III (Reprint; New York: The Humanities Press, 1968), 347-67. See also Hegel's *Vorlesungen über die Geschichte der Philosophie,* ed. Karl L. Michelet, III (Berlin: Duncker und Humblot, 1836), 164-69, trans. by E. S. Haldane and F. H. Simson as *Hegel's Lectures on the History of Philosophy* (Reprint; New York: The Humanities Press, 1968), 61-67.

[71]Cf. *L'Action* (Reprint of 1893 edition; Paris: Presses Universitaires de France, 1950), p. 348. See also James M. Somerville, *Total Commitment: Blondel's L'Action* (Washington, D.C.: Corpus Books, 1968), pp. 221-23. For a study of Blondel's original way of arguing to God see the present writer's article, "Maurice Blondel: The Method of Immanence As an Approach to God," in *Twentieth-Century Thinkers,* ed. John K. Ryan (Staten Island, N.Y.: Alba House, 1965), pp. 37-58.

[72]Koyré, *L'idée de Dieu, op. cit.,* p. vii.

[73]*Ibid.,* pp. 228-30.

[74]*Ibid.,* pp. 231-40.

is the neo-Platonic principle of perfection, which makes it possible to assert a priori a real existence and to argue from perfection to being. Although it is a demonstration a priori, it is not an ontological proof in the strict sense of the term. Moreover, contrary to what is being held by many commentators, there is no textual evidence to the effect that Anselm would have identified being and perfection. What he says is that a being endowed with perfection and existence is more perfect than a being with the same nature but without existence. This does not imply in any way that existence itself is a perfection.[75]

By combining the principles of perfection and contradiction, Anselm endeavors to prove not only the metaphysical impossibility of the nonexistence of God but also, and even more so, the logical impossibility of conceiving his nonexistence. It is precisely by showing the impossibility of denying the existence of God that he argues to its affirmation. This, contends Koyré, is the characteristic of Anselm's proof that distinguishes it from the Cartesian proof based on clear and distinct ideas of the divine nature.[76] Furthermore, Anselm's proof is autonomous, in the sense that it presupposes neither the existence of creatures nor any concept derived from them. Its only basis is the concept of God.[77]

If the proof does not convince the fool, and if it is unable to convert an unbeliever, to do so is not the purpose in the mind of its author. His purpose is to show to a believer that no argument can ever undermine his belief in God simply because no argument affects or even touches upon the content of his faith.[78]

Koyré believes, as do many other commentators, that Anselm's debate with Gaunilo is not only extremely enlightening, but that it contains the answer to most of the objections raised against the argument since Gaunilo's time. Anselm's demonstration, as evidenced by his *Reply* to Gaunilo, can be synthesized in the formula: if God is possible, he exists necessarily. The inference from possibility *(posse)* to existence *(esse)* is made through the impossibility of conceiving the nonexistence of the being in question *(non posse concipi non esse)*, from which it follows the necessity of conceiving it as existing *(necesse concipi esse)*, or, if one prefers, the necessity

[75]*Ibid.*, pp. 195-98.
[76]*Ibid.*, pp. 200-201 and n. 1.
[77]*Ibid.*, p. 202.
[78]*Ibid.*, pp. 204-205.

of existence can be inferred directly from the impossibility of non-existing *(non posse non esse ergo necesse esse)*.[79] We can therefore distinguish two different parts or moments in the Anselmian argument: the hypothetical part, which is the a priori element of the proof, and the synthetic part—Koyré calls it *thétique*—which is a factual truth. The first part of the argument contains an absolutely necessary truth, namely, that if God is possible, he must exist. But this truth does not involve in any way the actual existence of God. It merely affirms the necessary relationship between possibility and necessity of existence in God: a unique and extremely interesting relationship whose discovery and formulation are a perennial credit to Anselm. Yet the actual transition from possibility to existence in God can only be made in terms of another premise that turns conceptual possibility into real, factual possibility. In other words, it is necessary to prove first that God is possible, unless of course one is willing to accept such possibility without the benefit of a proof.

As far as a believer is concerned, Anselm would say that the assurance of the possibility of God is given to him by faith. Hence for him the synthetic part of the argument needs no proof: all he needs is the hypothetic part. It is only for the fool or the unbeliever that the two parts of the argument are needed. The fool will no doubt be able to understand the absurdity of denying God, but there is no way to prove to him the possibility of God. All one can do is to reduce him to silence, and that is precisely what Anselm intended to do. However, Koyré suggests, if we consider the *Monologium,* where the possibility of God is solidly established, as a preparation for or an introduction to the *Proslogion,* then we have in the two works a complete demonstration a priori of the existence of God.[80]

On the strength of this analysis, it is only to be expected that Koyré will consider the *ratio Anselmi* a much better argument than the one transmitted to us by Descartes and Leibniz, especially the latter. It will also be easy for him to refute both Gaunilo's ob-

[79]Koyré bases his formula on Anselm's *Liber apologeticus,* chap. I; PL 158, 249: "Certe ego dico: si vel cogitari potest esse, necesse est illud esse . . . Si ergo potest cogitari esse, ex necessitate est. Amplius. Si utique vel cogitari potest, necesse est illud esse."

[80]Koyré, *L'idée de Dieu,* pp. 209-211.

jections to the argument to which he devotes the entire Chapter X of his work[81] and the criticism of Kant, whom he blames "for demanding something that is absolutely impossible and has no sense whatsoever."[82] This is a severe judgment to pass on so towering figure as Kant, but no more severe than the judgment Kant passed on the ontological argument when he termed it a waste of labor and effort. Such remarks are obviously due to radically opposed ideologies and call for no further comment at this time. Instead we shall proceed in our survey and consider another prominent and much better known figure, whose interpretation of the Anselmian proof has stirred a great deal of discussion and controversy.

Like Koyré, whom he frequently quotes, Karl Barth has made Anselm's argument the object of extensive study. Approaching the subject from the viewpoint of a theologian and within the context of Anselm's theological scheme, he prefaces his book, *Anselm: Fides quaerens intellectum,* by saying that Anselm's proof of the existence of God is "a model piece of good, penetrating and neat theology . . . that has quite a bit to say to present-day theology, both Protestant and Roman Catholic."[83] Barth does not consider the Anselmian *argumentum* as being limited to the proof of Chapters 2-4 of the *Proslogion,* but rather as a kind of *argumentatio* that extends throughout the entire work, even though the largest part of it is devoted to the study of the nature of God. However, for the purpose of his inquiry he confines himself to an analysis of the proof as set forth in *Proslogion 2-4*.

Beginning with the concept of proof, Barth claims that in Anselm the term has not precisely the meaning of *probare* but rather the more general connotation of *intelligere:* it is an *intelligere* that issues in a *probare*. Hence to prove means that "the validity of certain propositions advocated by Anselm is established over against those who doubt or deny them; that is to say, it means the polemical-apologetic result of *intelligere*."[84] Besides, the only *intelligere* that concerns Anselm is that which is aroused by faith. This, he says, is

[81] *Ibid.*, pp. 212-25.

[82] *Ibid.*, p. 234.

[83] Karl Barth, *Anselm: Fides quaerens intellectum* ("Meridian Books"; Cleveland and New York: The World Publishing Co., 1962), p. 9.

[84] *Ibid.*, p. 14.

the meaning of the Anselmian *Credo ut intelligam,* I believe in order to understand.[85]

Barth's initial position on the notion of the Anselmian proof affects his treatment of the *Proslogion* by limiting its scope and depriving it of that particular probative feature that, rightly or wrongly, has fascinated philosophers of different persuasions. In Barth's view only theologians will profit from Anselm's proof which, having been reduced chiefly to *intelligere,* "can consist only of positive meditation on the object of faith" but "cannot establish this object of faith as such."[86] Barth feels however that although Anselm's proof—if we can still speak of proof—is directed primarily to a believer, it remains the same even from the viewpoint of an unbeliever, for "the unbeliever's quest [for knowledge of God] is not simply taken up in a casual fashion and incorporated into the theological task but all the way through it is in fact treated as identical with the quest of the believer himself."[87]

Once the nature of the *Proslogion* has been defined in terms of *Faith in Search of Understanding,* which was indeed the original subtitle of the work, Barth goes on to analyze the relationship between *ratio* and *necessitas* in Anselm's approach to faith, with special reference to the problem of our knowledge of God. Here are some of his conclusions: (1) The *necessitas* that is characteristic of the object of faith is the impossibility of this object not to exist or to be otherwise than it is, as well as the impossibility for thought to conceive it as not existing or as existing differently. (2) The *ratio* peculiar to the object of faith is the fact that its existence conforms to law and that it exists in this particular way, along with the other fact that the knowledge of it is the conception of that conformity and of that particular kind of existence. From these considerations it follows that, with regard to the object of faith, ontic necessity precedes noetic necessity. This means that the rational knowledge of the object of faith is derived from the object of faith and not vice versa. Ultimately, both the object of faith and its knowledge are derived from Truth, i.e., from God and his will.[88]

On these premises Barth approaches the actual "proof" of *Pros-*

[85] *Ibid.,* pp. 16-18.
[86] *Ibid.,* pp. 39-40.
[87] *Ibid.,* p. 67.
[88] *Ibid.,* pp. 49-52.

logion 2–4, which he claims to be based on the assumption of a name of God whose meaning implies that the statement "God exists" is necessary. Anselm translates this name in terms of a being than which no greater can be conceived, but this is not a concept of his own; it is a revealed concept, just as the existence of God is a revealed doctrine. What Anselm tries to do is to show that the existence of God, which he accepts on faith, must be recognized and proved on the presupposition of the name of God likewise accepted on faith and must be understood "as necessary for thought."[89] Furthermore, he wants to show that the necessity of the existence of God that is forced, as it were, upon our mind, cannot be merely a conceptual necessity, but is such that belongs to God himself and makes it impossible for us even to think of his nonexistence. This is of course a development of the data of our faith and the particular contribution that Anselm has made to Christian theology.[90]

In his work Barth follows the various steps of the Anselmian proof, which he presents on the strength of the first chapters of the *Proslogion* and integrates with many valuable insights from Anselm's dialogue with Gaunilo. He concludes his analysis by saying that "the whole effort of *Proslogion 2–3* has been to prove conclusively that God cannot be conceived as not existing. The demonstration that this is impossible is Anselm's proof of the existence of God."[91] Then, summing up his understanding of the proof, he insists once more that "it is a question of theology; . . . a question of the proof of faith by faith which was already established in itself without proof."[92] Hence any interpretation of the Anselmian argument along the lines of Descartes and Leibniz is altogether inaccurate, while Kant's criticism of the proof "is so much nonsense on which no more words ought to be wasted."[93]

As was to be expected, Barth's theological interpretation of the Anselmian proof led a number of scholars to take a new look at the *Proslogion* and see whether his conclusions were warranted by the text. One of these scholars is Etienne Gilson, whose unique competence in the field of scholastic philosophy is universally recog-

[89]*Ibid.,* p. 78.
[90]*Ibid.,* pp. 94-95.
[91]*Ibid.,* p. 165.
[92]*Ibid.,* p. 170.
[93]*Ibid.,* p. 171.

nized. Gilson had already touched upon the *Proslogion* argument in other writings, but the appearance of Barth's volume induced him to take up the issue anew and give it a fuller consideration. In his article, *Sens et nature de l'argument de Saint Anselme,*[94] which contains the four last lectures of a course on the doctrine of Saint Anselm offered at the Collège de France in 1934, he presents first his own interpretation of the Anselmian proof, then he compares it with the theological and mystical interpretations of Karl Barth and Anselm Stolz respectively, and finally he concludes with a section on the nature of the *Proslogion.* Our concern here will be chiefly his understanding of the proof in relation to Barth's view of it.

Gilson agrees with Barth that the argument of the *Proslogion* presupposes a concept of God from revelation that represents an object or *res* by which the concept is determined. Hence, for Anselm the question of whether it is possible to draw existence from thought is irrelevant, since the starting point of the argument is a real concept and not merely a logical one.[95] Gilson also agrees with Barth's theory that for Anselm a truth of faith is independent of rational speculation, so that a doctrine of faith does not need to be understood to be believed but may nevertheless be an aid to our intelligence to understand it: *credo ut intelligam.* He goes further and grants Barth the fundamental point that for Anselm reason will never be able to create its own truth, as if it were possible to have a double set of truths, one from faith and one from reason. To hold the contrary is to directly contradict Anselm who admits that thought must submit to, or be determined by, the object. Having made these concessions, Gilson asks himself whether the *Proslogion* argument is merely a piece of theology, as Barth thinks it to be, and his answer is an unequivocal "No." Here are his reasons.

To begin with, Gilson remarks that Barth seems to have very little use for philosophy, which he considers to be a worldly subject foreign to God and whatever pertains to him. Because this Calvinistic attitude toward philosophy permeates his whole approach to Anselm, Barth is unable to see how it is possible to have a rational argument for the existence of God, such as that of

[94]The article appeared in *Archives d'histoire doctrinale et littéraire du Moyen Age,* IX (Paris: Vrin, 1934), 5-51.

[95]*Ibid.*, pp. 6-8.

the *Proslogion,* without falling into ontologism. Hence, if it is not an ontological argument, Barth sees no other alternative: it must be purely theological or, in other words, no argument at all, for one does not prove the existence of God which he accepts on faith as an assumption of his proof. All he can do is to show how God's existence is possible, and that is precisely what in Barth's view Anselm would have done.[96]

Yet, Gilson continues, this is not what we read in the *Proslogion,* where Anselm states explicitly his intention of producing an argument which alone could establish that God truly exists *(ad astruendum quia Deus vere est).* Likewise, in his *Reply* to Gaunilo he speaks of the force of his proof: *Tantam enim vim huius probationis in se continet significatio,* an expression that Barth, to Gilson's surprise, has wrongly translated to fit into his own preconceived theory. It is not true, therefore, that Anselm builds his argument on the *name* of God known to us by revelation, for nowhere in Scripture is God called "a being than which no greater can be conceived," which is Anselm's point of departure. If the argument were built on the name of God known by revelation, then it would be the name of a person and the existence of God would be assumed at the very outset of the proof. This is of course what Barth wants us to believe, but textual evidence seems to run against him. The truth is that Anselm's argument takes as its starting point the *concept* of God as the supreme conceivable being, which is quite different from what Barth says.[97]

This raises the issue as to whether or not, despite the concept of God that Anselm assumes from revelation, it is still possible to speak in terms of a demonstration of God's existence. This is an important issue that has to be solved in order to establish the legitimacy of his claim, especially because there are historians who refuse to see in Anselm's argument any attempt at a real demonstration of the existence of God. To solve this problem, Gilson suggests, one must go once more to Anselm himself and see what was his intention in structuring the argument.

Anselm tells us that as a result of his discourse on God he has shown that the being than which no greater can be conceived exists not only in our mind *(in intellectu)* but also in reality *(in re).* Besides, unless he wanted to deceive us about his intention, he has

[96]*Ibid.,* pp. 22-24.
[97]*Ibid.,* pp. 25-28.

also made it clear that by proving the rational necessity of affirming the existence of God, or the rational impossibility of denying it, he has truly proved God's existence. He must have been convinced therefore, if we are willing to grant him that minimum of logical coherence one can expect from a philosopher, that the necessity for reason to affirm an existence—the existence of God in this case—fully guarantees the fact of that existence. Short of this his whole demonstration becomes useless. This in turn leads us to admit that the necessity of the above affirmation supposes the necessity of its object. Hence, Gilson argues, "unless the argument of the *Proslogion* be devoid of meaning, it must necessarily be inserted within a doctrine of truth to be conceived in such a way that the very existence of truths always presupposes the existence of their objects." And that is precisely the case with the *Proslogion,* a work that presupposes Anselm's previous treatise *De veritate,* where he laid down the epistemological foundation of his entire doctrine, including his doctrine on God.[98]

In this sense Gilson endorses without reservation Barth's view that in Anselm's teaching there can be no question about the creative and normative role of human reason in regard to truth, because it has none. "There will never be a God," he rightly observes, "because our reason has devised proofs for his existence, but there are proofs for the existence of God because there is a God."[99] Where ontic necessity precedes noetic necessity, as Barth well states, truth is caused by its object, which in the case of Anselm's argument is God himself. Summing up Anselm's reasoning, Gilson writes that Anselm starts from the word "God," next proceeds to analyze the meaning of that word, and then, from the analysis of that meaning in terms of "a being than which no greater can be conceived," concludes that God, the being in question, cannot exist merely in our understanding but must also exist in actual reality. And since there is nothing to stand between our thought and God except the meaning of that term, the cause of the truth of the argument's conclusion can only be sought in God himself, the source of all truth.[100]

On the basis of this analysis of the Anselmian proof, which he offers as a counterpart to Barth's understanding of it, Gilson con-

98*Ibid.,* pp. 8-9.
99*Ibid.,* pp. 10-11.
100*Ibid.,* p. 12.

cludes that between the two interpretations there stands the whole distance that separates Catholicism from Calvinism. "There is one Catholic way of maintaining that the *Proslogion* is the work of a theologian," and this aims to safeguard the rights of God without jeopardizing the rights of a reason created by God. "There is a Calvinistic way of maintaining the same thing," and it consists in safeguarding the rights of God at the expense of human reason, whose only right, or rather duty, is to repeat the word of God. Gilson feels that Barth has committed the mistake of trying to draw Anselm over to his own side.[101]

If we now look back at these three last interpretations of the Anselmian argument, we can see that, despite their obvious differences, they have many points in common. For one thing, each of them attempts to visualize the argument from the perspective of its author's Platonic–Augustinian thought and present it as a reflection on a concept of God known by revelation and whose truth–value is ultimately determined by God himself. The three authors do not quite agree whether or to what extent the argument is a proof for the existence of God, but all of them are apparently convinced that the value of the argument cannot be determined merely on logical or empirical grounds. Moreover, it seems to be their common understanding, which Gilson for one states explicitly,[102] that for the complete argument both Chapters 2 and 3 of the *Proslogion* must be considered, the third chapter being the necessary complement of the second.

Recently some of these ideas have been challenged, especially since the advent of logical positivism and analytic philosophy, whose followers have submitted the argument to their own criterion of truth.[103] It would be a long and tedious task to make even a brief survey of the massive amount of contemporary literature on the

[101]*Ibid.,* pp. 28-29.

[102]"Le chapitre III du *Proslogion* ne doit, sous aucun prétexte, être considéré comme séparable du chapitre II, ni inversement." *Ibid.,* p. 13.

[103]Surprisingly enough, even Bertrand Russell thought at one time that the ontological argument was valid. He writes: "I remember the precise moment, one day in 1894, as I was walking along Trinity Lane, when I saw in a flash (or thought I saw) that the ontological argument is valid. I had gone out to buy a tin of tobacco; on my way back, I suddenly threw it up in the air, and exclaimed as I caught it: 'Great Scott, the ontological argument is sound.' " Cf. Bertrand Russell, "My Mental Development," in *The Philosophy of Bertrand Russell,* ed Paul A. Schilpp (Evanston and Chicago, Ill.: Northwestern University, 1944), p. 10.

subject.[104] We shall rather focus our attention on two recent interpretations of the argument whose originality and challenging nature make them particularly interesting and worthy of our consideration. These are the interpretations of Norman Malcolm and Charles Hartshorne.

V. *Malcolm and Hartshorne*

Malcolm contends that the *Proslogion* argument contains two distinct pieces of reasoning, and therefore two distinct arguments for the existence of God. Anselm's failure to make a proper distinction between them has caused great confusion among his interpreters.[105] The first argument is stated in Chapter 2 and is essentially the argument that later was taken up by Descartes and developed by him in his own way. It consists in saying that a being than which no greater can be conceived cannot exist in our understanding alone but must also exist in reality, since otherwise we could think of a greater being that would exist both in the understanding and in reality. Such reasoning presupposes the notion that existence is a perfection, a doctrine that Descartes shared with Anselm. This doctrine, says Malcolm, is not only strange but fallacious as well, and to this effect he quotes Kant's criticism as already

[104] A good collection of recent studies on the ontological argument can be found in *The Many-Faced Argument,* ed. John Hick and Arthur C. McGill (New York: Macmillan, 1967). The work has an excellent bibliography (pp. 357-70) covering the history of the argument from Anselm to the present time and including the principal studies of it by both European and American philosophers. A shorter but very useful collection of studies was edited by Alvin Plantinga under the title, *The Ontological Argument from St. Anselm to Contemporary Philosophers* ("Anchor Books"; Garden City, N. Y.: Doubleday, 1965). A special section of *Religious Studies,* IV (The Cambridge University Press, 1968-1969), is devoted to the ontological argument. It includes the following articles: Leroy T. Howe, "Existence as a Perfection: A Reconsideration of the Ontological Argument," pp. 78-101; David A. Pailin, "Some Comments on Hartshorne's Presentation of the Ontological Argument," pp. 103-122; Charles Crittenden, "The Argument from Perfection to Existence," pp. 123-32; M. J. A. O'Connor, "New Aspects of Omnipotence and Necessity in Anselm," pp. 133-46; Donald F. Henze, "Language-Games and the Ontological Argument," pp. 147-52. The ontological argument is also the subject of several scholarly studies in the *Analecta Anselmiana,* ed. F. S. Schmitt (3 Vols.; Frankfurt/Main: Minerva GMBH, 1969-1972).

[105] Cf. Norman Malcolm, "Anselm's Ontological Arguments," in Plantinga, *op. cit.,* p. 136. (The article is a reprint from *The Philosophical Review,* LXIX (1960), 41-62.

discussed. In doing so, Malcolm makes the interesting observation: "It would be desirable to have a rigorous refutation of the doctrine [that existence is a perfection] but I have not been able to provide one. I am compelled to leave the matter at the more or less intuitive level of Kant's observation."[106] We admire Malcolm's honesty in making such a concession, but we cannot but wonder how seriously his charge that the doctrine holding existence as a perfection is fallacious must be taken. To leave the matter at the intuitive level of Kant's observation is little comfort to those who lack such an intuition and even less to those who may disagree with Kant altogether.

Regardless of what one may think of this issue, which separates two distinct schools of thought and hence two distinct interpretations of the argument, Malcolm does not attach much importance to it, since he does not accept the "first" argument as a valid proof. He notes, however, that Gassendi had already anticipated Kant's criticism when he asserted against Descartes that "existence is a perfection neither in God nor in anything else"—a statement, incidentally, that amounts to a rejection of much of what Malcolm himself will try to defend.

The second ontological proof, Malcolm says, is to be found in Chapter 3 of the *Proslogion*. In it Anselm affirms two things: first, that a being whose nonexistence is logically impossible is "greater" than a being whose nonexistence is logically possible (and therefore that a being a greater that which cannot be conceived must be one whose nonexistence is logically impossible); second, that *God* is a being than which a greater cannot be conceived.[107] It is worth noting that Anselm never speaks of "logical" possibility or "logical" impossibility: the qualification is Malcolm's own addition. This may appear to be a minor point, but in the light of his subsequent observation it is not. In fact, commenting on the second assertion, he remarks that the statements to be drawn from it, namely, that "God is the greatest of all beings," "God is the most perfect being," and the like are *logically* (italics are his) necessary truths in the same way that the statement "A square has four sides" is a logically necessary truth.[108] We do not question the truth of Malcolm's remark. What we do question is the correctness of approaching the

[106] *Ibid.*, p. 140.
[107] *Ibid.*, p. 141.
[108] *Ibid.*

Anselmian proof exclusively from the viewpoint of a logician, as he seems to do.

Going back to Anselm's alleged first assertion, namely, that a being whose nonexistence is logically impossible is greater than a being whose nonexistence is logically possible, Malcolm finds it difficult to accept in this connection the term "greater," which means of course superior or more perfect. This should not come to us as a surprise, since he has already rejected the idea that existence is a perfection. But what puzzles us is his inference from the above assertion that Anselm does not say that existence is a perfection, but rather that *the logical impossibility of nonexistence is a perfection* (Malcolm's italics). In other words, *necessary existence* is a perfection, not existence as such. From which Malcolm concludes that, whereas the first ontological proof rests on the principle that a thing is greater if it exists than if it does not exist, the second proof rests on a quite different principle, namely, that a thing is greater if it necessarily exists than if it does not necessarily exist.[109]

This line of reasoning seems to imply that Anselm has used the term "greater" in two entirely different ways, since in Malcolm's view only the latter use of the term is justified, while the former rests on a faulty principle. However, a reading of Anselm's text does not seem to bear out Malcolm's view, nor does the general context of the *Proslogion* where "greatness" stands for perfection and refers, although in different degrees, to both contingent and necessary existence. Is it not perhaps Malcolm's concern to safeguard, on the one hand, the value of the argument and, on the other hand, the soundness of his own principle, inherited from Kant, that existence is not a perfection that led him to interpret Anselm the way he did? This, at least, it seems to us, is a good question to ask of him.

To illustrate his point, Malcolm has recourse to the concepts we have of God as an absolutely independent and unlimited being and shows that such a being cannot be thought of as dependent on any other being for his existence, any more that it can be conceived as nonexistent at any particular moment of time. Accordingly, he quotes Anselm's *Reply* to Gaunilo to the effect that the notion of contingent existence or contingent nonexistence has no application to God, and concludes:

[109]*Ibid.*, p. 142.

> His [God's] existence must either be logically necessary or logically impossible. The only intelligible way or rejecting Anselm's claim that God's existence is necessary is to maintain that the concept of God, as a being a greater than which cannot be conceived, is self-contradictory or nonsensical. Supposing that this is false, Anselm is right to deduce God's necessary existence from his characterization of him as a being, a greater than which cannot be conceived.[110]

The argument, Malcolm insists, is an priori proof, for "the proposition 'God necessarily exists' entails the proposition 'God exists,' if and only if the latter also is understood as an a priori proposition: in which case the two propositions are equivalent. In this sense Anselm's proof is a proof of God's existence."[111]

Malcolm must be commended for his ingenuity in defending what he considers to be the second Anselmian argument against the objection—the strongest proposed since Kant's time—that existence is not a perfection or a real predicate of an essence. By making a distinction between contingent and necessary existence and claiming for the latter the same role of predication as for the other perfections of God, such as necessary omnipotence and necessary omniscience, he seems to avoid the extremes both of those who identify existence with other perfections in God as well as in creatures, and of those who deny any possibility for existence to serve as a real predicate, even in the case of God. This compromising solution has been hailed by some authors as an important discovery that enhances the value of the Anselmian argument and one that escaped the attention even of its author. But is it really so? Is Malcolm's discovery really so important as to determine for the first time the precise nature and value of the argument and rescue it from the centuries-old attacks of its opponents? This question must be asked because, as will be seen in the next and last man to be dealt with in this survey, some rather strong language has been used to characterize those who still refuse to endorse Malcolm's line of reasoning. Our answer will be brief and right to the point. Any attempt to prove the existence of God solely from the analysis of an a priori proposition such as "God necessarily exists" is bound to fail. The gap between mind and reality outside it cannot be bridged by a logical concept, not even in the case of a necessary

[110] *Ibid.*, pp. 145-46.
[111] *Ibid.*, p. 147.

being. To bridge such a gap something is needed to transform a logical concept into a real, metaphysical concept, or, as in the case in point, a proposition about a real being, either physical or spiritual. An a priori proposition can only be an analysis of the meaning of its terms, and this will never give us a clue as to the actual existence of the being the terms are held to stand for.[112] Logic, after all, deals only with what scholastic philosophers, following Aristotle, have called beings of second intention, i.e., concepts of concepts. We must go beyond logic and even beyond physics to attain to the realm of existence; we must enter into the realm of metaphysics. True, the term "metaphysics" is not popular today, especially among logical positivists and analysts, but popularity is not always a criterion of truth. We submit that it is not in this case.

The way to rescue the Anselmian proof from apparent shipwreck, if we may use this expression, is either the way indicated by men like Koyré and Gilson, or the more sophisticated way of Duns Scotus. But since to Malcolm and those who agree with him both of these ways are systematically closed to their investigation, it makes little sense to proceed any further in our criticism. A final remark is in order. Malcolm's presupposition that [contingent] existence is not a perfection and his frank admission of not being able to refute the opposite "fallacious" doctrine, is a weak spot in his analysis. So also is the fact that he discusses at some length the notion of perfection but gives no definition or clear indication of

[112]That is why, incidentally, Findlay, arguing on purely logical grounds, has arrived at a conclusion exactly opposite to Malcolm's, namely, that the existence of God is impossible! Cf. J. N. Findlay, "Can God's Existence Be Disproved?" in Plantinga, *op. cit.*, pp. 111-22. (The article is a reprint from *Language, Mind, and Value* (New York: Humanities Press, 1963), but was originally published in *Mind*, LVII (1948), 176-83). Although Findlay later admitted that the conclusion of his argument could be reversed (*ibid.*, p. 121), the fact of having accepted it as a possibility shows the obvious limitations of logic and linguistic analysis in dealing with such metaphysical issues as the existence of God. When "necessity in propositions merely reflects our use of words, the arbitrary conventions of our language," one can hardly expect to see a proof of God's existence derived from the proposition "God necessarily exists," unless "we have made up our minds to speak theistically *whatever the empirical circumstances might turn out to be*" (italics in the text). *Ibid.*, p. 119.

what perfection is, let alone of what Anselm meant it to be. This is a weakness that is common to many other present-day analysts.[113]

No contemporary philosopher has written so much and so earnestly on the ontological argument as Charles Hartshorne and his thought will be discussed here as a fitting conclusion to our survey. Hartshorne approaches the argument systematically in two works, *Man's Vision of God* and *The Logic of Perfection,* and historically in a more recent volume, *Anselm's Discovery.* In addition to these extensive treatments, he has made the Anselmian proof the subject of many articles and papers.[114] Keeping to the nature of this study, we shall present only the basic features of his interpretation, which in many respects is similar to that of Malcolm. As a matter of fact, Hartshorne had already pointed out long before Malcolm the need of distinguishing between two different forms of the Anselmian proof and said that the standard criticisms are relevant only to the first of them, namely, that of *Proslogion 2.*

Despite their similarities, there are substantial differences between the two philosophers in their understanding of the argument, and such differences are determined by their diverse concept of philosophy in general and of metaphysics in particular. Also, the conclusion that Hartshorne draws from *Proslogion 3* is not in line with Malcolm's theism but with what he himself terms neoclassical theism, a view of God inspired mainly by the process philosophy

[113]Recently an attempt has been made to show that in the case of God there is no real distinction between factual (or ontological) necessity and logical necessity, so that the form of the ontological argument based on the logical necessity of God's existence is valid. Cf. Alan G. Nasser, "Factual and Logical Necessity and the Ontological Argument," *International Philosophical Quarterly,* XI (1971), 385-402.

[114]The following sources will be used in this paper: *Man's Vision of God and the Logic of Theism* (New York: Harper and Row, 1941), chap. IX, pp. 299-341; *The Logic of Perfection and Other Essays in Neoclassical Metaphysics* (La Salle, Ill.: Open Court, 1962), chap. II, pp. 28-117; *Anselm's Discovery: A Re-examination of the Ontological Proof for God's Existence* (La Salle, Ill.: Open Court, 1965); "Introduction" to *St. Anselm: Basic Writings,* trans. S. W. Deane (2d ed.; La Salle, Ill.: Open Court, 1962), pp. 1-19; "The Necessarily Existent," in Plantinga, *op. cit.,* pp. 123-35 (a partial reprint from *Man's Vision of God* mentioned above); "What Did Anselm Discover?", in Hick, *The Many-Faced Argument, op. cit.,* pp. 321-33 (an expanded version of a previous paper which appeared under the same title in *Union Seminary Quarterly Review,* XVII (1962), 213-22.

of Whitehead. Hartshorne does not conceal the fact that his interpretation is intended to be original and that it will shed new light on a subject that "has been scandalously mishandled" by "nearly all schools of philosophy which have attempted to deal with it."[115] He feels that Anselm himself, whom he credits with "a discovery greater than he knew," did not realize all the implications of his argument because he was "blinded" by "prejudices derived chiefly from Greek and Roman sources."[116] Whether such statements are fully justified or not it will be seen later.

Hartshorne correctly observes that Anselm's ontological argument presents a metaphysical issue that must be solved on metaphysical grounds.[117] This explains why those philosophers, especially in recent times, who dismiss the argument as a mere sophistry, also dismiss the possibility of metaphysical inquiry.[118] The argument centers on the unique relationship between possibility and actuality, essence and existence in God. With ideas of finite things there can be three distinct cases as to the nature and value of their contents: (1) the thing conceived is impossible and hence nonexistent; (2) the thing is possible but not actualized; (3) the thing is possible and actual. The ontological argument holds that with the idea of God only the first and third cases need be considered, since the second case is meaningless. Moreover, if there is no God, there is no possibility for him to come into existence, and thus the very concept of God is nonsensical. Finally, if it can be shown that the idea of God is not nonsensical but must represent at least a possible object, it follows that the idea must refer to an actual object, since a merely possible God is inconceivable. Hence "where impossibility and mere unactualized possibility are both excluded, there nothing remains but actuality, if the idea has any meaning at all."[119]

The argument, Hartshorne remarks, is not in itself sufficient to exclude the impossibility or meaninglessness of God; rather it shows the contradiction of a notion of God as a merely possible

[115]*The Logic of Perfection,* p. viii.

[116]Introduction to *St. Anselm: Basic Writings,* p. 4.

[117]"What Did Anselm Discover?", in Hick, *op. cit.,* p. 321.

[118]*The Logic of Perfection,* p. 30. Obviously, Hartshorne's statement refers to a trend among modern and contemporary thinkers who reduce philosophy either to scientific knowledge or to linguistic analysis.

[119]"The Necessary Existent," in Plantinga, *op. cit.,* p. 124. Hartshorne's line of reasoning is basically that of Scotus, Leibniz, and the more recent authors, Lepidi and De Munnynck. These latter present the ontological argument in

being. Once this is granted, the transition from possibility to actuality in God becomes evident. Indeed—and here Hartshorne uses the same line of reasoning as Malcolm—the idea of God is the idea of a being everlasting in duration and independent of any other being. For such a being to be produced would imply both dependence on the producer and limitation in its duration—Hartshorne excludes the possibility of an eternally dependent being admitted among others by Aquinas—two conditions that contradict the very nature of the being under discussion. Hence it is only logical to conclude that to think of God as a merely possible being is to think an impossible idea. God must be thought as existent or cannot be thought at all.[120]

At this point Hartshorne becomes aware that the argument's opponents will take issue to the inference of reality from mere logical possibility. All that can be inferred from it is self-consistency on a purely conceptual level. To this Hartshorne answers that self-consistency cannot be the referent of the meaning whose consistency is granted; it is rather the presupposition of there being any meanings, consistent or otherwise. "If a consistent meaning means something, but something not even possible, then it means something very odd indeed. If it means only its own consistency, then it is really meaningless."[121] To better explain his position, Hartshorne insists on the unique nature of God as existence itself. To think of God is not to think of a being that might exist; it is to think of what "existence" itself must be, unless the idea is devoid of any meaning. The God must be conceived this

---

the following terms: God is either a being of reason *(ens rationis),* whose nature is to exist only in our mind, or a real being, actual or possible. But God, the plenitude of being represented in our mind through a created likeness, cannot be merely a being of reason, for, if it were so, the objectivity of all our concepts would be endangered. Nor can he be a merely possible being, for his existence would then depend on the causality of another being, which is obviously wrong. Hence he must be an actual being. Cf. Alberto Lepidi, O. P., *Elementa philosophiae christianae* (3 Vols.; Paris: Lethielleux; Louvain: Peeters, 1875-79), Vol. II, pp. 14-17; Vol. III, pp. 348-54; *Idem,* "La preuve ontologique de l'existence de Dieu et Saint Anselme," *Revue de philosophie,* XV (July-Dec., 1909), 655-64; Marc De Munnynck, O. P., *Praelectiones de Dei existentia* (Louvain: Uystpruyst-Dieudonné, 1904), pp. 18-23; *Idem,* "L'idée de l'être," *Revue néoscolastique de philosophie,* XXXI (1929), 182-203.

[120] "The Necessary Existent," in Plantinga, *op. cit.,* pp. 124-26.

[121] *Ibid.,* p. 128.

way can also be proved by the fact that all other beings can only exist through him, while he in turn cannot exist through another being but must be self–existent, as the cosmological argument puts it. Besides, mere possibility of existence is inconceivable without a being in which such possibility is ultimately grounded, and since the possibility is real, the source of it must also be real; it must be reality itself. This is the argument from the possibles, that is, the ideological argument.[122]

Nor can it be objected that existence is not a predicate and hence cannot be implied by the predicate "perfection." For if existence is not a predicate, the "mode" of a thing's existence is included in every predicate. Thus contingency of existence is implied in every predication concerning creatures, whereas necessary existence or self–existence is a predicate that belongs exclusively to God. Hence "that God's essence should imply his existential status (as contingent or necessary) is not an exception to the rule, but an example of it, since the rule is that contingency or non–contingency of existence follows from the kind of thing in question."[123]

Further developing his notion of modality of existence as a property deducible from the definition of a thing, Hartshorne goes on to apply it to three specific kinds of existence proper to a definition. With the modality of *contingency,* existence and non-existence are equally conceivable; with the modality of *impossibility,* existence is not conceivable; but with the modality of *necessity,* only the existence, but not the nonexistence, is conceivable. In this latter case, and in this case alone, existence must be affirmed, since its denial is contradictory. This is the gist of the Anselmian argument and that is why it makes no sense to argue, as some of its critics do, that God's existence is necessary only upon condition that he exists. "God's existence can only be unconditioned. We assert it, or we ignore it; we cannot logically deny it."[124]

Yet, despite the apparent logic of this reasoning, Hartshorne concedes that the ontological argument is only hypothetical. "If 'God' stands for something conceivable," the argument holds, "it stands for something actual," an expression that reminds us of

[122]*Ibid.,* p. 129.

[123]*Ibid.,* pp. 129-30.

[124]"What Did Anselm Discover?", in Hick, *op. cit.,* pp. 325-27. See also "A Theory of Existential Modality," in *The Logic of Perfection,* pp. 84-89.

St. Bonaventure's statement, "If God is God, God exists." But this hypothetical character of the argument should not be construed in a way that would deprive the Anselmian proof of all demonstrative value, as it would be if one were saying, as previously stated, that if God exists, he exists necessarily. It must rather be understood in the sense that "if the phrase 'necessary being' has a meaning, then what it means exists necessarily, and if it exists necessarily, then, a fortiori, it exists." To deny this is to deny all value to our idea of God, which, for all practical purposes, would be less than an idea; worse than that, no idea at all.[125]

It has been our concern to present Hartshorne's interpretation of the ontological argument as faithfully as possible and to quote verbatim some of his most significant statements. If we follow carefully the dialectic of his reasoning, we cannot fail to see that, regardless of his introductory remark that the argument is a metaphysical problem, all we have seen thus far is an attempt to solve the problem on purely logical grounds. If this is the case, then his presentation of the Anselmian proof is not much different from that of Malcolm and hence open to the same kind of criticism. Hartshorne is too keen a philosopher not to have seen this obvious inconsistency with his claim about the metaphysical nature of the argument. As a matter of fact, this is precisely the reproach he makes—whether rightly or wrongly is not our immediate concern here—that Anselm attempts to derive the concrete actuality of God from a mere abstract definition.[126] Actuality, he says, is much more than bare existence, and while Anselm is right in deducing existence from the definition of God, he overlooks the enormous gulf between bare existence and actuality. Actuality can never be deduced from a definition, not even in the case of a supreme conceivable being.

If this sounds a little puzzling to a "classic theist" who is used to think of God as a most simple being in whom essence and existence are identified, Hartshorne explains that a distinction must be made between existence and actuality in God, existence being God's abstract nature and actuality his concrete reality. Thus "God merely qua 'necessarily-existing individual' is not God in his concrete actuality, but is merely the abstract necessity that there

[125] "The Necessary Existent," in Plantinga, *op. cit.*, pp. 134-35.

[126] "What Did Anselm Discover?", in Hick, *op. cit*, p. 329: "Here, I think, is the innermost reason for the opposition to Anselm's Proof. From an abstract definition it *seems* to derive a concrete actuality; for God is not supposed to be a mere abstraction."

be some such actuality."[127] On this assumption, the ontological proof for the existence of God will have to include two steps, one going from essence to existence and the other from existence to actuality. Anselm's mistake, as well as the mistake of his opponents, Hartshorne asserts, is to have reduced these two steps to one. While Anselm was right in showing that in God the step from essence to existence is a necessary one, his argument fell short of showing how God's existence is actualized in concrete reality.

If we ask Hartshorne whether actuality can ever be proved to follow necessarily from existence in God, he will tell us that that can never be the case, for divine actuality is not necessary at all, neither in itself nor for our knowledge. "I hold that the divine actuality must be contingent, not only for us, but in itself."[128] Quite consistently, he then claims that if God is contingent in his concrete actuality, he is also limited and able to surpass himself, as for instance by coming to know a greater and better world. Thus Hartshorne's God is a being that is at one and the same time, although not in the same respect—it would be openly absurd to hold this latter—both necessary and contingent, infinite and finite, immutable and mutable . . . and the list could go on![129] In short, it is a God that, while absolute and transcendent in his perfections, is at the same time "a living, sensitive, free personality, preserving all actual events with impartial care and forever adding new events to his experience."[130] Hartshorne holds that once this new concept

[127]*The Logic of Perfection*, p. 94.

[128]"What Did Anselm Discover?", in Hick, *op. cit.*, p. 331. See also *The Logic of Perfection*, p. 100: "God as necessary is not God in his concrete actuality."

[129]"What Did Anselm Discover?", in Hick, *op. cit.*, p. 331.

[130]Cf. Charles Hartshorne and William L. Reese, *Philosophers Speak of God* (Chicago: The University of Chicago Press, 1953), p. 514. For Hartshorne's concept of God and his relation to the world see the whole essay, "The Logic of Panentheism," *ibid.*, pp. 499-514. For a more comprehensive study of the subject see his major works: *The Divine Relativity: A Social Conception of God* (Third Printing; New Haven and London: Yale University Press, 1967); *Reality as Social Process: Studies in Metaphysics and Religion* (Glencoe, Ill.: The Free Press, 1953); *A Natural Theology for Our Time* (La Salle, Ill.: Open Court, 1967); *Creative Synthesis and Philosophic Method* (London: S. C. M. Press, 1970). The following articles are also worth consulting: "The Formal Validity and Real Significance of the Ontological Argument," *The Philosophical Review*, LIII (1944), 225-45; "God as Absolute, Yet Related to All," *The Review of Metaphysics*, I (1947), 24-51; "The Dipolar Conception of Deity," *The Review of Metaphysics*, XXI (1967), 273-89.

of God is accepted and the proper distinction between divine existence and actuality is made, then the ambiguity of the Anselmian proof is removed and the proof becomes very strong. However, he insists, it will be a proof of God's necessary *existence,* not of his necessary actuality.[131]

Such, then, is Hartshorne's understanding of the Anselmian proof. Needless to say, his approach to the argument raises so many issues that it is almost impossible to pass a fair judgment on it without getting involved in a much wider discussion than the present study allows. Thus in our criticism we will have to be selective and choose those points which in our estimation are particularly important for a proper evaluation of both Anselm's argument and Hartshorne's interpretation of it.

We feel that Hartshorne's interest in the argument—an interest that he describes as going back to his student days when he made the Anselmian proof the subject of a thesis written in 1923 at Harvard University—coupled with a sharp and original mind, makes him particularly qualified for a discussion of a topic whose complexity has baffled some of the greatest philosophers. It is refreshing therefore to see how a man like Hartshorne, whose cast of mind sets him quite apart from the eleventh-century's "father of scholasticism," has the courage to stand up and sustain the value of Anselm's discovery in an unfriendly philosophical climate and against logicians who, in his own words, "would rather be seen in beggars' rags than in the company of the ontological argument."[132] While we admire his courage and the depth and subtlety of his reasoning, we cannot ignore the challenge offered to us by certain of his new and daring ideas on the subject.

First of all, Hartshorne believes that the argument of *Proslogion 3,* implemented with elements from Anselm's *Reply* to Gaunilo, is a valid proof of God's existence, as distinct from divine actuality, on the strength of pure logical reasoning. We have discussed this problem in connection with Malcolm's view, and need only repeat what we said in his regard. As long as the starting point of the argument is found in ideas as pure mental entities or propositions looked upon merely from the viewpoint of their logical contents, there seems to be no way of reaching out to God as an extramental reality, even when he is conceived as a necessary

[131]"What Did Anselm Discover?", in Hick, *op. cit.,* p. 333.
[132]*The Logic of Perfection,* p. 57.

being. Hartshorne's subtle distinction between existence and concrete actuality in God is no solution to the problem, as long as existence is considered as a mode of the divine nature with its characteristics of necessity, independence, immutability, and the like. If, on the other hand, divine existence is a pure abstraction or concept of our mind with no foundation in the reality of God —which does not seem to be Hartshorne's understanding of it— then the argument has even a lesser chance of reaching out to God for the reason previously mentioned. On either alternative, then, the argument fails to meet the requirements of a proof of the existence of God, as Hartshorne intends it to be.

But what appears to us an even weaker point in Hartshorne's theory is his conception of God as the embodiment of all those contradictory attributes listed above. To conceive God a self-existent and necessary being, the absolute and independent cause of all other beings which owe him *totally* whatever they have in the way of essence and existence, and then to make this self-same being dependent on the effects of his creative act, and hence contingent, relative, and subject to the limitations and imperfections of his creatures,[133] is to suggest a notion of God that defies the most fundamental principles of metaphysics. There is always room for suggestions and ideas that may help us to better understand the mysterious nature of God and his relation to the world, but not at the expense of those principles that are the foundation of traditional natural theology, unless these principles are shown to be inadequate. In our opinion, Hartshorne has failed to show that they are. On the other hand, the panentheistic doctrine he proposes as a conciliatory theory between the "extremes" of classical theism and pantheism, raises more problems than it can solve. Hence his distinction between existence and actuality in God, which he presents as the key to the solution of the problems involved in the Anselmian proof, is either too subtle or too unrealistic. We submit that it is the latter.[134]

[133]*Philosophers Speak of God,* pp. 501-502. See also *The Divine Relativity,* p. 74, where Hartshorne speaks of God as being bound to create, although not necessarily this world or any given creature.

[134]For a more sympathetic but equally critical appraisal of Hartshorne's view see David A. Pailin, "Some Comments on Hartshorne's Presentation of the Ontological Argument," *art. cit.* in n. 104 above. See also Eugene H. Peters, *Hartshorne and Neoclassical Metaphysics: An Interpretation* (Lincoln: University of Nebraska Press, 1970). The author concludes his evaluation of

CONCLUSION

In an attempt to summarize the result of our inquiry, it can be said that Anselm's ontological argument has found supporters in Bonaventure, Descartes, Leibniz, and Barth, while its strongest opponents have been Gaunilo, Aquinas, and Kant. Between these two opposite positions, there is the view of Malcolm and Hartshorne, who see in the *ratio Anselmi* two distinct pieces of reasoning and claim that only that of *Proslogion 3* is valid. Koyré and Gilson do not really take a stand for or against the argument. Rather, they try to show how the argument should be understood by placing it within the context of the entire *Proslogion* and other Anselmian works, especially the *Monologium* and *De veritate.* In this sense Koyré and Gilson can be considered as being somewhat favorable to the Anselmian proof. Actually they assign to it greater philosophical value than Barth does, since Barth sees the proof merely within a theological framework. In some respects they even come closer to Anselm than Malcolm and Hartshorne, who refuse to grant dialectic value to the reasoning of *Proslogion 2.* Whatever their stand, all the authors discussed in this paper have contributed, either directly or indirectly, to a better understanding of the issue at hand.

Our appraisal of the position of each individual author, as well as our remarks on Anselm's own presentation of the argument, both in this and in our previous study, seem to dispense us from any further comment. However, there are a few observations that we wish to make by way of conclusion in an effort to bring forth,

---

Hartshorne's philosophy with the following statement: "He is to many of us the foremost of contemporary philosophers." *Ibid.*, p. 127.

One of the latest works on the ontological argument is *Le Dieu d'Anselme et les apparences de la raison* by Jules Vuillemin (Paris: Aubier Montaigne, 1971). In the first two parts of his volume (pp. 11-52) the author restates the usual objection that the ontological argument of the *Proslogion* is a rational proof based on rational data that involves an illicit transition from the concept of God in our mind to God's actual existence. In the third and fourth parts of the book (pp. 53-131) Vuillemin attempts to show the epistemological and mathematical antinomies that result from the "negative" concept of a being than which no greater can be conceived. Thus he rules out the argument as a valid proof for the existence of God. Vuillemin, like many other writers before him, does not seem to do justice to the inventive genius of Anselm.

even more effectively than we have already done, the positive aspects of the Anselmian proof.

The strong point of Anselm's reasoning consists in his attempt to show that it is impossible to form a proper concept of a supremely conceivable being and at the same time deny the existence of the being in question. Existence is indeed a necessary element of that concept. One may question the ontological value of the concept but not the logic of Anselm's reasoning, provided this is placed within the context of the ideological realism which he shares with Augustine and the Augustinian school.

In such a context ideas have a value of their own and cannot be considered as mere logical constructs. The idea of perfection as something that is better to have than not to have, which is the traditional understanding of the term, has a positive contents, and so too has the being understood as possessing that perfection. When the concept of perfection is raised to the highest possible degree and impersonated, as it were, in a being, as in the case of God, then the concept does not lose its ontological value. On the contrary, it acquires a new dimension, an infinite dimension, if we are allowed to speak in such terms in regard to the human intellect.

The idea of God, it is worth repeating, does not prove God's existence, but without existence the idea has no meaning. Worse than that, it is no idea at all; it is a contradiction. Indeed, if the notion of a supremely conceivable being does not stand for an actual reality, it becomes the notion of the least conceivable being, for such being, in addition to having no reality of its own, would never be able to receive one without losing its identity. The greatest conceivable being cannot possibly depend on another being for its existence and remain what it is supposed to be. Thus the human mind would be placed in the embarassing situation, already pointed out by Scotus, that it would be deceived in the attainment of that very object which seems best to satisfy its inner tendency as a knowing faculty. It becomes evident, therefore, that the validity of Anselm's reasoning is closely connected with the question of the objective value of our concepts and the related issue of the proper object of our intellect.

A final remark. The idea of the greatest conceivable being, and hence of a self-existent being, would be proved to be groundless, and consequently false, if to exist meant exclusively to exist by and because of another. Until this is done, and it may rightly be assumed that it will never be the case because contradictions are impervious to all proofs, the Anselmian argument will continue to fascinate philosophers as a unique piece of profound and original thinking whose logic it is easier to reject than it is to refute.

The Catholic University of America

7

PHILOSOPHY IN THE *GETA* OF VITAL DE BLOIS*

by John K. Ryan

Two Latin comedies by Vital de Blois, of whom little more is known than his name and the fact than he lived and wrote in the 12th century, throw light upon a certain aspect of the academic life of his time. Both of Vital's plays derive, at least collaterally, from Plautus, and both of them are designed for a public made up primarily, it must be assumed, of university teachers and students, although not excluding other educated men and women. The earlier of the two plays, *Geta*[1]—it was also known as *Amphitrion* and by other titles[2]—has passages containing philosophical terms and teachings, or distortions of them, and similar passages are found in Vital's *Aulularia*.[3] It is here intended to present and discuss the philosophical elements in *Geta,* but to do so requires some statement of the antecedents of the comedy in earlier literature and certain other things connected with it.

Vital de Blois did not at first attach his name as author to *Geta,* nor do the earliest manuscripts ascribe it to him. However, the prologue to *Aulularia* ends with the statement that

> Hec mea uel Plauti comedia nomen ab olla
> Traxit, sed Plauti quae fuit illa mea est.

* Copyright 1973 by John K. Ryan.

[1]Vital de Blois, *Geta,* texte établi et traduit par Etienne Guilhou in Gustave Cohen, *La "Comédie" latine en France au XIIe siècle.* 2 vols. (Paris: Les Belles Lettres, 1931), Vol. 1, pp. 1-57. Guilhou's text is used throughout this article and his introduction and translation have been helpful in writing it.

[2]In the manuscripts *Geta* is the most common title and *Amphitrion* is frequent. Among other titles are *Amphitrion et Geta, Amphitrion, Alcmena et Geta,* and *Geta et Birria. Ibid.,* p. 29, n. 1.

[3]The text of *Aulularia,* established and (poorly) translated by Marcel Girard, is in Cohen, *op. cit.,* pp. 73-104.

Curtaui Plautum: Plautum hec iactura beauit;
Vt placeat Plautus scripta Vitalis emunt.
Amphitrion nuper, nunc Aulularia tandem
Senserunt senio pressa Vitalis opem.

"My comedy," Vital says of his second play, "like that of Plautus, takes its name from an earthen pot, but what once belonged to Plautus has now been made my own. I have abbreviated Plautus, and Plautus has benefited by being thus shortened. Vital's version brings Plautus into favor. Two of his works, both burdened with age, have profited by Vital's helping hand: *Amphitrion* not long ago, and now his *Aulularia*."[4]

Manuscript copies of *Geta* belonging to the 13th century give the author's name as Vitalis Blexus, Blesis, or Blesensis, indicating that he either lived in or came from Blois. Since the earliest of the many manuscript copies of the play belong to the second half of the 12th century and because of bits of evidence, both internal and external, that have been gathered, it is concluded that Geta could not have been written earlier than 1150-1160.[5] While the words "*Amphitrion* nuper, nunc *Aulularia*," used by Vital in reference to the composition of the two plays, are not precise, it is probable that the *Aulularia* followed *Geta* by a few years.

That Vital de Blois was a scholar is seen in the fact that the two plays are written in Latin in correct if uninspired elegiac distichs, and in evidences of his knowledge of both classical literature and contemporary philosophy contained in them. Something of his character and interests is revealed by the prologue to *Geta*.[6] He states that although the poet writes in order to afford pleasure to others, he fails to find a responsive and appreciative public. Neither his verses nor the stories he tells are well liked. People are interested only in material things and love of money dominates them. It is not how much a man knows, but what he possesses that counts. If he is without money, he is nobody. Not even educated men appreciate the new poetry. They will praise the ancients but they lack understanding of the poets of their own

[4] Ll. 23-28. The translations in this article have been made by its author, unless otherwise noted.

[5] Cf. Guilhou, pp. 3-7 and E. Faral, "Le fabliau latin au moyen âge," *Romania*, L (juillet, 1924), pp. 321-385.

[6] Ll. 11-22.

time. The result is that the poet's work does not receive its meed of praise and the poet himself receives no monetary reward. It would be better for him not to publish at all and to write solely for his own pleasure, since he alone can recognize his talent and set proper value on what he has written.

There is a note of bitterness in these lines. Vital de Blois sees himself as a modern author and an innovator whose efforts have been neglected or condemned. *Geta* could hardly have been his first composition and perhaps earlier things had not won the favor that he thought they deserved. Aside from such a possibility, *Geta* itself contains passages that could arouse hostile criticism. Its source is a notorious tale of immoral pagan deities,[7] and, along with the two gods who figure in it, two other characters are estimable neither in words nor in deeds. There are a few lines in it that can be held offensive even when judged by our low standards. Moreover, Vital's abilities as a Latin poet are not of high order. Yet even if there were earlier works by him that were not acclaimed and even if some readers of *Geta* found fault with it, it is probable that *Geta* quickly proved to be a popular success. The tone of Vital's prologue to *Aulularia* is notably different from that to *Geta,* and its concluding lines imply that *Geta* had been well received. It established a new literary form and, as the numerous manu-

[7]Various early Christian writers denounced the immorality of the pagan gods and of productions that showed shameful deeds of both gods and men on the stage. The theatre had a part in the honors paid to the gods. Plots were taken from pagan mythology, and performances could be offensive not only to Christian morality but also to that of the better pagans. Writing in the late 3rd or early 4th century, Arnobius of Sicca, a convert to Christianity, refers to three plays by name, *The Trachinian Women* of Sophocles, the *Hercules* of Euripides and the *Amphitryon* of Plautus, and asks: "And what cause is there, again, that they [the gods] should be made calm, benevolent, and mild, if improper things are done and bold fellows act up before an onlooking crowd? Does Jupiter put away his anger if the *Amphitryon* of Plautus is acted out or declaimed?" *Adversus nationes libri VII,* ed. C. Marchesi, 2nd ed. (Turin, 1953), VII, 33. Arnobius also uses the Jupiter-Alcmena episode in IV, 22, 26, and 35. Augustine condemns an especially obscene incident in Terence's *The Eunuch* in his *Confessions,* I, 16, and again in Letter 202 (91 in Migne, P.L. XXXIII, 313-318), and tells how Jupiter's many adulteries were depicted in paintings and statues, and acted and danced out on the stage. It may well be that Augustine, in his youthful passion for the theatre, attended performances of *Amphitryon.* It is difficult to think that there would be no adverse criticism in the 12th century of Vital de Blois's use of Jupiter's visit to Alcmena in his *Geta.*

scripts indicate,[8] it was widely diffused. Geta and Birria became proverbial figures,[9] and, one would think, the play was not only read privately but often acted out in university circles. Passages in it were imitated in *Babio* and certain other comedies written in the 12th century.[10] In 1390 John Gower published his *Confessio Amantis*[11] in which Geta, Alcmena, and Amphitryon appear briefly, each playing a new role. At the end of the 14th or beginning of the 15th century appeared *Il libro del Gieta e del Birria,*[12] which was long incorrectly attributed to Boccaccio, and early in the 15th century Eustache Deschamps wrote his French paraphrase of Vital's play under the title of *Un traictié de Geta et d'Amphitrion.*[13]

The *Geta* of Vital de Blois has a long and illustrious ancestry in the literature of Greece and Rome, since it is in part a retelling of one of the greatest of Greek myths, the story of Amphitryon and Alcmena and of Alcmena's son Heracles. Noble in character, chaste in conduct, and beautiful in person, Alcmena, daughter of Electryon, high king of Mycenae, had been given in marriage to her cousin Amphitryon, king of Troezen, but she would not permit

[8]Guilhou writes: "Les manuscrits du Geta sont très nombreux; sans doute en existe-t-il encore d'ignorés." p. 20.

[9]One 13th-century Ms. is headed *Proverbia Gete* and another is made up of extracts from the text. It has been stated that each man was taken during the middle ages as representative of the "servus nequam" in the Gospel. Cf. W. B. Sedgwick, "The History of a Latin Comedy," *Review of English Studies,* III (July, 1927) 346-349. Each was a wicked servant, but in more ways than were the slaves in Matt. 18:23-35 and 24:28.

[10]Cf. Cohen, *op. cit.,* Vol II for the texts of *Babio* (pp. 1-59), *Pamphilus, Gliscerium, et Birria* (pp. 83-101), and *Baucis et Traso* (pp. 62-82).

[11]In John Gower, *Complete Works,* ed. G. C. Macaulay. 4 vols. (Oxford: At the Clarendon Press, 1899-1902), *The English Works,* including *Confessio Amantis,* are in Vols. 2 and 3. In Gower's poem (Book II, lines 2459-2499) Geta and Amphitryon are close friends, Alcmena is not married to Amphitryon and she and Geta are lovers. Amphitryon successfully impersonates his friend Geta and seduces Alcmena. While this is taking place, Geta comes to visit Alcmena, is told by her that Geta is already there, and is turned away in bewilderment. Gower devised his version of the story to illustrate the sin of "supplantatio," a violation of the tenth commandment (Cf. Vulgate, Exodus, 20:17 and Deuteronomy 5:21). Along with Birria, Jupiter, and Archas, philosophy has disappeared from Gower's use of Vital de Blois's material.

[12]C. Arlìa, ed., *Geta e Birria,* novella riprodotta da un antica stampa e riscontrata co' testi a penna. Bologna: Romagnoli, 1879.

[13]In *Oeuvres complètes.* Publiés d'après le manuscrit de Bibliothéque Nationale par Gaston Raynaud (Paris: Didot, 1893), pp. 211-246.

their union to be consummated until he had avenged the death of her eight brothers who had been slain by the Teleboans. Because Amphitryon had accidentally caused the death of Electryon, he had to flee, accompanied by Alcmena, to Thebes where he was ritually purified and granted permission by King Creon to raise an army and make war on the Teleboans.

While Amphitryon was engaged in fulfilling Alcmena's demand, Zeus, king of the gods, saw an opportunity to carry out a plan that he had in mind. This was to father the mightiest of heroes, whose mother he had already decided was to be Alcmena. Having turned himself into a duplicate of Amphitryon, Zeus deceived Alcmena, prolonged the night into the 36 hours needed to produce their heroic offspring, and then departed for Mount Olympus just before the return of Amphitryon, who had won a quick victory over the enemy. In time Alcmena gave birth to twin boys, Heracles, her son by Zeus, and Iphicles, his half-brother, son of Amphitryon. Zeus had boasted about the approaching birth of his latest and greatest son by a mortal and with malicious humor said that he would be named Heracles, "the glory of Hera." Completely innocent though she was, Alcmena, and so too Amphitryon, were now caught in the intrigues of the gods. When Hera, spouse of Zeus and defender of the marriage bond, learned of his newest amorous adventure, her hatred and jealously were aroused. After interfering with the birth of the twins, she tried to kill them by sending two fiery serpents into their crib. Iphicles cried out in terror, but the infant Heracles gleefully seized the immense serpents and strangled them. Which child was the son of Zeus and which was the son of Amphitryon was easily determined.

The legend of Amphitryon and Alcmena provides material for both tragedy and comedy. In the 5th century B.C. two of the three greatest Greek tragic poets used the story, Sophocles in his *Alcmena* and Euripides in his play, also named *Alcmena,* both of which works are lost, and in a later century Aeschylus of Alexandria wrote a tragedy entitled *Amphitryon,* of which fragments survive.[14] The story of Amphitryon and Alcmena would have been

[14]Sophocles (495?-406 B.C.), Euripides (480?-406 B.C.), Aeschylus of Alexandria. For their plays, and for the attribution of an *Alcmena* to Aeschylus (525-456 B.C.), see A Nauck, *Tragicorum Graecorum Fragmenta* (Leipzig: Teubner, 1889), pp. 6, 156, and 824. For Aeschylus of Alexandria see also Athenaeus, *The Deipnosophists,* with an English translation by C. B. Gulick (London: Heinemann, 1937), VI, 231.

kept before the public by such plays as these and also in other ways. The *Alcmena* of Euripides has a special relation to the *Amphitryon* of Plautus. According to tradition, Euripides had studied philosophy under Anaxagoras, and became known as "the philosopher on the stage,"[15] and there are elements in his writing that indirectly contributed to the development of the New Comedy of Menander, Philemon, and others. Philemon wrote a work entitled *The Night,* or *The Great Night,* which is thought to have been a burlesque of Euripides' *Alcmena,* and Rhinthon,[16] chief of the writers of hilaro–tragedies in southern Italy, wrote a parody of a tragedy which he entitled *Amphitryon.* Plautus knew Euripides' *Alcmena*[17] but in keeping with his practice of using Greek originals as the basis for his Latin comedies, his *Amphitryon* is perhaps based directly upon either Philemon's or Rhinthon's play. In the prologue to this masterly work, Mercury, son of Jupiter, refers to the play as a tragedy, notes that the audience scowls. and adds: "I'm a god. I'll turn it around, and, if you wish it so, I'll make a comedy out of this tragedy, while keeping all its lines . . . I'll mix things up and we'll have a tragicomedy . . . Don't be surprised at my costume . . . I'm going to offer you a new version of an old and oft–told tale . . . In it I've taken on the appearance of Amphitryon's slave Sosia."[18]

[15]Vitruvius, *De architectura,* VIII, p. 1. Euripides is also associated with the names of Socrates and certain other philosophers in the Athens of his time. Alexander of Aitolia refers to him as "the fledgling of brave Anaxagoras." See H. Diels, *Die Fragmente der Vorsokratiker* (Berlin: Weidmann, 1956), II, 12, 11. 16-19. In *Nicomachean Ethics,* VIII, 1, Aristotle quotes Euripides as a philosopher who, along with Heraclitus and Empedocles, had probed deeply into the nature of friendship.

[16]Their dates are: Menander (342?-291 B.C.), Philemon (c. 364-264 B.C.) and Rhinthon of Tarentum (early 3rd century B.C.). Before them Archippus (5th century B.C.), a representative of the Old Comedy, also wrote on the Amphitryon-Alcmena story.

[17]Plautus (c. 254-c. 184 B.C.), describing a bad storm in his *Rudens,* says, "It was no mere wind, but what Euripides sent Alcmena." (1. 87) This reference to Euripides' *Alcmena* indicates that it had a storm in it like the one Plautus has in his *Amphitryon.* Bromia, the maid, tells how Alcmena invoked the gods and her prayers were answered by a terrific storm during which Hercules and Iphicles were born. Cf. 11. 1061-1063 and 1091-1095). The Latin text of *Amphitryon* used here is that of Friedrich Leo (Berlin: Weidmann, 1895-1896) as given in *Plautus* with an English translation by Paul Nixon, Vol. 1 (London: Heinemann, 1956), pp. 1-121.

[18]Ll. 52-55; 116; 118; 124.

The *Amphitryon* of Plautus opens with Alcmena, already bearing Amphitryon's child, at home in Thebes. Jupiter, impersonating Amphitryon, is with her, says that he has returned victorious, and presents her with a golden bowl belonging to King Pterelas whom he says he had slain in battle. Amphitryon himself has arrived in the harbor and sends his slave Sosia into the city to inform Alcmena of his return. When Sosia tries to enter the house he is stopped by Mercury disguised as Sosia. In a long and brilliant scene Mercury–Sosia shows such knowledge of the true Sosia's character and career and is so like him in every detail of his body that Sosia wonders where he lost himself and became thus transformed. Although convinced that there are two Sosias, he cannot be convinced that he himself is not Sosia. Jupiter–Amphitryon departs, telling Alcmena that he must get back to his troops. Amphitryon cannot accept Sosia's strange story of the other Sosia at the house —"I am both here and there,"[19] Sosia says—nor, when he gets back home, can Amphitryon accept Alcmena's claim that he had already been with her, told her of his victory, and gave her the golden bowl. Alcmena is innocent but in the end it requires Jupiter's intervention to vindicate her honor and to reconcile Amphitryon both to Alcmena and to the will of the gods. To Jupiter he says both reverently and pointedly, "I will do as you command, and I pray that you will keep your promises."[20]

In addition to Amphitryon and Alcmena, Jupiter and Mercury, and Sosia, son of Davus, Plautus has two other characters in his play: Bromia, Alcmena's maid, who has one fine scene, and Blepharo, a pilot, some of whose lines are now missing. Each of the chief characters is convincingly drawn and they provide wonderful comedy, both high and low, and other passages that are more serious in mood.

Alcmena's lofty character is made clear throughout the action. Conscious of her innocence, she defends herself with dignity against the reproaches of her deceived and tormented husband. At the end, when she is resolved to leave their home, Jupiter, again pretending to be Amphitryon, intercedes in her behalf, and tells her that he is sure of her virtue. Invoking Jupiter, Jupiter–Amphitryon swears an oath: "If I deceive you in this, then do I beseech thee, O Jupiter

19L. 594.
20L. 1144.

almighty, to send down thy everlasting wrath upon Amphitryon." To this Alcmena answers, "Ah, no, not that, a blessing rather!"[21]

After the hurried visit and departure of the presumed Amphitryon, Alcmena meditates on how life is marked by alternate joys and sorrows. Great as was her joy at Amphitryon's return, her sorrow at his sudden leaving is still greater. She is thankful that Amphitryon has been victorious in battle and has come back a hero. Since he is a soldier, he may have to leave home many times, but she will persevere to the end, enduring his absences with a firm, strong heart if only she can see him return a victor. She describes valor, the soldier's special form of the virtue of fortitude, and tells how necessary it is. Valor defends and keeps our liberty, health, life, and property, our parents, fatherland, and children. Valor contains all things within itself, and he who possesses this virtue possesses all good things."[22]

This last passage has a relation to Greek ethical doctrine. It is in praise of one of the four cardinal virtues in action and to some extent illustrates the doctrine that each of the virtues, in its highest expression, involves the others. The man who has complete fortitude will likewise fulfill his obligations in justice to family and country, and he will be prudent and temperate. As a traditional Greek maxim puts it, a man can be evil in many ways but good in only one way.[23]

Vital de Blois thought that he based his play upon the *Amphitryon* of Plautus.[24] However, *Geta* differs in so many ways from the great comedy written more than thirteen centuries earlier that it is probably based not on the work of Plautus himself but on a later work wrongly attributed to him. Writing in the 5th century A. D., Sedulius refers briefly to pagan dramas in his *Carmen*

[21]Ll. 933-935.

[22]Ll. 650-652.

[23]St. Thomas Aquinas, *Quaestio unica de virtutibus in communi, Opera omnia,* (New York: Musurgia, 1945, reprint of the Parma, 1852-1873 edition) VIII, 626, 638, discusses the question of how the virtues are so interconnected that a person who has one will have the others also. In the case of the four cardinal virtues—prudence, temperance, fortitude, and justice—he points out that unless a man has prudence he cannot have the other three. He quotes St. Ambrose (*De officiis,* Book I, Ch. 1) on the virtues: "Connexae sunt et concatenatae, ut qui unam habuerit, omnes habere videatur."

[24]Cf. prologue to *Aulularia,* 11, 11-28. Lines 11-12 read, "A reader of Plautus will perhaps wonder when he sees names for characters different from those I have written."

paschale and gives as an example, "ridiculoue Geta," and in a parallel passage in his *Opus paschale* he uses stronger words, "seu ridiculi Getae comica foeditate."[25] There is a "foeditas" in certain passages in Vital's *Geta* for which Plautus' *Amphitryon* offers no antecedents, but they may well have been in the *Geta* that Sedulius condemns.

In Vital's retelling of the story Sosia has become Geta, a slave of much coarser clay than the Sosia presented by Plautus. Bromia, Alcmena's maid, has been replaced by Birria, a man servant, and the pilot does not appear. The principal characters are Geta and Birria, while Amphitryon, Alcmena, Jupiter, and Mercury—the last now called Archas, a name for him that did not become common until the late Roman empire—are less important than they are in Plautus.

Amphitryon is described as an old man, as he is in Plautus, but not as a general, although he gives evidence of military experience. But if he is an old soldier, he has been spending part of his retirement as a student of philosophy in Athens. He has a deep, chaste love for Alcmena, whom he describes as being part of his very life and whose death would mean that he too had died in part. He refers to a son, but it is not made clear whether the son is also Alcmena's or from some earlier union, and is fearful that this son as well as Alcmena may have died and that he himself will be childless. The long tradition of Alcmena's innocence and nobility is continued by Vital de Blois. She easily removes Amphitryon's doubts as to her fidelity, and husband and wife are reconciled, but not with Jove's help as they are in Plautus.

The two slaves are contrasting but complementary characters. Geta is a complete scoundrel: he is vain, boastful, foolish, and cynical, and he is also a liar, thief, lecherer, and atheist. Repulsive in appearance, he suffers from more than one disease, and anyone who has once met him does not want to repeat the experience Yet despite all his vices and other defects, Geta is a rogue who is laughed with as well as laughed at, and he evokes a certain

[25]*Carmen paschale*, I, line 19, and *Opus paschale*, I, i in Sedulius, *Opera omnia* . . . recensuit et commentario critico instruxit Iohannes Huemer (Vindobonae: apud C. Genoldifilium, 1885), pp. 16 and 176. CSEL vol. 10, E. Müllenbach, *Comoediae elegiacae* (Bonn: E. Weber, 1885), pp. 28-31, and F. Osann, *Vitalis Blesensis Amphitrion et Aulularia eclogae* (Darmstadt: E. Heil, 1836) p. xvii.

sympathy because of his bold and rugged character and his lot in life.

Birria too is base, cynical, and self-centered, but he is higher on the moral scale than Geta. He knows Geta from experience and therefore distrusts him. He disdains Amphitryon and he even suspects Alcmena of evil things. His place as a household servant is not easy, but he expects nothing better. Birria, he thinks, is born to hard luck and hard work, and one of his principles is to avoid work, or at least to put it off as long as possible. Some people, he says, like to work and others to play games, but he likes to sleep. He has no intellectual pretentions, as Geta foolishly has, but he is the embodiment of good sense. Without education or training in logic, he can recognize the flagrant contradiction in Geta's vapid philosophical musings. He has nothing but scorn for the heroics of Amphitryon and Geta as they prepare for battle. If there is any fighting to be done, Birria will keep well out of it and find a safe place for himself.

Geta and Birria belong to the long life of such characters who flourished in the Greek and Roman theatre and are found today on stage and screen, in comic strips, and elsewhere. Of the two, Geta is the sharp but shallow man who takes advantage of his simpler but solider associate, only to find in the end that Birria has come out better than he has. Appropriately, Vital de Blois gives Birria the last word in his play.

The play of *Geta* has only 530 lines, including the argument and prologue, and eight of them are held to be additions made by later hands, but in this short space Vital has presented living figures and compressed a good deal of action. The work may be divided into five acts, or quasi-acts, made up of thirteen scenes, Whether *Geta* was written as a closet drama or one designed to be read or acted out upon the stage is a debated point. Apart from the 22 lines making up the argument and prologue, and not counting the eight spurious verses, there are 500 lines in the play proper. Of these, 390, or 78%, are spoken in dialogue or as soliloquies by the various characters. Of the other 110 lines, some are in the order of stage directions, such as "Iupiter inquid," "Archas ait," "Continuat Geta," "Solus abit; secum queritur," and "Birria tunc sibi," while certain longer passages are explanatory of what is to come or of what has already taken place. It would have been a simple matter for a small group of players, six for the characters and a seventh to act as narrator, to offer an effective production of

Geta, and it would have been even simpler for a skilled actor or accomplished reader to give a lively reading of it.[26]

Vital de Blois opens his play with a passage in which he has Jupiter describe his lust for Alcmena. He makes no mention of the future Hercules as part of his plan, but feels himself to be less fortunate than Amphitryon in her regard. He decides that while Amphitryon is away in Athens philosophizing, reading his books, and engaged in disputations, he, Jupiter, will be engaged in another affair. "We'll let Amphitryon cultivate the liberal arts, while Jupiter cultivates his dear Alcmena," he tells his son Archas, and he describes "how great and good and beautiful Alcmena is," and how much better than his own Juno.[27] The father of the gods impersonates Amphitryon, his son and staff-bearer takes on the form of Geta, and the two depart upon their errand.

> The heavens are left behind, and earth breathes forth
> A springtime odor. It senses the presence of the gods.[28]

Alcmena had heard that Amphitryon was on his way home and calls to Birria to hasten down to the harbor and verify the report. True to his antipathy to work, Birria pretends to be asleep and does not answer but finally has to obey. He sets out on his errand, grumbling about his hard lot and voicing suspicions as to why Alcmena was getting him out of the house. Amphitryon had in fact already arrived in port and had ordered his slave Geta to take on a load of books, hasten home, and speed the good news to Alcmena. Birria sees Geta coming along the road and hides in a cave in order to avoid him, since he knows that Geta would contrive to get more work for him to do. However, Geta has

[26]Cf. Guilhou, pp. 16-20.

[27]Ll. 33-34 and 52-53.

[28]Ll. 57-58. They read in Latin:

> Deseritur celum, Vernali mitis odore
> Respirauit humus; sensit adesse deos.

Cf. Horace: "praesentia numina sensit" (Ep. II, 1, 134). In lines 495-498 Jupiter announces, "Duty calls—I left the ships unguarded at the shore. Geta, prepare for the journey." The passage continues: "He ceased speaking. Archas stands ready. The heavens rejoice at Jove's return, but earth laughs less gaily; it senses the departure of the gods." In Latin:

> Dixerat; Archas adest, gaudetque suo Ioue celum;
> Ridet terra minus, sensit abesse deos.

already caught sight of him, stops at the entrance to the cave, and soliloquizes for Birria's benefit.

> It's a long story to tell about how many hardships of every sort I endured in Athens. Cold, constant hunger, bitter thirst, only a little sleep at night, and wretched food wore me down. It wasn't first grade bread that the master lived on, but only second rate stuff. What he fed me was hardly fourth rate.
>
> But as recompense for such hardships, I've brought back a lot of marvelous sophisms. I can now prove that a man is a little donkey. When I get back to my pots and pans, hearth, and greasy kitchen, I'll prove that some men are asses and others oxen. I am a logician. I'll turn them all into whatever animals I like. Birria, who's so extremely slow, will be a little donkey.[29]

On hearing this, Birria says to himself, "What's this? Is Birria going to be turned into a little donkey? Will that fellow deprive me of what nature gave me?" He resolves that no matter what Geta is up to, "Birria will always remain a man."[30] Geta sets forth more of his philosophy:

> I have also learned this truth, that no real thing can perish. What is once something cannot be nothing. It is impossible for what is once endowed with being ever to cease to be. It merely changes.

Birria dryly comments, "Geta will live forever, if he's only telling the truth.[31]

> Death (says Geta, continuing his reflections) takes away all things. They say that the learned Plato is dead, and that Socrates himself has passed away. My fame will live, but it too

[29]Ll. 158-169. John of Salisbury describes certain anti-humanists as holding that a man who studies the ancient classics is clearly "slower than an Arcadian ass, thicker than lead or stone, and an object of general derision." The words "asello Archadie tardior" derive from Persius, *Satire,* iii, 9. Cf. John of Salisbury, *Metalogicon* Libri IIII, recognovit . . . Clemens C. I. Webb (Oxford, 1929) I, iii, p. 11. Also *The Metalogicon . . . a Twelfth-Century Defense of the Verbal Arts of the Trivium.* Translated with an introduction and notes by Daniel D. McGarry (Berkeley and Los Angeles: University of California Press, 1955). Geta's words "pane secundo," here translated as "second-rate stuff," come from Horace, *Epistles* II, 1, 123. Other classical authors used by Vital are Vergil, Ovid, and Lucan.

[30]Ll. 169-172.

[31]L. 178.

> will perish in death. Death destroys all things. All things fall before death.[32]

Upon this Birria observes: "The fellow contradicts himself. First he proves that all things are without end, and now he laments that all things perish in death."[33]

After failing to get Birria to relieve him of his load of books, Geta continues on his way, reflecting on the great future that lies before him now that he has learned how to philosophize. His name will become famous; he will be called Master Geta,[34] and the other slaves[35] will stand up and applaud when he gets back. Adapting a line from Lucan, he states that the shadow of his name will overawe them all.[36] He will be set free, have slaves of his own, and teach them great doctrines.[37]

But when Geta arrives at the house in Thebes, he is astounded to find that it is closed and silent and that Alcmena does not appear. Still more astounding, a strange porter refuses to let him in, states that Amphitryon is back at home, and claims that he himself is Geta. Dumbfounded at all this Geta says:

> The man speaking to me is Geta in voice and body. Who except Geta could speak with Geta's voice? But the logicians teach that there can be a single voiced word for two things, and that the same name will signify two different men.[38]

[32]Ll. 179-182.

[33]Ll. 183-184. In his translation of Aristotle's *Nicomachean Ethics,* the first translation of one of Aristotle's works into a modern language, Nicole Oresme (c. 1323-1382), bishop of Lisieux, refers to Geta's fallacious arguments and Birria's dimissal of them: ". . . et neant moins le simple homme scet bien que telz conclusions sont fausse. Et tele chose est en la fable de Birria." Maistre Nicole Oresme, *Le Livre de Ethiques d'Aristote.* Published . . . with a critical introduction and notes by Albert Douglas Menut (New York: Stechert, 1940), pp. 486-488.

[34]Geta's expectation of acceptance as a teacher is a reflection of an academic abuse condemned by John of Salisbury, according to whom young and untrained teachers were promoted to professorial chairs. Cf. *Metalogicon,* I, 3 and 4.

[35]Geta names three of his fellow slaves: Samnio, Sanga, and Davus. Davus is used as a slave's name in various Roman comedies; Sosia states that he is "the son of Davus" in Plautus's *Amphitryon,* 1, 395.

[36]Cf. 11. 231-238. L. 236 reads, "Terrebit cunctos nominis umbra mei," and seems to echo Lucan's "Stat magni nominis umbra" in reference to Pompey in *Pharsalia,* I, 135.

[37]Ll. 229-238.

[38]Ll. 257-260.

When Geta repeats his demand to enter the house, Archas repeats his statement that he is Geta and that Amphitryon is inside the house. He adds that Birria, who was terrified by the way he threatened him and by the rocks he threw at him in the cave, is also back. Geta says, "His acts and words prove that this fellow is the true Geta," and wonders how he has been led astray and whether Birria got back ahead of him by some shorter route. It is all very perplexing:

> It is I who speak to myself, but I don't know how it is that he who before was one man has been made into two. Whatever is, is one; but I who speak am not one; therefore Geta is nothing—and yet nothing cannot be.
> I was one when I raised my voice outside the closed entrance, but the other fellow replied to me as myself. Did I answer myself? Did the house return my voice, borne back by an echo, as happens out in a forest?[39]

Geta returns to the attack, pleads with Archas, threatens to batter down the door, is frightened off, and then asks Archas for further information:

> Tell me, I beg of you, what is the cast and color of your countenance, and add on the peculiar marks of all your members. Run through them one by one, because I'm trying to find if anyone besides myself can be me.[40]

Archas agrees to do this, but sternly tells Geta not to believe that he (Geta) is Geta. "I don't think that you do believe it. Believe me straight off. Greece recognizes no other Geta except myself. You've sought to trick me by using a name that is in fact my own. I alone am Geta."[41] He proceeds to describe himself. His whole body has a strange black hue and it is afflicted by a chronic mange. His head is crowned by a thick mat of hair, his brow is low, and his eyes are red. He has a heavy beard, long neck, narrow shoulders, bloated belly, shaggy loins, short, fat legs and crooked feet. So repulsive is Geta in appearance that people turn away in disgust

[39]Ll. 277-284.
[40]Ll. 321-324.
[41]Ll. 327-331.

After hearing this detailed description of himself, Geta admits that whoever the man is, he's Geta, "for such am I!"[42]

When Geta asks for an account of things that he has done, Archas tells of Geta's insatiable lust and of the women who like him in spite of his repulsive appearance but for other reasons. "Amphitryon," says Archas–Geta, "was kept busy by his studies, Geta by his Thais. When I travel from one country to another I look out for a new Thais. I chase after the Thaises, and a good many of them chase after Geta. I conquer them by my gifts. It is by gifts that love conquers."[43] But money is needed for all that, and Geta gets the money by robbing Amphitryon, something not hard to do, because, as he says, "It's easy to cheat foolish old men." Sometimes he's caught and punished for his misdeeds, but then he denies everything and calls upon the gods as his witnesses. "I don't scruple to call in the powers above as false witnesses. A man who believes that there are gods dares do nothing great."[44]

After hearing this description of what he is in body and soul and the account of his misdeeds, Geta says, "This is certainly proof enough. You may be me. I may be nothing,"[45] and dejectedly begins his journey back to Amphitryon. Alone with his thoughts, Geta laments the fate that has befallen him. "Alas, alas for me! Alas for me who once was but now have become nothing." He looks for consolation in philosophy and tries to reason things out. The problem, as he sees it, is, "Geta, who can you be?" and his answer is, "You are a man." But logic refutes this. "Not so, by

[42]Ll. 331-354. This passage has been thought to be patterned after the description of the Gothic king, Theodoric II (reigned 453-466), by Sidonius Apollinaris, in that the description moves from the head on down to the feet. As pictured, Theodoric and Geta were very different in physique. The description of the Huns by Sidonius may also be noted. Cf. *Poems and Letters,* tr. W. B. Anderson. 2 vols. (London, Heinemann, 1936), I, 335 and I, 29-31.

[43]Ll. 375-378. Geta's "munere uincit amor" is his restatement of Vergil's "Omnia vincit amor" in *Bucolics,* X, 69. Thais is here used as a name for any prostitute. In *The Eunuch* by Terence, Thais, a courtesan, is a leading character, and there were famous courtesans in Athens and Rome who took the name.

[44]Ll. 384; 387-390. There is a double irony in this episode. Archas, the patron of liars and thieves, falsely claims to be Geta but gives a truthful description of the slave's thefts, and Geta, an atheist, agrees with the opponent whom he does not know to be one of those gods whose existence he scoffs at.

[45]Ll. 391-393.

Hercules, for if Geta were a man, who would he be except Geta?"[46] Since the question is still open, another answer presents itself:

> I'm Plato! Perhaps the liberal arts have turned me into Plato. Certainly, I'm not Geta, and yet I'm called Geta. I was called Geta. What will my name be now? There won't be any name, because I am nothing. Alas for me, I am nothing. Yet I speak and see, and touch myself with my hand. By Hercules, I touch myself! A thing that can be touched won't be nothing, by Hercules.
>
> Whatever was is something, and doesn't cease to be. Moreover, what once has been always is. Therefore, I am, and therefore I am not. Perish the dialectic by which I've thus perished completely! Now I am one who knows, and to know hurts. When Geta learned logic, he forthwith ceased to be. An art that turns other men into oxen has turned me into nothing. In fact those sophisms have had a more destructive effect on me than on the others. While I'm only changing the others, the sophisms have taken my very being away from me. If such is the case, it's a terrible thing for all logicians.[47]

At this point Geta sees Amphitryon and Birria approaching and he thinks:

> But hey, look, here comes Amphitryon back again. I wonder whether he too is nothing. He approaches, and he's nothing! But is it possible for nothing to move? By Hercules, things have left their accustomed ways. From the fool that I was dialectic has turned me into a madman. It can be proved that Geta is and that he is not. I am, if he greets me by the name of Geta. If he remains silent, I'm dead.[48]

Amphitryon is alarmed by Geta's gloomy appearance, fears that he is a bearer of bad news, that either Alcmena, his "better half," or his son is dead, and cries out, "Come, speak up, speak up, Geta!" At this Geta says to himself. "By Hercules, I am Geta—for he calls me Geta! It's impossible for a thing that's not real to have a name.[49] He then informs Amphitryon about the situation back

[46]Ll. 395-398.

[47]Ll. 399-415. When Geta says, "Nunc scio"—"Now I know," or "Now I am one who knows,"—he employs a medieval definition of the philosopher, the man who knows, as in Dante's praise of Aristotle, "il maestro di color che sanno," the master of those who know, in *Inferno,* IV, 131.

[48]Ll. 415-422.

[49]Ll. 437-438.

at the house and the strange porter who told him that Amphitryon is already home and in bed, and that he, Geta, didn't even exist. Hearing this Birria laughs to himself and says:

> When Greece took them in, they were same men, but she sends them back madmen. It's dialectic that turns fools into madmen. Birria, never let yourself learn such an art. It's well to be ignorant of an art which by some fantastic means makes men become either asses or nothing at all. Let him who will be a logician. You, Birria, shall always be a man. May their studies be their delight, and yours a fine greasy kitchen.[50]

Amphitryon, who is equally matter of fact, but in another way, tells Geta, "You've been tricked into thinking you're nothing. Some adulterer who knows you well has gotten into my bed."[51] He calls for his armor, tells Geta and Birria to arm themselves so that they can storm the house, and he and Geta rush to the assault. Birria continues in character and has no intention of being a hero or of risking life or limb. He reflects:

> By Hercules, I was right about this whole affair! When I set out for the ships, the adulterer was already inside the house. That's why I was sent away. Nobody fools Birria. Rage over that they've endured has made those two men insane. Let them wage war. In battle nothing is safe. If I can help it, Birria will never fall victim to Mars.[52]

When Amphitryon shouts defiance and calls out, "To arms! Charge!" Birria claims that his pack slows him down and that he he'll bring up the rear. Ordered to throw away the pack so that they can catch and kill the adulterer, Birria answers:

> Throw it down? It's bad business to add injuries to injuries. Hercules, we're not their equals. Perhaps there are many of them inside. The adulterer won't be captured without putting up a stiff fight. Adulterers carry arms, I'll follow you. You go first. In war the sword has great effect in close combat. I'll support you from a high spot, where I'll roll down rocks. Surprise attacks often do the worst damage.[53]

[50]Ll. 451-458.
[51]Ll. 461-462.
[52]Ll. 469-474.
[53]Ll. 478-484.

Amphitryon and Geta brandish their weapons, shout threats, and call on Jupiter for help. Birria laughs at them and soliloquizes:

> Whence this bravado? What is this madness? Oh, if the adulterer only knew them! Oh, men quick to turn tail! If Greece in olden times had sent forth such soldiers, Troy would still stand. Birria, if you're smart, you'll be the first to flee, the last to take a stand. For a timid man there's nothing safer than flight.[54]

After Amphitryon, Geta, and Birria have charged into the house, they find no adulterer there but only Alcmena. At first she is surprised and happy at seeing Amphitryon who, as she thought, had just left, returning so soon, but she is quickly shocked at his charge, "By Hercules, there was an adulterer here!"[55] Happily, the misunderstanding is cleared up by Alcmena's explanation that she actually saw both Amphitryon and Geta in the house, to which she adds, "At least I thought I saw you. I have often been deceived by my dreams."[56] On hearing this, Birria interrupts with the observation:

> Dreams they are, by Hercules! Geta raves, and by those studies of his he's been made even more foolish than before. Away with these crazy quarrels! I'm going down to the kitchen. May Amphitryon be filled with joy—and may Geta become a man.[57]

Vital closes his play with a final distich addressed to his readers and hearers:

> Letatur sponsa Amphitrion, nidore coquine
> Birria, Geta hominem se fore. Queque placent.[58]

It may be translated:

> Glad is Amphitryon, his spouse rewon,
> And Birria, his pots and pans among,
> And Geta, man once more—glad everyone!

[54]Ll. 487-492. Vital's lines.
O faciles dare terga uiri! Si Grecia tales
Misisset quondam, nunc quoque Troia foret,
are imitated in *Babio*, 11, 177-178.
Hostes si tales sensisset, Troia, maneres,
Nec raperent Danai Tyndaridem Paridi!

[55]L. 522.

[56]Ll. 523-524.

[57]Ll. 525-528.

[58]Ll. 529-530.

Vital de Blois's adaptation of the Greek legend is addressed to a mature and educated audience that spoke and read the Latin language it is written in, had more than a little knowledge of ancient literature, and could understand the characters of his play and appreciate its distinctive wit and humor. For such an audience Geta is not so much a man of that little learning which is so dangerous a thing, but rather a man of no learning whatever who has picked up a few scraps of logic and metaphysics which he does not understand and can only misuse. He has heard something about the doctrines of prime matter and substantial form, Democritean atomism, and the conservation of matter, and about being, unity as a transcendental attribute, and the problem of nonbeing. He has also learned a little of the philosophy of language and epistemology, and a few things about the syllogism and various fallacies. Being particularly entranced by logic, he first wishes to use it to the discomfiture of Birria and other associates and later for a more serious purpose.

When Geta is informed that another man has usurped his job, name, appearance, and personal history, he turns to logic for help. He argues that while every being is one, Geta is not one but two; therefore, Geta is not a real being. Again: a real being has a name, but Geta now has no name; therefore, Geta is not real. Employing a hypothetical syllogism, he sees that if Geta is a man, he is Geta, but since he is not Geta, he is therefore not a man. Metaphysics teaches that whathever once was continues to be, and since Geta once was, Geta therefore continues to be. Thus these syllogisms prove both that Geta exists and that he does not exist. Just as Birria spontaneously, if unknowingly, invokes the principle of noncontradiction when he notes that Geta proves both that nothing ever ends and that death destroys all things, so too Geta makes use of it when he exclaims, "Perish the dialectic by which I've thus perished completely."[59]

Although the *Geta* of Vital de Blois is far removed in many ways from the masterpiece of Plautus, Vital has retained the essentials of the confrontation between the slave Sosia and Mercury–Sosia as described by Plautus. The climax of the scene in Plautus is a statement of special interest to the historian of philosophy. Sosia makes a close inspection of Mercury–Sosia and says:

[59]Cf. 11, 409-410.

> He's got the same hat and clothes as I have. He's just like me—legs, feet, height, hairdo, eyes, nose, lips, jaws too, chin, beard, neck—the whole works. There's no use talking. If he's got a whip-scarred back, there's no one could be liker me.
>
> But when I think, I'm sure that I'm the same man I always was. I know my master, I know our house. I think and feel like a sane man.[60]
>
> In the Latin these last words are:
>
> > Sed quom cogito, equidem certo idem sum qui semper fui.
> > novi erum, novi aedis nostras; sane sapio et sentio.

This clear statement of the Cartesian "Cogito ergo sum," made by Plautus more than 1800 years before the publication of the *Discours de la méthode* with its "ie pense, donc ie suis," is employed by Vital de Blois. Geta has wondered about who he is, whether he has a name and whether he is. He proceeds:

> Alas for me, I am nothing. Yet I speak and see, and touch myself with my hand. Then touching himself, he exclaims, By Hercules, I touch myself! A thing that can be touched won't be nothing, by Hercules! His Latin words are:
>
> **"Heu mihi, nil sum!**
> **Iam loquor et uideo, tangor et ipse manu."**
> Seque manu tangens sic intulit: "Hercule, tangor!
> Quodque ualet tangi non erit hercle nichil."[61]

Geta's principle may be stated as, "Valeo loqui, videre, et tangi, ergo non sum nichil." "I can speak, see, and be touched, therefore I am not nothing." Or, affirmatively and more generally, it may be stated as "Sentio, ergo sum." "I sense, therefore I am."

[60]*Amphitryon,* 11, 441-448. The question of Sosia's sanity had already been challenged by Mercury who observes in 1, 401: "Hic homo non est sanus," When Mercury-Sosia says, "This fellow's crazy," Sosia retorts, "You're the one who's crazy, and you're imputing your sickness to me."

[61]Ll. 403-406. In the original Geta's words for "I am nothing" are "sum nichil" and "nil sum." They repeat St. Paul's "nihil sum," as given in the Vulgate: "Factus sum insipiens . . . tametsi nihil sum signa tamen apostolatus mei facta sunt super vos: I have become a fool . . . although I am nothing, yet the signs of my apostolate have been wrought on you" (2 Cor. 12:11), and "Et si habuero omnem fidem ita ut montes transferam, charitatem autem non habuero, nihil sum: And if I have all faith so that I might move mountains but do not have charity, I am nothing." (1 Cor. 13:2) St. Paul, of course, does not speak of personal nonexistence but of his nothingness apart from grace.

For Plautus's Sosia, his "Cogito equidem certo idem sum qui semper fui" is a recognition not only of the fact of his existence but also of his self-identity. In like manner, Vital's Geta recognizes both that he is and who he is.

Geta's concern over the seeming loss of his name to another, speculation as to who he is and what he is to be called if he is not Geta, and conviction that if Amphitryon addresses him as Geta it will be proof that he is not only real, but really Geta, are all related in his muddled thought to a medieval listing of individuating notes.

Forma, figura, locus, tempus, stirps, patria, nomen,
Et ea sunt septem quae non habet unus et alter.

Each individual man can be identified by his bodily form and appearance, his time and place of existence, his lineage, country, and name. No two men have exactly the same set of these seven marks. However, Geta's "forma et figura" apparently belong to another man, as do his time and place of activity. Moreover, for Geta the strong claim to his name that Archas has made creates a difficulty that is compounded by what he had picked up in the Athenian schools of philosophy. He had heard that one word, one name, can signify two beings, and that every real being is one. It appears, therefore, that he, Geta, is two and that the other Geta is only too real and is rightly called Geta, while he himself is now nothing, and being nothing has no name. Happily for Geta, this intellectual difficulty is also solved by an appeal to experience. Amphitryon calls him Geta by name, and he thus has further and final proof both that he is and that he is really Geta. It may be thought that here his principle is in the way of "percipi est esse." "If I'm perceived and addressed as Geta," he thinks, "then I am Geta."

Vital's account of Geta and his gaucheries is a form of comedy that is for the most part broad and obvious, but it is at times light and subtle. Geta's statements, "They say that the learned Plato[62] is dead, and that Socrates himself has passed away," and

[62]Horace uses the phrase in *Satires* II, iv, 2-3:

ponere signa novis praeceptis qualis vincent
Pythagoram Anytique reum doctumque Platonem

In this passage he has Catius say that he is compiling a set of new precepts that will surpass Pythagoras, the man against whom Anytus brought charges, i.e., Socrates, and the learned Plato. John of Salisbury quotes the

"I'm Plato! Perhaps the liberal arts have turned me into Plato," must have brought a special response from Vital's audience. The flourishing 12th-century school of Chartres placed great emphasis on Plato's thought, and it may well be that Vital de Blois had studied at Chartres or was connected in some way with its school. The audience must also have savored Geta's recital of the hardships he suffered while Amphitryon pursued his philosophical studies in Athens. Cold, hunger, thirst, lack of sleep, and poor food were all well known to medieval students, and they would have been a strange breed if they did not complain, especially about the food. Professors no doubt fared better at the table than the students did, but they had to endure the same cold. Scholars who have spent winters in the unheated or barely heated buildings of modern Europe have some knowledge of what it must have been like in the middle ages. These are jokes for initiates and are shared alike by Vital de Blois and his audience.

Geta's arguments are formally correct: two categorical syllogisms are in "barbara" and one in "camestres," and his two hypothetical syllogisms obey the rules about affirming the antecedent and denying the consequent. His boast that as a logician he has the power to turn men into oxen, asses, and other animals has reference to a logical scherzo familiar to medieval students. In the following century St. Thomas Aquinas in his *De fallaciis*[63] states that the fallacy of amphibology is of three kinds, the second of which is

---

lines by Horace and also uses the words "doctus Plato" in his *Policraticus*. Cf. Ioannis Saresberiensis episcopi Carnotensis *Policratici, sive de nugis curialium et vestigiis philosophorum libri VIII*. Recognovit . . . Clemens C. I. Webb (Oxford: 1909) VIII, 8 and VII, 12.

[63]*De fallaciis, ad quosdam nobiles artistas,* XVI, pp. 377-387. Cf. Ch. V, *De amphibologia,* p. 380.

It may be noted that the fallacy is used by the author of the 16th-century interlude *Jack Juggler,* which is based directly on Mercury's deception of Sosia in Plautus. In lines 1188-1189 he writes:

> As a cunning Sopist (sic) will by argument bring to passe.
> That the rude shall confesse and graunt him selfe an Asse.

See *Jack Juggler (Third Edition)* (Oxford: The Malone Society Reprints, 1936), prepared by B. Ifor Evans and W. W. Greg, whose prefatory note indicates that it was probably printed after 1568-69 but not later than 1582. They also state: "If the piece was indeed written by Nicholas Udall, the author was dead before the first edition appeared, and may have been dead a quarter of a century before the revision was made." (pp. v-vi) The author's reference to the sophistry of changing a man into an ass and certain other passages reveal familiarity with *Geta.*

found in propositions that can be construed grammatically in different ways. As an example he gives the syllogism: "Quicumque sunt episcopi sunt sacerdotes; isti asini sunt episcopi; ergo isti asini sunt sacerdotes." Although the major premise is true, the syllogism is fallacious because the minor premise can be construed in two ways. If the word "episcopi" is taken as in the nominative plural case, then the minor premise means, "These donkeys are bishops" and is false. If "episcopi" is taken as in the genitive singular case, so that "Isti asini sunt episcopi" means, "These donkeys are (the property) of a bishop," then the minor premise could be true. In the middle ages donkeys of a certain type came to be called "episcopi."[64] With this meaning the syllogism would still be invalid because of its equivocal middle term. Perhaps Geta's argument against Birria would have taken some such form as "Donkeys are slow-moving animals; Birria is a slow-moving animal; therefore Birria is a donkey." The undistributed middle term in his syllogism would hardly have disturbed Geta, while Birria would have rejected the argument for less technical reasons.

Vital plays with considerable skill upon the theme of Geta's self-supposed annihilation. Archas never tells Geta that he no longer exists, and his nothingness is strictly a conclusion that reliance on his knowledge of logic has led him to. Early in the play there is some preparation for the theme, and both Birria and Amphitryon have reflections on their personal continuance in being. When

[64]This syllogism is also used by a contemporary of Aquinas, William of Sherwood, in his work on logic, where it is given as an example of equivocation. Cf. M. Grabmann, *Die Introductiones ad Logicam von Wilhelm von Shyreswood +nach 1267* (München: Sitzungsberichte der Baierische Akademie, 1937), p. 87; N. Kretzmann, tr. and ed., *William of Sherwood's Introduction to Logic* (Minneapolis: University of Minnesota Press, 1966), pp. 136-137; and V. J. Bourke, *Aquinas's Search for Wisdom* (Milwaukee; Bruce, 1964), pp. 30-31.

The use of burros by religious leaders has a long background in history. An example is the Messianic text, Zachary, 9:9-10: "Rejoice greatly, O daughter Sion, shout for joy, O daughter Jerusalem! Behold, your king shall come to you. A just savior is he, meek, and riding on an ass, on a colt, the foal of an ass. He shall banish the chariot from Ephraim and the horse from Jerusalem. The warrior's bow shall be banished, and he shall proclaim peace to the nations." See also Matt. 21:1-9; Mark 11:1-10; Luke 19:29-38; John 12:12-15. Hence because of its association with Christ and peace, the burro was much used by ecclesiastics in preference to the horse, and a species of burro came to be called "episcopi." It is said that Pope Pius IX (died 1878) rode a white burro during the summers he spent before 1870 at Castel Gandolfo near Rome.

Birria, who loves life in spite of his fatalism and pessimism, is sent down to the harbor by Alcmena, he fears that he might be swept down into a watery grave, and that his epitaph would be pronounced by Amphitryon, his master, as "Birria nullus erat."[65] Birria would be remembered as a nobody, a nonentity, a zero. Birria protests to Alcmena that he will not live to return from his mission, yet whether he does or does not return, she must remember that Amphitryon will return if he's going to return. Later Amphitryon so identifies his own being with that of Alcmena that if she were to die, he would at least in part cease to be.[66]

Birria hopes that Geta will perish, while he himself will live on as a man. When he hears that by Geta's art of logic he will be changed into a donkey, he asks, "Is that fellow going to deprive me of what nature gave me?"[67] He laughs at Geta's conflicting pronouncements that everything ends in death and that while Geta will live on in fame yet his fame too will die. When hiding in the cave, he laments that in trying so hard to be completely safe and escape death, he is likely to lose his life and have the cave as his tomb. When Birria pleads, "I'm Birria. My dear Geta, I beg you spare me, your friend," Geta answers, "You're not Birria,"[68] just as later Archas will tell Geta that he is not Geta. At the end of the play Amphitryon tells Geta that he had been deceived into thinking that he was nonexistent, and adds that those whom the adulterer "proved to be nothing will make him feel that they are something."[69] A little later, when no evidence of an adulterer can

[65]L. 78.

[66]Ll. 430-436.

[67]L. 170.

[68]Ll. 201-202.

[69]L. 465. Amphitryon's words in the original text, "Quos nichil esse probat, aliquid iam sencient esse," parody St. Paul's words: "Nam si quis existimat se aliquid esse, cum nihil sit, ipse se seducit: For if anyone thinks himself to be something, whereas he is nothing, he deceives himself" (Gal. 6:3).

There also seems to be a use of Scriptural thought and Vulgate phraseology in certain of Birria's lines. In 1. 111 he says of himself, "Ad mala natus ego crucior cum cuncta quiescunt: Born to hardships, I'm tortured while all other things are at rest," and in 1. 129 he describes Geta as "homo natus pondere ferre: a man born to bear burdens." Both lines reflect Job 5:7: "Homo nascitur ad laborem": "Man is born to labor." In 1. 225 Birria says of himself, Birria cogetur montes transferre: Birria is compelled to move mountains," recalling St. Paul's "ita ut montes transferam: so as to move mountains" (1 Cor. 13:2). Cf. also Mt. 21:21 and Mk. 11:23.

be found, Geta boldly cries out, "Where's the adulterer? He'll soon fall beneath my sword!"[70] In various ways Vital has Geta, Birria, and Amphitryon illustrate the maxim, "Contra factum non valet argumentum."

There are further comic elements in *Geta* that would appeal to sophisticated readers and listeners. One of them is the use and misuse of oaths. At the play's supposed time of action Hercules, the future hero, was hardly more than a gleam in Father Jupiter's eye and he was not to see the light of day for at least seven months. Yet the just conceived and still unnamed Hercules is invoked by all the characters except Alcmena and Jupiter himself. "By Hercules" is used nine times by Geta, three times by Birria, once by Archas, the unborn Hercules' half-brother, and once by Amphitryon.[71]

Jupiter and Juno are also invoked, but in prayers rather than in oaths. "Adsis, bone Iupiter!"—"Be with us, good Jupiter!"—Alcmena prays, and Archas-Geta observes sardonically, "Adest!"—"He's here, all right!"[72] When he fears that Geta brings bad news about Alcmena's health and life, Amphitryon cries out, "Proh maxime Iupiter! . . . Fac, bona Iuno, precor, nunciet ille bonum."—"Jupiter almighty! . . . Grant, good Juno, I pray three, that he may bring good news."[73] Speaking as commentator, Vital notes that when Alcmena compares the one she mistakenly thinks to be Amphitryon to Jove, she likens "Jove to Jove," and he points out that when Amphitryon and his two warriors pray for the help of Jove in their search for the adulterer, they invoke Jove against Jove.[74] Archas–Geta, a god, with deliberate irony prays, "May the gods punish me if I don't let you know what Geta can do." Since a chief duty of Mercury was to bear Jove's staff, he was called, "Caducifer," the staff bearer, and it was therefore a special blasphemy for Geta to call Archas–Geta a "furcifer,"[75] a yoke bearer, i.e., criminal or gallows bird, while Archas–Geta could tell Geta, "I've often deserved the cross," i.e., to be tortured as a criminal,

[70]L. 512.

[71]Plautus makes use of oaths in his *Amphitryon,* especially "pol," "edepol," and "ecastor," forms of "By Pollux" and "By Castor." "Hercle" is used twice by Amphitryon and three times by Sosia, and twice by Mercury.

[72]Ll. 85-86.

[73]Ll. 425-528.

[74]Cf. 98 and 486.

[75]L. 312.

"still oftener to be put in chains."[76] There are also places in *Geta* that no doubt brought forth laughter and perhaps applause for lower reasons. These are the passages where the lustful Jove appears and in certain gross lines in Archas–Geta's description of the true Geta.

It is erroneous to think that Vital de Blois satirizes logic and logicians by his creation of Geta with his stock of "wonderful sophisms" and efforts at syllogistic reasoning.[77] He lived and wrote in a time of accomplishment in logic, but it was also a time when logic was subject to a twofold threat. One danger came from various professors of logic, and the other from a sect of philosophers, or pseudo philosophers, who rejected logic as special and necessary discipline. The first danger was a form of "malice domestic," perhaps unmeant but yet real, on the part of overspecialized teachers of logic, while the second could be classed as "foreign levies," or attacks made by nonlogicians. Both abuses had to be faced and answered, and this was done at the very time *Geta* was being written by one of the greatest of Vital de Blois's contemporaries. In his *Metalogicon*—it is a defence of the trivium, to which the study of logic belongs, a treatise on education, and much else besides—John of Salisbury[78] discusses the nature and function of logic and gives effective criticism of both those who in their devotion to logic have lost hold of its true character and those who reject it altogether.

[76]Ll. 381-382.

[77]Against such misunderstanding Guilhou correctly writes: "L'auteur ne se moque pas de la dialectique et de la philosophie scolastiques en elles-mêmes; ce serait une lourde erreur de le croire, et l'on sent bien que notre poète, qui est un clerc, possède, à fond ces sciences, les révère, et reste persuadé qu'elles sont le patrimoine des esprits supérieurs." p. 8.

[78]John of Salisbury was born at Salisbury between 1115 and 1120 went to France in 1136, studied at Paris and Chartres under some of the leading teachers of the time—Abelard, Thierry of Chartres, and Gilbert de la Porrée among them—was ordained a priest, held a place in the papal court, returned to England in 1154 as secretary to Theobald, archbishop of Canterbury, wrote his *Policraticus* and *Metalogicon*, and after Theobald's death in 1161 continued as secretary to the new archbishop, Thomas Becket, whose martyrdom he witnessed in Canterbury cathedral on December 29, 1170. In 1176 John of Salisbury was made bishop of Chartres, where he died on October 25, 1180. Cf. D. M. McGarry's translation of the *Metalogicon*, pp. XVI-XIX, and E. Gilson, *History of Christian Philosophy in the Middle Ages* (New York, Random House, 1955), pp. 150-153, 619-625.

Teachers of logic who do a disservice to their subject are shown to be culpable because they have forgotten that logic is for use. They are too much concerned with matters that are of no value in the real world. Logic has become their sole concern and their only topic of conversation. For them it has usurped the place of every other branch of philosophical knowledge. They neglect the great sources of logic, "the ancient authorities," while indiscriminately compiling every new opinion and counter opinion. They are "forever learning but never attaining to knowledge" and never really possess what they pretend to teach. To paraphrase John of Salisbury, it is a matter of logic for logic's sake and of the means becoming the end. He observes that "it is very easy to talk about definition, proofs, genera, and similar subjects, but it is far more difficult to carry out this art by finding such things in the various branches of learning."[79]

John of Salisbury has even more severe words for the declared enemies of logic. As the leader of this movement he names "Cornificius," a teacher whose real name has been lost to history, and describes him as "an uneducated foe of studies that inculcate eloquence," "a foolish old man" who had been badly educated and now "rails at those who respect the founders of the liberal arts, since he himself could see nothing useful in the arts when he was pretending to study them." Cornificius refuses to debate with others and can offer no proofs for his positions. He claims that he can teach students to speak well without any art, i.e., without training in grammar, logic, and rhetoric, and that he can show them how to become philosophers without work. The attack made by Cornificius and his followers is in fact upon all culture and organized society. An immediate result of this anti-intellectualistic movement is that its members have deserted philosophy. Some of them have turned to medicine, others have taken government jobs, stlll others have gone into business, and some have even become usurers. Certain of them have entered the cloister, and of these latter, some have seen the error of their Cornifician ways, while others, "having once usurped the professor's chair are now ashamed to descend to the learner's bench."[80]

[79]*Metalogicon,* Cf. 11, Chs. 7 and 9. It may be that John of Salisbury, the practical Englishman, was too critical of the highly specialized logicians and that there was a value in their investigations that he did not perceive.

[80]*Ibid.,* I, chs. 1-4.

Writing in the great tradition, John of Salisbury points out that logic is concerned with making correct divisions and definitions and with argumentation, that is, strict demonstrations, which lead to certitude, dialectical arguments, which lead to probability, and sophistical arguments. While logic is neither the oldest branch of philosophy nor the first to be systematized, it has a twofold primacy: it must be learned first by those who wish to take up philosophy and it must be used in the study of all other branches of philosophy.[81] Even a knowledge of sophistical arguments is useful, for although sophistry is deceptive, it still employs reason. It sometimes uses true or probable arguments in order to deceive and "thus transforms itself into an angel of light." Sophistry is not true but only apparent wisdom. If a man has knowledge of the tricks of the sophist, he will not be deceive by them.[82]

In a passage that is an answer to the two groups of extremists, to the Cornificians with their claim that study of the linguistic arts is unnecessary and should have no place in the philosophical curriculum, and to those for whom logic is the be-all and the end-all of philosophy, John of Salisbury emphasizes that dialectic is of the very greatest help to a man of great and genuine knowledge but of very little use to a man of little learning. In a celebrated simile he states that just as the sword of Hercules is useless in the hand of a pygmy or dwarf but invincible in the hand of an Achilles or a Hector, so too with dialectic. Dialectic must be nourished by other studies, and if so nourished it becomes a powerful instrument for refuting errors. A mastery of dialectic enables a man to argue with probability on any subject, but that is the least of its merits. On the other hand, dialectic is not great if it is concerned only with itself and with things that are of no practical value at home, or in the army, forum, cloister, court, or church. The dialectician must thus be more than a dialectician if he is to get the great benefits that dialectic promises and provides.[83]

In his play Vital de Blois shows himself to be neither a follower of Cornificius nor a pedant who has nothing but logical interests. His Geta, newly returned from Athens with a smattering of dialectic

[81]Cf. Book II, prologue and chs. 1-5.
[82]Cf. Book II, ch. 5.
[83]Book II, ch. 9.

and no knowledge of the rest of the trivium or of the quadrivium, must have been looked on by John of Salisbury as a prime instance of the pygmy trying to wield Hercules' sword.

The Catholic University of America

8

A PROBLEM IN PROPOSITIONS

by John J. Doyle

Some years ago this writer devised a figure, which he called the hexagon of relations, intended to illustrate the relations between pairs of propositions and the relations of these relations to one another.[1] In its provision for equivalence and independence, which find no place in the square of opposition, the figure seems to have some merit. Among its examples, however, there is an inconsistency of which the writer became aware only later on. In extenuation of his error, it could be said that the same inconsistency appears in many textbooks purporting to present the logic of Aristotle. In the hexagon the inconsistency is between the examples of equivalence and those of superimplication. These are:

Equivalence
All men are mortal
No men are immortal

Superimplication
All men are mortal
Some men are mortal

From the point of view of common sense there is nothing the matter with these pairs, whether taken singly or together: they are both in accord with colloquial usage. The first pair seem to be but different ways of expressing the same thought, and in the other the I proposition seems to follow from the A. But if common sense is to be the final arbiter of our thinking and if we are to rely on colloquial usage to determine the correctness of our reasoning, the study of logic is pointless.

[1]John J. Doyle, "The Hexagon of Relations," *The Modern Schoolman*, XXIX (January, 1952), 93-97.

The crux of the matter lies, of course, in the fact that obverse propositions, such as "All men are mortal" and "No men are immortal," are equivalent only if they are alike in having or in lacking existential import, and that a universal proposition implies the corresponding particular only if *they* are alike in existential import. It is the modern convention to interpret particulars, I and O, as asserting the existence of what their subjects name, and universals, A and E, as making no such assertion. Since by this convention propositions alike in quantity are also alike in existential import, nothing prevents any proposition from being equivalent to its obverse. Hence the modern logician would readily accept the examples of equivalence. On the other hand, since for him the universal is not existential and the particular is, he would reject the illustration of superimplication, holding that A no more implies I than I implies A.

So natural does this convention seem, so closely does custom bind us, that it is difficult for anyone nowadays, even though intending to follow the scholastic tradition, to see that this convention is only a convention, or to conceive that another convention could find acceptance. Yet the logicians of others times interpreted categorical propositions quite differently. For them, the proposition's quality determined its existential import: the affirmatives, A and I, were existential, the negatives, E and O, were not. Following this interpretation, we should say that if there are no men, "All men are mortal" is false and its contradictory, "Not all men are mortal," is true. Since the obverse of the latter is in this case false because it is affirmative, it is obvious that obverses are not equivalent. As those writers explained categorical propositions, appealing to Aristotle as their authority, the affirmative implies its obverse but is not implied by it. Therefore if this writer wished to present the medieval tradition he should not have used obverse propositions to illustrate equivalence. He might have employed an E or an I with its converse, such as:

No men are mortal
No mortals are men

The situation is similar, but with a reversal of roles, if one adheres to the modern convention, basing existential import on quantity and thus retaining obverses as the example of equivalence. Since on this interpretation, the only relations that obtain between categorical propositions are contradicition, equivalence, and independence, one would have to introduce either compound or existence propositions to exemplify the other relations. These might serve:

Contrariety
There are no men
Some men are mortal

Subcontrariety
All men are mortal
There are men

Superimplication
There are no men
All men are mortal

The hexagon of relations ought therefore to conform to one of these conventions and to exclude the other. Employing obverses to illustrate equivalence, it ought to look for examples of the other relations that conform to the modern convention; making the A proposition the superimplicant of the I, it ought not to present obverses as equivalent to each other. As noted, however, there is an excuse for the mistake in that many texts professing to follow the scholastic tradition straddle the issue, maintaining both the equivalence of obverses and the validity of the relations of the square of opposition. The reading of Moody's *Truth and Consequence in Mediaeval Logic*[2] led this writer to suspect that there was something amiss in the combination of these positions in one system.

Some textbook writers seem not to consider the possibility of basing the distinction between existential and nonexistential propositions on their quality rather than their quantity. Thus Copi,[3] after calling attention to the difficulties arising from the doctrine that A implies I and E implies O, finds no escape from them except "to presuppose that the classes to which they refer do have members." Following this suggestion, he encounters even greater difficulties. He does not observe that by making affirmatives existential and negatives nonexistential he could obtain all the rela-

[2]Ernest A. Moody, *Truth and Consequence in Mediaeval Logic* (Amsterdam: North-Holland Publishing Company, 1953).

[3]Irving M. Copi, *Introduction to Logic* (New York: The Macmillan Company, 1968), 142-144.

tions of the square of opposition. The switch would cost him the equivalence of obverses, but only seldom can we get something for nothing.

Cohen and Nagel[4] point out certain fallacies that result from the operations described in texts purporting to present the traditional logic. One instance is the inversion of the A proposition. In "All physicists are mathematicians" the predicate is undistributed, while in its partial inverse, "Some nonphysicists are not mathematicians," this term is distributed. For the modern logician there is here no violation of the principle concerning distribution of terms because, in order to make the limited conversion of "All nonmathematicians are nonphysicists" to "Some nonphysicists are nonmathematicians," he must add the premise "There are nonmathematicians," which implies "Something is not a mathematician" and thus supplies the distributed term. These writers fail to note that if one holds the affirmatives to be existential and the negatives to be nonexistential one must add the same premise in order to infer "All nonmathe-

[4]Morris R. Cohen and Ernest Nagel, *An Introduction to Logic and Scientific Method* (New York: Harcourt, Brace and Company, 1934), 61-63. Apparently the authors nodded at this point, for they wrote: "Consequently, a particular can never be validly inferred from a universal . . ., *unless* the premises include a proposition asserting that the classes denoted by the terms of the universal contain at least one member. And specifically, the conversion of *A* is valid only if the predicate denotes such a class." Accordingly, they add the premise "Some men are nonphysicists" to achieve the converse of "All nonmathematicians are nonphysicists." Obviously, this addition does not accomplish the desired result of distributing "mathematicians." What the modern convention requires for the conversion of the A proposition is a premise asserting the existence of members in the class denoted by its *subject.* The inadequacy of the authors' procedure is evident from the other case they cite: the inversion of "No mathematicians are circlesquarers." The obverted converse of this is "All circlesquarers are nonmathematicians." The addition of a premise asserting that the predicate denotes a class containing at least one member, namely, "Someone is a nonmathematician," would not free us from the embarrassment of inferring an absurd conclusion from true premises, for the added premise would generally be taken to be as true as the original. What is needed is the assertion that the subject class of the A proposition contains members: "There are circlesquarers." That the statement specifying that a premise asserting the existence of members of the predicate class should be added and the subsequent carrying out of this injunction are due to a momentary inadvertence is evident from the discussion by Cohen and Nagen of existential import on pages 41-44 and from their explicit statement on page 58: "But as we saw before, no inference *per accidens* is valid without the assumption that the class denoted by the subject has members."

maticians are nonphysicists" from "No nonmathematicians are physicists." As will appear, the scholastic doctrine explicitly requires this addition.

It is not at all surprising that modern writers take the position they do. In the English language at least, obversion is so obvious and natural a procedure that to question it seems implausible. Indeed some declare that obverses are not distinct propositions but merely variant expressions of a single one, not taking into account that they contain different terms. Not in every language, however, does obversion seem so obvious, for when the Spaniard says, "*No dice nada*" his meaning is "He says nothing" or "He doesn't say anything," whereas the word-for-word translation of his sentence is "He doesn't say nothing," which we, accustomed to the English idiom, might be tempted to tell him is the contradictory of what he intends. Be that as it may, it is quite certain that for the scholastic logicians professing to follow Aristole's teaching obverse propositions are not equivalent.

In his *Summa Logicae*[5] William Ockham states that an affirmative proposition can be true only if its subject has supposition, that is, if what its subject names exists. In one passage he states that "A chimera is a not-man" is false because the indefinite predicate makes it to be in effect a compound proposition, one of whose

[5]William Ockham, *Summa Logicae,* 2 vols. (St. Bonaventure, New York: The Franciscan Institute, 1951), Vol. II, 256-257. Et si dicatur, quod secundum Aristotelem alterum contradictorium dicitur de quolibet, si igitur chimaera non sit non-homo, igitur chimaera est homo. — Dicendum est secundum intentionen Aristotelis, quod non de quolibet termino significative sumpto dicitur alterum contradictoriorum incomplexorum, sicut de hoc nomine "chimaera" significative sumpto nec dicitur "homo" nec "non-homo"; tamen de omni termino supponente significantive non includente aequivalenter aliquod syncategorama vel aliam determinationem, de quo praedicatur vere "ens" vel "aliquid," dicitur alterum contradictoriorum. Unde si haec esset vera: "Chimaera est aliquid," altera istarum esset vera: "Chimaera est homo"; "Chimaera est non-homo." Et ideo concedendum est, quod non de quolibet significative simpto dicitur alterum contradictoriorum. Tamen hoc non obstante de quolibet tali quodlibet vere affirmatur vel negatur. Et hoc intendit Aristoteles, quando dicit: De quolibet affirmatio vet negatio et de nullo eorum ambo. Unde quamvis nec "homo" nec "non-homo" dicatur de chimaera, tamen "homo" vere affirmatur vel vere negatur de chimaera. Unde altera istarum est vera: "Chimaera est homo"; "Chimaera non est homo." Similiter altera istarum est vera: "Chimaera est non-homo"; "Chimaera non est non-homo."

components is the false statement "A chimera is something." He goes on to say:

> Someone may object that according to Aristotle one of a pair of contradictories must be asserted of anything, and hence if a chimera is not a not-man it is a man. My answer is that it is not Aristotle's meaning that one or the other contradictory term is to be asserted of every significant subject; in fact, neither "man" nor "not-man" can be asserted of "chimera". It is indeed the case that of every significant term, except the syncategorematic or other modifiers, of which one can truly say that it is a being or something, one of the contradictory predicates must be asserted. Hence if "A chimera is something" were true, either "A chimera is a man" or "A chimera is a not-man" would be true. We must admit though that not of every significant term must one or the other of contradictories be asserted. Nonetheless, of any such term either the affirmation or the denial of any predicate is true. This is the meaning of Aristotle's principle: "Of anything either an affirmation or a denial and of nothing both." Therefore, while neither "man" nor "not-man" is to be asserted of a chimera, yet "man" is either truly affirmed or truly denied of it. Hence either "A chimera is a man" or "A chimera is not a man" is true, and likewise either "A chimera is a not-man" or "A chimera is not a not-man."

So firm is Ockham's conviction that no affirmative is true whose subject lacks supposition, as in the case of fictitious beings, that he does not accept "A chimera is a chimera" as a true proposition; this would be true, he says, only if "A chimera is something" were true.[6] He even frowns on definitions of such fictions in the form

[6] *Ibid* 259-260. Et si dicatur: Numquid ista est vera: Chimaera est chimaera?" Videtur, quod sic, eo quod praedicatur idem de se, et Boethius dicit, quod nulla propositio est verior illa, in qua idem praedicatur de se. — Dicendum est, quod de virtute vocis ista est falsa: "Chimaera est chimaera," is termini supponant significative, eo quod falsum implicatur. Et ad Boethium dicendum, quod Boethius intendit, quod nulla propositio, in qua aliquid praedicatur de aliquo, est verior illa, in qua idem praedicatur de se; quia tamen ista est negativa, cum ista stat, quod nulla sit vera, nec illa, in qua idem praedicatur de se, nec illa, in qua praedicatur aliud. Si tamen illa esset vera, in qua praedicatur aliquid de aliquo, ista esset vera, in qua idem praedicatur de se. Sicut si haec esset vera: "Chimaera est aliquid," haec esset vera: "Chimaera est chimaera." Et ita nulla propositio, in qua praedicatur aliquid de hoc nomine "chimaera" significative sumpto, potest esse verior illa, in quo hoc nomen "chimaera" praedicatur de se ipso. Cum hoc tamen stat, quod nec ista nec illa sit vera.

"A chimera is an animal, part goat and part ox," granting the truth of such a statement only as a paraphrase of " 'Chimera' and 'animal, part goat and part ox' have the same meaning."[7]

The doctrine that Ockham propounded in the 14th century John of St. Thomas propounded and defended 300 years later. There is indeed a passage in *Ars Logica* in which he appears to accept the equivalence of obverse propositions. In arguing for his thesis, to which he attaches considerable importance, that there is an essential difference between affirmatives and negatives and not a mere accidental difference as there is between universals and particulars, he takes note of this objection[8]:

> . . . An affirmative and a negative can be synonymous, as "Man is rational" and "Man is not irrational." Hence they are specifically the same.

His reply is that while these propositions are of the same species on the part of the matter and the subject materially considered, they

[7]*Ibid.*, Vol. I, *Pars* I, *cap.* 26, 80. Ex quo sequitur, quod sic accipiendo definitionem aliquando praedicatio definitionis de definito per hoc verbum "est," utroque significative sumpto, est impossibilis. Sicut haec est impossibilis: "Chimaera est animal compositum ex capra et bove" — sit haec eius definitio. Et hoc propter implicationem impossibilem, qua scilicet implicatur componi ex capra et bove. Tamen propositio, in qua illi termini materialiter supponunt: " 'Chimaera' et 'animal compositum ex capra et bove' idem significant," vera est. Et per istam primam communiter loquentes intelligunt istam secundam, quae tamen secundum proprietatem sermonis est alia . . . Verumtamen conditionalis ex tali definito et definitione composita vera est. Ista enim vera est: "Si aliquid est chimaera, ipsum est compositum ex homine et leone," et e converso," Ockham's lack of interest in the chimaera is manifest, since he assigns several combinations of animals to its composition: goat, cow, man, lion.

[8]Ioannis de Sancto Thoma, O. P., *Ars Logica seu de Forma et Materia Ratiocinandi* (Roma: Marietti, 1948), *Pars* I, *Qu.* V, *art.* iv, 165-166. Et confirmatur, quia propositio affirmativa et negativa possunt esse synonimae, ut "homo est rationalis,"; "homo non est irrationalis"; ergo sunt eiusdem speciei. Patet consequens quia respiciunt idem obiectum, ab obiecto autem sumitur species . . .

Ad confirmationem respondetur, quod illae duae propositiones licet eiusdem speciei exparte materiae seu subiecto materialiter considerati, tamen ex parte formae et artificiosi modi enuntiandi sunt diversae, quod est esse eiusdem speciei posterioristice, diversae autem prioristice; sicut ex eodem obiecto et materia potest fieri enthymema et syllogismus, quae in ratione artificiosae orationis et consequentiae sunt diversae speciei, posterioristice autem erunt eiusdem rationis.

are nonetheless diverse in form and manner of expression, which is the determinant of the species; *a posteriori* they are the same, *a priori* they differ. His meaning appears to be that, since we know that men exist and are rational, we perceive that both statements are true, but that without the knowledge of the facts in the case we could not ascertain from the form of the statements whether or not they agreed. At any rate, in the light of his clear and constant teaching that affirmatives require supposition for their subjects and negatives do not, it is certain that John of St. Thomas holds that the affirmative implies its obverse and that the negative does not.

Two objections may be raised against this statement. One is that while there is no mention of obversion in *Ars Logica,* there is in the following passage an explicit description of contraposition:

> Conversion by contraposition is the transposition of subject and predicate with the interchange of definite and indefinite terms, as from "Every man is an animal" there follows "Every not-animal is a not-man."[9]

Then comes the rule still to be found in Latin textbooks:

> FECI simpliciter, EVA per accidens,
> ASTO per contra, sic fit conversio tota.

Since contraposition is effected only by means of obversion, it may appear that in accepting the one, John of St. Thomas must accept the other also. If he said no more about contraposition we should have to conclude that he does consider obverse propositions to be equivalent.

But he has more to say about the matter. Sometimes textbook writers, in their zeal to simplify logic and make it easier for the student, actually falsify it. Perhaps John of St. Thomas fails in this respect when in the first part of his book he presents contraposition so starkly, making no qualifications concerning its validity, but reserving for the *Quaestiones Disputatae* his more complete and careful discussion. There, however, he does make an important qualification, which some writers professedly in the scholastic tra-

[9]*Ibid., Pars* I, *Lib.* II, *cap.* xix, 47. Conversio per contrapositionem est mutatio praedicati in subiectum variatis terminis penes finitum et infinitum, ut si dicas: "Omins homo est animal," sequitur bene: "Ergo omne non-animal est non-homo"; "quidam homo non est albus," "ergo non-album non est non-homo."

dition say nothing about. After justifying the simple conversion of E and I and the conversion of A, he continues:

> Conversion by contrapositions is based on two rules laid down by Aristotle. First: From the affirmative to the negative with the interchange of definite and indefinite terms there is an implication, as "Man is white, therefore man is not not-white." Second: From the negative to the affirmative with the interchange of definite and indefinite terms and the insertion of the *constantia,* there is a valid inference, as "Man is not a stone, and man exists (this is the *constantia,* declaring that there is such a subject), therefore man is a not-stone."[10]

In his examples he is careful to supply the *constantia* whenever he passes from a negative to an affirmative, whether the proposition is universal or particular and whether the subject is a definite or an indefinite term. It should be noted that he appeals to Aristotle as the source of his rules.

The other objection has the authority of eminent logicians, whom I should be slow to gainsay if they were not so clearly mistaken. Both Joseph[11] and Joyce[12] identify the *aequipollentia* of the medieval writers with the obversion of modern logic. If they are correct, the statement that there is no mention of obversion in *Ars Logica* is in error, for this work devotes a chapter to this topic of *aequipollentia.* It would be strange indeed if the earlier writers, while stoutly maintaining that affirmatives are true only if their subjects have supposition and that the absence of supposition for the subjects of negatives insures their truth, should accept a doctrine inconsistent with that one. Nevertheless, since the study of logic forbids us to take anything for granted, least of all may we do so when logicians are concerned. It is necessary to examine

[10]*Ibid., Pars* I, *Qu.* VII, *art.* iii, 194. Conversio per contrapositionem fundatur in illa duplici regula tradita ab Aristotele: Prima: "Ab affirmativa ad negativam, variato praedicato penes finitum et infinitum, bona est consequentia, ut: homo est albus, ergo homo non est non albus." Secunda: "A negativa ad affirmativam, variato praedicato penes finitum et infinitum, et posita constantia subiecti in affirmativa, valet consequentia, ut "Homo non est lapis, et homo est (hoc dicitur constantia, quia constat dari tale subiectum) ergo homo non est non-lapis."

[11]H. W. B. Joseph, *An Introduction to Logic* (Oxford: at the Clarendon Press, 1950), 237.

[12]George Edward Joyce, *Principles of Logic* (New York: Longmans, Green and Co., 1926), 98.

aequipollentia as John of St. Thomas presents it. If Joseph and Joyce had done so, they would have been convinced that it is a purely verbal operation, not producing a new proposition, but merely showing another way to state a given one.

The rules are simple.[13] For contradictories, one places *non* before one of the pair to obtain the *aequipollens* of the other. For contraries, one places *non* after the subject of the one to obtain the *aequipollens* of the other. For subalterns, one performs both these operations on the one to obtain the *aequipollens* of the other. Subcontraries have no *aequipollentes.* In stating the rule for contradictories, John of St. Thomas warns that the negation is to be taken as precisely that and not as producing an indefinite term. This caution must apply to the other cases too, for in the examples the predicates are verbs and elsewhere in *Ars Logica* there is a chapter proving that an indefinite verb cannot serve as a predicate, as is noted below.

John of St. Thomas gives some examples of the application of the rules but he does not carry out the rules for all cases. The following list contains his illustrations as well as examples that result in the cases he omits. The only change is the use of *currit* in all instances in place of *disputat,* which he uses in some of his examples. Since the rules do not have the same effect when applied to English sentences as they do when applied to Latin, it is neces-

[13]Ioannis a Sancto Thoma, *op. cit., Pars* I, *Lib.* II, *cap.* xviii, 46. Aequipollentia nihil aliud est quam "propositionum oppositarum penes variationem negationis aequivalentia et eiusdem sensus significatio." Ad hoc autem sunt tres regulae: Prima: Propositis duabus contradictoriis, si uni illarum praeponatur negatio, redduntur aequipollentes. Intelligitur: dummodo negatio teneatur neganter, et non infinitanter . . . Secunda regula: Positis duabus propositionibus contrariis fiunt aequipollentes postponendo negationen subiecto propositionis ante copulam . . . Tertia regula est pro subalternis ut "Omnis homo disputat"; "aliquis homo disputat": fiunt aequipollentes per praepositionem et postpositionem; ut si dicas: "Non omnis homo disputat" aequipollet huic: "Aliquis homo disputat", et "Non aliquis homo non disputat" aequipollet illi: "Omnis homo disputat . . . De suncontrariis non dantur aequipollentiae, quia non sunt capaces. Si enim praeponas negationem, redditur universalis propositio et consequenter non aequipollens particulari, ut "Quidam homo est albus"; "Quidam homo non est albus." Si dicas: "Non quidam homo est albus," est idem quod nullus. Si postponas negationem subiecto in affirmativa, fiet non aequipollens, sed formaliter negativa, ut "Quidam homo est albus," si postponas negationem fiet negativa: "Quidam homo non est albus," non autem aequipollens negativae. Si vero ipsi negativae postponatur, fiet repetitio inutilis: "Quidam homo non non est albus."

sary to give the examples in the original. The first and second columns contain: the contradictories, (1), (2), (3), (4); the contraries, (5), (6); and the subalterns, (7), (8), (9), (10). The sentences in the third column are the *aequipollentes* of those in the second.

	I	II	III
(1)	Omnis homo currit	Aliquis homo non currit	Non omnis homo currit
(2)	Aliquis homo non currit	Omnis homo currit	Non aliquis homo non currit
(3)	Nullus homo currit	Aliquis homo currit	Non nullus homo currit
(4)	Aliquis homo currit	Nullus homo currit	Non aliquis homo currit
(5)	Omnis homo currit	Nullus homo currit	Omnis homo non currit
(6)	Nullus homo currit	Omnis homo currit	Nullus homo non currit
(7)	Omnis homo currit	Aliquis homo currit	Non omnis homo non currit
(8)	Aliquis homo currit	Omnis homo currit	Non aliquis homo non currit
(9)	Nullus homo currit	Aliquis homo non currit	Non nullus homo non currit
(10)	Aliquis homo non currit	Nullus homo currit	Non aliquis homo non non currit

That John of St. Thomas attaches but little importance to this matter is evident from his silence regarding (10), which is not one of his examples. In that *aequipollens* there is a repetition of *non,* which is one reason for the exclusion of subcontraries from this operation. He argues that if *non* is prefixed to *Quidam homo est bonus* the resulting sentence is the same as *Nullus homo est bonus;* if *non* is placed after the subject the result is the subcontrary itself, not its *aequipollens;* if *non* is placed after the subject of *Quidam non est bonus* the result is but a useless repetition of *non.* To attach *non* to *bonus,* thus forming the indefinite *non-bonus,* would violate the caution that the negation should not be taken to form an indefinite term. More importantly, it would be contrary to the principle that affirmatives and negatives differ in essence.

Obviously then *aequipollentia* is quite different from obversion; obverses are opposite in quality, while *aequipollentes* are either both affirmative or both negative. It is likely that the only instances that interested John of St. Thomas are (1), which gives an alternative way of expressing the O proposition, and (5), which he himself often employs instead the form "No S is P."

The importance to John of St. Thomas of determining the quality of compound propositions appears in another passage in which he discusses the quality of compound propositions. He states this rule: If both members are affirmative, the compound is affirmative; if both are negative, the compound is negative; if the members differ in quality, then the compound implying an affirmative is affirmative, the compound implied by a negative is negative. Thus "Peter was not white but is white" is affirmative because it implies "Peter is white"; while "Either Peter is white or he was not white" is negative because it is implied by "Peter was not white." There can scarcely be any doubt that the importance to this question arises from the doctrine that affirmatives require supposition for their subjects while negatives do not.

In his discussion of contradiction John of St. Thomas answers certain questions, one of which concerns the statement "Peter who flies is a man." His reply is that this may be reworded to say "The flying Peter is a man." Its contradictory is "The flying Peter is not a man," which is true because the subject is one of which any denial is true. Another example is "Every irrational man is a man." Its contradictory is "Some irrational man is not a man," which is true because the predicate is denied of a fiction, of which any denial is true. In the light of the discussion that follows it is interesting that this proposition is particular and that its subject is an indefinite term.

Perhaps the most convincing evidence that John of St. Thomas does not accept the equivalence of obverse propositions is that he continues to adhere to the rule concerning the reduction of Baroco and Bocardo. Many writers point out that these are subject to direct reduction by means of obversion and contraposition. In his *Elements of Logic,*[14] first published in 1826, Richard Whately works out what he calls the ostensive reduction of these moods. Still he follows the tradition of accepting the validity of the relations of the square of opposition and of the strengthened moods of the syllogism, a position not compatible with the direct reduction of Baroco and Bocardo. John of St. Thomas is aware of contraposition. If he recognized is as a formally valid procedure it is highly unlikely that he would fail to suggest it as a means of such direct reduction. Instead he simply states that these moods are to be reduced indirectly because they cannot be reduced in any other way.

[14]Richard Whately, D. D., *Elements of Logic, Containing the Substance of the Article in the Encyclopaedia Metropolitana with Additions &c,* (London: B. Fellowes, 1844), 95-96.

It would be interesting to know when logicians began to accept the equivalence of obverses, whether Whately broke new ground or merely fell in line with a practice already begun. At any rate, after his time and until quite recently, logicians seem to have taken such equivalence for granted along with the validity of the relations of the square of opposition. Some even attribute the doctrine to Aristotle. As has been noted, both Ockham and John of St. Thomas appeal to Aristotle as their authority for treating affirmatives as existential and negatives as nonexistential. Some recent investigators of Aristotle's teaching have reached conclusions that agree in large measure with the older writers' position.

One such interpretation is that of Manley Thompson, who has made an analysis of *De Interpretatione* which is in many respects similar to that of Ockham and John of St. Thomas. He writes:

> Aristotle does not say explicitly that a universal affirmative or A statement is false when nothing of the kind named exists, but what he does say about the logical relations of quantified statements seems to me to make the best sense when we take this interpretantion of the universal affirmative . . . With this interpretation of the square, the existential import of a statement is determined by its quality rather than by its quantity.[15]

Still Thompson is not in full agreement with the writers in the scholastic tradition, as this summary of his conclusions shows:

> I believe that there is little room for doubt about the following two points: (1) Whenever a statement containing no indefinite terms and representing one of the four categorical forms is logically related to another statement containing indefinite terms, the relation seems to be implication rather than equivalence. (2) In every case the affirmative statement is the antecedent of the implication.[16]

The difference of this interpretation from that of the scholastics lies in its restriction of the rule to pairs of propositions one of which contains no indefinite terms. Thompson understands that for Aristotle statements with indefinite subjects are governed by the same principle as are all categoricals in the modern convention,

[15]Manley Thompson, "On Aristotle's Square of Opposition," in J. M. E. Moravcsik, *Aristotle* (Garden City, New York, 1967, 51-72), 59-60. (The article is reprinted from *The Philosophical Review,* LXII (1953), 251-265).
[16]*Ibid.,* p. 62.

particulars being existential and universals nonexistential. In consequence, statements like "Every not–man is not just," which he takes to be a universal affirmative, "do not have existential import in so far as they are assertions about the members of a collection that are not such and such," while "particular statements with indefinite terms as subjects, on the other hand, are always equivalent to compound assertions of existence, even though they appear to be particular negatives." He goes on to state:

> An A statement implies, but is not equivalent to, its observe, its partial contrapositive, and its full contrapositive . . . "No not-P is S" is equivalent to its observe, because it has an indefinite term as subject so that neither it nor its obverse has existential import. The inference from "Every not-P is not-S" to "Some not-S is not-P," the so-called full inverse of "Every S is P," is illegitimate because the antecedent in this case does not have existential import while the consequient does.[17]

Thompson adduces several reasons to support his thesis that for Aristotle propositions with indefinite subjects depart from the general rule. First, while Aristotle presents a group of propositions with indefinite subjects, just as he does for those with definite subjects, he does not in the former case, as he does in the latter, follow it with quantified propositions. Indeed Aristotle refers to "not–man" somewhat slightingly as "a kind of subject," and in regard to the propositions he remarks, "This last group should remain distinct from those which preceded it, since it employs as its subject the expression 'not–man.' " Thompson argues at some length that such statements are naturally diverse from those having definite subjects, in much the same way that John of St. Thomas argues in support of his thesis concerning the essential difference between affirmatives and negatives. Thompson writes:

> From this point of view, the statements are compound denials rather than affirmations—they deny that there is at least one member of the collection which is . . . not-man and just. This equivalence to a compound denial is again the result of the peculiar signification of indefinite terms, and is no less the case when the statement appears to be a universal affirmative. "Every not-man is just" is equivalent to the denial that there is at least one thing which is both not-man and not just.[18]

[17] *Ibid.,* 66-67.
[18] *Ibid.,* 64.

In what appears to be the clinching argument Thompson quotes this statement of Aristotle's *De interpretatione,* 20 a 40:

> On the other hand, the proposition "Everything that is not man is not just" is equivalent to "Nothing that is not man is just."

He makes this comment:

> Yet if treated as an ordinary categorical statement, the first member of this equivalence is ambiguous and might mean "Not every not-man is just" instead of "No not-man is just." In order for the equivalence to hold, "every" and "no" must be taken with the force of everything and nothing.[19]

Here Thompson understates the extent of the ambiguity. Besides meaning "Not every not-man is not just" and "Every not-man is not-just," it can mean "Every not-man is not just" as simply an alternative to "No not-man is just." As a matter of fact, this is often the meaning such sentences are meant to convey in ordinary speech; it is not easy to dissuade the college student of logic from employing this form to express the E proposition. No doubt it is in this sense that John of St. Thomas understands the sentence. In view of his reference to Aristotle as the source of his rules for contraposition, we may be sure that he read the statement in question. But his understanding of it is not the same as Thompson's. For him the two sentences mentioned are not equivalents but *aequipollentes,* variant expressions of a single proposition rather than two propositions implying each other. One of his examples of *aequipollentia* in the list given above, namely, (5), is in precisely this form. Moreover he frequently uses this form to express the E proposition. One instance of this use occurs in the illustration of contraposition.

> "Every man is white, therefore every man is not not-white" by the first rule, "Therefore every not-white is not man" by conversion of the universal negative. By the second rule: "Every not-white is not man, and there is a not-white, therefore every not-white is a not-man," which is the converse of the original, "Every man is white."[20]

[19]*Ibid.*

[20]Ioannis a Sancto Thoma, *op. cit. Pars* I, *Qu.* VII, *art.* iii. 194: Ex quibus probatur converti *universalem affirmativam* sic: "Omnis homo est albus, ergo omne non-album est non-homo" quia bene valet: "Omnis homo est albus,

The example shows that on this interpretation, a categorical, while it implies its obverse and its partial contrapositive, does not, as in Thompson's analysis, imply its full contrapositive; and that a statement in the form "No not–P is S" is not equivalent to its obverse, as it is for Thompson. For John of St. Thomas finds it necessary to supply the *constantia* in order to obvert "Every not–white is not man" and so infer the full contrapositive, "Every not–white is a not–man." Besides illustrating this writer's use of the form "Every S is not P" for the E proposition, the example demonstrates that the scholastics' understanding of categorical propositions does not expose them to the peril of inferring absurd statements from a true one, as in the case of "Some nonmathematicians are circle–squarers,"the inverse of "All mathematicians are noncircle–squarers." For before reaching the inverse, they find it necessary to infer "All circle–squarers are nonmathematicians" from "No circle-squarers are mathematicians," a step they cannot take without supplying the *constantia,* "There is at least one circle–squarer."

It has been this writer's intention to outline the scholastic theory of propositions as it is taught by Ockham and John of St. Thomas and to show that it is a consistent one, not entailing the fallacies that result from combining it with another system. His purpose is not to vindicate their appeal to Aristotle as the source of their interpretation. Nevertheless, it may not be out of place to remark that there is something to be said for the construction John of St. Thomas puts on Aristotle's statement with regard to "Everything that is not man is not just" and "Nothing that is not man is just." The version quoted is that of the Oxford edition. In the Loeb translation the statement reads,

> "Everything that is not man is not just," which amounts to the same thing as saying that "Nothing that is not man is just."

This seems to be closer to the Greek ταυτον σημαινει the literal rendering of which is "means the same." "Means the same as" is surely stronger than "is equivalent to." Equivalent propositions imply each other, but they do not mean precisely the same. *Aequipol-*

---

ergo omnis homo non est non-album" per primam regulam. Rursus: "Ergo omne non-album non est homo" per conversionem universalis negativae. Rursus per secundam regulam positam valet: "Omne non-album non est homo, et non-album est, ergo omne non-album est non-homo," quae est convertens illius primae: "Omnis homo est albus."

lentes, on the other hand, are identical in meaning, since they are but variant expressions of a single proposition. Unlike obverses, which have different predicates, *aequipollentes* have the same predicate. Furthermore, in the context, Aristotle appears to be concerned more with what propositions mean than with what they imply. When he writes that "Every not-man is just" and "Not every not-man is just" do not mean the same as any previous examples, he may well be warning the student against becoming confused by the frequent repetition of οὐκ and οὐ.

John of St. Thomas is well aware of the distinction between definite and indefinite terms, which in Thompson's view is the reason for Aristotle's excepting statements with indefinite subjects from the general rule for existential import. A chapter of *Ars logica* is devoted to proving that such terms, while they can serve as subjects and predicates, are not truly names *(nomina)* because they tell only what a thing is not, and not what it is.[21] Another chapter argues that, while a verb taken by itself may be indefinite, it is never such when it serves as the predicate of a proposition; in such a case, the negation applies only to the relation between subject and predicate and does not adhere to the verb.[22] Nowhere, however, is there a suggestion that the presence of an indefinite term affects the nature of the proposition of which it is the subject or predicate. Aristotle's remark about viewing propositions with "not-man" as subject as distinct from those with definite subjects, which Thompson finds so significant, draws no comment from John of St. Thomas. Difference in quality is essential, difference in quantity is accidental, but difference in the kind of subject seems to have no effect on the proposition. Nor is there among the numerous objections to his teaching that he answers any that proposes to treat statements with indefinite subjects differently from others.

[21] *Ibid., Pars* I, *Qu.* II, *art.* ii, 114-118: His positis dico: Nomen infinitum excludi a ratione nominis per illam particularem "finita." To the objection that indefinite terms should be accounted to be names because they serve as subjects and predicates of propositions, he replies: Possunt enim multa poni in propositione ut extrema, non quia sunt nomina, sed quia tenentur in vi nominis . . ., ut si dicas: "currere est moveri."

[22] *Ibid., Pars.* I, *Qu* III, *art.* ii, 125-128: Unde tenet ratio S. Thomae, quod quia in propositione negatio verbi removet unum ab alio, non potest infinitari verbum. Extra propositionem, autem, cum non teneatur in vi copulantis, infinitari potest.

Neither the proofs advanced by John of St. Thomas in support of his thesis concerning the essential diversity of affirmatives and negatives nor Thompson's reasons for his belief that "the peculiar signification of indefinite terms" calls for a different interpretation of statements with such subjects from that of statements with definite subjects appear to be very convincing. As to the former, logicians today find no difficulty in calling propositions of opposite quality equivalent; as to the latter, these logicians argue in much the same manner that all universals are naturally nonexistential as Thompson does in the case of those having indefinite subjects. The truth of the matter seems to be that there is no one correct interpretation of categorical propositions. What is important in any convention is that it should be consistent. The modern system, which rejects the relations of the square of opposition and accepts the equivalence of obverses is consistent. So also is that of Ockham and John of St. Thomas, which accepts the relations of the square and sees obversion as a one-way street, the affirmative implying the negative but not being implied by it. So also is the somewhat cumbersome system of Manley Thompson. There is no reason to doubt that Aristotle's system is consistent also, whether it is one of these or still another one. The scholastics' system seems to lack the flexibility and power of the modern one, but that is a practical matter. In consistency it yields nothing to any other.

Whether William Ockham and John of St. Thomas are correct in their understanding of Aristotle is unimportant. It is important that their system entails no fallacies. In it all the moods of the syllogism, including those with strengthened premises, are valid; the rules of the syllogism regarding quality and quantity are sufficient, with no need for another forbidding a particular conclusion to be drawn from universal premises. All that is required is that A and I shall have existential import and that E and O shall not. In this system, A implies I, E implies O, and both A and E imply their limited converses. On the other hand, neither obverses nor contrapositives are equivalent to each other; an affirmative implies its obverse, but is not implied by it. The A proposition implies its partial, but not its full, contrapositive; full contrapositives are independent of each other.

It would be well for writers in the scholastic tradition to take account of these distinctions and not to present obversion and contraposition without the qualifications John of St. Thomas so carefully makes. It is unfortunate that writers in the modern tradition represent the older logicians as so lacking in logical insight as to state principles that lead to palpable fallacies. But their misunderstanding is hardly surprising when the supposed representatives of the scholastic tradition misrepresent it. Logic is not an easy subject. To attempt to teach it by means of a few rules of thumb without pointing out the changes that result from shifts in the interpretation of propositions hardly serves the purpose that logic has in the philosophy curriculum.

In conclusion it may be noted that there is no metaphysical implication in the different ways of interpreting propositions. Either way of understanding categorical propositions is compatible with any system of metaphysics. Still it is difficult to free ourselves from the conventions of our time. Perhaps this is the excuse for writers of scholastic texts who attempt to fuse the old interpretation with the new. Horace asked his readers

Humano capiti cervicem pictor equinam
iungere si velit . . .
spectatum admissi risum teneatis, amici?[23]

Could you keep from laughing if you saw a painter putting a man's head on a horse's neck? The joining of two interpretations of propositions is not a matter for laughter but rather for tears.

Historian and Archivist
Archdiocese of Indianapolis

[23] *Ars poetica*, lines 1-5.

9

THE INTERIOR METAPHYSICS OF PLOTINUS

by John E. Kelly

In every philosophical epoch, whether ancient, medieval, or modern, the metaphysician is faced with the task of reconciling being and thought. The search for being in an unqualified, absolute sense is that toward which thought unceasingly moves but can never adequately grasp.[1] Further still, in order to be effective in this mediating process, the metaphysician must find an adequate central point of reference which will give meaning to and thereby show the positive content of his basic philosophical concepts.[2] This undertaking is crucial, for there are always philosophers of other persuasions who feel most uncomfortable with the way the metaphysician utilizes such all-embracing concepts in an attempt to grasp reality in its most fundamental aspects.[3] The point is inevitably raised that perhaps these abstract concepts and elaborate schemes of the metaphysician are empty formulations with no existential foundation in the real.

[1]Martin Heidegger, *Was ist Metaphysics,* 5th ed. (Frankfurt A.M., Klostermann, 1949), p. 46. "Das Denken, gehorsam der Stimme des Seins, sucht diesem das Wort, aus dem die Wahrheit des Seins zur Sprache kommt."

On this same point, G.W.F. Hegel stresses that ". . . Nature and the world or history of spirit, are the two realities . . . The ultimate aim of philosophy is to reconcile thought or the Notion with reality." G.W.F. Hegel, *Lectures on the History of Philosophy,* trans. E. S. Haldane and F. H. Simson (London: Routledge and Kegan Paul, 1955), III, 545.

[2]Kenneth Schmitz emphasizes that ". . . the supremacy of a metaphysical insight may be gauged by its ability to absorb within itself all other metaphysical insights. In its absorption, furthermore, the others ought to receive their proper intelligible location, realize their ontological identity, maintain their integrity, and be charged with a profundity which is not theirs alone." "Metaphysical Restoration of Natural Things" in *An Etienne Gilson Tribute,* ed. Charles J. O'Neil (Milwaukee: Marquette University Press, 1959), p. 261.

[3]For example, such concepts as being, unity, goodness, and substance.

On the contemporary scene, the existentialist tradition attempts to come to grips with this problem by bringing under tighter control the creative tension between thought and being. By a more careful analysis of the tentativeness of the self or spirit in all its lived experiential immediacy, are they not suggesting that the centrality of the dynamic subject is a more privileged vantage point than we realize for gaining insight into the causes or principles beyond the reach of direct human experience? The aspect of the self to which we must appeal, therefore, is the innate dynamism of the mind itself as it points beyond itself toward a source which will make the world of our immediate experience adequately intelligible.[4] In a sense one must learn to live consciously the relation of the incomplete self to the Absolute or run the risk of remaining sterilely formal and empty of insight.[5]

The genius of the Greek philosophers is marked by an ability always to preserve this vital union of reason and life.[6] Within the tradition of antiquity there is no figure who crystallizes this "way" more consciously and with greater rigor and control than Plotinus. In the field of mystical theology, in his role as philosophical theologian, Plotinus makes important contributions toward a better understanding of what he considers are the two basic realities in a philosopher's quest for wisdom; these realities are God and the soul.[7] He attempts to metaphysically ground with an all-embracing and directive principle, this cosmic force, this source and impulse to movement and activity which is so fundamental to the finite

[4]Cf. Alexander Kojève, *Introduction to the Reading of Hegel,* trans. James Nichols (New York: Basic Books, 1969), p. 4. "In contrast to the knowledge that keeps man in a passive quietude, desire dis-quiets him and moves him to action. Born of desire, action tends to satisfy it and can do so only by the 'negation,' the destruction or at least the transformation of the desired object."

[5]W. Norris Clark, "The Self as Source of Meaning," *Review of Metaphysics,* 21 (1968), 604.

[6]C.J. de Vogel, "The Concept of Personality in Greek Thought," *Studies in Philosophy and the History of Philosophy,* II (1963), 20-60, see also her "What Philosophy Meant to the Greeks," *International Philosophical Quarterly,* I (1961), 55.

[7]St. Augustine, whose debt to the philosophy of Plotinus is very great, writes that ". . . philosophy has a double question, one of the soul, the other about God." *De ordine* II, xviii, 47 ed. P. Knoll, *Corpus scriptorum ecclesiasticorum latinorum* (Vienna, 1922), LXIII, 180.

world.[8] His entire system is based on a mediating process which seems to consist in the expansion of consciousness until the subject or knower is no longer aware of the limits of individuality, but becomes in some way united with the absolute source of being. Until the soul has reached this state of absorbed contemplation it can only be described as a striving, a tendency, a dynamic direction of consciousness.[9]

It can be stated with a reasonable amount of certitude that Plotinus always formally remains a Platonist as far as his general orientation is concerned, but he does not hesitate to modify Plato's meaning and to go beyond it, if that is warranted in order to develop his own line of thought.[10] Almost always he will try to weave original elements of his own thought into the Platonic superstructure.

Plato's passion for the divine, and his desire for unity certainly influenced Plotinus. The *Phaedrus* and *Symposium* give us an ordered analysis of spiritual reality striving toward fulfillment. The conception of *Eros* as developed in these two dialogues presents spiritual reality as dynamic, as striving, as loving. Spirit is encountered here as reason filled with aspiration for unity. All these elements could not help but aid Plotinus in his own development, where all being derives from a single infinite force which communicates

[8]*Ennead* III, 5, 1-9. References to the *Enneads,* unless otherwhise cited, are to the edition of Paul Henry and Hans-Rudolf Schwyzer, Editio maior I-II (Paris: Desclée de Brouwer, 1951-59). Use has also been made of the edition of Emile Bréhier, text and French translation with introductory notices to the treatises. (6 vols. in 7, Paris: Budé, 1924-38) 3rd edition, 1960. See also Marsilio Ficino's Latin translation, *Plotini Enneades* (Paris: Didot, 1855).

[9]Henry Duméry, commenting on the attitude of the finite subject toward the Absolute, writes: "One does not know God (as an object). But because being situated with relation to him and being spirit are the same thing, all orientation toward him (that is, the manner in which the spirit masters its own experience in order to open itself to him) entails various and complex approaches within the heart of consciousness. In short, the spirit is relation to God; the spiritual life is the concrete 'exercise' of this relation, the knowledge of God is reflection on this exercise." Henry Duméry, *The Problem of God in Philosophy of Religion,* trans. Charles Courtney (Evanston: Northwestern University Press, 1964), p. 115, n. 23.

[10]In *Ennead* VI, 2, 22, Plotinus stresses that Plato sometimes speaks in riddles, that he leaves us to work out its meaning for ourselves. See also V, 8, 4 and IV, 4, 22.

itself to all subsequent levels of existence.[11] However, on closer scrutiny of the Absolute in Plato and the subject's relation to it, we find a gulf between the two thinkers. Plato does not go far enough in working out the implications of this center or ground of being and the degree to which the subject can reach union with it. Paul Friedländer comments that Plato seems uneasy remaining on this highest of metaphysical regions for too long.[12] Plato speaks of "touches" and "flashes" of the divine, rather than of a sustained vision. There seems to be more concern for intuitive apprehension rather than genuine and lasting union.[13] Plato had to take this more restrained position precisely because his thought lacks a vision of the world as an organic whole. The levels of being in Plotinus' system, reaching its ultimate source in "the One,"[14] never entail that disparate quality, that inability to completely erase the dual view of the universe which permeates the thought of Plato. Resistance to the reality of the sensible world and the exaltation of the Ideas as transcendent objects of contemplation intensified the Platonic split between the so-called perishable and imperishable worlds—the concrete world and the world of forms—making the gap between knower and object of intellection more profound. In the final analysis Platonism ends with Form, external, ineffable,

[11]*Ennead,* VI, 5, 12 (5). Plotinus speaks here of a "δυναμιζ Βυσσοθεν απειρσζ." See also P. Hadot, "Etre, vie, pensée chez Plotin et avant Plotin," *Les Sources de Plotin* (Genéve: Hardt Fondation, 1957), V, 107-137.

[12]Paul Friedländer, *Plato, An Introduction* (New York: Harper Torchbook, 1958), pp. 59-84.

[13]*Ibid.,* p. 82. In his *Eros and Psyche—Studies in Plato, Plotinus and Origen* (Toronto: University of Toronto Press, 1964), J. M. Rist comments upon the tension between the two forces in the soul of Plato: one is pure reason, the other is more personal. For an excellent account of the more animistic or personal force in Plato, see J. Pieper, *Divine Enthusiasm: A Study of the "Phaedrus"* (New York: Harcourt Brace, 1946). Consult also A. H. Armstrong and R.A. Markus, *Christian Faith and Greek Philosophy* (New York: Sheed & Ward, 1960), esp. chapter 7, "Love and Will," pp. 78-96.

[14]*Ennead* VI, 4 and 5. One of the pivotal features in the Plotinian system is insistence on the highly dynamic role which the One or Good plays in uniting the entire neoplatonic cosmogony. All being derives from a single infinite source which in no way is diminished as it causes lesser traces of itself. Complementing this procession there is an upward, ordered impulse or tendency in being to become identified with its source by imitating, as completely as possible, the perfect unity found in the One. (III, 8, 9; V, 4, 1.)

yet still form, limit, determination. The Absolute of Plotinus can participate in none of these qualities if it is to be called "the One."[15] Plotinus' supreme principle cannot be a limited, determined form; if such were the case, the One would merely be the complement of our deficiences rather than the spring of our energy, the condition of the possibility of being in the first place. Finite, determined being implies participated being. The self will not be satisfied until this limited status is completely justified.[16]

Plotinus' ultimate concern, then, is not with the Forms but rather with the cause of their very existence, which demands a quality superior to anything that even the highest of forms could enjoy. This seems to demand going beyond the world of form and determination.

Plotinus' entire life and work, therefore, is an attempt to arrive at the presence of the Absolute, the source of the Forms.[17] He is trying, then, to do more than undercut the dualism in the systems of his predecessors. Of greater importance is the consideration of this central intuition of the One as ultimate actuality and source

[15]*Ennead* VI, 8, 7 (49-54).

[16]Summarizing Pseudo-Dionysius and explaining how he subordinates ideas and being to God, Etienne Gilson writes, "the ideas, then represent divine rays, which are scarcely removed from their center, but are, however, already distinguished from it, since they are like the second revelation of the unity within number. The important thing to retain here is that God produces being as his first participation. Thus being is dependent on God, but God is not dependent on being." *(La philosophie au moyen âge,* 2nd ed., [Paris, 1944], p. 84).

[17]VI, 9, 6 (Bréhier, Vol. 6, part II, p. 179). Although we stress that Plotinus always formally remained a Platonist, it should not be thought that the works of Aristotle went unnoticed. Plotinus' knowledge of Aristotle and the commentators appears to have been extensive. Cf. Paul Henry, "Une comparison chez Aristote, Alexandre et Plotin," *Les Sources de Plotin,* 429-449. Of special interest to Plotinus must have been Aristotle's analysis of how the mind becomes the object, as well as the role of active reason as impersonal and universal. We find there the identity of divinity and intelligence, the belief in the supremacy and transcendence of the life of Nous. (*Nicomachean. Ethics* 1177b-1178a.)

In the final analysis, the Aristotelian *Nous* is found defective. True, there is found here a union of thought and object of thought; however, Plotinus fears to admit that the Absolute has knowledge even of itself, is to allow us to see it not as simply itself, but as a duality. The Plotinian Absolute is more unitary and more absolutely itself than man can conceive. See *Ennead* V, 6, 4 and especially *Ennead* III, 9, 9.

of power on all subsidiary levels of reality.[18] We sense through Plotinus' resistance to what he considers still the world of determination that the infinite is the inaccessible and compelling force of all intellectual activity. This urge for further contemplation beyond the world of form is made quite explicit in V, 1, 7 (10). Stressing *Nous* as the place of Forms, Plotinus remarks that Nous perceives these things by splitting them up in some way. If it did not do so, it would not be a Nous. And, furthermore, Nous derives from itself a kind of consciousness of this power of the One, a consciousness that the One brings being into existence.[19] This comes down to recognizing that the Absolute cannot be held in any determinations.[20]

Plotinus' treatment of the "Indefinite Dyad" or "Intelligible Matter" and its relation to the One serves to explain the higher unitary source, and why there is a weakening of its influence in successive emanations.[21] The Indefinite Dyad serves as the paradigm of nature's striving for unity.[22] In *Ennead* II, 4, 3 (4 & 5) there is a detailed analysis of the relationship of Intelligible Matter and Nous to the One. Plotinus shows in these passages how the Dyad is so fundamentally a part of Nous. We see that the Dyad is Nous at its more primal stage.[23] The role of the Dyad is brought into sharper focus through a consideration of the nature of this "effluence" from the One when it first appears before it has returned

[18]VI, 4, 3 (12); VI, 4, 11 (12).

[19]V, 4, 2 (14-25).

[20]The ontological argument moves in this vein. It can succeed as a proof by relying on the prior conviction that God cannot be an idea among others. In reference to the ontological argument used by St. Bonaventure, Gilson writes, "Saint Bonaventure does not pass from the idea to being, since for him the idea is only the being's mode of presence in his thought. Thus there is no real transition to be affected between the idea of a God whose existence is necessary and the same God necessarily existing." (*La philosophie de saint Bonaventure,* 2nd ed., Paris, 1943, p. 110.)

The passage, then, is no longer from the idea to the being of God, but from his necessarily lived presence to his existence freely and consciously acknowledged.

[21]IV, 4, 36 (9).

[22]II, 4, 3.

[23]J.M. Rist, "The Indefinite Dyad and Intelligible Matter in Plotinus," *Classical Quarterly,* n. 2, 12, (1962), 99-107; also see A.H. Armstrong, *The Architecture of the Intelligible Universe in the Philosophy of Plotinus* (Cambridge: Cambridge University Press, 1940), 65-81.

in contemplation upon its source and becomes informed. Plotinus is concerned therefore, not with a description of Nous but, rather, with the rationale for its existence in the first place,—an existence which can best be described as tendency or urge for contemplation.

In speaking of the first effluence from the One, we learn that this process is an openness toward determination, it is unlimited—a potentiality for plurality. How does it function as a potentiality for plurality? What is involved in this active function, constantly being specified by the One? In II, 4, 3, Plotinus introduces us to the main feature of the Dyad, viz., it has a certain capacity of "offering itself to what is metaphysically prior."[24] He also stresses that this indetermination is not as in matter in the sensible world, for it has a certain sameness and stability.[25] It has the same form and is in a sense all things at once so that it cannot change into anything which is not itself. The foundation seems laid, then, to describe the Dyad as a kind of unity of openness to all things. Indeed because of its radical openness or shapelessness, there is found a unity and closer affinity to the infinite than Nous enjoys when it is taken in itself. Plotinus calls it a unity which accepts diversification and says that this unity must be matter.

A further development of Intelligible Matter is advanced in V, 4, 2. Plotinus makes use of the metaphor of sight to describe the activity when considered in its undetermined stage.[26] Plotinus states that Intellect is undetermined like sight (a vague readiness for any and every vision) and is determined by its object.[27] Its object is, of course, the One which is above all determination and form. In V, 3, 11 Nous is sight which has not yet seen. It is a potency with no impression yet made upon it. This impression must come from the One.

We can see then, that the contemplation of the One by Nous in the form of Intelligible Matter is the cause of the very existence of the Second Hypostasis. At the same time, the more active char-

[24]II, 4, 3 (1-3).

[25]*Ibid.*, lines 12ff.

[26]In regard to the use of the sight metaphor in Plotinus see R. Ferwerda, *La signification des images et des metaphores dans la pensée de Plotin* (Groningen: Wolters, 1965).

[27]V, 4, 2 (5-15).

acter of Nous is stressed. Nous is not only regarded as prior to the Intelligibles but generates them.[28]

The distinction between Nous and the Dyad or Intelligible Matter therefore is employed to demonstrate the full impact of the Second Hypostasis as an essentially active entity which needs a higher Principle to complete itself. When treating of the already established Second Hypostasis, one can simply say Nous. But when seeking the condition for the possibility of the existence of Nous in the first place, or for its continuous operation, one has to break down this level of reality into its more fundamental aspect. This is the level of Nous as Dyad, as openness to and desire of specification.

In *Ennead* III, 8, 11, the entire tract emphasizes how the One is the ultimate foundation of intelligibility. It will be granted that the Forms have their natural place in the Second Hypistasis, but their status in the final analysis depends upon the One as ultimate source.

Plotinus begins by comparing the Second Hypostasis with sight, explaining that, like sight, it must have both potentiality and actuality.[29] If such is the case, Plotinus continues, "this implies the distinction of Matter and Form in it, as there must be in all actual seeing."[30] The next line is the key to the entire passage. Plotinus stresses that "the Matter in this case is in the intelligibles which the Second Hypostasis contains and sees."[31] It would appear that the so-called material element of the Second Hypostasis is not simply in Nous or Mind as seer, but in the Forms as the objects of vision. It can be maintained, then, that this implies a certain priority of Nous to the Intelligibles or Forms. The Second Hypostasis regarded as Mind is the representative at a more advanced stage of Intelligible Matter, which itself looks back at the One.[32] Indeed the remainder of III, 8, 11, is concerned with precisely this point.[33]

[28]V, 8, 12. Bréhier translates this passage as follows: "il se complèt en ce qu'il engendre."

[29]III, 8, 11 (1-2).

[30]*Ibid.*, line 3.

[31]*Ibid.*, line 4.

[32]*Ibid.*, lines 5-10.

[33]Cf. III, 8, 11 (9ff). "Now as our sight requires the world of sense for its satisfaction and realization, so the vision in the Second Hypostasis demands for its completion, the Good."

By associating the Forms with the material aspect of the Hypostasis, Plotinus brings into clearer perspective that when taking the Second Hypostasis as a completed whole the Forms stand in an inferior position to Mind, and the entire Hypostasis is dependent upon a higher unity.[34]

The One or the Good is the real object of the Divine Mind's intellection. The Forms are only a second best. Nous sees the One as the Forms, but the intelligibility of those Forms is supplied by the One. Nous can not grasp the complete unity as found in the One, but expresses or mirrors the simplicity of the Highest order by means of the Forms.

The Dyad (or "earlier stage" of the Second Hypostasis) turned toward the One is compared "to an eye that has not yet seen." In its return, it is an eye possessed of the multiplicity which it has itself conferred: it sought something "of which it found the vague presentment (phantasma)."[36] The Dyad cannot adequately grasp the "simplex" or most simple of entities and can only make for itself a vision of multiplicity.[37]

In *Ennead* VI, 7, 15, Plotinus presents an excellent picture of the relation of the One to the second Hypostasis.

> But the Good comes to it not as it was in its primal state but in accord with the condition of the Intellectual Principle . . . but the Good bestows what itself does not possess.[38]

It is multiplicity, of course, which is not part of the world of the One.

Although the Dyad is not plurality, it is the cause of multiplicity simply by being other than the simplicity of the One. The Dyad, then, in its striving toward Unity, cannot support the Unity it is permitted to see. It can only accept this Unity in the form of multiplicity, thus "allowing" the Nous–Intelligibles complex, i.e., the fully developed Second Hypostasis now comes into existence. It would appear, therefore, that Nous is prior to the Forms. A more active role is in order for Divine Mind than a simple coincidence of knower and object known, i.e., the sight that sees no impressions now sees the One, but only through the medium of its own

[34]V, 3, 11.
[36]V, 3, 11 (5-10).
[37]*Ibid.*, (30ff).
[38]VI, 7, 15 (12ff).

otherness. Nous responds to the One not as pure Unity but as the world of Forms. Both the Forms and the One, then, may be described as the Intelligible. Nous sees the One as the Forms, but the intelligibility of those Forms is supplied by the One.[39] The Dyad can only grasp the One as multiplicity. This multiplicity constitutes the World of Forms, and these Forms can be said to define the previously undefined Dyad. The *cause* of the Dyad's being defined is the One, but what existentially define it are the Forms.[40]

In *Ennead* II, 4, 4, Plotinus maintains that if there are Forms, they must have both an element in common and a particular characteristic which distinguishes them one from the other. The distinguishing characteristic is that of shape (μορφη), and if they have shape, there must be something to receive the shape. The character common to all which receives the shapes must be Matter.[41] It is clear, then, that if there is Form in the Intelligible World, there must be Matter too.

> And how can you predict an ordered system without thinking of form, and how think of form apart from the notion of something in which the form is lodged.[42]

Plotinus continues that the Intelligible realm in the strict sense is utterly without parts, but in some sense there is part there too; this Intelligible realm is diversified and so there must be a basic shapelessness which can be the unifying force which accepts diversification; this unity must be Matter.[43]

The analysis of the double aspect of Nous tends to reinforce the demand of Plotinus that we go beyond the kind of knowledge involved in Aristotle's self-thinking mind. By suggesting that Nous is prior to the forms and indeed generates them through the specification of a higher principle, Plotinus attempts to show that there must be a more fundamental principle than that which is found in the Aristotelian account of God's knowledge; for even though there is unity in Aristotle's conception of God as the identity of knower and object of intellection, this union is formed by the resolution of a duality. Therefore, it is still a unity of plurality, and

[39]III, 8, 11.
[40]II, 4, 5; V, 1, 5.
[41]II, 4, 4 (1-10).
[42]*Ibid.*, (11-15).
[43]II, 4, 4 (20-30).

not simple enough to be the truly first Principle of the cosmos. Demonstrating further that this undetermined aspect of Nous (the Dyad) makes for a kinship with the One (which the Forms as such do not have since they are restricted to one form)—Plotinus can emphasize that there is a capacity in spirit to expand and go beyond the subject and apprehend and appropriate the whole. There is in Nous then, an immanent unity and structure which constantly is striving for further completion. Plotinus refers to this element as the supreme aspect of Nous.[44] This higher element in Nous will become a crucial issue for Plotinus when he attempts to explain the experience of union with the One.[45]

The most fruitful conception of Plotinus, then, is the dynamic unity of his metaphysical world. There is a transparency in it that permeates his entire system. Plotinus would offer a more pliable field of influence of one level of reality on another. With material being no longer dramatically opposed to spiritual reality the order of descent from the One becomes a question of a fragmentation of spirit rather than a sharp dichotomy between the mutable and immutable worlds.[46] The gradual deteriorization or determination of being is a *natural* consequence of emanation from the One the *or the first* where each level of reality stabilizes itself by imitating as best it can, the world of true being.[47] In *Ennead* III, 4, 2 (15) Plotinus claims that our life must be directed toward what is intellective, toward Nous and toward Theos. However, as has been seen, in the final analysis, this imitation or "mirroring" demands going beyond the world of true being or Theos (i.e., if Theos is associated with Aristotelian Nous).[48]

The kind of activity involved would seem to exceed mere discursive knowledge. It seems that the word επιβολη is Plotinus' favorite word for the knowledge enjoyed by the One which we must attempt to imitate.[49] Sinse επιβαλλειν can carry the meaning "attend", or "think on", Deck translates επιβολη of the One as a

[44]VI, 9, 3 (27) (edition Bréhier Vol. 6 part II, p. 175).

[45]V, 9, 4 (3) (ed. cit. p. 176).

[46]*Ennead* II, 3, 17 (21); III, 8, 10.

[47]VI, 7, 9.

[48]J.M. Rist, "Theos and the One in Some Texts of Plotinus," *Medieval Studies,* 24 (1962), 169-180.

[49]III, 8, 9 (20ff); IV, 4, 1 (2); IV, 4, 8 (6); VI, 8, 11 (23).

simple thrust towards itself.[50] Marsilio Ficino translates επιβολη "intuitus *(si deus non intelligit se ipsum, qua ratione bonum, quaeri potest, qua potissimum ratione. Ac respondere quis potest, nihil aliud adesse deo: sed simplicem quendam intuitum ipsi exsistere ad se ipsum.)*[51]

This certain "thrust" or "intuition" beyond the world of form or essence toward its ultimate Source helps us to focus on the central perspective in Plotinus' thought, viz., the diffusive character of the One or the Good.

This significant aspect of Plotinian thought follows from the author's insistence concerning the "trans-formal" character of the One. By locating the Supreme principle "beyond being," while at the same time developing a highly systematic theory of emanation, Plotinus is able to perfect the work of his predecessors. There unfolds a more intelligible link between the infinite and finite or lower levels of reality.[52]

By critical rethinking of Platonic and Aristotelian theology, Plotinus demonstrates how the One or Good can be a genuine creator or giver of being. Further still, by stressing the organic unity through all the levels of being, it can be shown how that which flows from the Source is a dynamic being which looks, strives and finally can achieve its total return and completion.[53]

In the purview of Plotinus, then, there unfolds an entirely new approach to the concept of being. Due to the detailed analysis of the hierarchy of being and his positing of the One "beyond being," Plotinus is able to systematically develop a more rigorous and meaningful theology of derivation and return.[54]

The difference and interplay between the One and Nous allows Plotinus to outline more tightly the dynamic and organic character

[50]John N. Deck, *Nature, Contemplation and The One* (Toronto: University of Toronto Press, 1967), p. 18.

[51]*Ennead* VI, 7, 39 (1-2) Ficino, p. 505.

[52]VI, 7, 31 (17-18); VI, 7, 22. Cf. also J. Peghaire, "L'axiome, 'bonum est diffusivum sui' dans le néoplatonisme et le thomisme," *Revue de l'Université Ottawa,* Section spéciale, Vol. I (1932), 5-32.

[53]I, 6, 7 (1-10).

[54]III, 8, 11 (14-15). Cf. E.R. Dodds, "The Parmenides of Plato and the Origin of the Neoplatonic One," *Classical Quarterly,* 22 (1928) 129-43. H.R. Schwyzer, "Die Zwiefache Sicht in der Philosophie Plotins," *Museum Helveticum,* I (1944), 87-99. C.J. de Vogel, "On the Neoplatonic Character of Platonism and the Platonic Character of Neoplatonism." *Mind,* 62 (1955), 43-64.

of being. His main concern, however, will not be with Nous, but rather with the third Hypostasis (Soul). Nous, in a certain sense, goes into the background, for Soul is Nous or intelligibility, though it is a more diminished aspect of it.[55] I stress that *Nous* enters the background, because at the level of *Nous,* being is more or less at one with itself and hence it is in the nondialectical stage; with soul, however, we are more directly in touch with the dialectical stage, for there is evidence here of the oscillation of consciousness as it attempts to attain unity within the order of being. The self or soul here is found attempting to reestablish consciously a closer identity with its Source. As Hazel Barnes has noted, "the unity already exists, but Soul, on the lower realms of the hierarchy, is unaware of it. Therefore, whether we speak of "ascent to higher spheres' or 'descent into the deeper realms of consciousness,' the same meaning is intended."[56]

In *Ennead* IV, 8 (1-5) Plotinus maintains that there can be a spiritual continuum extending through a definite series of degrees of intelligible clarity from its highest focus in "the Supreme God" to the most restricted confines of matter.[57] Soul functions as the interlacing link between the two extreme poles. There is an overflow of a single infinite source. This initial dynamic force communicates itself to all subsequent levels of existence by means of

[55]In order to categorize the three Hypotases, we might label the One as *radical unity,* Nous as *unity in multiplicity* and Soul as *unity and multiplicity.* Commenting on this oriented dynamism," and drawing a parallel between Plotinus and John Scotus Erigena, Henry Duméry says this: ". . . it seems that God can perfectly be the One without creating (thus he is transcendent); but because he is a 'Nihil per excellentian,' he cannot know himself (knowledge implying detour) without creating. By creating spirits that aim toward him, he creates being and thought in them. They, being given this intention, leave their mystical intedermination and create themselves as spirits by making themselves theophanic in the most rigorous sense." *The Problem of God, op. cit.,* p. 103, n. 7.

[56]Hazel Barnes, "Neoplatonism and Analytical Psychology," *Phylosophical Review,* 54 (1945), 560-561.

Cf. *Enneads* VI, 9, 7; VI, 7, 21 (2-7) (11-17); VI, 7, 22 (1-21).

[57]It must be stressed, however, that even should soul become attached to body it still keeps some higher principle (Nous) within itself and thereby never completely loses contact with the spiritual world. IV, 8, 4 (1-23). Cf. also Jean Trouillard, *La procession plotinienne* (Paris: Presses Universitaires de France, 1955), p. 15.

Soul;[58] for Soul's function is to see a lower realm which Nous does not see.[59]

The doctrine of an orderly descent of parts of Soul in the thought of Plotinus is given a more solid foundation through the significance of *Logos* (intelligibility of world) in the overall structure of the Neoplatonic universe; for the Neoplatonic emphasis on Logos brings to fuller consciousness how parts of soul establish these various spiritual connections all down the line, and provide the framework for the ultimate transparent view of the universe as a spiritual whole.[60]

By remolding the Stoic doctrine of spermatic logos[61] into a more specifically noetic logos, Plotinus is able to drastically

[58]IV, 8, 3 (21-31).

[59]Soul "sees" a lower realm because it governs, illuminates, or "creates" the lower regions (sensible world) by retaining contact with Nous. As phro nesis soul is opposed to physis, which does not possess any intelligence. IV, 4, 3 (1-8).

[60]Cf. P. Hadot, "Etre, vie, pensée chez Plotin et avant Plotin," *Entrétient Hardt* V, p. 135. "Le mouvement tonique qui assure la consistance du *Pneuma* est dirigé alternativement vers l'extérieur, et vers l'intérieur produit la grandeur et les qualités des individus. Le mouvement dirigé vers l'intérieur produit leur unité et leur substance." Cf. IV, 7, 2.

[61]The Stoic doctrine of "logos spermatikos," or seminal reason, is designed to explain both plurality and teleology in a monistic system. The Logos, considered as a unified entity, contains within itself, on the analogy of animal sperm, the growth powers for all aspects of the Cosmos (Cf. J. Von Arnim, *Stoicorum Veterum Fragmenta* [4 vols., Leipzig, 1903-1924], II, 1027.) The Stoic point of departure on Logos is Heraclitus' doctrine of an all pervasive formula of organization which was considered divine. It is the active force in the universe created in the fashion of sperm. (Cf. Diogenes Laertius, *Lives of the Eminent Philosophers*, edited and trans. by R.D. Hicks [London: Loeb Classical Library, 1925], VII, 134.) As in Heraclitus, it is material and identified with fire (Von Arnim, II, 1027). It is also identical with nature. Cf. Heraclitus, frs. i, 2, 50 *Diels* VS; frs. 8, 51, 53, 60.

This pervasive presence in the universe develops in several directions. Since it is a unity it grounds the theory of cosmic sympathy, (i.e., a mutual interaction of all the forces of the universe. The universe is compared to an organic and rational living thing in which all aspects of the entity are akin to each other,) as well as the theory of natural law and the ethical imperative "to live according to nature." (For an analysis of the Stoic doctrine of *physis* as an immanent logos, cf. Seneca, *De beneficiis*, IV, 7-8; for the definition of virtue as "living according to nature," cf. Diogenes Laertius, VIII, 86-87. Nature here is to be understood in both its cosmic and individual sense, VIII, 89; cf. also Cicero *De legibus* II, 4, 8; and *De republica*, III, 33.) This throughgoing determinism caused Christian thinkers to look

transform the former. The Neoplatonic perspective stresses that logos is the diversifying aspect of intellectuality issuing not from matter (since logos is pure form) but from Nous; it is as an irradiation of intellectuality from Nous and reaches to matter itself. Logos, therefore, becomes a creative, intellectual force, which, through its "coordinated intellectual interplay"[62] is the condition of the possibility for a descent from the realm of being as such to the world of becoming. While working out the implications of creation the terms Dynamis or Dynameis and Logos (or Logoi) are used. Nous gives something of it itself to Hyle, and this is Logos. It flows eternally from Nous, containing the multiplicity and the opposites that are found in the material world exactly as the Logoi Spermatikoi contain in themselves the multiplicity and opposites that are in individual living beings.[63] It is the main link, then, and unifies the many heterogeneous elements in Plotinus' theory of orderly irradiation of spirituality;[64] for although Logos is not another hypostasis, it is an aspect of Nous, an aspect of Soul, an aspect of Nature. Logos therefore, is intellectuality on whichever level one finds it.[65] Again, it is described as a rational principle in life, coming forth from Nous and Soul without being identical with them,

---

unfavorably upon the Stoic deoctrines. However, the idea of a law running through nature, and of the minds' affinity to it made a lasting impression of Christian thought. Cf. T. Deman, "*Le De Officiis* de saint Ambroise dans l'histoire de la théologie morale," *Revue des sciences philosophiques et théologiques*, 37 (1953), 409-424; M. Spanneut, *Le stoicisme des pères de l'église* (Paris, 1957), especially pp. 231-269; John Ferguson, *Moral Values in the Ancient World* (London: Metheun and Co., 1958).

[62]J.N. Deck, *Nature, Contemplation and The One*, p. 62.

[63]III, 2, 2 (15-33); see also R. E. Witt, "The Plotinian Logos and its Stoic Basis," *Classical Quarterly*, 25 (1931), 103-111; Willy Theiler, "Plotin Zwischen Platon und Stoa," *Entrétiens Hardt* V, pp. 65-86. The discussion following Theiler's paper, concerning the precise status and role of Logos in the thought of Plotinus is most illuminating.

See also, R.E. Witt, "Plotinus and Posidonius," *Classical Quarterly*, 24 (1930), 198-207.

[64]Witt maintains that in two aspects the Stoic and Plotinian theories are similar. In both systems Logos in an ontological conception of fundamental importance. In both systems Logos is developed with the desire which a monistic attitude toward the universe promotes for a rigidly consistent doctrine of creative activity. R.E. Witt, "Plotinian Logos an its Stoic Basis," *art. cit.*, p. 111.

[65]II, 9, 1 (31-33); III, 2; cf. also J.M. Rist, *Plotinus: The Road to Reality* (Cambridge: at the University Press, 1967), chapter 7, pp. 84-102.

containing in itself all opposites, uniting them into a harmonious whole.[66] Just as there is an urge for *diversification* as well as for *unity* in intellectuality itself, Logos becomes this diversifying aspect of intellectuality.

In the treatises on Providence we see Logos referred to as the intellectuality of world—which is what providence entails, viz., an intellectual ordering.[67] Logos, then, is found on every level. It is always "le principe de l'épanouissement."—"L épanoiussement aussi du raisonnement par rapport à l'intuition, d'une dispersion toujours plus grande par rapport à l'unité précédente, plus serrée."[68]

Logos, consequiently, is found on every level. It is not itself a hypostasis but the reflection on each level of the preceding hypostasis.

Such an orientation provides Plotinus with sufficient flexibility to preserve the important metaphysical factor of participation. It is through his doctrine of Logos that Plotinus can account for the multiplicity of Souls as the multiplicity of one cohesive spiritual whole.[69]

Through a consideration of the ordered relation of being and intelligibility in the Neoplatonian system, Plotinus describes how mind or spirit achieves an appreciation of being as relatable to intellect. Intellect is always co-relative with being, and in the case of Nous, one finds the complete self collectedness of being and intelligibility.[70] In the exposition of the "descent" Plotinus captures the more diminished thrusts of intelligibility and explains how the

[66]III, 2, 16 (12-54) and (56-58).

[67]III, 7, 11 (20-23) the soul as a Logos and sum of logoi is unquiet VI, 2, 5 (12-15).

[68]Cf. the discussion section of Theiler's paper, "Plotin zwischen Plato und Stoa," *Entrétiens Hardt* V, p. 98.

[69]Cf. the important chapter on Logos in Deck's *Nature, Contemplation and The One,* pp. 56-63, esp. n. 7, p. 63. Professor Bréhier in his edition of Plotinus (Plotin, *Ennéades* texte établi et traduit, Vol. III, p. 19) suggests that the Logos doctrine in Plotinus is taken from Philo of Alexandria. However, C.J. de Vogel claims that such a position would be misleading. De Vogel emphasizes, that for Philo, Logos was not only the Stoic notion of universal law, immanent in nature; it was also the Platonic world of transcendent paradeigmata the χοσμοζ νοηγοζ. For Philo the Logos is primarily the "Divine Mind," or what Plotinus calls Nous. For Plotinus it is not; Logos is a much more expansive notion in the Plotinian theory. Cf. C.J. de Vogel, *Greek Philosophy, op. cit.,* pp. 354-375; also p. 522 col. 1427.

[70]V, 6, 1 (5-14).

principle of intelligibility is grounded in a transcendental relation. This is achieved by maintaining that Soul or consciousness on every level is still co-related with the First Principle.[71]

With such a pattern already outlined, it was not difficult for Plotinus to introduce and stress the unique viewpoint of soul as a limited consciousness, rather than that of an individual substance. The limitation of consciousness therefore can be explained by its having been turned toward the material. But Plotinus will emphasize that however entwined soul becomes with matter, it can never be separated from its intelligible core—not subject to quantity but such that though you divide it mentally forever you still have the same power, infinite to the core.[72] Our ultimate unity and individuality as centers of consciousness are images of the perfect unity of Nous. It follows, then, that if there is any genuine unity and identity in ourselves, it must come from the realm of pure spiritual activity which we imitate through our own qualitative identity with Nous.[73]

Plotinus' primary concern is to make soul completely similar to its Source, which is the One, infinitely active and self-collected. Since there cannot be two things so characterized, the result was bound to be an attempt toward union.[74] Soul systematically advances into a higher realm toward a relation and hopefully union with the "trans ordinal" character of the One. Plotinus stresses that soul's desire for unity will not be satisfied by a mere coincidence with Nous. The contemplation of the One by Nous is never the same as the soul's vision of this highest principle; for the former demands a certain separation which soul will not grant. Soul demands a further unification for its well being, than the seeming duality of the Nous. There is the suggestion of an even higher unity, indeed even a coalition with the One,[75] (unity as such rather than unity in multiplicity). Plotinus concurs that soul, while it remains within the sphere of Nous, shares or mirrors the self-identity of the intellectual order, but it tends toward a still higher

[71]V, 1, 4 (10-29).

[72]VI, 5, 12 (1 5).

[73]VI, 5, 12 (10ff).

[74]Cf. A.H. Armstrong, "Plotinus and India," *Classical Quarterly*, 30 (1936), 27. A. Ed. Chaignet, *Histoire de la psychologie des grêcs* (Paris: Hachette, 1892), 331.

[75]VI, 7, 35.

order where Soul is not the Nous contemplating, but the One itself.[76]

By exploiting more rigorously the dynamism of soul toward not only noetic but indeed ontological identity with the One, Plotinus expands upon his predecessors toward a more viable analysis of the self. This is reinforced by his important distinction between soul (psyche) and self or ego consciousness (hêmeis). "The Ego" becomes for the first time a philosophical term.[77] By developing the implications of the difference and interplay within the various levels of consciousness, Plotinus can more convincingly work out a fuller metaphysics of return as he traces the expansion of the self toward further unification.

Plato's impossible ideal, then, has been brought within the realm of possibility due to the capacity of the Plotinian individual soul to attain the hyperintelligibility of the One.[78] This conviction

[76]VI, 7, 8 (1-22).

[77]Cf. E.R. Dodds, "Tradition and Personal Achievement in the Philosophy of Plotinus," *Journal of Roman Studies,* 50 (1960), 6: Hémeis or "the We" refers to our intellectual life or state of consciousness and ranges from the level of discursive reasoning to perfect union with the One. At this higher level hémeis usually connotes the infinite or true self, or the transcendental ego. Cf. *Ennead* I, 1, 7 (15-17); I, 1, 10 (3-4).

Duméry, in his analysis of reduction (i.e., the movement that seeks to pass through the different levels of consciousness in order to secure, step by step their foundation) remarks that transcendental intentionality no longer says "I," but "We" although the plural must be attributed to each singular, *op. cit.,* 45-46. Hémeis is not so much a pronoun as a technical philosophical term to emphasize the necessity of tracing the ego in dynamic terms in its striving attention toward its source.

[78]This can be realized as due to the more positive stand toward soul, i.e., rather than viewing soul as "fallen" (cf. Orphic tradition on fall of Soul and the moral peregrinations involved) Plotinus prefers to view it as the last emanation of reality. To a great extent, Plotinus' philosophy is an attempt to integrate the religious and metaphysical points of view. Cf. A.H. Armstrong, *The Architecture of the Intelligible Universe,* especially Chapter III, pp. 29ff.

Bréhier on this point suggests that there is a definite Oriental influence here, rather than an internal development of Hellenic thought. Cf. E. Bréhier, *The Philosophy of Plotinus, op. cit.,* p. 107.

A.H. Armstrong in "Plotinus and India," *Classical Quarterly,* 30 (1936), 22-38, comments that Bréhier's theory in itself involves no impossibility. Further still, Armstrong quotes the work of Charlesworth, *Trade-Routes of the Roman Empire,* (Chap. 4) and Warmington, *Commerce Between the Roman Empire and India,* (conclusion) in order to corraborate that there was communication between Alexandria and India. However, Armstrong

concerning the ability of individual soul to attain coalition with its Source leads into the doctrine of the "infinite" self. In the same frame of reference there unfolds the full import of his doctrine of levels of consciousness; for it is through a detailed analysis of the range of consciousness that Plotinus is able to systematically demonstrate how finite self or empirical ego becomes infinite self or transcendental ego while still retaining continuity with the three fundamental hypostases or realities (Soul, Nous, and One).[79]

What then is the role of consciousness in the sytem of Plotinus? Further still, what is the significance of *the self* which is drawn outside itself toward further perfection and ultimate fulfillment?[80] Manifested in different forms and on a variety of levels, consciousness serves as the expression of the continuous identity of the self in its ascent toward the One.[81]

---

emphasizes that we can find within the Hellenic tradition an attempt to overcome the limits of the self and be "oned" with the Divine. In Heraclitus we have the explict assertion that the soul has no discernible limits. This theme is given added impetus with Aristotle's doctrine that mind becomes what it thinks. This was one of Plotinus' most powerful weapons in breaking down the rigorous subject-object distinction in the spiritual world; for in the Aristotelian setting consciousness becomes its object and therefore there are no limits to soul's expansion.

The Orphic view of the soul, which Plato seems to embrace, is something pure, divine, and immortal and radically separate from the material world. The problem of the religious life in this setting is not so much how to overcome the limits of self and to be unitied with the infinite, but rather primary concern is given to the problem of how one can escape from the body.

[79]The three hypotheses stand in static relationships. They are all eternal and never alter their nature. Although it is true that the cognitive condition of these relations is extraordinarily significant for Plotinus' objective reality, it is more revealing of Plotinian thought and intent to reveal the *bearer of cognition, the self,* which becomes conscious in men and whose salvation Plotinus attempts to describe. Cf. E.G. Warren, "Consciousness in Plotinus," *Phronesis,* IX (1964), p. 92. For a less enthusiastic approach to the value of a study of the relation of the self, see A.H. Armstrong, *Architecture of the Intelligible Universe, op. cit.,* p. 119: "The relation between the Absolute and relative and derived beings must always remain mysterious because one term of it is inaccessible to our knowledge and because it is necessarily a unique relation about which we can form no general concept. The wise philosopher will be content to note that there is at this point a gulf or cleft in being and leave it at that."

[80]IV, 8, 8.

[81]To experience unification is to experience the highest of all forms of life. Cf. IV, 8, 6. Cf. also A.H. Armstrong, *Architecture of the Intelligible Universe,* p. 48.

Plotinus seems to emphasize, sometimes explicity, more often implicitly, that the factor which determines one's conscious experience is the peculiar power that enables the self to turn toward its object and cognize it. The self refers primarily to the bearer of cognition, the agent performing the particular conscious activity. Empirical self or the empirical ego refers to self on the lower levels of conscious experience. The transcendental ego refers to the higher realms of consciousness.[82]

The word consciousness in this context may be used to mean an awareness of any sort.[83] The most general expression for consciousness is antilepsis. Sensory perception, (aisthesis) discursive thought, (dianoia) and intellectual knowledge properly so called (noesis) are squally types of antilepsis, differing only in the form in which this awareness occurs and in the degree of truth–value which it represents; further still, on each of these levels of psychic awareness, there is involved a mental synthesis appropriate to that level, by which the content of consciousness is apprehended as a unity.

It is through a consideration of self as dynamic agent, point of attention, or center of consciousness, operating on a variety of cognitive levels that Plotinus is able to emphasize how unity can remain intact. One's noetic life in Nous is eternal but more fragmented as one declines from and "forgets" the life of Nous.[84] The self can operate roughly on five different levels.[85] These stages are characterized by the direction and activity of consciousness. On the lowest level, that of Nature (Phusis), the self's attention is wholly

[82]II, 3, 9 (27-31). It is most common for Plotinus to speak of the self as "higher man" or "pure soul." ". . . or a man becomes bereft of this soul (the higher Soul turned toward Nous) and live governed by fate, and here the stars for him not only are signs, but he himself becomes a part, as it were, and follows along with the whole (universe) of which he is a part. For each man is double, the one something composite, the other himself."

[83]Edward Warren, Consciousness in Plotinus," *Phronesis*, IX, n. 2 (1964), page 97.

[84]VI, 7, 7 (24-31, 24ff). Our psychic activity on lower levels is a reflection of the reality of Nous which possesses its object directly. Cf. Jean Guitton, *Temps et l'Eternité chez Plotin et Saint-Augustin* (Paris: J. Vrin, 1959), p. 106. For him antilepsis "est la prise en possession d'une pensée, l'intuition, l'intermédiaire du sensible ou il se refléte."

[85]III, 4 (1-6). Also cf. E.W. Warren, *Phronesis*, IX (1964), esp. pp. 94-96. "Das Wesen des Menschen erstreckt sich ja . . . von der Materie bis hinauf

directed to the material world such that it is, in a sense, noetically that material world.[86] Unaware that it is a cognitive power, it would nonetheless find its proper activity in contemplating the physical world. The subject of the knowing experience, the self, would be asleep. It should be emphasized, however, that the rational powers, which are rooted in eternity, would always function; but the self, attending only at the level of phusis, would not identify itself with these higher activities.[87]

On each level, consciousness involves a type of mental synthesis appropriate to that level, by which the content of consciousness is apprehended and its unified. The term synesis is the understanding or comprehension by which particular objects on their respective levels are grasped in their relation to the conscious subject. That this process of conscious activity is regarded as the function of a metaphysical subject with a continuous self-identity is demonstrated by the terms synaisthesis and parakalouthesis. They express a reflexive awereness of subjective states and activities. Synaisthesis is the term employed for the functioning on the level of perception, while parakalouthesis functions on the level of ratiocination.

In *Ennead* V, 3 Plotinus elaborates upon consciousness in the sense of synaisthesis. It has the task of describing the tension between cognitive unity and multiplicity. There is a grasp of unity here that transcends the narrow unity of the particular world. There is a further straining in which its activity points toward the whole and how all particular facets participate in the whole. We might say with Professor Chaignet that synaisthesis consists in the knowledge that being has of the unity of the parts which compose it.[88] The term is one of the most difficult terms in Plotinian vocabulary and cannot be translated by one formula. It can mean simply consciousness.[89] Together with the reflexive pronoun it connotes "self-consciousness" of some type.[90] It may mean merely sympathy

---

zur Gottheit. Ein Jeder von uns ist gewissermassen zusammengesetzt (1) aus dem Korper oder der gestalten Materie, (2) aus dem phutikon, (3) der aisthetikon, (4) der Denkseele (5) dem Nous und uber diesem steht noch (6) die Gottheit oder das Eine, mit dem wir auch alle innerlich verknupft sind . . ." H. von Kleist, "Zu Plotinus *Ennead* III, 4" *Hermes,* 21 (1886), 478.

[86]III, 4, 1.

[87]III, 4, 2 (15ff).

[88]Chaignet, *op. cit.,* p. 90.

[89]IV, 4, 8.

[90]II, 2, 1; III, 4, 4; IV, 4, 2; V, 8, 11; VI, 7, 16.

or awareness of the mutual interaction of the various levels of intelligibility.[91] On this same theme, Jean Guitton suggests that synaisthesis "n'est pas seulement un caractère de l'âme: ce terme désigne aussi toute entente sympathique entre les parties d'un tout."[92]

In regard to parakalouthesis this term is the properly human form of consciousness. However, true self-consciousness emerges only at the next level as νοησις εαυτον, in which the reflexive activity of consciousness presents the subject as the object of its own immediate awareness. Parakalouthesis, therefore, is properly applied to human consciousness. Having derived from the notion of "following along with" it emphasizes the force of the subject–object duality on the sporadic human level, where there is a combination of sensory and intellectual powers.

Ontologically, then, the self appears as fragmented on different cognitive levels. But subjectively it always preserves it unity in the content of experience.[93] There seems to be no sharp boundaries within the Neoplatonic view of being as realities merge imperceptively. The self can regain vision of the eternal essences, and consequently, its ontological solidarity (which is characteristic of the higher realms), by adapting to the various levels of being, and by attempting to recall its higher state.

The ascent from empirical ego to transcendental ego is a long and arduous one. But the time bound ego is able by an effort of will, to identify itself with the higher part of soul which is "always already" present to Nous.

When the self is bent toward body it has ceased to be All and becomes a someone; consequently, self is more fragmentary and there develops a narrowing of consciousness.[94] Human existence, therefore, acquires value as it becomes closer to Nous.

It is imperative that consciusness disengage itself from the passions and all the conditions of space and time in order to engage in the one activity which experience shows to be free from the world of multiplicity. Empirical self is, therefore, a fall from higher spiritual activity. Genuine unity is realized in the realm of pure spiritual energy, where there are no restrictions, and where subject is the object of its own contemplation.

[91]I, 1, 11; IV, 4, 45; IV, 5, 5.
[92]J. Guitton, *Le temps et l'eternité,* p. 108.
[93]III, 8, 4 (14-31).
[94]VI, 5, 12.

Our unity as centers of consciousness becomes an image of the perfect unity of the Absolute as we attempt, as Henry Duméry emphasizes, "to live consciously, the relation of the spirit to the One."[95]

Through a careful delineation of the parts of soul expanding in infinite open-endedness toward its Source, Plotinus is able tc describe the full import of self as center of consciousness. Salvation for Plotinus becomes not so much a matter of being rid of the body. It is primarily a matter of will and attention to its Source.[96] By close elaboration upon the levels of consciousness, as the central psychic power of attention, Plotinus finds "the locus of the self and the true measure of our identity."[97]

Finite spirit in the final analysis, must be correlative with Absolute Being, for only this state of total actuality and simplicity will satisfy the soul's quest for self realization.

Plotinus, more than any of his predecessors, is able to move toward the attainment of this goal. He is successful in this endeavor due to the distinction between the soul and ego-consciousness, plus his conception of the universe as an unbroken chain emanating from the One to all the lower levels of Being. Finite spirit in the Plotinian system, can expand its attention to the point where it literally returns or receives the Ground of its own consciousness and is oned with the Divine.[98]

The pivotal feature in the study of the philosophy of Plotinus, then, must be his insistence concerning the highly dynamic role which the One or Good plays in uniting the entire Neoplatonic cosmogony. All being derives from a single infinite source which in no way is diminished as it causes lesser traces of itself.[99] Complementing this procession, there is an upward, ordered impulse or tendency in being to become indentical with its Source by imitating, as completely as possible, the perfect unity and intelligibility found in the One.[100] The Plotinian conception of being assumes

[95]H. Duméry, *The Problem of God in Philosophy of Religion, op. cit.*, p. 104.

[96]IV, 4, 16.

[97]E. Warren, "Consciousness in Plotinus," *Phronesis,* IV (1964), 97.

[98]III, 4, 3.

[99]III, 8, 9.

[100]V, 4, 1. For a central study of "being as tendency," cf. R. Arnou, *Le désir de dieu dans la philosophie de Plotin* (Paris: Alcan, 1921).

at this point a double aspect—being as total actuality and being as aim or end.[101] Being as perfection and as object of desire, then, are intimately linked; for once outside the radical unity of the One, Plotinus directs all his energy toward coming to grips with the fragmentary world of multiplicity. At the same time he must demonstrate how these lesser aspects of consciousness share in the unified totality of which they form a part.

In this relationship between the One or Good and mind, Plotinus emphasizes that to think the One is first of all to think *by means of the One*, that is to employ intelligible meditations that permit the mind to return toward the One from which it proceeds.[102]

Objects are real, then, in the manner and to the extent to which they converge toward the total unity of the One, or rather, objects are unreal only in the manner and to the extent to which they diverge from it.[103]

The crux of the problem in our consideration of the desire for self completion is to ascertain precisely how the One or Good as object of love or tendency exercises its attraction. What precisely is the causal relationship between the self and the Absolute which allows for this movement of desire for perfection? What is the peculiar character of the One that it can lead lower segments of reality toward further perfection?

Plotinus develops a study of Being as love, therefore, which opens up for us a more thorough understanding of Soul or self's conversion to its Source. Involved here, will be a treatment of Being from the perspective of its goodness; for love involves inclination toward the perfection of a thing, which is its good. Being, from the perspective of Goodness, connotes a positive rela-

[101]V, 2, 1 (1-4). "The One is all things and no one of them; the Source of all things is not all things; and yet it is all things in a transcendent sense. All things, so to speak, having run back to it; or more correctly, not all as yet one within it, they will be."

[102]Cf. Jean Trouillard, *La purification plotienne* (Paris: Presses Universitaires de France, 1955), p. 100. "L'être simple est celui qui n'est que soi dans une intensité indistincte: μονον αυγο (VI, 8, 21 [32]). Il est atteint en lui-meme et par lui-meme, ou il n'est pas atteint. Notre façon de le viser, c'est donc l'attitude qui nous fait rejeter tout ce que nous lui ajoutons et nous ajoutons à nous-mêmes pour le penser, et qui nous fait retrouver le point originaire ou nous coincidons avec lui, puisque tous les esprits sont concentriques à Dieu."

[103]VI, 9, 9.

tion to the soul.[104] It is a relation which is recognized as a unique aptitude to perfect the soul; the precise recognition of this capacity on the part of Being to perfect soul initiates the experience of love.[105]

In the Sixth *Ennead* Plotinus remarks that:

> . . . Every one of those Beings exists for itself but becomes an object of desire by the color cast upon it from The Good, source of those graces and of the love they evoke. The Soul taking that out-flow from the divine is stirred. Seized with a Bacchic passion, goaded by these goods, it becomes Love.[106]

In a mysterious way, then, the Good sets its mark on the basic tendency of our intelligence.[107] The intuition of love would seem to be the prime step along the way to metaphysical knowledge. It is an intuition of the intellect which enables us to seize upon the reality of things which lie outside ourselves. Plotinus stressess that one will find the prime source of love in a tendency of the Soul toward pure beauty.[108] Love allows us to cross the boundaries of our own subjectivity.[109] What is not clear, however, is how this presence of the Good to intellect is seized upon, thereby allowing Soul to strive for further perfection. What stimulates Soul to assimilate itself to being purely and simply?[110] This is no small problem, for Soul's journey into the interior and the recovery of the true self does not depend on any type of divine grace in the Christian sense of the term, but simply on the Soul's choice alone.[111] To further emphasize the antithesis between Plotinian self-dependence and Christian grace, Professor Dodds quotes *Ennead* V, 6, 12, where

[104]In an attempt to define the Good positively, Plotinus describes it as the light by which the intelligible world becomes desirable and Soul is awakened and gets wings. VI, 7, 21 (2-7; 11-17); VI, 7, 22 (1-22).

[105]P. Hadot, *Plotin ou la simplicité du regard,* p. 69. "L'experience de l'amour! C'est d'abord l'impression d'un elan infini."

[106]VI, 7, 22 (5-8).

[107]VI, 7, 31.

[108]III, 5, 1. Cf. Bernard Diggs, *Love and Being* (New York: S. Vanni, 1947), p. 55.

[109]V, 3, 17.

[110]VI, 9, 11. Cf. also F. O'Farrell, "The Dialectic of the Affirmation by Fr. André Marc—an Analysis," *Gregorianum,* XXXV (1954), p. 482.

[111]M. de Gandillac, *La Sagesse de Plotin* (Paris: J. Vrin, 1952), p. 27.

Plotinus assures us that the One does not need its products and would not care if it had no products.[112]

The great difference between Plotinus and Christian thinkers is the former's more optimistic view of human capabilities. When man is produced in the Plotinian world, he is a being capable of returning to his source. He can attain it precisely because part of his soul has not fallen but remains above in the intelligible world.[113] We are always conscious of the activity of this higher self when we direct our whole personality in accordance with it.

There is a sense, however, in which we can speak of the "grace" of the Plotinian One; for in some way there exists a power of Divine initiative which seems responsible for Soul's capacity to be and to return to its Source. Plotinus emphasizes that the soul which has never strayed from this love (love of the Supreme Good) waits for no reminding from the beauty of our world.[114]

There is, then, a pointing beyond oneself, and this élan toward the One can be called a kind of grace; further still, Plotinus stresses that this intense love of the One is due not to what we are but rather is caused by receiving from above something quite apart from our nature.[115]

Professor Hadot, in speaking of this élan towards the One will maintain that the desire for the truth and achievement of it is a power available to the purified soul. The only factor preventing man from achieving this goal would be a restriction due to the passions and impediments of the material world. It is precisely these material conditions which prevent man from understanding and willing the god-given root of his nature. Until the soul can reach this stage, he will never be free, for freedom is not simply equivalent to the power of choice; it is freedom from that necessity of choice which the passions impose. Only when Soul is in possession of the One will perfect freedom be achieved.

> . . . Il lui apparaitra que toute necessité et toute devoir supposent avant eux l'initiative absolute d'une liberté et d'un amour originale.[116]

[112]E. Dodds, "Tradition and Personal Achievement in the Philosophy of Plotinus," *Journal of Roman Studies,* 50 (1960), p. 4.

[113]II, 9, 2.

[114]VI, 7, 21 (18ff).

[115]VI, 7, 21. Cf. J. Trouillard, *La purification plotinienne* (Paris: Presses Universitaires de France, 1955), pp. 156-162.

[116]P. Hadot, *Plotin ou la simplicité de regard,* p. 68.

In Plotinus' world, salvation by any miraculous act of God is excluded. As De Gandillac emphasizes, "Salvation is the work of the saved."[117]

At this point Plotinus has yet to resolve the difficulty in regard to the relation of Soul to its source. How does Soul gradually come to rediscover the Fatherland?[118] The question is reduced to discovering where the ascent to the Supreme begins. It becomes evident that the things of this world are but effects of the Supreme's work.[119] The Soul cannot be in itself beauty or wisdom. There must exist a principle as source and giver of wisdom; this will be "the Intellectual Principle, the veritably intellectual, wise without intermission, and therefore beautiful of itself."[120] Indeed, we must even look beyond the Intellectual Principle for the supreme source of Being. This is achieved by looking within, for he who discovers himself will know the source from whence he came.[121]

Perhaps the most significant Plotinian text for an appreciation of the actual ascent is the treatise *On Beauty*. Plotinus conceives God as lying beyond the Intellectual Principle and radiating beauty itself.[122] A thing is beautiful when it communicates in the thought which flows from the divine.[123] The Soul experiences a weight which points to a beyond.

> What is this Dionysian exultation that thrills through your being; this longing to break away from the body and live sunken within the veritable self.[124]

It is evident that the notion of love and its precise relation to the Good is of crucial importance in developing a "metaphysics of return"; for what has to be demonstrated is how the Good is able to be present to the will or appetitive power in man. The main thrust of the system of Plotinus moves toward a clarification of this problem. Behing the difference and interplay of the three Hypostases lies an attempt to understand the relationship of the One to

[117]M. de Gandillac, *La sagesse de Plotin*, p. 8.

[118]V, 9, 3.

[119]V, 9, 2. ". . . the guiding thought is this that the beauty perceived in material things is borrowed."

[120]*Ibid.*

[121]VI, 9, 7.

[122]I, 7, 1.

[123]I, 7, 2.

[124]I, 6, 5.

Eros together with the significance of that relationship.[125] With Plotinus, there is an attempt to develop the doctrine of love as outlined in Plato's thought., The *Symposium* treats of the problem confronting Plato as he attempts to develop a comprehensive definition of love.[126] Plato emphasizes that we cannot simply equate love with the Good-in-itself. Indeed, Diotima stresses that we cannot even consider love as a God, since it is impossible that the God's should be deficient in goodness and beauty. Love, therefore, becomes a great spirit and is a member of that class of semi-divine beings which includes the human soul, or at least the rational part of it, constantly aspiring toward the perfection of its nature. At the same time, it must be kept in mind that Plato suggest that love is something more than a violent sense of need, or a pointing beyond oneself. The theme of "the perfection of love" is never completely forsaken in the *Symposium*. It is granted that here Socrates does refute the eulogies of Phaedrus and Agathon when they praise love as Goodness itself; but Diotima herself, (after 210a) speaks of a love that is "desire to give rather than to receive," that is a kind of generosity rather than a kind of need.[127] Plato suggess, then, that the relation of lover and object of love is no small difficulty to resolve. Implied here is that "la nature synthetique de l'amour fait de lui un intermédiare entre las qualites opposées que cette nature a pour fonction d'unir."[128]

In the *Timaeus* Plato attempts to tie together more systematically these two faces of love. We are told that the Demiourgos, whose outlook is that of a God, is the creator of the order of the world. He creates the world because he is "good and has no envy."[129] The Demiourgos was good and in him that is good no envy can ever arise. Since he was without envy, he desired that all things should be as like himself as possible.[130] This theme can be developed further in the thought of Plotinus, for though Plotinus thought he found his emanation theory in Plato, there is a definite metaphysical advance in the Neoplatonic setting. The more advanced

[125]V, 8, 15.

[126]*Symposium* 201a-204d.

[127]R. Markus, "The Dialectic of Eros in Plato's *Symposium*," *Downside Review*, 233 (1955), p. 227.

[128]Léon Robin, *La théorie platonicienne de l'amour* (Paris: Presses Universitaires de France, 1922), p. 129.

[129]*Timaeus* 29e.

[130]*Timaeus* 30a.

theory of emanation as developed by Plotinus allows us to picture more clearly the association of the "over-flowing" of the Good with the notion of love.[131]

The notion of love in the philosophy of Plato is expanded by Plotinus; for the Neoplatonic doctrine of emanation allows for more detailed analysis of the precise nature and role of the Good. Markus and Armstrong among others, maintain that the germ of the Plotinian doctrine of emanation is to be found in Plato's account of Eros.[132]

At the heart of the Plotinian system is the attempt to understand the full import of this diffusion or dissemination of Being from its Source. Involve here, of course, is a consideration of efficient causality.[133] But at the same time the element of final causality is frequently and strongly affirmed in the *Enneads*. The Good, in giving itself, is also the end of all which flows from it.[134]

The philosophical problem facing Plotinus, then, will be to determine exactly why the Good is what it is, for if we know why

[131]We do not mean to say that the entire Neoplatonic theory of emanation is found in Plato; but as Professor Trouillard has stated, "On trouverait également dans la théorie platonicienne de l'amour, qui n'est pas seulement aspiration mais génerosité an sens plain, un germe de procession." J. Trouillard, *La procession plotinienne,* p. 60.

[132]A. H. Armstrong and R. A. Markus, *Christian Faith and Greek Philosophy* (New York: Sheed and Ward, 1960); Paul Henry, "The Place of Plotinus in the History of Thought," in *The Enneads* trans. by S. MacKenna, 3rd edition revised by B. S. Page (New York: Pantheon, 1962), xxxv-lxx; J. Souilhé, *La doctrine platonicienne d'intermédiaires* (Paris, 1919), p. 253. "Il faut reconnaître que la thèse philonienne ou plotinienne de la procession des êtres dérive légitimement du Platonisme le plus pur."

[133]III, 8 10; V, 1, 6; V, 4, 1.

[134]III, 8, 10. This notion of the "diffusive" character of being is developed in the thought of St. Thomas Aquinas. Aquinas describes the meaning of good as diffusion in both a final and an efficient way. In a final way the Good diffuses the goodness it has by moving those who lack it to desire it and by moving the efficient cause to remedy this deficiency through its agency. Thomas Aquinas, *Questiones Disputatae,* Vol. I; *De Veritate* edited by R. Spiazzi, editio VIII revisa (Romae: Marietti, 1949), q. 22, a2. Cf. Julien Péghaire, "L'axiome Bonum est diffusivum sui dans le néoplatonisme et le thomisme," *Revue de l'Université d'Ottawa,* II (section speciale, Vol. I, 1932), p. 12. The author discusses the meaning of the axiom and sees efficient causality primarily intended by the Neoplatonists.

> Nous pouvous donc conclure qu'aux yeux de Plotin, le Bien est cause efficiente, pourvu que l'on ne mette pas dans ce mot la precision que plus tard y introduiront les Scholastiques.

the Good is what it is, we shall also know why it does what it does.[135]

The main concern at this time, than, is to study the doctrine of emanation in the hope of grasping the cause of this procession from the One. The fact of emanation is well known to us. At the summit of being is the One which Plotinus also calls the First. This "First" is properly neither being nor thought but beyond all being and thought. By a necessity of nature, the One gives birth to Mind or the world of intelligibility. From Nous, or the seat of the eternal Ideas, there emanates in turn, Soul which is the active principle, organizing and vivifying the world of nature.

We might press further, however, and ask what is involved in the internal structure of the One that enables it to produce the world of Nous.

In *Ennead* V, 4, Plotinus undertakes to probe how "the Secondaries rise from the First."[136] He emphasizes that from our limited awareness of nature–in–process, we are able to grasp the purposeful activity of the Cosmos. All things are unable to remain self–enclosed; but rather, they impart something of themselves as much as they are able. Fire warms, snow chills, and drugs have their own outgoing efficiency. All things then, imitate their source to the extent of their capabilities. "All things to the utmost of their power imitate the Source in some operation tending to eternity and to service."[137] If such is the case, Plotinus continues, how is it possible that the First Good, the One itself which is perfect, could remain enclosed within itself as though it were jealous or powerless?[138] It is necessary then, that the One, too, be productive, and in a pre–eminent way, for

> . . . if things other than itself are to exist, it must produce since there is no other source. And further, this engendering principle must be the very highest in worth.[139]

In V, 4, 2, Plotinus reinforces the connection of the One with its effects. He maintains that "there is in everything the Act of the Essence and the Act going out from the Essence: The first Act

[135]VI, 7, 37 (29-31); V, 5, 12 (40ff).
[136]V, 4 (1-2).
[137]V, 4, 1 (35ff).
[138]*Ibid.*
[139]*Ibid.*, 1, 40.

is the thing itself in its realized identity, the second Act is an inevitable following outgo from the first, an emanation distinct from the thing itself."[140]

Plotinus always comes back to the necessary connection of the One with its effects. The effects feel the continual and illuminating presence of the cause. To clarify this problem, Plotinus relies heavily on the analogy of light and the sun. The entire intellectual order may be considered as a kind of light with the One in repose at the summit of the system.[141] This intellectual order or light stands as an image of the One because there is a certain necessity that the First should have offspring, carrying onward much of its quality;[142] for just as light preserves much of the character of the sun, the Nous imitates the total unity of the One. The very nature of the One or Good, therefore, is to produce expressions of itself.[143]

In *Ennead* VI, 8, entitled "On Free Will and The Will of the One," Plotinus moves toward a resolution of the necessary procession of the One. He maintains that the One is what it is because it wills to be so. It is to be conceived as the "total power toward things, supremely self-concentered, being what it wills to be or rather projecting into existence what it wills."[144] The nature of the One, therefore, is to be seen as its will. What he says is that the One itself is the end of its own infinite will, not as the object of appetition, but as the object of infinite fruition. It is the enjoyment of perfection possessed, or we might say that "there is to be no distinction between the will and its accomplishment."[145]

> The Good is what from always it wished and wishes to be. For the Good is precisely a willing toward itself . . . The Good is what it chose to be and, in fact, there was never anything outside it to which it could be drawn.[146]

Only in a very special sense, then, can we consider the One determined or necessitated. Since the One is infinitely perfect, it is "necessitated" to be above external constraint. The only internal

[140]V, 4, 2 (27ff).

[141]V, 3, 12 (38ff) ". . . the only reasonable explanation of act flowing from it lies in the analogy of light from the sun . . ."

[142]V, 1, 7 (1-5).

[143]III, 8, 10; IV, 8, 6 (1-3) (12-13); II, 9, 3 (8).

[144]VI, 8, 9 (41ff).

[145]Cf. also J. Trouillard, *La procession plotinienne,* pp. 77-79.

[146]VI, 8, 13 (33ff).

constraint would be that it be itself, which it cannot help but be. "We cannot think of it as a chance existence; it is not what it chanced to be but what it *must* be—and yet without a Must."[147] In answer to the question why the One is as it is, Plotinus would declare that it has willed to be so. And it would not and could not act in any other way; for being perfect and possessing the fulness of actuality the One is a total love of itself. "Lovable, very love, the Supreme is also self-love in that He is lovely not otherwise than from Himself and in Himself."[148] The One and its will, therefore, are identical. Plotinus continues this theme by maintaining that "all that ensued upon that willing was what that definite willing engendered; *but it engendered nothing new;* all existed from the first."[149] What seems to be suggested here is that the result of willing itself is the cause of the production of the world of participated being. "All the rest is maintained in virtue of Him by means of a certain participation."[150] The One communicates a likeness of its perfection to its effect, which as a distinct reality participates in the perfection of the Source.

Since the Plotinian One as an emanating Being is itself, in a sense, the product of its own will we can conclude that the One's willing of its own nature is the direct cause of an emanation from that nature. The One, enjoying total perfection and unity does not concern itself with the Second Hypostasis. It concerns itself, as we have seen, only with itself. But the result of willing itself is the production of the Second Hypostasis. There will always be an element of mystery regarding the creation of plurality; but it is impossible to deny that a procession has taken place. The alternative would entail an opting for nothingness on the finite level.

> Something besides a unity there must be or all would be indiscernibly buried, shapeless within that unbroken whole: none of the real beings (of the Intellectual Cosmos) would exist if that unity remained at halt within itself: the plurality of these beings, offspring of the unity, could not exist without their own next taking the outward path.[151]

[147] VI, 8, 9 (14ff).
[148] VI, 8, 15 (1-2).
[149] VI, 8, 21 (17).
[150] *Ibid.*, lines 21ff.
[151] IV, 8, 6 (1-5); cf. also VI, 4, 14.

What is more, there is found here at least the suggestion of a creation motif. In VI, 8, 19, Plotinus maintains that the One's making of being is "no action in accordance with his Being."[152] Plotinus seems to be saying that the One is not necessitated to produce.

> He is Principle to Essence and not for Himself did He make it; producing it He left it outside of Himself. He has no need of being, who brought it to be.[153]

It might be straining the texts to press the notion of free creation too strongly;[154] for the above text could refer merely to the One as having infinite status, i.e., that it is a different kind of being than finite being. However, from an analysis of the act of procession Plotinus has outlined for us the very active role played by the One or Good. By developing how Absolute Goodness diffuses itself, Plotinus is able to clarify the precise relation between the transcendent and immanent fields of reality. Involved in this perspective is not merely a consideration of the nature and role of the First Principle, but also how the finite world of being derives from and can imitate and return to its Source.

Being as Love, therefore, can be expanded to include more than the aspirations of inferior grades of reality for perfection. Plotinus sees more in love than mere self-seeking, or a tendency to become one with the larger whole.[155] He will express the connection that God or the Good itself can be spoken of as love; indeed, he is love in a pre-eminent degree. In a sense we can say that love (Eros) is a tautalogous description of the One's nature; for the effect of the One's self-sufficient unity and creativeness is the creation of the world of finite being; this limited and determined world expands in the perfection of its nature by imitating the infinite perfection of the One.[156] All things are phases of the One; this is evident from the obscure instinct-like contemplation of Nature, to the infinite consciousness of the One.

[152]VI, 8, 19 (cf. entire chapter).

[153]VI, 8, 19.

[154]Cf. for example Paul Henry, "La liberté chez Plotin," *Revue Néoscholastique de Philosophie*, 33 (1931), p. 339. ". . . sur la liberté de la creation Plotin a donc garde le silence."

[155]I, 6.

[156]VI, 5, 10 (1-4); VI, 7, 32.

The essence of love in the Plotinian cosmogony, therefore, is participation. That is why it is unnecessary to press the distinction between the lower Eros (mere desire) and the other (the Good itself as Love), which is more akin to giving, perhaps even to creation. L. Eborowicz remarks on this point that Plotinus makes little distinction between the two aspects of love (that of desire and that of joyful union with the self-sufficient creativeness of the One).[157] Rist quite correctly remarks that in the Plotinian system the two kinds of Eros complement one another. They are not entirely separate; rather, the higher is the logical and best possible result of the lower.[158] The Eros of the mystic union is the actuality of the Eros which as mere potency, is still at the stage of desire.[159] The key to actualization of love is that it is caused in some way by the actual vision of the One. Since the text is so significant, we quote at length:

> Therefore we must ascend again to the Good, the desired of every soul. Anyone that has seen this, knows what I intend when I say that it is beautiful. Even the desire of it is to be desired as a Good. To attain it is for those that will take the upward path, who will set all their forces toward, who will divest themselves of all that we have put on in our descent . . . And One that shall know this vision—with what passion of love—shall he not be seized, with what pang of desire, what longing to be molten into one with This—what wondering delight. If he that has never seen this Being must hunger for it as for all his welfare, he that has known must love and reverence It as the very Beauty.[160]

Of special interest in this passage is the fact that the awarenness of the Good is grasped not only at the moment of total union but also in all acts of purification or contemplation on the ascent to

[157] L. Eborowicz, "Le sense de la contemplation chez Plotin et St. Augustin," *Giornale Metaphysica,* XVIII, 1963, p. 221. "Plotin exprime donc la conviction que Dieu est l'eros par rapport à lui même, et c'est ainsi que l'eros embrasse tout, sans excepter l'absolu. Toutefois, lorsqu'il s'agit de Dieu, l'eros s'en rapporte à lui dans un autre sens qu' aux êtres, car l'amour de Dieu pour lui-même ne ports préjudice ni à son bonheur ni a son independence intégrale."

[158] J. M. Rist, *Eros and Psyche: Studies in Plato, Plotinus and Origen* (Toronto: University of Toronto Press, 1964), p. 99.

[159] VI, 7, 22 (10); I, 6, 7 (14-19).

[160] VI, 7, 22.

the Divine.[161] Of course, it is a much more pervading influence at the moment of vision, but we would distort the spirit of Plotinus if we did not see the picture as a whole. Perhaps the preliminary steps in the ascent can be put under the category of mediate vision.[162] Once we grasp the significance of these more or less shadowing visions of the One, we can proceed to the immediate vision, to direct grasps which were given to Plotinus on various occasions.[163]

The link, then, which binds the finite and infinite order is precisely love; for love is the only quality in us that is truly akin to the One. On the finite level we have witnessed a striving of spirit for further determination and unification. On the infinite level there resides an entity which contains all determinations, by being above all determination. The One is purely in act, absolutely simple, and contains these perfections as intellected and willed. All lesser aspects or qualities stand in a situation of participation to this most perfect and absolutely simple of entities.

The Supreme Hypostasis as Infinite Goodness, is love itself. In the lower Hypostases, there is still love of the Good, but it is an analogical good, or imitation of the self-sufficiency of the source.[164] It would seem that the only justification for Plotinus' procedure in this regard would appear to be due to some kind of doctrine of analogy.[165]

[161]Cf. the distinction between Eros-god and Eros-daemon in III, 5, 4 (23-25).

[162]V, 8, 10.

[163]Joseph Maréchal develops this point of mediate and immediate vision as love expanding toward further integration while dealing with this point in the thought of St. Augustine. In "La Vision de Dieu au sommet de la contemplation d'après saint Augustin," he comments upon this precise point: ". . . Dans l'acte meme de sa contemplation effectivée sous la motion des trois personnes divines, l'âme sainte recontre donc de Dieu l'image tant palpitaté encore de la vie divine qui s'y donne réelement. 'Vision d Dieu?' Oui, selon la terminologie Augustinienne, mais toujours encore vision, (mediate) dans une image dans le miroir de l'âme: vision (per speculum, in aenignate), dit le saint docteur, repernant l'expression Paulinienne.

"Mais saint Augustine parle aussi d'une vision de Dieu au sens le plus strict d'une vision immediate." Cf. *Nouvelle Revue Théologique,* 57 (1930), p. 109. Cf. also *Ennead* VI, 9, 4

[164]III, 8, 10.

[165]V, 3, 14. See how Porphyry in his *Commentary on the Parmenides of Plato* handles the tension between finite and infinite being, in P. Hadot, *Porphyre et Victorinus II Texts* (Paris: Etudes Augustiniennes, 1968), esp. pp. 67-113.

Due to the elaborate presentation of the One and the systematic unfolding of his theory of emanation, Plotinus is able to set a foundation for some kind of doctrine of analogy; by so doing there is a more viable connection of finite being to the infinite order. This can be achieved due to the developed character of the One as Exemplar Cause.

The One as Exemplar Cause tends to order and reinforce the roles of efficient and final causality as they are presented in the Neoplatonic system. For by analyzing precisely what the One is, and how plurality proceeds from and returns to the Source, Plotinus demonstrates how the One as Supreme Exemplar, causes by a guiding action. He presents the One as an original Form or IDEA, if you will, in whose likeness finite beings are made. Exemplarity reinforces final causality, then, by showing how all finite beings can be reduced to a higher principle which guides each thing to its end. The exemplarity of the One also grounds efficient causality, for these partial expressions of the One depend upon the efficient action of the Source which as first agent produces effects resembling, though deficiently, the One.

> Imagine a spring that has no source outside itself. It gives itself to all the rivers, yet is never exhausted by what they take, but remains always integrally as it was; the tides that proceed from it are at one within it before they run their several ways, yet all in some sense, know beforehand down what channels they will pour their streams.[166]

The exemplarity of the One, therefore, diffuses itself as final and efficient cause. As final cause it attracts finite being to perfection by moving those who lack it to desire it, and moves the efficient cause to remedy their particular deficiencies by imitating as best they can, the contemplation of the One.

> In sum—the loveliness that is in the sense-realm is an index of the nobleness of the Intellectual sphere, displaying its power and its goodness alike; all things are forever linked; the one order Intellectual in its being, the other of sense; one self-existent, the other eternally taking its being by participating in that first and to the full of its power reproducing the Intellectual nature.[167]

[166]III, 8, 10.
[167]IV, 8, 6.

There is not involved here just a desire for fulfillment but also a love of the object for itself. The dynamic element of will is predicated upon its having present to tiself something which remains on the part of the object quite distinct; yet while being distinct, its presence is most certainly felt on the finite world.

Plotinus suggests a relation of all being to Absolute Being. This Absolute or infinite Being does not stand as the most abstract of beings, but rather there is a relationship to a Being which is all perfect and contains all determinations of being—purely in act, absolutely One and contains them as intellected and willed.

The systematic analysis of the reciprocity of exemplar, efficient and final causality in the Neoplatonic system, allows for a coherent development of the Plotinian "metaphysics of return."

The exemplarity of the One seems to give to the world of finite being the unity of a whole; for by demonstrating how all aspects of being mirror and imitate the absolute perfection of the One, Plotinus shows how the movement to further perfection reflects, indeed is initiated by, a certain connaturality between finite agent and Ultimate End. This connaturality is completely achieved only after mystical union with the Divine has been realized, and we are that which we desire and that which we look at.

At this point soul grasps the unity of the whole. There is a simplification of consciousness until all distinctions and multiplicity disappear and the self has become absorbed into its transcendent Source. The self approaches the One and then becomes "oned" with it.[168] All otherness seems to have been transcended and the soul is "no longer himself, nor self belonging; he is merged with the Supreme, sunken into it."[169]

To conclude we can say that the most profound insight in the thought of Plotinus is that no meaningful and adequate grasp of reality can be achieved without a rigorous deciphering of the spiritual experience of the self and its intense living relationship with its source. There can be no sharp dichotomies in the life of the self. Self is always one, yet capable of going through various stages as it proceeds from and converges toward its ground. He suggests that a more accurate relation with the Divine can best be served by looking upon the One not so much as *external to* or *in front of*

[168]VI, 9, 11 (6-7).
[169]VI, 9, 10 (18).

finite consciousness, as *in* consciousness, as a unity richer than we can immediately grasp, and which will be comprehended through natural affinity. Plotinus advocates a kind of intuitive or connatural knowledge. This contact is beyond the order of explanation for the One is not an object but that *by which* objects are. Plotinus shows, however, how we can read or comprehend this transcendent Source through the dynamic immanence of the self tending toward total actualization. In order to justify intellectually this dialectic of love which allows the self to attain such complete unification with its Source, Plotinus develops a highly original and sophisticated account of an eternal, unlimited, and totally unified spiritual world. This is accomplished through his emphasis on the very active character of the First Principle and its intrinsic relation to the lower hypostases. This hierarchical structure gives a more dynamic unity to his metaphysical world.

Through the careful analysis of the difference and interplay of One to Nous, and Nous to Soul, Plotinus can work out how natural agents strive to produce similitudes in their natural effects. This striving must be reduced to a higher principle which guides each thing to its end. We have such a guide or supreme exemplar in the infinite character of the One, who as true creator of the finite world gives it being, direction and meaning.

Continuity between the One or Good and the lower levels of reality is reinforced through a distinction between Soul and Ego consciousness. Through an analysis of parts of soul expanding in infinite openendedness toward its Source, Plotinus can establish how the self as center of consciousness is defined and develops according to the object of its attention.

By metaphysically establishing how the self is capable of such infinite expansion, Plotinus demonstrates how the metaphysical and mystical realms are inextricably mixed in his system and shows how the Absolute can be present at the heart of spirit while not being enclosed there. The all-embracing concepts employed by the metaphysician to describe this unified vision of the real are prevented from becoming empty of content if we consider the self as the most important and intimate access we have toward an understanding of the real, or rather, an "instanding in" the real.

Canisius College

10

ST. AUGUSTINE AND ARISTOTLE ON TIME AND HISTORY

by Bernard Huddlestun

The purpose of this study is to raise questions about typical modes of treating certain aspects of time and history in the writings of St. Augustine and Aristotle.[1] It is customary to contrast the two in terms of a rectilinear versus a circular view of history and of the possession or lack of a concept of history. Here it is maintained that the difference between a rectilinear and circular view of history is not the decisive difference between Augustine and Aristotle, but rather that the difference poses a question about human proportion and human relevance. Further, to ask whether Aristotle has a concept of history or whether Augustine has "the modern concept of history" is, philosophically speaking, to beg a question.

It is here assumed at the beginning that the issues of time and history are associated, in that time is generally thought to be a generic issue, specifiable in many ways, of which one is the question of the nature of that "history" which has to do with groups of human beings or with humanity over a period of time. This being

[1]Among the works of Augustine we will consider the *Confessions* and *De civitate Dei*. The Bekker edition of Aristotle has been used, and for the text of the *Confessions*, the following: *Las Confesiones*, edición crítica y anotada por el padre Angel Custodio Vega, O.S.A., quinta edición, in *Obras de San Agustín, texto bilingüe* (Madrid: Biblioteca de Autores Cristianos, 1968), and the English quotations from Augustine are from *The Confessions of St. Augustine*, Translated, with an Introduction and Notes, by John K. Ryan (Garden City, N.Y.: Image Books, Doubleday & Company, 1960).

I wish to acknowledge my debt to Professor Francis Slade of St. Francis College, Brooklyn, N.Y., and to Professor Thomas Prufer of the School of Philosophy, The Catholic University of America, for some of the essential points of this study.

said, there is more truth in the affirmation than in the denial that while Aristotle maintains that in the ultimate sense time is circular, yet specifically human time, which we will use the term "history" to refer to, is not. The evidence for this is strong: where Aristotle concludes that time is circular, history is not a topic (cf. *Physics,* IV, 14, 223b12-224a2). In *De generatione et corruptione,* II, 11, 338b7 ff., Aristotle states that the generation and corruption of a species of living things are cyclical in nature; however, no individual recurs. Without abusing the customary sense attached to the word "history," one may say that what for Aristotle distinguishes an individual in relation to the species is the fact that an individual has a history, whereas the species does not. This is indeed the language we use to characterize the Darwinian revolution over against Aristotelian biology. For Darwin, we say, species too have histories. Further, the fact that time as such is not a systematic theme of inquiry in Aristotle's works concerning man in his distinctiveness implies that time in its essentiality (circularity) does not, in Aristotle's mind, define the human. Finally, we note that Aristotle criticizes Socrates in the *Republic* for taking too logical a view of fundamental changes in constitutional forms (*Politics,* V, 12, 1316a1724). In other words, Aristotle rejects those notions which we customarily associate with a cyclical view of history.

Although Aristotle's writings seem to be in harmony with the sentiment expressed in the adage, "History repeats itself," the weight and sense of such a statement may vary significantly. Thus, while Aristotle speaks of the recurrent loss and recovery of the arts and sciences, he also speaks of the man who first founded political communities (*Ibid.,* I, 2, 1253a30-31), of the time when men first began to philosophize (*Metaphysics,* I, 2, 982b13), and of the discovery of certain arts (*Ibid.,* I, 1, 981b23-25). From the point of view of the cyclic nature of all becoming, these latter remarks are incorrect. But if taken seriously, it appears that depending on context Aristotle conceives time in two radically different ways. For Aristotle, it appears that when one speaks of time in terms of human possibilities, there is no such thing as a "concept of history," if by that one means an idea to which corresponds a temporal whole, revealed to the inquiring mind, and embracing and expressing humanness.

That Aristotle has no special word for what we call history is not sufficient reason for saying that he has no conception of history in another sense. After all, the nonspecialized term *historein* came to signify for us specifically human (economic and political) history because of its association with a distinctive and definitive kind of inquiry originating with Greeks earlier than Aristotle.

In our attempt to outline some differences between Aristotle and Augustine on time and history, it is necessary to keep in mind two pairs of contrasting phenomena described by Aristotle: the first is the contrast between theoretical knowledge and practical understanding, the second is that between what may be called a process, motion, or change *(kinesis)* and an activity in a strict sense *(energeia* or *praxis)*.[2] Although these distinctions are well known, they will be reviewed with a view to our purpose. Both Aristotle's and Augustine's views will be considered insofar as differentiation of these phenomena is presupposed.

Ordinary experience teaches that there are some things that are not within our power. Insofar as we try to extend the scope of our power, our concern is practical, and knowing the limits of the sphere of human action is part of practical wisdom. When we are interested in understanding things that are beyond our power to change, curiosity has superseded practicality. The practical is discovered in the doing; curiosity is, as it were, led by the nose. A man does not so much discover as forget himself as a practical, political being when he becomes absorbed in what happens and goes on without him. Such things are looked at, and even touched and grasped, but not with the hand. Since, on the other hand, the limits and the aims of the practical are discovered in the doing, such things are not manifest, they are not phenomena, to the contemplative eye.

Although we may contemplate things not within our power, not all such things are objects of theoretical knowledge in a distinctive sense. For example, although an American cannot change the Russian constitution, nevertheless if he wants to understand that constitution, he has to look at it in practical terms. Apart from things which are of their very nature practical even though we cannot do them, many things can be contemplated which are not objects of knowledge in a strict sense. Such are things that occur by chance: having understood one chance event, we do not thereby understand a multitude of other events. In contrast theoretical knowledge is possessed in the discovery of what defines a multitude of phenomena. Finally, the human portion, as defined by the

[2]As explained in *Met.* IX 6, 1048b18ff.

practical, is small, while the sphere of things that do not originate with us is vast. It is in this encompassing sphere that the origins of all things are sought by the theoretical scientist. In classical literature, the most fundamental of such things are called "divine."[3]

An activity in a strict sense differs from a process in being essentially nontemporal. For example, if one is watching a film, the activity of seeing is fulfilled at every moment, not at one moment more than at another. Such activities are nontemporal even though they are continuous rather than momentary. They are nontemporal because they do not come to be or pass away: they exist and then they exist no longer. When an observer judges how long they last, he refers to concommitant changes because he cannot say how long in terms of the activities themselves. A process, on the other hand, makes sense only if it is a movement from one state to another. It is difference from moment to moment—the differences are its moments—that makes a process a process and movement from one state or place toward another state or place that makes it a single, identifiable process. The growth of a living thing, for example, and the making of a chair are both processes.

Some activities, called such in a broad sense, that seem to be essentially processes, can also sometimes be activities in the strict sense. If legs are for taking us where we want to go, then walking is a process. But if we sometimes walk for the enjoyment alone, then in that case walking is an activity in the strict sense. The difference is as real as experience can deliver. To maintain that one must always walk primarily with a view to getting somewhere is to show a certain kind of ignorance.

Both Augustine and Aristotle maintain that there is an absolute time in terms of which all other times and corresponding motions are measured or are measurable. For both men this absolute time is not absolute in itself, but is such on the basis of something else.

In Aristotle's view, absolute time is a cosmic time, i.e., the time of the eternal and regular motion of the heavenly bodies. One and the same motion recurs, and therefore one and the same time (*Physics*, IV, 13, 222a32-33). This time is manifest to perception, just as motion is, and affects the soul in its "aisthetic" reality (*Ibid.*, IV, 11, 219a30-31). It is the context and clearing in which the motion of animals, not only their movement in place but also their

[3]For example see *N.E.* VI 7, 1141a34-b2.

growth and decay, takes place. "Man is begotten by man and by the sun as well" (*Ibid.,* II, 2, 194b13). The years, seasons, and days measured out by the motion of the sun are the absolute, i.e., the final and unchanging, measure of life as the time between birth and death. The absolute heavenly motions set the rhythm of all sublunary life-processes.[4]

Augustine does not see any absoluteness in the motions of the heavenly bodies. For him what primarily characterizes these bodies is not the seeming regularity of their motions and their significance for the system of earthly life-processes, but just their changeableness. Changeableness is the essence of all bodies. Any regularity in the motions of bodies is therefore deemed to be itself transient (see *Confessions,* IV, 10 [15]). This changeableness is a datum of perception which Augustine connects directly to his theological idea that all things, other than God, are created by God:

> Lo, heaven and earth exist: they cry out that they have been created, for they are subject to change and variation. Whatever has not been made, and yet exists, has nothing in it which was not previously there, whereas to have what once was not is to change and vary. (*Ibid.,* XI, 4 [6])

Since Augustine has a supracosmic explanation for the cosmos, he does not seek cosmic explanations for it.

In contrast, Aristotle takes account of the apparent regularity of cosmic changes because, as one who seeks to give a natural explanation of motion, this regularity offers a clue to the principles of cosmic motion. What is primary for Aristotle are the forms of change; for Augustine it is changeableness as such.

Augustine does not ignore but deemphasizes the function of heavently motions relative to living things on earth. The motion of the sun measures the lifetimes of living things, and Augustine does not go so far as to say that this measure can be exchanged for the rotating motion of a potter's wheel:

> The stars and the lights of heaven are "for signs, and for seasons, and for days and for years". Truly they are such. Yet I should not say that the turning of that little wooden wheel constitutes a day, nor under those conditions should that learned men say that there is no time. (*Ibid.,* XI, 23 [a 29]).

[4]See *Physics* VIII 9, 265b8-11; *De gen. et cor.* II 10, 336a15-337a33; 11 338b4-6.

The cycle of years, seasons, and days is matched by the cycle of generation and decay, of birth and death. In a basic sense, birth and death mark the boundaries of a human lifetime. In Aristotle, the cycle of birth and death is understood as an integral part of the larger cosmic motions. For Augustine, on the contrary, death is not natural but rather, the consequence of sin (*Ibid.*, X, 42 [67]-43 [68]). Therefore the tie between the cycle of birth and death, the individual lifetime, and the cycle of years, seasons, and days is considered accidental, not essential. Thus the inquiry into the nature of time leads, on the one hand, beyond the cosmos (to the Creator) and, on the other, away from the cosmos to the human soul (cf. *Ibid.*, X, 7 [9]).

If what characterizes all bodies and man *qua bodily* is changeableness, what characterizes soul is desire or longing for cessation of change, for stability, sureness, and completeness.[5] Time is therefore not only a theoretical problem but also a practical one: time is the measure of the distance between desire and satisfaction. It is unfulfilled desire that cries out, "How long, O Lord?".[6] Since what is beyond the cosmos is timeless, and since it is the human soul that struggles to overcome time, it is by understanding the soul in relation to the eternal that time can be understood.

The crucial thesis in Augustine's account is that human desire cannot find fulfillment in this life. Since death is a punishment for sin, it is not just the cessation of natural life after the Fall, but rather that in terms of which this life is understood. Life after the Fall is a living death.[7] Since death is not a fulfillment but a mere cessation, life defined by the inevitability of death means a meaningless process precisely because the life-process does not reach fulfillment. On the other hand, since faith also teaches that fulfillment lies in the next life, this life is a means to the happiness of the next and a pilgrimage to it. On that account it is still a process,

[5]The *Confessions* is more than anything else an expression and exploration of manifold longing. In fact, Augustine states the themes of several of its books as different kinds of longing. See, in particular, I 1 (1); II 1 (1)-2 (2-4); III 1 (1); IV 1 (1)-2 (2); VI 1 (1); VIII 1 (1-2)- 2(3-5); IX 1 (1)-2 (2-3).

The completeness Augustine has in mind, which we judge by his characterizations of divinity, is not static but active. It is a living that is not a process.

[6]Consider together *Conf.* XI 2 (2) and 29 (39).

[7]". . . Nescio, unde venerim huc, in istam dico vitam mortalem an mortem vitalem" (*Conf.* I 6 [7]).

though not a meaningless one. In sum, life is essentially a process on two accounts: (1) because the final truth is that life ends in death, and (2) because this life is a path to another life beyond. This process is either a meaningless process for those who tread the path without knowing that it is merely a path, or it is a meaningful process for those who do. Hence, life is in every respect temporal:

> But now "my years are wasted in sighs," and you, O Lord my comfort, my Father, are eternal. But I am distracted amid times, whose order I do not know, and my thoughts, the inmost bowels of my soul, are torn asunder by tumult and change, until being purged and melted clear by the fire of your love, I may flow altogether into you. (*Ibid.,* XI, 29 [39]).

The process which is human life articulates itself in Augustine's account, as it does in Aristotle's, into three ways of life: (1) the life given over to the pursuit of bodily pleasure, (2) that given over to the pursuit of honor, and (3) that given over to the pursuit of knowledge for the sake of knowing (*Ibid.,* X, 30 (41) ff.; *N.E.* I, 5). Since the first is not distinctively human, only the second and third ways need be considered. Augustine is concerned with the temporality of *human* life (*Ibid.,* XI, 15 [19]). In *De civitate Dei,* it is primarily the deeds and thoughts of men and cities that constitute history. If all activities in this life are processes, then action, the fiber of political life, and thought too are essentially processes. The search for honor for virtuous deeds does not lead to true immortality, and theoretical inquiry does not lead to knowing.

These human activities are, however, anticipations of fulfillment in the next life. The just will be rewarded by God and the desire to know will be satisfied. In the light of this datum of faith, the time of human life takes on definitive and determinate dimensions. This time is seen to be absolute because it is the measure granted for each human life and for the "age of the sons of men" to complete their course (cf. *Ibid.,* XI, 28 [38]). This time is the time, i.e., every moment, between the predetermined beginning and the predetermined end of the life of each man and the history of all men. In Augustine's account, the concept of an absolute time is a deduction from the belief in an eternal God who takes human life, and indeed all creation, into his care:

[8]See also *De civitate Dei* IV 33.

> Surely, if there is a mind possessed of such great knowledge and foreknowledge, so that to it are known all things past and future, just as I know one well-known psalm, then supremely marvelous is that mind and wondrous and fearsome . . . Far, far more wonderfully, far more deeply do you know them! It is not as emotions are changed or senses filled up by expectation of words to come and memory of those past as in one who sings well-known psalms or hears a familiar psalm. Not so does it befall you who are unchangeably eternal, that is, truly eternal, the creator of minds. (*Ibid.*, XL, 31 [41]).
>
> ". . . although free from care, yet (you) care for us. (*Ibid.*, XI, 2 [3]).
>
> "Behold, O Lord, I cast my cares upon you so that I may live." (*Ibid.*, X, 43 [70]).

In sum, what is emphasized here is (1) that for Augustine, time, as a comprehensive or absolute phenomenon, comes to light not in the perception and contemplation of cosmic, natural, or human reality, when considered from a natural, i.e., political and philosophical, point of view, but in theologically enlightened reflection on the human soul in its moral and intellectual striving, and (2) that the life of each individual and history in general do not form a coherent and comprehensive whole but are a multitude of processes, aiming everywhere and leading nowhere without the comprehensive and all–powerful divine care.

It must now be added that Aristotle's account of time in the *Physics* concerns time in the final and ultimate sense, but not time in every sense. His access to time in its ultimate sense is, in the *Physics,* through what time is for us,[9] as it is in Augustine's account.[10] But for Aristotle, what time is for us is not what time ultimately is in itself. Now though this is also true in a sense for Augustine, because for him it is what it is for God who creates it, the path to the final truth about time is for Augustine coextensive with the ultimate problem of time. Time in the ultimate sense comes to light for Augustine in the investigation of what the Greeks

[9]See, for example, IV 11, 218b21-23; 219a27-29, 30-31; 13, 222a20-29.

[10]One cannot say that for Aristotle time exists somehow independent and outside of soul in general for (1) it is through the effects of time in the human soul that what time is is manifest to us (see note 9), (2) it is soul which takes the measure of motion (*Phy.* IV 14, 223a21-29), and (3) in the *Metaphysics* Aristotle conjectures that *life* is the cause of the regular, eternal cosmic motions (XII 6, 1071b3-12; 7, 1072b14, 25-31).

called "the human things." On the contrary, for Aristotle, insofar as time can be a systematic theme of inquiry as an object of theoretical knowledge and therefore in its ultimate sense, it is not part of the inquiry into human things, but into nonhuman and divine things. The divine things *qua* moving and therefore *qua* temporal, do not measure action and thought as described in the *Nicomachean Ethics*. This is in fact a way of saying why physics, the science of the moveable *qua* moveable, is not the highest science (cf. *Physics,* VIII, 6, 258b10-13). There is, for Aristotle, no absolute time for action and thought. They are not defined by time in any sense at all because they are not themselves motions or processes, even though they involve motions or processes. Such activities are continuous, but yet not temporal. The time they take is an external consideration. This truth is manifest, as we have said, in experience rather than through discursive analysis.[11]

Aristotle develops fully the meaning of time for us, i.e., in the properly human sense as distinct from the temporality of mere life-processes, in his ethical–political works. But with the most elementary of the virtues, viz., courage, one is already in the process of overcoming temporality, although it is always along with one. Courage is most of all courage in the face of death for the sake of the political community (*Nicomachean Ethics,* III, 6, 1115a32-35). As in Augustine, it is anticipation and remembrance that constitute distinctively human time.[12] But though birth and death set limits to human life, they are not the limits which define it. The limits which define it are the goals which distinguish the various ways of life.[13]

[11]"If we take eternity to mean not infinite temporal duration but timelessness, then eternal life belongs to those who live in the present." "Our life has no end in just the way in which our visual field has no limits" (Ludwig Wittgenstein, *Tractatus logico-philosophicus,* 6.4311, trans. by D.F. Pears and B.F. McGuinness (London: Routledge, 1963).

[12]As for anticipation, consider these texts together: *De interpretatione* IX 18b27-36; 19a7-9; *N.E.* VI 2, 1139a31-b11 (esp. 1139b5-11); III 2, 1111-b19-29; 1112a16-17. This last text suggests to us that *proairesis* and "anticipation" have the same literal meaning. As to remembrance, one would have to consider the full implications of the following passages: *N.E.* VI 5, 1140a24-25; 2, 1139b10-11; I 5, 1195b22-26; *Pol.* I 2, 1253a30-31.

[13]Life is inherent completeness of activities (see *N.E.* I 10, 1100a10-14). In the same vein Wittgenstein writes "Death is not an event in life: we do not live to experience death" (*loc. cit.*). Again, Aristotle says that "we must not follow those who advise us, being men, to think of human things, and,

Political life is closer to temporality than the life of thought. The unalterable fact of birth and death sets the stage for the man of action, whose primary concern is the creation and preservation of communities in which noble deeds like his own are cherished. These deeds constitute the common goods of such communities and also ensure their survival. Thus, insofar as the man of action seeks undying fame, his action is temporal or, better, historical because he *looks foward to* being *remembered*. Yet, if a deed is honored by posterity, it is not honored primarily in virtue of the temporality of the deed. Its being past, present, or yet to be, or its having results to which it leads as the process of work leads to a product, or its representing an ongoing change or process of moral growth in a man does not constitute its nobility. It is primarily in virtue of its inherent completeness that it is deemed worthy of remembrance (see *Ibid.*, I, 5, 1095b26-31; VI, 5, 1140b6-7).

The activity of thought is relatively immune from the temporal contingencies of political activity. Nothing is taken away from the knower, although something is lost to the man, if he goes unrecognized and leaves no trace behind him, nor is anything added to his wisdom if he is known and remembered.

Hence, time is not a distinct theme of inquiry in Aristotle's ethical-political works because for us time is understood and comprehended in what are the distinct themes of ethical-political inquiry, viz., moral and intellectual excellence. Insofar as time can be the object of theoretical inquiry, the question of time is like that of the absolute good, the good without qualification as distinct from the good for man; both are irrelevant to the inquiry into human affairs (*Ibid.*, I, 6, 1096a29-b8; 1096b30-35). In other words, the starting points of ethical-political inquiry exist independently of the starting points of strictly theoretical inquiries like physics. Their principles are therefore grasped independently and in different ways (*Ibid.*, I, 3, 1095a1-6; 4, 1095b2-6). Theoretical knowledge does not intrude upon practical knowledge, which is

---

being mortal, of mortal things, but must, so far as we can, make ourselves immortal (*athanatizein*) . . ." (*op. cit.* X 7, 1177b31-33, Oxford translation). This obviously does not mean that we should search out the knowledge which will enable us to do away with physical death, as Descartes might be taken to suggest. Cf. *Discours de la méthode* VI, pp. 61-62, in *Oeuvres* . . . , vol. VI, ed. by Adam and Tannery (Paris: Léopold Cerf, 1902).

what ethical-political knowledge is (*loc. cit.*), nor is practical knowledge deducible from theoretical knowledge.

This is not the case for Augustine, if we judge by the *Confessions*. For him all the knowledge we possess in this life is practical and none of it strictly theoretical. Nevertheless this practical knowledge is a function of anticipated theoretical knowledge and in principle deducible from it. In the light of the completeness of the next life granted by the absolute Good, this present life is seen as a process toward that end, and anticipated knowledge of the nature of that end is the basis for action now directed to the achievement of that end. Augustine never says, as Aristotle does, that the inquiry into the absolute good is not relevant to the inquiry into human affairs.

In Aristotle's account, then, the independence of the practical is the principle of the possibility of any real history, which is the nonnecessary sequence of noteworthy deeds. Whatever order the sequence may have, i.e., to whatever extent it is indeed a sequence and forms one history, originates out of the genius of individual actions through which political communities cohere. Hence the prominence of founders of cities and the importance of preserving constitutional forms which are a function of the recognition of virtue. The word "history," insofar as it refers to reality, applies to a plurality of histories.

It is said that Augustine raises the individual act and history in general to a level quite beyond that allowed by the Greeks.[14] This contains an essential irony, for (1) it is only in virtue of the creative contemplation of the individual act by God that history takes on cosmic, or rather, supracosmic dimensions, and (2) in general, God is said to countenance acts in inverse ratio to their political importance, as the ancients understood it.[15] In Augustine's view, it is in virtue of God's graciousness, and not in virtue of the inherent quality of deeds themselves, that they acquire transcending value and that universal history exists. Primarily, it is not men who

[14]For example, Jean Guitton, *Le temps et l'éternité chez Plotin et saint Augustin* (Paris; J. Vrin, 1959), pp. 400-401, 403, and C.N. Cochrane, *Christianity and Classical Culture: A Study of Thought and Action from Augustus to Augustine* (New York: Oxford University Press, 1957), pp. 479-484.

[15]See *Conf.* X 36 (58-59). That Augustine understood that his view does away with political life as the ancients saw it is clear from *De civitate Dei* V 12 & 15.

deserve honor for their actions, but God. If, then, human actions have greater meaning because they are accepted by God for justification, they have, at the same time, less apparent worth because the political world which is established through them is outshined by the next world which is established through grace.

It is not clear what is meant by assertions that Aristotle lacks an adequate appreciation of the individual and of history.[16] For him, human action and political history represent the ephemeral, not because the individual lacks reality but because the individual dies. To the extent that a man becomes preeminent as an individual, he is not identified with those aspects of reality which are enduring or recurrent. Hence, when a man dies, all of his preeminence is gone except insofar as it is remembered. For this reason, political history is of the utmost importance within a political perspective, and it would be difficult to deny that of all political philosophers, including the most recent, Aristotle holds the most uncompromising view of the independence and distinctive character of the political realm.

This independence is such that even if the human species has evolved, its evolution is irrelevant to human history because it does not fall within the scope of that remembrance and anticipation which set the limits of political life. Insofar as one looks at man from the transcending theoretical view—and this is made possible not through remembering but through the discovery of universals—one's humanity is transcended, perhaps for something better, because one surrenders the limited perspective within which the distinctively human becomes visible.

Augustine's concept of history, although concerned with humanity in its humanness,[17] likewise escapes the power of human remembrance and anticipation. This is the more obvious in that, unlike the cycles of Polybius, it is less a generalization from experience than a deduction from firmly held beliefs. Augustine's concept of universal history is not a knowledge of history that Augustine has but a belief in a knowledge that God is thought to have, and yet Augustine wants to make practical sense of human life with this concept. If, as Augustine recognizes, human time, or history, is a function of human remembrance and and anticipation, how can he

[16]For example, cf. Mary T. Clark, *Augustine, Philosopher of Freedom* (New York: Desclée, 1958), pp. 13, 15-16, 37-38, and Guitton, *loc. cit.*

[17]A theory of evolution, for example, is not.

maintain against Aristotle the relevance of a universal history? If this is indeed the true locus of the argument between Augustine and Aristotle on history, then it is not a theoretical argument about the nature of the divine or about whether history is rectilinear or circular, but an argument about human proportion and human relevance.

If the sense of this argument is grasped, then the function of the Incarnation in Augustine's theology of history becomes clear, and further, one can explain Augustine's seemingly naive appeal in *De civitate Dei* to the success of Christianity as a mark of its truth. If God, in an act of providence, becomes man, he then lives within the dimensions of human practical concern. If through his actions the establishment of a community is inspired, this community can literally remember the actions of God in his person. Since its originating actions occurred in plain sight only once and for all, this community as time goes on develops its ways of remembering and of introducing new members to its ways. When these ways develop to the extent that one can speak of a Christian view of justice, Christian education, and Christian thought embodying a depth and range of experience approaching that of ancient civilization, then one is speaking of what we call a culture.

If Augustine thought along these lines, then he saw the spread of Christianity not merely as the espousal of the new creed by an increasing number of individuals, but a progressing redefinition of ancient culture. If the Incarnation implies that a Christian culture must embody an understanding of history in the distinctive sense, then neither fantasy nor a system of ideas can supply for the genuine remembrance that characterizes a living historical tradition. Perhaps in adopting for Catholicism many of the classical instruments of cultural continuity and tradition Augustine believed that beyond the limits of a culture's extended memory Christianity is in danger of dissolving into an empty play of concepts and the grossest fantasy.

NOTES ON CONTRIBUTORS

Felix Alluntis, O.F.M. has published books and articles on philosophy in Spanish and English, edited and translated into Spanish the text of Duns Scotus's *Quodlibetal Questions* (Madrid: 1968), and with Professor Allan B. Wolter, O.F.M. has done further work on the Latin text and made an English translation of it. He is completing a work on Ortega's thought.

Bernardino M. Bonansea, O.F.M., author of *Tommaso Campanella: Renaissance Pioneer of Modern Thought* (1969) and other books and articles on medieval and modern philosophy, is completing a work on the character and history of the Anselmian argument.

John J. Doyle, Professor Emeritus, Marian College, is archivist and historian of the Archdiocese of Indianapolis and has published on philosophy and on early Indiana history.

John Driscoll is a doctoral candidate at the University of Michigan, Ann Arbor, where he has held scholarships and taught courses in philosophy.

Thomas R. Flynn, Assistant Professor in the School of Philosophy, CUA, studied at Columbia University (Ph.D., 1971) and at the Gregorian and other European and American universities.

Bernard Huddlestun has studied at the New School for Social Research and in the School of Philosophy, CUA, where he earned the M.A. and Ph.D. degrees.

John E. Kelly studied at the Pontifical Institute of Medieval Studies, Toronto, and at CUA, and teaches philosophy at Canisius College, Buffalo, New York.

John K. Ryan is Elizabeth Breckinridge Caldwell Professor of Philosophy Emeritus and formerly Dean of the School of Philosophy, CUA.

Marius G. Schneider, O.F.M. is professor of philosophy in the School of Philosophy, CUA, and has published many articles on psychology and philosophy in German and American philosophical journals.

George J. Stack, a member of the philosophy faculty of the State University of New York College at Brockport, has published in American philosophical journals.

INDEX